Dear Jay

You always ~~g~~
fantastic books.
I hope you'll find
this book fantastic!

From Jarry

LETTERS TO AUNTIE FORI

OTHER BOOKS BY MARTIN GILBERT
ON JEWISH THEMES

LETTERS TO
AUNTIE FORI

*The 5000–Year History of
the Jewish People and Their Faith*

MARTIN GILBERT

Weidenfeld & Nicolson
LONDON

First published in Great Britain in 2002
by Weidenfeld & Nicolson

Copyright © 2002 Martin Gilbert

A CIP catalogue record for this book
is available from the British Library.

ISBN 0 297 60740 5

Printed and bound by
Butler & Tanner Ltd, Frome and London

Weidenfeld & Nicolson
The Orion Publishing Group Ltd
Orion House
5 Upper Saint Martin's Lane
London WC2H 9EA

To Auntie Fori

CONTENTS

(the New Moon)—Purim—the Rabbi and Other Synagogue
Officials—the Torah and Other Books of the Jewish Faith—Joseph
Caro—Kashrut (the Dietary Laws)—Gematria (Numerology)—
Mitzvot (Good Deeds)—Tzedakah (Charity)—Lashon Ha-Ra (Bad
Mouthing)—Rituals and Practices of the Life Cycle: Birth; Coming of
Age; Marriage and Divorce; Death and Burial—Religious Symbols and
Artifacts—the Reform Movement—the Sabbath—the Jews of Alaska—
Final Letter

ACKNOWLEDGMENTS

Erica Hunningher and Kay Thomson read these letters as I was writing them, and gave me the benefit of their wisdom, as did Rabbi Louis Jacobs, who read the letters dealing with the Bible, faith and tradition; Ralph Blumenau, who helped me with regard to many historical questions of fact, interpretation and balance; and Esther Poznansky, a wise guide. Auntie Fori has certainly been the gainer from their scrutiny.

INTRODUCTION

In the summer of 1957 I found myself in the Garden of Eden. Having left the army, where I had been a National Serviceman for two years, I travelled southward through the Balkans and into Turkey, earning money by teaching English, and using it to travel further. After a month wandering through southern and central Anatolia I reached the most easterly eastern region of Turkey, almost a thousand miles from Istanbul. There I found myself in sight of the 15,500-foot snow-capped conical peak of Mount Ararat, the peak on which Noah's Ark is said to have alighted as the flood waters receded.

Four rivers flow from the high plateau which I had reached: the Euphrates, the Tigris, the Coruh and the Aras. In the words of the Bible: 'And a river went out of Eden to water the garden; and from thence it was parted and came unto four heads.' The Bible gives the names of these four heads, or tributaries, as Euphrates, Pison, Gihon and Hiddekel—'that which goeth south towards the east of Assyria'. The Hiddekel is the river Tigris of today.

So here I was in the Garden of Eden, standing by the banks of the River Aras, a mere twelve miles from the upper reaches of the Euphrates. Nearby were two Kurdish camel drivers. Contemplating the isolation and grandeur of the scene, I felt that I was at the very end of the road, at its remotest, most adventurous point. Then, in the far distance, I saw a small car making its way along the rough road in my direction. Eventually it arrived at the point in the roadside where I was sitting. Two German students got out. Pointing eastward, where the road continued, one of them demanded: 'Is this the road to India?' I was mortified. It was indeed the road one would take to India, if one continued eastward for another two thousand miles. But I had imagined, sitting there in Eden, that I was at the end of the road, not at a mere way-station along it. At that moment I determined that one day I would continue along that eastern road and reach India.

In Athens, on my way back to England, I met Neil Malcolm, a young man—my age—who was also going to Oxford. I told him of my experience in the Garden of Eden, and he agreed to go back with me the following summer, to try to reach that spot where I had sat within sight of Mount Ararat, and then to continue on to India—however long or rough the road might be, however many rivers, deserts and borders had to be crossed. When Neil and I took the Channel ferry from England to France in the early summer of 1958, each of us had several letters from Indian students whom we had met at university. One of my letters was from my friend Ashok. 'If you find yourself in Delhi,' he said, 'do look up my mother.'

A student feels he can navigate the world without letters of introduction to other people's parents. But long before reaching Delhi, Neil Malcolm and I had both become quite ill. A potent mixture of kaolin and morphine, provided in a Teheran hospital by an American nurse, Nurse Choate—who was said to have been the Shah's nurse—helped ward off the worst, but her magic potion had run out by the time we left Afghanistan and crossed the Khyber Pass, to make our way across Pakistan by train to Lahore, and then on to Delhi. There, Neil and I set off in different directions, having agreed to meet in Bombay, to return to Britain by sea, which we did. Forty-three years later, telephoning Neil to tell him about the book which was the final end-product of our long-ago Indian journey, I was shocked to learn that he had died three months earlier. He was my contemporary and friend.

Neil set off for other Indian cities, and I made my way to Ashok's mother's door in Delhi. Welcoming me as if I were her own son, she introduced me to her two younger sons, Aditya and Anil, and to her strikingly handsome husband. His name was Braj Kumar Nehru—

known colloquially as BK, and affectionately as Bijju. He was a cousin of Jawaharlal Nehru, then Prime Minister of India.

BK's wife, Mrs Nehru—who insisted that I call her Auntie Fori—nursed me back to health. I had felt so ill when I reached her front door that I have no doubt she saved my life. Her medicine was not the kaolin and morphine concoction of Nurse Choate in Teheran, but an equally effective mixture of rice and yogurt. Within a week I was no longer weak or groaning. Within two weeks I was cycling along the broad avenues of New Delhi, and even penetrating the maze of Old Delhi. One morning I went to the vast open space in front of the Red Fort and stood with an estimated one million Indians to hear Jawaharlal Nehru speak to the hushed multitude—a vast sea of white stretching, as it seemed, to the horizon. It was the eleventh anniversary of Indian independence.

As soon as I was completely recovered, Auntie Fori gave me her own letter of introduction and packed me off by train to the Hindu holy city of Benares, where I stayed for a while, working in an orphanage. On my return to Oxford, we kept in touch by letter and postcard. In the 1960s I visited her in Washington, where BK—whom I was bidden to call Uncle Bijju—was India's Ambassador. Later, when he was Indian High Commissioner in London, we saw a good deal of each other.

Auntie Fori was a warm Indian woman, beautiful in her sari, deeply concerned about the welfare of India. Before being posted to London, Uncle Bijju—with Fori at his side—had been governor of the most easterly region of India, stretching to the Chinese and Burmese borders: the 'Seven Sisters' of Assam, Nagaland, Manipur, Tripura, Mizoram, Meghalaya and the North East Frontier Agency. Leaving London, he still had a distinguished career in front of him, first as Governor of Jammu and Kashmir, then as Governor of Gujarat. He also served as Chairman of the Investments Committee of the United Nations, and was at one point spoken of as the next Secretary-General of the United Nations. At the age of eighty-two he had been asked to become India's Foreign Minister. 'My ego was greatly titillated,' he wrote in his memoirs, 'but I retained enough common sense to refuse the offer on grounds of age.'

Auntie Fori and I had continued to correspond since 1958—I have a large box crammed with her letters—but after the mid-1970s we did not see each other again for more than two decades. In 1998 Auntie Fori and Uncle Bijju both reached the age of ninety. My own son David was then twenty-one, my age when I had gone to India. He and I travelled to India together, flying rather than going by road and rail—neither Iran nor Afghanistan being as inviting to travellers as they had once been. I wanted him to meet the ninety-year-olds who had been so good to me forty years earlier.

That December, during one of our chats, Auntie Fori asked me if I knew of a history of the Jews that she could read. 'I know nothing of Jewish history and Jewish life, that is a fact,' she said. But why did she want to read such a book? She told me her story. She was not Indian at all—except by passage of time and her love for the people of India: of the country, of BK and their sons, and of the large Nehru clan. She was Jewish, and Hungarian. Her parents, the Friedmanns, had been born, like her, in the Austro-Hungarian Empire. They had been members of the Budapest Jewish community. Her father had a seat in the Dohany Street Synagogue, the largest synagogue in Europe. In 1928, when Fori was twenty, her application to study at Budapest university had been turned down because of the strict quota established for Jewish students—the notorious *numerus clausus.* Her parents had sent her to study first in France and then in Britain.

In Britain, in 1930, Auntie Fori met BK, then a student preparing for the Indian Civil Service examination and for a life of dedication to the welfare of India. They had wanted to marry. But Fori's parents were worried, in BK's own words, that he was 'a black man'. Even more alarming for Fori's parents, his cousin Jawaharlal Nehru was, as BK expressed it, 'a jailbird'. The British had already imprisoned him more than once, and were to do so several more times.

'Not only was the Hungarian family worried about this Indian black prince,' Ashok told me when we discussed his parents' love match, 'but the Indians were equally worried—who was this girl who was taking away their darling son?' True love prevailed, however. Auntie Fori went to India. The Nehru family fell in love with her. And she and BK were married in 1935. Two years later my friend Ashok was born, followed within five years by his two brothers, Aditya and Anil. According to Jewish religious law, because their mother is Jewish all three boys are also

Jews: Israel's Law of Return, promulgated in 1950, entitles them—and of course their mother—to Israeli citizenship if they should request this on reaching its shores. 'I never knew' was Fori's comment when I told her this.

Auntie Fori wanted to learn the history of the people to whom she belonged, but from whom, sixty-seven years earlier, she had moved away, to the heat and dust and challenges of India. I told her that as soon as I was back in Britain I would write to her, setting out each week, in letter form, a segment of the Jewish story, starting with Abraham, or perhaps with Adam. Two and a half years later the last letter was put into the post. Auntie Fori was then ninety-two. My hope was that the Jewish story, despite its moments of sadness, internal divisions, war and suffering—sometimes terrible suffering—would reveal the tenacity of her people's survival and achievement, its communal life and creativity, and the attempt by each generation to follow the advice which Moses transmitted from God to the Children of Israel, as recorded in the Book of Deuteronomy: 'I have set before you life and death, blessing and cursing: therefore choose life, that both thou and thy seed may live.' The injunction 'choose life' became the Jewish religious, communal and national imperative. These letters to my Indian aunt trace its course through five thousand years.

Merton College,
Oxford
14 August 2001

LETTERS TO AUNTIE FORI

By air mail
Par avion

50ᴾ

Part One

THE BIBLICAL ERA

No. 1

Dearest Auntie Fori,

So you are now ninety-one years old, a great and wonderful age. And the Jewish people, of whom you are a part, are more than five and a half thousand years old. According to the Jewish calendar—the oldest calendar in the world—this present year is the year 5759.

The Five Books of Moses, the core of the Jewish Bible, begin with the story of Creation, which, based on the Biblical narrative, is calculated by Orthodox Jews as having taken place 5759 years ago. That narrative begins in the most precise way, which any historian could envy: (I will use in these letters the seventeenth-century King James version, on which all schoolchildren, myself included, were brought up in England half a century ago): 'In the beginning God created the heaven and the earth.' The Bible goes on to say that the Creation took God six days, during which time he created day and night, land and water, grass and trees, sun and moon, 'great whales, and every living creature'—including cattle—and man.

'God created man in his own image, in the image of God he created him; male and female created he them.' He then blessed the man and the woman and told them: 'Be fruitful, and multiply.' This—as recorded in the Book of Genesis, chapter 1, verse 28—was thus God's first command to man and woman. He then told them to 'replenish the earth, and subdue it: and have dominion over the fish of the sea, and over the fowl of the air, and over every living thing that moveth upon the earth.' Next he gave them all the herbs and the fruit of every tree, to be their food.

'And God saw everything that he had made, and, behold, it was very good.'

Six days had passed since the start of creation. On the seventh day

3

God rested 'from all his work'. His day of rest is the origin of the Sabbath, which Moses was to institute during the exodus from Egypt in around 1250 BC. Every week of the year, every year of their lives, Jews—starting at sunset on Friday and going on until sunset on Saturday—are told to rest also. Practising Jews do no work that day, do not drive cars or carry money or transact business or turn on lights, or cook, because all these activities constitute work.

The story of God having created man and woman during the six days of creation is how the Bible begins—in verses 26-27 of chapter 1 of the Book of Genesis. The Bible continues, however, with a different version of the story. According to this second version, in the aftermath of creation, and following his day of rest, plants and herbs were in the earth but had not yet grown, because it had not rained.

God, we are told, 'had not caused it to rain upon the earth because there was not a man to till the ground'. It was only then—according to verse 7 of chapter 2 of Genesis—that he formed man 'of the dust of the ground, and breathed into his nostrils the breath of life; and man became a living soul'.

Following the creation of man—but not yet of woman, according to this second Biblical version—God brought rain in the form of 'a mist from the earth', and then planted a garden, the Garden of Eden—in Hebrew the word *eden* means fruitful or delightful. God then put the man he had created into the garden. 'And out of the ground made the Lord to grow every tree that is pleasant to the sight, and good for food; the tree of life also in the midst of the garden, and the tree of knowledge of good and evil.'

God told the first man—whose name was Adam—that he could eat the fruit of all the trees, but that he must not eat the fruit of the tree of knowledge of good and evil. The reason which God gave was that 'in the day that thou eatest thereof thou shalt surely die'. God then formed 'every beast of the field and every fowl of the air', after which Adam gave them all their names. But Adam was lonely, one man amid the wonders of creation. Seeing this, God said: 'It is not good that man should be alone; I will make him an help meet for him.' God then put Adam to sleep and while he slept 'took one of his ribs' and made woman.

One result of the creation of a female partner for man was set out with stark clarity: 'Therefore shall a man leave his father and his mother, and shall cleave unto his wife; and they shall be one flesh.' The perpetuation of the species was paramount.

The Garden of Eden figures in Jewish rabbinical tradition and prayers. One of the blessings recited at a marriage is to ask that the bride and groom may rejoice 'even as of old thou didst gladden thy creatures in the Garden of Eden'. In prayers for the dead one asks that the soul of the departed should rest in Eden. Rabbi Yosef Hayyim of Baghdad, who died, dearest Auntie Fori, the year after you were born, believed that the Garden of Eden was a real place, even though it had not yet been discovered by explorers. In one of the central books of Jewish rabbinic reflections, the Ethics of the Fathers, compiled two centuries after Jesus, it is said that those who were modest in their lifetime are destined for the Garden of Eden while those who were without shame will go to a place of torment—*Gehinnom* in Hebrew, the valley where, in pagan times, children were burned in fire by those who worshipped the idol Moloch.

Adam and Eve lived in the Garden of Eden, naked and unaware of sin, until a serpent tempted Eve to eat the forbidden fruit of the tree of knowledge of good and evil. This tree was in the middle of the garden. Eve ate the fruit: the Bible does not say what fruit it was. Jewish tradition holds it to be the grape—possibly intoxicating wine. Later Christian writers and painters made it an apple! Eve then gave some to Adam, and suddenly they became conscious of being naked, and so ashamed that they made themselves clothes out of fig leaves.

God was extremely disappointed that Adam and Eve had chosen to disobey him, and explained to Eve the three consequences of this—consequences, it seems to have been intended, for all women through the ages. He would 'multiply' her sorrow so that 'in sorrow thou shalt bring forth children'. She would have a craving for her man. And her man would rule over her.

As for Adam, he would have to work hard in order to live off the soil: 'In the sweat of thy face shalt thou eat bread'. Adam's life (and Eve's presumably) would not be perpetual, 'for dust thou art, and unto dust shalt thou return'. In Hebrew, the words for 'man' and 'ground' have the same root: 'adam' and 'adamah'. In colloquial Hebrew today, 'ha-adam' means 'the person', as in the sentence, 'the person I was talking to . . .'.

Adam and Eve were sent away from the garden—driven out, the Bible tells us—and had to work the fields elsewhere, but not before God made each of them a 'coat of skins, and clothed them'. He also explained that, as far as the future of mankind was concerned, 'man is become as one of us, to know good and evil'. According to rabbinic tradition, the first laws laid down by God for human conduct were given to Adam—and later given to Noah.

No. 2

Dearest Auntie Fori,

After being driven from the Garden of Eden, Adam and Eve had two children. They were indeed the first parents of the human race—in that regard, both your predecessors, Auntie Fori, and mine. Their first-born, Cain, was jealous because his younger brother Abel's sacrificial offerings—'the firstlings of his flock'—had been more acceptable to God than Cain's offering of the 'fruit of the ground'. Cain then killed Abel. When God, who knew of course of Abel's murder, asked Cain where Abel was, Cain replied by asking God: 'Am I my brother's keeper?'

According to Jewish tradition the rest of the Bible is God's attempt to emphasise that the answer to this question is 'yes', to teach us that every one of us is responsible for all others.

In anger at Cain's fratricide, God cursed him and made him 'a fugitive and a vagabond'. But he also put a protective mark on him 'lest any finding him should kill him'. And he warned that if anyone killed Cain, 'vengeance will be taken on him sevenfold'. Even the outcast was to be protected.

Cain and Abel's fatal quarrel has been the subject of much rabbinical reflection. Some saw it as a dispute over land, one of the brothers taking all the land and ordering the other off it—telling him to fly in the air. Others said it was as a dispute over women—Abel having claimed their two sisters for himself. A third tradition is that they quarrelled over where the Temple should be built, each wanting it on his own land.

Other traditions abound. Jews love to try to illuminate obscurity and build ornate palaces on simple hovels. According to Jewish mystical tradition—the *kabbalah*—Cain's soul belongs to the demonic aspect of mankind, while Abel's soul came down to earth again as the soul of Moses. Was this not a type of Hindu-style re-incarnation? Another legend, reiterating the demonization of Cain, places his descendants in the netherworld as two-headed monsters. There are also Jewish commentators who point out, not so much in justification as in explanation of the deed, that Cain had no experience of the fact or nature of either death or killing: Abel's is the first recorded death and the first recorded murder.

Cain later married. The Bible does not tell us that Adam had daughters or how otherwise Cain's wife had come into existence, but it does say that Cain and his wife had a son, Enoch, and that Cain then 'builded a city' which he named after his son. Enoch is the first recorded city, though its whereabouts remain unknown. Like the Garden of Eden, it has never quite been discovered.

No. 3

Dearest Auntie Fori,

After Abel's killing, Adam and Eve had a third son, named Seth. According to one Jewish tradition, he inherited the clothes God had made for Adam. Another tradition asserts that Seth will be one of the seven shepherds advising the Messiah after the resurrection of the dead. Seth is also a figure in Muslim tradition: Arab genealogists trace the descent of mankind through him, his name believed to mean 'a present from Allah'—God's present to Adam after the murder of Abel, thus perpetuating the human race.

Seth's descendants, each of whom is named in the Bible, included Methuselah, who, the Bible tells us, lived to the age of 969—the longest-living person in recorded history.

How to explain Methuselah's longevity? The Psalmist—Methuselah's descendant King David—refers to a thousand years being a day in God's eyes ('For a thousand years in thy sight are but as yesterday when it is past, and as a watch in the night.'). Hence, despite his longevity, Methuselah did not live for even one whole day—he would have had to live to the age of 1,000 for that. Rabbinical tradition asserts that this curtailing of Methuselah's age was done deliberately, in order to counteract the heathen concept of human beings being admitted to the ranks of gods by virtue of their longevity.

Methuselah's descendants included his grandson Noah—a direct descendant of Adam. Before the great flood which covered all the earth, God instructed Noah to make an ark and take on board a few—some in sevens and some in twos—of every creature on earth, as well as his wife, his three sons (Shem, Ham and Japheth) and their wives. The flood was God's punishment for man's wickedness, because 'every imagination of the thoughts of his heart was only evil continually'. Noah, however, 'found grace in the eyes of the Lord' and was to be saved. God gave him the exact specifications of how to build the ark—length, breadth, height (three storeys), the type of wood—and it proved seaworthy.

It rained for forty days and forty nights. When the rains ceased the whole earth was covered in water, and all its inhabitants and creatures had drowned. 'And all flesh died that moved upon the earth, both of fowl, and of cattle, and of beast, and of every creeping thing that creepeth upon the earth, and every man: All in whose nostrils was the breath of life, of all that was in the dry land, died.'

Only the ark was afloat; only those whom Noah had brought into it were alive. After seven months and seventeen days the floodwaters began to subside, and the ark came to rest on Mount Ararat—the very mountain whose conical snow-capped peak I have seen twice, first on my Turkish travels in 1957 and again on my way to India a year later.

The creatures on Noah's ark, saved from the flood that killed everything else, re-populated the earth. A rainbow appeared, which God explained as 'a token of a covenant between me and the earth' that he would never again bring a flood on such a scale. God then promised that while the earth remained in existence 'seedtime and harvest, and cold and heat, and summer and winter, and day and night shall not cease'.

God then blessed Noah and his sons, telling them: 'Be fruitful, and multiply, and replenish the earth.' This they did: the Bible lists Noah's male descendants generation after generation. One of them, Terah, was the father of Abraham, about whom I will write in my next letter.

God had already given Adam a set of laws, and he now gave them to Noah. There were seven in all, known as the Noahide Laws. Six were prohibitions: against idolatry, blasphemy, murder, adultery and incest (counted as one) and the eating of flesh torn from a living animal. One was a positive law: to establish a system of justice. These are not, of course, Israelite or Jewish laws, since God had yet to 'choose' Abraham for the special task of creating a nation, but laws for all peoples. In Hebrew 'son of Noah' is the name given to any non-Jew, or Gentile. Non-Jews who keep the Noahide Laws are considered among 'the righteous of the nations of the world' who have a share in the world to come.

The Babylonians also recounted the story of a flood in their legends, and there was in fact a great flood around 3000 BC. But whereas the legendary hero of the Babylonian flood, Ut-Napishtim, eventually became a god, Noah remained a man, saved because he was righteous, but not elevated beyond the realms of humanity.

No. 4

Dearest Auntie Fori,

According to the Biblical chronology, Abram, the son of Terah (later known as Abraham), was born in Mesopotamia, some four thousand years ago. His birthplace was the town of Ur, on the River Euphrates, less than two hundred miles from the head of the Persian Gulf, at the eastern end of the Fertile Crescent, which stretched as far as Canaan on the Mediterranean Sea. From the social system described in Genesis, scholars deduce that the story of Abraham took place around 2000 BC. The BC–AD dating, incidentally, is the Christian one, Before Christ and Anno Domini, the Year of the Lord. In recent years Jews have come increasingly to prefer BCE and CE—Before the Christian Era, and the Common Era.

As a young man, Abraham turned against the idols worshipped by his tribe, one of many dozens of small communities of farmers and shepherds. According to rabbinic tradition, when he found himself alone with the idols of his father he took hold of an axe, smashed all but the largest, and then, in a gesture of contempt, rested the axe on the arm of the largest idol.

When Abraham's father saw the destroyed idols he was deeply distressed. What has happened? he asked. Abraham replied that it was the
largest idol—still holding the axe—which had destroyed the others. 'If
you don't believe me, ask him.'

'You are telling lies,' Abraham's father replied. 'These are only wood
and stone which I made myself.' To which Abraham answered: 'So how
can you worship these idols who have no power to do anything?'

Abraham then heard the words of a greater God, a singular God, and
became the first person to understand—and believe in—monotheism.
The Bible records that God then said to Abraham: 'Get thee out of thy
country, and from thy kindred, and from thy father's house, unto a land
which I will show thee.' Obeying God's call, Abraham left the fertile
lands of Mesopotamia with his family and flocks. His father went with
him. They travelled northward and eastward, following the fertile valley
of the Euphrates, towards a land—Canaan, later known as Palestine—
which God promised to Abraham's descendants.

During the journey to Canaan, Abraham's father died. Abraham continued southward. 'I will make of thee a great nation,' God told him, as
recorded in the Bible, 'and I will bless thee, and make thy name great;
and thou shall be a blessing: And I will bless them that bless thee, and
curse him that curseth thee: and in thee shall all families of the earth be
blessed.'

Still following the Fertile Crescent, Abraham reached the town of
Bethel, in Canaan, where he built an altar to God. But because of famine
in Canaan, he decided to continue, taking his family further southward,
into Egypt, a journey of more than 150 miles. There they lived for several
years, until, 'very rich in cattle, in silver, and in gold', he went back to
Bethel. By then the famine in Canaan had passed.

After Abraham had returned to Bethel, God said to him: 'Lift up now
thine eyes, and look from the place where thou are northward, and
southward, and eastward, and westward: For all the land which thou
seest, to thee I will give it, and to thy seed for ever.' God's promise continued: 'I will make thy seed as the dust of the earth: so that if a man can
number the dust of the earth, then shall thy seed also be numbered.'
Arise, walk through the land in the length of it and in the breadth of it;
for I will give it unto thee.'

Abraham travelled southward, reaching the town of Hebron (the scene of so much Arab-Jewish violence nowadays!), where he built another altar to God. He and his wife Sarah were puzzled as to how God's promise about their descendants could be fulfilled: they had no children, and Sarah was past child-bearing age. It was Sarah who then suggested to Abraham that he have a child with her Egyptian maidservant, Hagar. But of this child, whose name was to be Ishmael, the Angel of the Lord told Hagar: 'And he will be a wild man; his hand will be against every man, and every man's hand against him.'

God then spoke to Abraham again, telling him again 'thou shalt be a father of many nations', and that his name would henceforth be Abraham, not Abram—'for a father of many nations have I made thee'. God then repeated his promise yet again: 'And I will make thee exceeding fruitful, and I will make nations of thee, and kings shall come out of thee.' This was more than a promise of descendants: there was also to be a direct link between God and the children of Abraham. As God went on to explain to Abraham: 'And I will establish my covenant between me and thee and thy seed after thee in their generation for an everlasting covenant . . .'. As a sign and reminder of this covenant, every male was to be circumcised when he was eight days old.

God also explained that his covenant would not be with the descendants of Ishmael, Hagar's son—who was then thirteen years old—but only with those of Sarah. Incredulous, the aged Abraham asked God, 'Shall a child be born unto him that is an hundred years old? and shall Sarah, that is ninety years old, bear?'

Their son, Isaac, was born as predicted. After Isaac's birth, Ishmael was sent away into the desert. There, as he lay dying of thirst, God told Hagar: 'Arise, lift up the lad, and hold him in thine hand; for I will make him a great nation.' She then opened her eyes and 'saw a well of water'. Ishmael drank, and survived. Later he married an Egyptian woman. They made their home in the desert.

The Arabs of today claim their descent from Ishmael, and are proud that he was Abraham's first-born son. According to Muslim tradition— which my own rabbi, Hugo Gryn, a leader in Jewish–Muslim dialogue, always liked to recall—Abraham made his way across the deserts of Arabia to visit Ishmael, who was then in Mecca, and together they built the

Ka'aba, which became the centre of the annual Muslim pilgrimage, the Haj.

No. 5

Dearest Auntie Fori,

We now come to a moment when God decided to destroy two cities at the Dead Sea, Sodom and Gomorrah, 'because their sin is very grievous'. Abraham, a humane man, was uneasy at this. 'Wilt thou also destroy the righteous with the wicked?' he asked God, and urged God to spare the cities, however few righteous there might be in them. Even if there were only fifty—or forty—or thirty—or twenty—or even only ten, he pleaded, the cities should be saved. Moved by Abraham's concern for the lives of the righteous, God agreed to spare the two cities even if only ten good men could be found. But even that small number were not there.

Abraham's nephew Lot—who lived in Sodom, and had protected two angels, who visited him in disguise, from the rapacious carnal desires of the Sodomites—was allowed to leave the city before its destruction, together with his wife and daughters. They were told not to look back, not to gaze at the scene of destruction, but his wife could not resist the temptation to do so. She was immediately turned into a pillar of salt.

Sodom and Gomorrah were completely destroyed. No one was spared: 'Then the Lord rained upon Sodom and upon Gomorrah brimstone and fire. . . . And he overthrew those cities, and all the plain, and all the inhabitants of the cities, and that which grew upon the ground.' Abraham witnessed the destruction from afar. 'And Abraham got up early in the morning. . . . And he looked towards Sodom and Gomorrah, and towards all the land of the plain, and beheld, and, lo, the smoke of the country went up as the smoke of a furnace.' His plea to save the cities had failed, through no fault of his own, only through lack of men of goodness.

No. 6

Dearest Auntie Fori,

Last week I wrote about the destruction of Sodom and Gomorrah, and Abraham's humanity. This week his story takes a dramatic turn. The story, though short, is decisive in its implications. When Isaac was a young man, the deeply God-fearing Abraham was told by God to sacrifice him on a mountaintop. Hitherto, child sacrifice was part of the accepted ritual of pleasing and placating the gods. Abraham therefore obeyed. He made all the necessary preparations, had already bound Isaac as ordered to do, and was about to kill him when a voice from heaven called to him to stop.

A new ethic was about to be created. The voice was that of a deity that did not want child sacrifice as part of the code of practice of his people: a unique God for those times. He had intervened to halt a hitherto accepted practice.

God's words to Abraham were: 'for now I know that thou fearest God, seeing thou has not withheld thy son, thine only son from me'. God then repeated his promise again with regard to Abraham's descendants: 'By myself I have sworn, saith the Lord, for because thou hast done this thing, and hast not withheld thy son, thine only son; That in blessing I will bless thee, and in multiplying I will multiply thy seed as the stars of the heaven, and as the sand which is upon the sea shore; and thy seed shall possess the gate of his enemies . . .'.

The near sacrifice of Isaac was and remains a defining one for the Jewish religion. Each year Jews recount it in synagogue, not only as part of the annual cycle of weekly readings of the Bible, but also on the second day of Rosh Hashanah, the Jewish New Year, when it is central to the day's liturgy. At that moment Jews feel in the presence of a decisive moment. God had called for total obedience. One Jewish tradition sees the Binding of Isaac as the first Jewish willingness to give up life itself for the sake of the sanctification of God's name.

Each year, on Rosh Hashanah—which is not only New Year's Day but also Judgment Day—Jews in synagogue ask God to remember how

Abraham 'suppressed his compassion in order to perform Thy will with a perfect heart. So may Thy compassion overbear Thine anger against us; in Thy goodness may Thy great wrath turn aside from Thy people, Thy city, and Thine inheritance.'

Isaac lived. His descendants became the Jews of history. The descendants of his half-brother Ishmael became the Arabs of today, for whom Islam was to become the dominant religion. The 'sons of Abraham' are the Jews and Arabs of today. There was also another line of descent. After Sarah's death Abraham married Keturah, by whom he had six more children. Having given Isaac 'all that he had', he gave gifts to his six children by Keturah and 'sent them away from Isaac his son . . . eastward, unto the east country'. Abraham wanted no conflict between these six sons and Isaac, his heir.

In later years, people in many lands, including southern Arabia, claimed to be descendants of Abraham through his six children with Keturah, and their children, ten of whom who are named in the Bible.

Abraham died in Hebron. Isaac and Ishmael were together at his funeral. His burial place, the Cave of Machpelah in Hebron—where Sarah was already buried, and where according to legend Adam and Eve are also buried—is holy to Jews and Muslims. It is also the scene, in the twenty-first century—more than four thousand years after Abraham's death—of continuing physical confrontation and ideological conflict.

In Jewish tradition Abraham is a God-fearing man of no great pretensions or brilliance. In an old Jewish story a man says he does not necessarily want his son to be famous, but 'a simple Jew like our father Abraham'. Above all Abraham is the model of a hospitable person—like you, Auntie Fori!

The Bible describes Abraham sitting at the door of his tent in the heat of the day when three men approached. He urged them to rest, called for water to wash their feet, told Sarah to make cakes for them, and prepared them a meal: butter, milk and a tender calf: 'and he stood with them under the tree, and they did eat'. A hundred years ago and more, in the Jewish heartland of Eastern Europe, a house known for its hospitality was called 'a house with Abraham's doors'.

When describing the visit of the three men, the Biblical account shifts from singular to plural. This led to the rabbinical suggestion that the three men were in fact God himself. A leading Jewish thinker, Philo of Alexandria (who died in about 50 AD), suggested that the three guests were God and his two divine powers of Mercy and Justice.

No. 7

Dearest Auntie Fori,

My last letter ended with Abraham, the patriarch to whom Jews, Christians and Muslims are all beholden. His son Isaac married Rebecca, Abraham's great-niece. The blessing with which Rebecca's brother and mother blessed her as she set off to meet Isaac for the first time is recited before a Jewish wedding ceremony, at the moment when the groom places the veil over his bride-to-be's face, as Rebecca veiled herself when she first saw Isaac: 'Thou art our sister, be thou the mother of thousands of mothers, and let thy seed possess the gate of those which hate them.'

Isaac and Rebecca had twin sons, Esau and Jacob. When Rebecca asked God why, before they were born, they 'struggled within her', he replied: 'Two nations are in thy womb, and two manner of people.' God also told her that 'the one people shall be stronger than the other people; and the elder shall serve the younger.'

Esau was the elder. As the boys grew up, Esau became 'a cunning hunter, a man of the field'. Jacob, by contrast, was 'a plain man, dwelling in tents'. One day Esau came in from the fields, faint with hunger. He begged Jacob to give him some food. Before agreeing to do so, Jacob drove a hard bargain, asking Esau to sell his birthright. Esau agreed, telling his brother: 'Behold, I am at the point to die: and what profit shall this birthright do to me?' Jacob then gave his brother 'bread and pottage of lentiles' and Esau went away.

Esau later married two Hittite women, much to the 'grief of mind' of both Isaac and Rebecca. Later, when Isaac was old 'and his eyes were dim, so that he could not see', he called for Esau, his first-born, to bless him. With Rebecca's urging, Jacob then tricked Isaac into giving him and not Esau his blessing. 'Let people serve thee, and nations bow down to thee: be lord over thy brethren, and let thy mother's sons bow down to

thee: cursed be every one that curseth thee, and blessed be he that blesseth thee.'

As soon as Esau discovered the deception, Jacob fled from his father's
house and went to live with Rebecca's brother, his uncle Laban, whose
two daughters, Rachel and Leah, he later married. They are the third and
fourth (and last) Jewish Matriarchs, Sarah being the first and Rebecca
the second. Isaac also had two concubines, Bilhah and Zilpah. From
these four ladies he had twelve sons.

Rachel, known to Jews as *Rahel Imenu,* Our Mother Rachel, is the
'mother of the sorrows' who weeps in prayer over the Jewish people. It
was while giving birth to Jacob's son Benjamin that she died. Her tomb
on the road from Jerusalem to Bethlehem is a place of pilgrimage for
Jews, Christians, and Muslims. In the words of the Prophet Jeremiah:
'Thus saith the Lord; A voice was heard in Ramah, lamentation, and bitter weeping; Rahel weeping for her children refused to be comforted
for her children, because they were not.' Jews believe that because of
Rachel's merit, God will intervene for the good of the Jewish people,
especially Jewish women. From Byzantine times until the modern era,
women who could not have children, and those suffering pain or sorrow, would surround Rachel's tomb with a red thread and then tie the
thread to their elbows or necks, in the hope that Rachel's merit and the
sanctity of the tomb would permeate their lives and souls.

Jacob—Abraham's grandson—continued to live in the land of
Canaan which God had promised his grandfather. It was to Jacob that
God made a further promise, concerning his descendants: 'A nation and
a company of nations shall be of thee, and kings shall come out of thy
loins, and the land which I gave Abraham and Isaac, to thee I will give it.'

God also said to Jacob: 'Thy name shall not be called any more Jacob,
but Israel.' Thus was born the name by which the Jewish people were
known, the Twelve Tribes of Israel—the descendants of Jacob's twelve
sons. The name given to them was Israelites, members of the House of
Israel. The name given to Canaan was the Land of Israel. And Israel was
the name given in 1948 to the Jewish State.

The names of the twelve sons of Jacob have been popular Jewish
boys' names throughout the ages. His sons by his first wife Leah were
Reuben, Simeon, Levi, Judah, Issachar and Zebulun. His sons by Leah's

maidservant, Bilhah, were Dan and Naphtali. His sons by his second wife Rachel were Joseph and Benjamin. His sons by Rachel's maidservant, Zilpah, were Gad and Asher. Each of the tribes who descended from the twelve sons were to be given a portion of the Promised Land, with the exception of the descendants of Levi, who were delegated to serve God and teach the people the tenets of the religion.

No. 8

Dearest Auntie Fori,

In my last letter I wrote of how Jacob had twelve sons. One of them, Joseph, was his father's favourite, making the others so jealous that the Bible tells us 'They hated him, and could not speak peaceably unto him'. When Joseph told his brothers of a dream he had, that one day they would bow down to him and pay him homage, 'they hated him yet the more'. When he told them of a second dream, which he interpreted that not only his brothers but also his parents would bow down to him, even his father was angry, asking: 'Shall I and thy mother and thy brethren indeed come to bow down ourselves to thee to the earth?'

The brothers decided to kill Joseph, and throw his body into a pit. But one of them, Reuben, the eldest, said they should not kill him but leave him in a pit to die. This they did. They then sat down a little way off and ate their food. Luckily for Joseph—and for Jewish history—at that very moment some Ishmaelite merchants came by—cousins in fact, the descendants of Abraham's brother. It was Judah who suggested that, instead of leaving Joseph in the pit to die, they sell him into slavery. This they did, for 'twenty pieces of silver'.

Joseph was seventeen years old. His brothers, returning to their father, reported that the young man had been killed and eaten by wild beasts. As proof of Joseph's death they showed Jacob his son's coat of many colours—one of the gifts that had made them jealous—and which they had dipped in the blood of a young goat.

Those who bought Joseph as their slave took him to Egypt, where he was sold again, this time to the captain of Pharaoh's guard, Potiphar. Joseph was diligent, and became 'a prosperous man', becoming the overseer of Potiphar's house. Then disaster struck. Potiphar's wife asked Joseph to sleep with her. He refused. Once she grabbed hold of his robe, pleading with him, 'Lie with me', but he fled from the room, leaving his robe in her hand. She then accused him of having molested her, and Potiphar sent him to the royal prison. For resisting the sexual advances of Potiphar's wife, the rabbis gave Joseph the name 'righteous'.

While in prison, God showed Joseph mercy, and 'gave him favour in the sight of the keeper of the prison', so much so that the prisoners were committed to his charge. Two of the prisoners were Pharaoh's chief butler and chief baker. Joseph successfully interpreted their dreams, that the butler would be released three days later, and that the baker would be hanged. He then asked the butler: 'Think on me when it shall be well with thee, and show kindness, I pray thee, unto me, and make mention of me unto Pharoah, and bring me out of this house: For indeed I was stolen away out of the land of the Hebrews: and here also have I done nothing that they should put me into the dungeon.'

The butler was indeed released and returned to Pharoah's palace. The baker was hanged. As for Joseph's request that the butler tell Pharaoh about him, the Bible tells us in a brief sentence that the butler did not remember him 'but forgat him'. Two years passed. Pharaoh himself then had a disturbing dream—seven thin ears of corn eating seven full ears— which none of those near him could interpret, neither the wise men nor the magicians. Then the chief butler remembered Joseph and his successful interpretation of the dreams in prison, and told Pharaoh, who called for Joseph, 'and they brought him hastily out of the dungeon: and he shaved himself, and changed his raiment, and came in unto Pharaoh.'

Joseph then interpreted the royal dream as meaning that seven years of plenty would be followed by seven years of drought, and advised Pharoah to gather up all the surplus food in the seven good years, and store them for the seven bad years 'that the land perish not through the famine'. Pharoah was so impressed that he appointed Joseph ruler of Egypt, telling him: 'Thou shalt be over my house, and according unto thy word shall all my people be ruled: only in the throne will I be greater than thou.' Henceforth, Joseph rode in the second most important chariot in the land, second only to that of Pharoah. The Bible tells us how, when Joseph rode past, the people of Egypt 'cried before him, Bow the knee'.

Joseph married the daughter of an Egyptian priest. They had two sons: Manasseh ('For God, said he, hath made me forget all my toil') and Ephraim ('For God hath caused me to be fruitful in the land of my affliction'). For thousands of years, every Sabbath, a Jewish father puts his hands on his sons' heads and says: 'May you be like Ephraim and Menasseh'—that is, may you be a blessing to your father. As the first of Jacob's grandchildren to be born outside Canaan, Ephraim and Menasseh were the first Jews of the Diaspora; that dispersion, first of a family, then of a tribe, and finally of a whole people, has characterized Jewish history until today.

After seven years, as Joseph had predicted, famine came. It affected the whole region, including Canaan. Ten of Jacob's sons made their way to Egypt in search of corn. One, Benjamin, stayed with his father, Jacob. The brothers had no idea that Joseph was alive, let alone in such high office. Joseph was still Pharoah's regent. His prudence in storing grain had averted the worst of the famine. His power was immense. His brothers came to him, to ask to buy corn, and did not recognize him. Hiding his identity, and speaking through an interpreter, he accused them of being spies, imprisoned one of them—his brother Simeon—and gave the rest food to take back to Canaan, insisting that only if they returned with Benjamin would Simeon be released.

The brothers did return, and Joseph gave them more food and sent them on their way. But he had put his own silver cup in Benjamin's sack, and had the brothers brought back, accusing Benjamin of stealing the cup. Judah, still not realizing that Joseph was his brother, pleaded with him that Benjamin could not have stolen the cup. Joseph decided to end their torment, and told them who he was—to their utter amazement. They should not be angry that they had sold him into slavery, he said, 'for God did send me before you to preserve life'. His own relief was enormous that his father, Jacob, was still alive.

At Joseph's suggestion, his brothers moved to Egypt, together with their father, Jacob, and their families. 'Fear not to go down into Egypt,' God told the old man Jacob, 'for I will make of thee a great nation.' Pharaoh accepted the newcomers with enthusiasm, telling Joseph: 'The land of Egypt is before thee; in the best of the land, make thy father and brethren to dwell.'

For many years—for three whole generations—the Jews remained in Egypt, in the land of Goshen in the Nile Delta. Life was pleasant for them. 'And the children of Israel were fruitful, and increased abundantly, and multiplied, and waxed exceeding mighty, and the land was filled with them.' That might have been the end of the story, as far as geography and Jewish heritage were concerned, had God (or fate, or history) not had a different future in store for the Jews.

But that story is for my next letter.

No. 9

Dearest Auntie Fori,

Last week, after Joseph's successes as Pharaoh's favourite, the Jews in Egypt flourished, and were content with their lives. But, the Bible tells us, in due course 'there arose up a new king over Egypt, which knew not Joseph'. He was upset because, he told the Egyptians, 'Behold, the people of the children of Israel are more and mightier than we.' This new Pharaoh, probably Rameses II (1290-1223 BC) used the Jews as slave labourers, forcing them to build two cities for the Egyptians: Pithom and Rameses. The more the Egyptians afflicted the Jews, however, 'the more they multiplied and grew'.

There is a Hebrew word, *habiru,* which referred to a certain kind of slave. An Egyptian decree, issued by Pharaoh Merueptah (1223-1214 BC) refers to 'the Habiru, who carry stones for the great pylon of the great city of Rameses'. Some scholars think this may be the origin of the word 'Hebrew'.

The Bible relates how the Egyptians made the lives of the Jews 'bitter with hard bondage', making them work both at building and in the fields, 'with rigour'. Then, to reduce the Jewish population—to destroy the perpetuation of the Jewish people—the new Pharoah determined on a drastic course, to kill every new-born Jewish male child. His order was succinct: 'Every son that is born ye shall cast into the river, and every daughter ye shall save alive.'

Mothers sought to avoid the harsh decree. One Jewish infant—a great-grandson of Jacob through his third son, Levi—was hidden by his mother Jochebed for three months after his birth. 'And when she could not longer hide him, she took for him an ark of bulrushes, and daubed it with slime and with pitch, and put the child therein; and she laid it in the flags by the river's brink.'

That tiny child was Moses. Miriam, his older sister, watched from a distance to see what would happen. She saw Pharaoh's daughter come down to the river to bathe. Seeing the basket, the princess asked her maid to bring it to her. 'And when she opened it, she saw the child: and, behold, the babe wept. And she had compassion on him, and said, This is one of the Hebrews' children.'

The young Miriam then came forward, and asked Pharoah's daughter if she would like a Hebrew nurse for the child. Pharoah's daughter said yes, whereupon Miriam went and brought back Moses' mother. 'And Pharaoh's daughter said unto her, take this child away, and nurse it for me, and I will give thee thy wages.' So it was that his mother took Moses away and nursed him. Then, when the baby grew, she took him back to Pharaoh's daughter, and he became her son: it was indeed she who gave him the name Moses—the Egyptian word for 'son'.

This fortunate survivor of Pharoah's anger became one of the great figures of history, known to the Jews as *Moshe Rabbenu*—Moses our Teacher. The modern Hebrew name for ladybird—a name popularized by the Yiddish writer Mendele Mocher Sforim a hundred years ago—is *parat Moshe Rabbenu,* the cow of Moses our teacher, a term of endearment for that delightful little creature. But that is a digression!

Saved from an early and terrible death, Moses lived as a young man in the palace of Pharoah's daughter, becoming a prince in Egypt. But at the same time, 'he went out unto his brethren, and looked on their burdens'. Seeing an Egyptian striking a Hebrew with intent to kill him, Moses killed the Egyptian and hid his body in the sand. Pharaoh, hearing of this, tried to put him to death, but Moses managed to flee into the distant land of Midian. There he came to the rescue of the seven daughters of Jethro, the priest of Midian, when shepherds tried to drive them away from the well where they were watering their father's flock. The priest gave Moses one of his daughters, Zipporah, as his wife. She bore him a son, Gershom, a name meaning 'stranger in a strange land'.

Pharaoh died, but under his successor, probably Merueptah, the Jews in Egypt remained in bondage. Moses, still in Midian, was confronted by 'a flame of fire' that wreathed a desert bush in flames but did not consume it. From the middle of the bush, God told Moses that he knew of the suffering of the Jews in Egypt, telling him: 'And I am come down to deliver them out of the hands of the Egyptians, and to bring them up out of that land unto a good land and a large, unto a land flowing with milk and honey.' Moses would be God's instrument. 'I will send thee unto Pharaoh, that thou mayest bring forth my people the children of Israel out of Egypt.'

Moses protested that he was a poor speaker: 'I am not eloquent, neither heretofore, nor since thou has spoken unto thy servant: but I am slow of speech, and of a slow tongue.' Some say this means that Moses was a stutterer; more likely, it means that he was not a man of eloquence. After all, he later speaks at great length to the Children of Israel in the wilderness, as he articulates God's will.

God suggested that Moses should be helped by his older brother Aaron, who could 'speak well'. Moses was then eighty and Aaron eighty-three. God told Moses: 'See, I have made thee a god to Pharaoh: and Aaron thy brother shall be thy prophet.' It was not to be a simple task. Speaking through Aaron, Moses urged Pharaoh to 'let my people go', but Pharaoh refused. God had other plans in mind, telling Moses: 'And the Egyptians shall know that I am the Lord, when I stretch forth mine hand upon Egypt. . . .'

The first sign of power was an impressive demonstration: Aaron threw down his rod in front of Pharaoh and it turned into a snake. Pharoah's magicians then did the same, but Aaron's snake ate up all their snakes. Pharaoh was impressed, but then God hardened his heart so that he refused to let the Children of Israel go. God wanted to show him more of 'my signs and my wonders'. These were the plagues, which some modern scholars suggest could have been the result of a serious flooding of the Nile. The first was turning all the rivers of Egypt into blood, 'and the fish that was in the river died; and the river stank, and the Egyptians could not drink the water of the river.' Once more, Pharaoh's magicians were able to emulate this, and once more Pharaoh hardened his heart.

And after each further plague, Pharaoh still refused to let the Jews go. Aaron's rod was used again, to produce a plague of frogs. Then, again using his rod, Aaron produced a plague of lice. This was followed by a plague of flies, then by a disease which affected all the Egyptian horses, cattle, camels, oxen and sheep—but none of the Israelite livestock—then a plague of boils on man and beast, then a ferocious hailstorm with 'fire mingled with the hail', then a plague of locusts that ate 'every herb of the land, and all the fruit of the trees which the hail had left', then darkness for three days—'but all the children of Israel had light in their dwellings'. After each plague Pharoah at first told the Children of Israel to go, but then rescinded his order.

Once again, the Jewish story might have ended: an implacable Pharaoh, and a people with no way out of their slavery. But, as we shall see next week, the final plague proved too much, even for the fiercest of Pharaohs.

No. 10

Dearest Auntie Fori,

After nine plagues had failed, there came what proved to be the final plague, the death of all first-born Egyptians. Before the deaths took place, and determined not to be caught out by any further change of mind by Pharaoh, the Children of Israel made preparations for a rapid departure. There was no time to bake bread properly, so unleavened bread was prepared: dry and flat: the bread, called *matza,* that Jews eat throughout the week of the Passover celebrations. I wonder if you remember the matza of your youth, Auntie Fori?

God caused the Israelites to put the blood of a lamb on the doorposts and the lintel of their houses—so that the Angel of Death would pass over their houses and their own first-born would not be killed. This gives the festival its name: Passover: 'I will pass over you, and the plague shall not be upon you to destroy you, when I smite the land of Egypt.'

As the final plague was about to take place, and as the Israelites were making preparations for departure, God told Moses and Aaron: 'And this day shall be unto you for a memorial; and ye shall keep it a feast to the Lord throughout your generations; ye shall keep it as a feast by an ordinance for ever.'

Pharaoh's own oldest son was among the thousands of Egyptian first-born to die. Horrified, Pharaoh summoned Moses and Aaron and told them: 'Rise up, and get you forth from among my people, both ye and the Children of Israel; and go, serve the Lord, as you have said.' He also told them to take their flocks and herds, 'and be gone; and bless me also'.

Moses led the Jews eastward fifty or sixty miles, to the Red Sea. This is widely believed to have been the Reed Sea, a brackish sheet of water some five to ten miles wide, separated from the Mediterranean by a thirty-mile-long sand spur, not far from today's Suez Canal. When the Jews reached the sea, however, Pharaoh changed his mind again about letting them go, and set out in pursuit with six hundred chariots. As the Egyptian charioteers confronted the Jews, Moses 'stretched out his hand over the sea'. The waters divided and the Children of Israel crossed over to the far shore on dry land: the waters of the sea formed a wall on either side of them.

According to Jewish tradition, attributed to the second century Rabbi Tarfon, although the parting of the sea was a result of Divine intervention, the first act of advancing into it was taken by an individual Jew, Nahshon, the head of the tribe of Judah, who alone among the Israelites obeyed Moses' command to enter the water before it parted, and was followed by his tribe. Another version of the story is quite different: that the tribe of Benjamin jumped first into the water, whereupon the tribe of Judah, angered by this, attacked them with stones.

The Children of Israel having crossed, the waters still held back, whereupon the Egyptian charioteers followed in pursuit. Moses stretched out his hand again, the sea returned, and the Egyptians were drowned. The Bible recounts that the Jews 'saw the Egyptians dead upon the sea shore'. The story of how the Children of Israel left Egypt and escaped through the Red Sea is recounted every year at Passover by every Jewish family, as a crucial moment of national liberty, and as proof of God's concern. I will write you a special 'Passover' letter later on.

The story of the parting of the Red Sea is told on the seventh day of the festival. Some extremely devout Jews even pour water on the floor of their home that day, and then walk through it, as a re-enactment of the final Passover miracle. In synagogue, the triumphant Song of Moses is sung, the first, but not the last moment in the Bible when the Jews expressed their feelings in song:

> *I will sing unto the Lord, for he hath triumphed gloriously: the horse and his rider hath he thrown into the sea.*
>
> *The Lord is my strength and song, and he is become my salvation. . . .*
>
> *The Lord is a man of war: the Lord is his name.*
>
> *Pharoah's chariots and his host hath he cast into the sea: his chosen captains also are drowned in the Red sea.*
>
> *The depths have covered them: they sank into the bottom as a stone. . . .*
>
> *Thou in thy mercy hast led forth the people which thou hast redeemed: thou hast guided them in thy strength unto thy holy habitation. . . .*
>
> *Thou shalt bring them in, and plant them in the mountain of thine inheritance, in the place, O Lord, which thou hast made for thee to dwell in, in the Sanctuary, O Lord, which thy hands have established.*
>
> *The Lord shall reign for ever and ever.*

That Sanctuary was the Temple and 'the place' was Jerusalem. But it was to be a long journey.

No. 11

Dearest Auntie Fori,

How extraordinary to think that Moses was in his eighties when he led the Children of Israel through the inhospitable Sinai desert for forty years, surely forty 'long' years if ever one set of years was longer than another. From the Red Sea they probably made their way down the west coast of the Sinai Peninsula (past today's Egyptian oil town of Abu Rudeis) and then up the east coast, from oasis to oasis.

From the earliest days of their wandering the Jews complained— 'murmured against Moses'—first because the waters at one oasis were too bitter to drink. Moses appealed to God, who showed him a tree which he then threw into the waters, making them sweet. God then promised that if the Jews did 'that which is right' in his sight he would put none of the diseases on them 'which I have brought upon the Egyptians: for I am the Lord that healeth thee'.

More complaints came at the next oasis, when the Israelites again 'murmured' against Moses and Aaron in no uncertain terms, telling them: 'Would to God we had died by the hand of the Lord in the land of Egypt, when we sat by the flesh pots, and when we did eat bread to the full; for ye have brought us forth into this wilderness, to kill this whole assembly with hunger.' God again came to Moses' rescue, bringing the Children of Israel meat in the evening and bread in the morning 'whether they will walk in my law, or no'. The meat was quails, the bread was manna—'like coriander seed, white; and the taste of it was like wafers made with honey'.

A third rebellion came when, at yet another oasis, this one in the north-east of the Sinai Peninsula, there was no water. God told Moses to speak to the rock and it would produce water. Moses, in a moment of frustration, struck the rock instead. Water flowed, but God did not forget Moses' lack of faith: so much so that Moses was not allowed to enter the Promised Land. It was at the moment when Moses struck the rock that the Amalekites attacked the Israelites. Joshua was chosen to lead the fight against Amalek: Moses, on a hilltop, lifted up his hands, helped by Aaron on one side and an Israelite called Hur on the other, and brought victory. God then told Moses: 'Write this for a memorial in a book . . . for I will utterly put out the remembrance of Amalek under heaven.'

The time had come for God to make a promise to the Israelites, one which was to define the Jewish people's relationship with him for all time. Three months after the Israelites left the Nile Delta they reached Mount Sinai. God then told Moses to tell the Children of Israel: 'Ye have seen what I did unto the Egyptians, and how I bare you on eagles' wings, and brought you unto myself. Now therefore, if ye will obey my voice indeed, and keep my covenant, then ye shall be a peculiar treasure unto me above all people . . .'

With these words, God made the Children of Israel his 'chosen' people, and great has been the discussion about what that chosenness meant. Chosen to serve God? Chosen to conquer others? Chosen to be an example to others of goodness and fair dealing? Chosen to rule, or to serve? Not only to serve, the commentators tell us, but to regard service—serving God and serving Man—as a privilege.

That concept of serving God in a special—indeed a unique—way began when Moses was at the top of Mount Sinai and God gave him two tablets of stone: the Ten Commandments. On them were inscribed the basic tenets of the Jewish moral code. Yet when Moses came down from the mountain with the tablets he found the children of Israel were worshipping a golden calf.

The pagan calf had been fashioned from the gold ornaments of the people, who had prevailed on Aaron, Moses' brother, to help them gather the gold while Moses was up the mountain. Furious at seeing this idol worship, Moses smashed the tablets and destroyed the golden calf—burning it and stamping on it and reducing it to powder and throwing it into the brook that flowed from Mount Sinai.

Frightened by the thought of God's anger, Moses fasted for forty days and nights. 'I did neither eat bread, nor drink water,' he recalled just before he died, 'because of all your sins which ye sinned, in doing wickedly in the sight of the Lord, to provoke him to anger.'

God wanted to destroy Aaron, but Moses successfully intervened on his brother's behalf. Returning up the mountain after forty days, Moses then made two new tablets of stone, on which God rewrote the Ten Commandments. These tablets, kept in an ark which Moses made before climbing the mountain again, were accepted by the people. They included God's injunction to have 'no other gods before me', or to take God's name in vain.

The Jews were also told to remember the Sabbath day and keep it holy—to work for six days but to rest on the seventh. They were told to 'Honour thy father and mother: that thy days may be long upon the land which the Lord thy God giveth thee.' Each commandment sought to change the prevailing morality of those ancient times: 'Thou shalt not kill. Thou shalt not commit adultery. Thou shalt not steal. Thou shalt not bear false witness against thy neighbour. Thou shalt not covet thy neighbour's house, thou shalt not covet thy neighbour's wife. . . .'

The Ten Commandments were to set the standards to which each generation of Jews would aspire. Over a hundred other laws of personal and communal conduct were passed on by Moses to the Jews—125 are to be found in the Book of Exodus. To this day, these laws form part of several of the weekly Bible readings in synagogue during the Sabbath service. The rest of the 613 laws to which Jews adhere are 'post-Mosaic', from the Books of Leviticus and Deuteronomy.

Here is a curious repercussion of the Biblical story of Moses when he came down from the mountain. The Bible tells us that his face was 'radiant', since he had spoken with God. The Hebrew word for 'radiant', *karan,* was mistranslated in the Christian eleventh-century Latin Vulgate version as *keren,* meaning horn. This gave rise to the Christian portrayal of Moses—and later of Jews generally—as having horns, a sign of ugliness and evil. Of course, Michelangelo's horned Moses at the church of San Pietro in Vincoli in Rome is a masterpiece.

As the Israelites continued their travels in the wilderness, discontent against Moses grew among those who felt he was taking too much on his shoulders. They complained that, together with Aaron, he was lifting himself 'above the congregation of the Lord'. When Korah, a member of the tribe of Levi, led a revolt, he was joined by 250 'princes of the assembly, famous in the congregation, men of renown'. Their main complaint was that Moses had brought them 'out of a land that floweth with milk and honey'—Egypt—only to 'kill us in the wilderness'. He had not brought them into a land of milk and honey, 'or given us inheritance of fields and vineyards'.

Moses was very angry, as was God. The malcontents were gathered together with their families, and then 'the earth opened her mouth and swallowed them up . . . and they perished from among the congregation'. Many of the Israelites protested at this, telling Moses and Aaron: 'Ye have killed the people of the Lord'. For that protest, plague 'was begun among the people': 14,700 of them died—that is the figure the Bible gives—before the plague ended. There were no more rebellions, for a while.

Another incident during the years in the wilderness shows God's sense of punishment—and as my rabbi, Hugo Gryn, used to remark, his wry humour. During the journey Moses married a black woman from Ethiopia. Both Miriam and Aaron were critical of their brother's choice. God punished Miriam by turning her skin even whiter than it was: 'and behold, Miriam became leprous, white as snow.' For seven days she was made to stay outside the Israelite camp. Only when Moses prayed for her was she cured.

The Ark of the Covenant travelled with the Israelites through the wilderness. According to second century AD translations of the Bible in Aramaic—the Onkeles—it was the dwelling place of the Shekhinah, the Divine Presence. The word Shekhinah comes from the Hebrew verb *shakhan,* to dwell, God having told Moses: 'And let them make me a sanctuary, that I may dwell among them.' It was at this sanctuary that the Israelites brought their thank offerings, including 'gold, and silver, and brass, And blue, and purple, and scarlet, and fine linen, and goat's hair, And ram's skins dyed red . . .' and oil and spices, and constructed the Tabernacle. It was at the Tabernacle that Aaron—whom Moses had appointed High Priest—and the other priests conducted their services.

Each of Aaron's four sons were priests in his lifetime. But two of them, Nadab and Abihu, were killed by Divine intervention after an incident at the Tabernacle. They had incurred God's anger after appearing at the Tabernacle and putting what the Bible calls 'incense' and 'strange fire' in their father's priestly censer.

After forty years, the Children of Israel reached the plains of Moab, on the eastern bank of the River Jordan, facing the land which God had promised to Abraham and his descendants. There, Balaam, a heathen prophet, was asked by the King of Moab to curse them. Instead, he blessed them. 'The people shall dwell alone', he said, 'and shall not be reckoned among the nations'; the Lord 'hath not beheld iniquity in Jacob; neither hath he seen perversness in Israel.' Then, after declaring 'Blessed is he that blesseth thee, and cursed is he that curseth thee', Balaam spoke the words which, in future ages, every Jew was to speak on entering the synagogue—or in touching the mezuzah at the entrance to each home: 'How goodly are thy tents, O Jacob, and thy tabernacles, O Israel!' and he went on to prophesy a triumphant future for Israel: 'there shall come a Star out of Jacob, and a Sceptre shall rise out of Israel, and shall smite the corners of Moab, and destroy all the children of Sheth. And Edom shall be a possession . . . and Israel shall do valiantly.'

Throughout their journeying, Moses had urged the Jews to keep God's commandments, not to lose faith, not to turn their back on God, not to abandon their belief in the promised land. The Ten Commandments, kept inside their special Ark, had travelled with them from Sinai. Finally they came to a hillside overlooking the Dead Sea from which could be seen, to the west, the mountains of Judaea—the very hills around Hebron where Abraham had lived and died so many generations earlier.

In this final year of wandering, Aaron died. He was 123 years old.

Two of Aaron's sons, Nadab and Abihu, had, as you saw, incurred God's wrath and been killed. His two other sons, Eleazar and Ithamar, who had behaved with propriety in the Tabernacle, secured the succession of the priesthood, Eleazar becoming High Priest on Aaron's death.

By Jewish tradition, the priesthood has continued to this day through Aaron's descendants, the *Cohanim,* the Cohens. Not only has the priestly ritual in synagogue devolved on Cohens since Biblical times, but the most recent DNA research has shown that seventy per cent of today's Cohens—two and a half thousand years after Aaron—have one identical gene. Many varieties of the name have come into use, among them Cohen, Kahan, Kagan, Kohn, Kun—as in Bela Kun, who led the Communist revolution in Hungary in 1919, when you were a young girl. I wonder if you have any memories of those dramatic days in Budapest, when a Jew came so near to imposing Communism on the Danube.

No. 12

Dearest Auntie Fori,

In my last letter, the Children of Israel had reached the eastern shore of the Dead Sea after forty years of wandering through many inhospitable deserts.

More than forty years earlier, before the Exodus from Egypt, Moses had married a Midianite. As the Israelites approached the Promised Land, some of them committed 'harlotry' with Midianite women there. God told Moses to take action, after which, God told him, 'Thou shalt be gathered unto thy people'.

Moses despatched an Israelite army—a thousand men from each of the Twelve Tribes—together with the priest Phineas (Pinhas), Aaron's grandson, 'with holy instruments, and the trumpets to blow in his hand'. The army killed every Midianite male, including the five Kings of Midian, burned all the Midianite cities, and returned to Moses with 'all the spoil, all the prey, both of men and beasts'. The Bible lists the spoils of war, including 675,000 sheep. Moses then told the army to 'kill every male among the little ones, and kill every woman that hath known man by lying with him'. The young women 'that have not known a man by lying with him, keep alive for yourselves.'

The last battle of the wilderness years was over. There, overlooking the lowest spot on the surface of the earth (more than a thousand feet below sea level—in Biblical times as today), God then told Moses to speak to the Children of Israel.

These were God's words: 'When ye are passed over Jordan into the land of Canaan; Then ye shall drive out all the inhabitants before you, and destroy all their pictures, and destroy all their molten images, and quite pluck down all their high places: And ye shall dispossess the inhabitants of the land, and dwell therein: for I have given you the land to possess it: And ye shall divide the land by lot for an inheritance among your families.'

Moses then repeated the Ten Commandments, using words which are at the centre of every Jewish prayer service, the words which a pious Jew recites several times each day: '*Shema Yisroel*—Hear, O Israel: The Lord our God is one Lord. And thou shalt love the Lord with all thine heart and with all thy soul, and with all thy might.'

In a final address to the children of Israel, Moses set out in detail the laws that they must follow. These repeated and fortified the laws they had received in the Sinai desert. They contained many injunctions that were to establish a new ethic for those violent, often lawless times. They included: 'Cursed be he that maketh the blind to wander out of the way' and 'Cursed be he that taketh reward to slay an innocent person'.

Moses understood that the will of the people to obey the written law could not be taken for granted. 'For I know thy rebellion and thy stiff neck,' he exclaimed to the Levites—whose task was to attend to the Ark of the Covenant—'behold, while I am yet alive with you this day, ye have been rebellious against the Lord; and how much more after my death?' Pessimistically, he told them: 'For I know that after my death ye will utterly corrupt yourselves, and aside from the way which I have commanded you; and evil will befall you in later days, because you will do evil in the sight of the Lord, to provoke him to anger through the work of your hands.'

In one last plea to the Children of Israel to serve God and obey his commandments, Moses told them that God would be their saviour. 'Happy art thou, O Israel: who is like unto thee, O people saved by the Lord, the shield of thy help. . . .'

Moses then went from the plains of Moab to a mountaintop over-looking the promised land. From that high vantage point God showed him the whole region, stretching westward from the river Jordan to the Mediterranean Sea sixty miles away, and a few miles to the north, far below across the river Jordan, the city of Jericho: 'the city of palm trees'. God then said to Moses: 'This is the land which I sware unto Abraham, unto Isaac, and unto Jacob, saying, I will give it unto thy seed'. As for Moses himself, God told him: 'I have caused thee to see it with thine eyes, but thou shalt not go over thither.'

Then Moses died. He was a hundred and twenty years old. To this day, when Jews want to wish somebody long life, they say: 'May you live to be a hundred and twenty'. So you, Auntie Fori, have at least another thirty years to go—or as Jews say to those who are venerable like your-self, 'May you live till the Messiah comes'.

No. 13

Dearest Auntie Fori,

This letter is about the moment when a wandering group of tribes—the Israelites—ceased their wandering and found a patch of land—not much larger than Wales or Massachusetts, in which they could become a nation, and establish national institutions, first in Biblical times and then, a long time in the future, during your lifetime and mine.

The death of Moses did not impede the progress of nationhood, although his death was a blow to the Israelites whom he had led for so long, and with such determination. The Bible records that the children of Israel 'wept for Moses' for thirty days in the plains of Moab. Henceforth, thirty days was to be the period of mourning when a Jew died. Of all the figures of Biblical and later Jewish history, Moses was the one most highly regarded: the outstanding leader. Naming a Jewish boy Moses (Moshe, Moishe, Moise) was to wish him a fine life in service of his people.

The mourning for Moses did not hold up the imminent transformation of Jewish history—the search for nationhood, and its rapid achievement. Immediately after the death of Moses, the Jews entered their promised land, under the leadership of Joshua.

Living in the area which God had promised to the Children of Israel were many tribes which sought to bar their path. Among them were the Amorites, Ammonites, Jebusites and Canaanites. The first city to fall to the Israelites—to the sound of their trumpets—was Jericho. Gradually, as a result of many battles, probably over a period of about 200 years between 1250 and 1000 BC, the whole of the land of Canaan had come under the rule of the Israelite tribes.

Despite the ferocity which had been needed to conquer Canaan, the Jews settled down to a pastoral life, content to graze their sheep and cultivate their fields, and hoping to be unmolested by their neighbours. What marked them out as different from their neighbours was their belief in a single deity, the belief which had sustained them during their years in Egypt, and been fortified during their forty-year wanderings in the desert. The laws of Moses were their guide, the story of the Exodus their inspiration, the Sabbath day their focal point of prayer and rest and relaxation, the Ark of the Covenant the centre of their religious worship. Their belief in one God continued for many hundreds of years to be a curiosity at a time when larger and more powerful groups in the region boasted many gods, large numbers of impressive golden images, and fine temples in which to worship them.

No. 14

Dearest Auntie Fori,

For two hundred years the children of Israel, dwelling in Canaan, were ruled, not by soldiers or kings—as were their neighbours—but by

Judges, chosen from among the leaders of the twelve tribes. The Bible tells of one Judge—his name was Jair—who had 'thirty sons that rode on thirty ass colts, and they had thirty cities'. Jair ruled for twenty-two years. Another Judge was a woman prophet, Deborah.

Life for the Israelites at the time of the Judges was constantly threatened by the tribes living around them. One such enemy was Jabin, the King of Canaan. Deborah ordered one of the leading Israelite soldiers, Barak—the name, as I write this letter, both of the present Prime Minister of Israel and of the Israeli Chief Justice—to go to war against Jabin's military captain, Sisera. Barak agreed to do so, but on condition that Deborah accompany him.

So it was that Deborah gave Barak the decisive order to attack, urging him: 'Up; for this is the day in which the Lord hath delivered Sisera into thine hand.' Sisera's army had nine hundred iron chariots, Barak's had none. But Deborah, noticing that the nearby Kishon brook was flooded, devised a strategy whereby Sisera's chariots were caught in the waters and his army defeated. Deborah and Barak then sang a song of triumph, recalling how 'the stars in their courses fought against Sisera. The river of Kishon swept them away. . . .'

The victory was a complete one: 'all the host of Sisera fell upon the edge of the sword; and there was not a man left'. Sisera himself sought refuge in the tent of Jael, a local Kenite woman. Being desperately thirsty after the battle and his flight, he asked Jael for water. The Bible recounts that 'she gave him milk; she brought forth butter in a lordly dish'. Then, as soon as Sisera was asleep, 'she took a nail of the tent, and took an hammer in her hand, and went softly unto him, and smote the nail into his temples, and fastened it to the ground: for he was fast asleep and weary. So he died.'

In their song of triumph Deborah and Barak recounted each phase of Jael's action, including the last, 'she smote off his head, when she had pierced and stricken through his temples'. Their song ended: 'So let all thine enemies perish, O Lord: but let them that love him be as the sun when he goeth forth in his might.' For the children of Israel, forty years of peace followed the defeat of Sisera.

Alternating with persistent regularity, war and peace became the pattern of life for the Israelites, as they were for all the tribes who made up the nations of what we now call the Middle East. The wars were fierce; peace a treasured possession when it came.

No. 15

Dearest Auntie Fori,

In my last letter, the Israelites were in their own land, and it was a time of peace. Flocks of sheep, groves of trees, orchards, vegetables, corn, fresh-water springs, cities—more like the small hill villages of France and Italy today than the great cities where we live—were given a cohesion by the worship of the one God, known in the liturgy as the God of Abraham, Isaac and Jacob.

But life was precarious amid so many warring and competing nations, and the Israelites' God was one who punished as well as rewarded. The Bible tells us that after the Children of Israel 'did evil again in the sight of the Lord' they found themselves under the rule of the Philistines for forty years. The Philistines were a sea-faring and warrior nation living along the Mediterranean coast, whose chief city was Gaza. It was on one occasion while the Philistines had 'dominion over Israel' that a young Israelite, Samson, sought to restore Israelite independence.

Samson's first military expedition was against the Philistine coastal city of Ashkelon, where he killed thirty Philistine soldiers. In one of his ensuing battles, armed with 'the jawbone of an ass', Samson killed a thousand men. But he was betrayed by a Philistine woman, Delilah, with whom he had fallen in love. In response to her pleading—and in Saint-Saëns's nineteenth century opera as a result of her treachery and deceit—he told her the secret of his power: his long hair, which he had grown in seven flowing locks; and that if it were to be cut, his power would disappear. While Samson was sleeping, Delilah called a man who shaved off all seven locks.

The Philistines captured Samson, put out his eyes, took him to Gaza 'and bound him with fetters of brass; and he did grind in the prison house'. To entertain themselves, the Philistines then tied Samson to two pillars of a house. All the leading Philistines came to watch the spectacle: 'and there were upon the roof about three thousand men and women, that beheld while Samson made sport'. They did not know that, as his hair had begun to grow again, his strength had started to return.

Calling on God to let him be avenged for the loss of his sight, and exerting all the strength he could find, Samson pulled down the pillars, and was crushed and killed, 'and the house fell upon all the lords, and upon all the people that were therein. So the dead which he slew at his death were more than they which he slew in his life.'

The Israelites broke free from the Philistine yoke, but later they fought against each other in a violent civil war. In one such violent encounter, according to the Bible, more than 25,000 members of the tribe of Benjamin were killed. Then, once again, the Philistines attacked, and in the course of their victories captured the Ark of the Covenant, which they took back to Ashdod, another of their coastal cities.

For seven months the Philistines kept the Ark. During that time, thousands of Philistine men were taken ill—the Bible makes no bones about the illness—haemorrhoids. Hundreds died. In an attempt to shake off the cursed illness the Philistines moved the Ark to another of their cities, Gath. There too, hundreds of men were taken ill, also with haemorrhoids, and many died.

In despair the Philistines returned the Ark. But the Israelites, cast down by the loss of their sovereignty and burdened by the Philistine occupation, had begun to worship other gods—an echo of the worship of the golden calf at the foot of Mount Sinai some two hundred years earlier. In urging them to return to the one God, the prophet Samuel gathered them together at Mizpeh, in the hills of Samaria, and told them: 'Prepare your hearts unto the Lord, and serve him only: and he will deliver you out of the hands of the Philistines'.

Samuel's appeal was successful. When the Philistines attacked the assembled multitude they were 'smitten before Israel'. Then the Israelites, advancing from Mizpeh, pursued and defeated them, 'and the hand of the Lord was against the Philistines all the days of Samuel'.

When Samuel was old he appointed his two sons to be Judges over Israel. They, however, were far removed from his stature and wisdom: they 'walked not in his ways, but turned aside after lucre, and took bribes, and perverted judgment'.

These were bad days for the Israelites. In search of a better system of government, they appealed to Samuel to turn from the system of Judges by which they had been ruled for so long. They wanted to have a king instead, 'like all the nations; and that our king may judge us, and go out before us, and fight our battles'.

Samuel was reluctant to create a king: tradition maintained that God was the King of the Israelites. No mortal could take that place. But public pressure was considerable: kingship was clearly a central element in the nationhood of all the neighbouring peoples. The Jews also wanted to be a nation, not just a confederation of tribes.

Eventually Samuel deferred to public pressure. Saul, a member of the tribe of Benjamin, was chosen as the first king. Samuel anointed Saul's head with oil, 'and kissed him and said, Is it not because the Lord hath anointed you to be captain over his inheritance?'

In future centuries, for worshippers of a Christian Trinity, and for nations that had not existed in Biblical times—including France and Britain—the 'divine right of kings' was to be maintained through a similar procedure of anointing each new king, following Samuel's example.

No. 16

Dearest Auntie Fori,

My last letter brought the Israelites to their first King, Saul, and to the era of the Jewish kingdoms. Saul's rule began in approximately 1029 BC. He brought great prosperity to the land of Israel. But war against the neighbouring Philistines and Amalekites was his main preoccupation. He fell foul of Samuel after capturing the Amalekite king, Agag.

Samuel, in conformity with God's command that the Amalekites should be wiped out, insisted that Agag be killed, and also all the Amalekite cattle and sheep. Saul wanted to spare his captive's life, and that of his livestock. Furious at being disobeyed, Samuel summoned Agag, intending to kill him.

Pleading for his life, Agag asked Samuel: 'Surely the bitterness of death is past,' but Samuel replied: 'As thy sword hath made women childless, so shall thy mother be childless among women.' After which pronouncement, Samuel himself 'hewed Agag in pieces'.

Never again did Samuel visit Saul—the man he had made 'king over Israel'—for, as Samuel himself explained, 'rebellion is as the sin of witchcraft, and stubbornness is as iniquity and idolatry.'

The Israelites, even in the earlier, dangerous years when they had left Egypt under Moses and wandered in the desert, were noted for their rebelliousness and stubbornness. These were not characteristics that could easily be eliminated, if at all.

Among those in Saul's royal court was a shepherd boy and musician, David, of the tribe of Judah. Born in Bethlehem, he had been marked out for a special part in Jewish history. Indeed, he was anointed by Samuel as Saul's future successor while still tending his sheep. In court he played music to the king, who suffered from periodic depressions.

After David, in single combat, had killed the Philistine giant, Goliath, he was made Saul's armour-bearer, and later one of his military commanders. David married Saul's daughter Michal, and was on terms of the closest friendship with Saul's son Jonathan. But as Saul's mind became more and more unbalanced he tried to kill David, making repeated attempts on his life.

For self-preservation, David fled from the court and from the land of the Israelites, and took refuge among the Philistines. There, he even offered to join the Philistines in their attack on Saul, but they were uneasy about enlisting his help, and sent him away from the battlefield.

In the twenty-first year of his reign, Saul was killed in battle, having first witnessed the deaths of three of his sons, including Jonathan. 'And it came to pass on the morrow, when the Philistines came to strip the slain, that they found Saul and his three sons fallen in Mount Gilboa. And they cut off his head, and stripped off his armour, and sent into the land of the Philistines round about, to publish it in the house of their idols, and among the people.'

Saul's body and that of his sons were then 'fastened to a wall' of the city of Beth-shan. When the Israelites of a nearby town heard of this, they travelled through the night and took the bodies down, took them back, buried them under a tree, and fasted for seven days. The Bible calls them 'valiant men'.

On learning of the death of Saul and his sons, David—despite Saul's earlier attempts on his life—lamented (in another of the songs which beautifully elevate the biblical narrative):

The beauty of Israel is slain upon thy high places: how are the mighty fallen!

Tell it not in Gath, publish it not in Ashklelon; lest the daughters of the Philistines rejoice. . . .

Saul and Jonathan were lovely and pleasant in their life, and in their death they were not divided; they were swifter than eagles, they were stronger than lions.

Ye daughters of Israel, weep over Saul, who clothed you in scarlet, with other delights, who put on ornaments of gold upon your apparel.

How are the mighty fallen in the midst of the battle! . . .

How are the mighty fallen, and the weapons of war perished!

With Saul's death, David became king. But that story must wait a while, until the next letter.

No. 17

Dearest Auntie Fori,

What can one write of King David: he was one of the giants of Jewish history: a Biblical figure, and yet for the Jews a man of flesh and blood, of passions and sensitivities—and not a few faults either!

At first not all Israelites accepted David as their ruler, and after a short while civil war broke out between his house and that of Saul. 'But David waxed stronger and stronger, and the house of Saul weaker and weaker.' After much bloodletting, David triumphed. In Hebron, he was anointed king by the elders of Israel. The year: about 1005 BC. He was thirty years old.

From the start of his reign, David's achievements were considerable. He set up a fair and effective administration, 'executed judgment and justice unto all his people', and rebuilt the army, introducing new weaponry including, according to one tradition, body-armour. At the head of

his soldiers, he drove the Philistines out of the Land of Israel, and defeated the Moabites to the east.

The fighting with Syria was more prolonged. Early in his reign,
David killed 22,000 Syrians near Damascus, 'and the Syrians became servants to David, and brought gifts'. Later they fought him again, but this
second time the result was decisive: 'And the Syrians fled before Israel;
and David slew the men of seven hundred chariots of the Syrians, and
forty thousand horsemen'. The Syrian commander was also killed.

David not only ruled over Damascus, but in due course extended his
rule eastward to the River Euphrates, not so far from where his own
ancestor Abraham, the father of the Jews, had begun that first journey of
Jewish history.

For seven years David ruled from Hebron, the city where Abraham
was buried. Then he captured the Jebusite city of Jebus, which had
remained since the conquest of Canaan a Jebusite enclave in the middle
of the Israelite territory. Renaming the city Jerusalem ('city of peace'), he
made it his new capital. Itself built on a hill, Jerusalem was surrounded by
hills, and thus invisible from afar to those approaching it. David's City—
as it became known—was protected on the east by the deep ravine of the
Kidron valley, and to the south-west by the Hinnom valley—the first
'hell', where in times ancient even by David's era child sacrifice had
taken place.

David brought the Ark of the Covenant to Jerusalem, and announced
that the city, having never belonged to any of the twelve tribes, would
be detached from the tribal boundaries: it would be an independent
capital—not unlike Washington, D.C., in the United States, Canberra in
Australia, and Islamabad in Pakistan.

With great energy, David set about strengthening Jerusalem's walls
and building strong houses within it. He also bought a threshing field
from a Jebusite woman, a field that was at the highest point of the city,
and designated it the place for the eventual building of the Temple, to be
the resting place of the Ark of the Covenant, the physical centre of Jewish worship.

For forty years David was king over Israel. In the very first weeks of
his reign, his allies had hastened to send him gifts: Hiram the King of
Tyre, on the coast of Lebanon, sent him cedar trees and carpenters, who

built him a house. As well as being a soldier—and extending his rule to Damascus and the River Euphrates—he was an accomplished administrator, and also a poet. The Psalms are his poetic legacy. There is a common phrase among Jews, advice given to those in distress: 'Forget miracles, recite Psalms!'

In captivity in a Soviet prison in the 1970s, Anatoly Shcharansky—whose desire to live in Israel had led to his incarceration in solitary confinement for many years, and to a campaign throughout the Jewish world for his release—found solace in a small book of Psalms which he was able to keep with him, despite the hostility of his Russian captors.

While David's soldiers were busy fighting the Ammonites, he fell in love with Bathsheba, a married woman, whom he saw one evening when he was unable to sleep. From the roof of his palace, the Bible tells us, 'he saw a woman washing herself; and the woman was very beautiful to look upon'.

Making inquiries, David was told that the woman was Bathsheba, the wife of Uriah the Hittite. Despite this, David then slept with her. Soon afterwards she sent a message to David, 'I am with child.' David then ordered Uriah into battle against the Ammonites, writing to the commander of the Israelite army, Joab: 'Set ye Uriah in the forefront of the hottest battle, and retire ye from him, that he may be smitten, and die.'

Joab did not obey David to the letter, but he did send Uriah into the thick of the battle 'where he knew that valiant men were', and Uriah was among those killed. David then married Bathsheba. For his duplicity, he was punished by the death of their first child when he was just seven days old. He was also warned by God that the sword would never depart from the House of David.

This warning came swiftly to pass, when Absalom, David's eldest son from an earlier marriage, raised the standard of revolt against his father. With considerable difficulty, David's army commander, Joab, crushed the rebellion. Absalom was killed—his head struck the branch of an oak tree as he was riding on a mule: later his body was thrown into a deep pit and covered with stones. David was distraught when he was brought the news, wishing that he had been killed instead of his son. 'O my son, Absalom, my son, my son Absalom!' he lamented, 'Would God I had died for thee, O Absalom, my son, my son!'

David understood the fragility of life. Before his own death he addressed God in words which echo across the ages: 'But who am I and what is my people. For we are strangers before Thee, and sojourners, as were all our fathers: our days on earth are as a shadow, and there is none abiding.'

After Absalom's death, another of David's sons, Adonijah, was pushed forward as heir to the throne by his mother, Hagith, who enlisted the support of Joab, the army commander, and Abiathar, the High Priest. But Adonijah was challenged by Solomon, the second child of Bathsheba and David, who enlisted the support of the prophet Nathan. In the ensuing struggle for the succession—while David was still alive, but by then old and frail—Solomon prevailed. He then ruled as co-regent with his father.

On David's death, in about 965 BC, Solomon was anointed King. Following his father's deathbed wish, he took swift revenge on those who had earlier tried to take the throne. Joab and Adonijah were killed, and Abiathar exiled.

These were violent times, and yet the dynastic royal inheritance continued—and was to mean a great deal in future ages. When in later centuries the Jews were enslaved by other nations—the Babylonians, Hellenes and Romans—they expected God to send a Messiah: the word to the Jews meant an anointed king, to rescue them from oppression, and they believed that this Messiah would be a descendant of King David. The writers of the New Testament, aware of this, stressed that Jesus was a direct descendant of David. Even Queen Victoria—Queen-Empress of India when 'your' Nehru family was coming into prominence—was presented with a chart showing her own lineage going back to King David.

No. 18

Dearest Auntie Fori,

King David was dead, his memory cherished by all subsequent Jewish generations as 'the sweet singer of Israel'. Under the rule of his son Solomon, an Israelite empire was maintained from Gaza—formerly the

Philistine capital, today the chief city of the Palestine Authority—to the River Euphrates, the eastern border of Syria, which David had conquered. Those whom Solomon defeated in battle 'brought presents, and served Solomon all his life'. He also made an alliance with Pharaoh and married Pharaoh's daughter 'and brought her into the city of David'. Her dowry was the former Philistine city of Gezer, on the road from Jerusalem to the coast. When Pharaoh had conquered it, he had killed all its inhabitants.

Solomon's achievements were considerable. 'And the Lord gave Solomon wisdom, as he promised him'. The best-known example of his wisdom was when he was confronted by two women—the Bible identifies them as 'harlots'—each of whom claimed that they were the mother of the same child. Solomon listened to their respective stories, and then, calling for a sword, said: 'Divide the living child in two, and give half to the one, and half to the other.'

One of the women reacted by saying that she would rather renounce her claim to the child than allow it to be cut in half. Solomon immediately identified her as the true mother, and ordered her to be given the child. 'And all Israel heard of the judgment which the king had judged; and they feared the king: for they saw that the wisdom of God was in him, to do judgment.'

Early in his reign, Solomon established peace and a binding alliance with King Hiram of Tyre, to the north. Hiram sent Solomon as much timber as he needed for whatever he wished to build, chiefly the long-awaited Temple. In return, every year Solomon sent Hiram large quantities of wheat and olive oil.

In Jerusalem, Solomon built himself a magnificent palace, using hewn stones and cedars from Lebanon. Within the palace was a throne from which he gave judgments. He also built new walls for the city. But his greatest building achievement was in the service of God: on the threshing floor which his father David had bought many years before, Solomon built the Temple, raising its foundations on a high platform.

The foundations of the Temple were laid of 'great stones, costly stones, and hewed stones', quarried by Jewish labourers in the mountains of Lebanon. Building began in the fourth year of Solomon's reign. It was almost five hundred years (480 to be more precise) since Moses had brought the children of Israel out of Egypt. While the Temple was being constructed, God told Solomon: 'If thou wilt walk in my statutes, and execute my judgments, and keep all my commandments to walk in them; then I will perform my word with thee, which I spake unto David thy father: And I will dwell among the children of Israel, and will not forsake my people Israel.'

It took seven years for Solomon to complete the Temple. Its gold and its masonry and its decorations were remarkable. Among its noted features were four hundred carved stone pomegranates, and twelve carved oxen, as well as many carved lilies and carved lions. 'I have surely built thee an house to dwell in,' Solomon told God, 'a settled place for thee to abide in forever.' At the heart of the Temple was the Ark: 'the Ark of the Covenant' which God had made through Moses with the children of Israel.

In building a strong army, Solomon had not only foot soldiers, but cavalrymen and horse-drawn chariots. In the 1960s, archaeological excavations at Megiddo (Armageddon) at the edge of the Plain of Jezreel revealed an enormous stable with stalls for 450 horses. Solomon also built a navy, through which he embarked on a vigorous sea-borne trade. Ships sailed from ports on the Mediterranean and from the southernmost town of Solomon's dominions, the port of Etzion-Geber, at the head of the Gulf of Akaba. It is located a few miles to the east of present-day Eilat.

Solomon's ships, whose crews were sailors provided by Hiram, sailed through the Red Sea to the Indian Ocean, trading with southern Arabia, eastern Africa, and even with distant India. From the land of Ophir (possibly present-day Ethiopia) they brought Solomon large quantities of gold. From this he made two hundred shields of gold, covered his ivory throne with gold, and drank from golden goblets. Also brought from afar were apes and peacocks.

From distant Sheba (possibly present-day southern Yemen), the Queen herself came, drawn by the fame of Solomon and the stories about his God. 'She came to prove him with hard questions. And she came to Jerusalem with a very great train, with camels that bare spices, and very much gold, and precious stones.' After seeing Solomon's court, and his judgments, and the Temple, she exclaimed: 'Happy are thy men, happy are these servants, which stand continually before thee, and hear thy wisdom.' She then gave Solomon gold, spices and precious stones: 'There came no more such abundance of spices as these which the Queen of Sheba gave to king Solomon.

'So Solomon exceeded all the kings of the earth for riches and for wisdom'. The pastoral life led by the twelve Jewish tribes, who had settled on both sides of the River Jordan, their cities and their religious worship, were protected by Solomon's wealth and alliances. Based on his judgment, the laws were fair. For protection against any possible attack from outside his borders, he built three strong fortresses: at Hazor, Megiddo and Gezer. To this day their ruins show just how substantial they had been.

Solomon also built several cities for his stores, chariots and horsemen. 'And the king made silver to be in Jerusalem as stones.' Horses and linen were brought from Egypt. Agriculture flourished, though the ten northern tribes of his kingdom resented the taxes that he imposed on them. The two southern tribes had been exempted because, on the death of Saul, they had chosen David as their king, whereas the northern tribes had initially opted for Saul's son Ishbaal. Only after Ishbaal was murdered, seven years into his reign, had the elders of the northern tribes invited David to rule over them also.

There was one burden imposed by Solomon on all citizens, north and south. To pay for his many building projects, he obliged every Israelite to spend a third of every year in the royal service.

For the authors of the Bible there was a further, even more serious problem: 'Solomon loved many strange women'. Not only did he marry Pharaoh's daughter, he also married women from nations that worshipped pagan gods: Moabites, Ammonites, Edomites, Sidonians and Hittites. The Bible recounts that he 'clave unto these in love'.

In all, Solomon had seven hundred wives—all of them princesses— and a further three hundred concubines. When he was an old man these myriad women 'turned away his heart after other gods'. Among these alien deities were Ashtoreth, the goddess of the Sidonians; Chemosh, the god of the Moabites; and Milcom, described in the Bible as 'the abomination of the Ammonites'. For another of these pagan gods, Moloch— 'the abomination of Ammon'—Solomon built an altar. 'And likewise did he for all his strange wives, which burned incense and sacrificed unto their gods.'

The remains of the palace of Solomon's wives and concubines is on Ramat Rahel, a hill three miles to the south of Jerusalem: from their roof-top garden they would have been able to see from afar the glistening edifice of Solomon's Temple. In 1948 these ruins were the scene of fierce fighting between the newly created Israeli forces, which were holding out in them, and the Egyptian army, which had advanced from the south to within sight of Jerusalem, but was halted at that very spot.

Today, the visitor can wander over both the ruins of Solomon's pagan palace, and the trenches defended by the Israeli soldiers in the mid-twentieth-century battle. Pine trees give welcome shade, and flowering shrubs a sweet scent.

No. 19

Dearest Auntie Fori,

Despite Solomon's worship of other gods when he was old, which led God to stir up rebellion against him, the Bible recounts how under his rule the children of Israel 'were many, as the sand which is by the sea in multitude, eating and drinking, and making merry'. Commerce flourished. Peace reigned. It was, for all the old King's waywardness, a golden age of Jewish history.

Solomon died in about 933 BC—2,863 years before you were married, and 2,869 years before I was born! He was succeeded as king by his son Rehoboam, whose mother was from a non-Israelite tribe, the Ammonites—against whom David had warred so fiercely. Rehoboam's rule began badly. When he went to the city of Shechem, north of Jerusalem, to obtain allegiance from the ten tribes living in the north, they asked him—in return for recognizing him as King—that he 'lighten' the weight of taxation which Solomon had put on them.

After asking the northern tribes to wait for three days for his reply, Rehoboam, who had building and fortifications plans that needed to be paid for, declared that he would not lessen their burdens. Indeed he told them: 'Whereas my father laid upon you a heavy yoke, I will add to your yoke; my father chastised you with whips, but I will chastise you with scorpions.'

The ten northern tribes raised the standard of revolt. They chose one of Solomon's former ministers, Jeroboam, as their king, and repudiated Rehoboam: 'What portion have we in David?' they asked, and then called out in defiance: 'To your tents, O Israel: now see to thine own house, David.' Despite the danger, Rehoboam ordered his principal tax gatherer, Adoram, to gather the taxes against which the northerners had protested. Adoram was immediately stoned to death. Fearful of what might happen to him, Rehoboam hastened to his chariot and fled to Jerusalem.

The lands that had been ruled by David and Solomon as a unified Jewish entity were suddenly and disastrously divided into two separate kingdoms. Jeroboam's kingdom took the name 'Kingdom of Israel': it included the mountains of Samaria, the Galilee, and the Mediterranean shore. Rehoboam—David's grandson—continued to rule over the southern area, including Jerusalem and the mountains of Judaea. The southern kingdom took the name 'Kingdom of Judah'—the tribe of Judah had remained loyal to Rehoboam and the House of David.

Rehoboam and Jeroboam are today the names of especially large bottles of red wine—a Rehoboam is the equivalent of six ordinary bottles of wine, a Jeroboam of four bottles—a 'magnum' being a mere two. Such is the way in which historical figures became remembered, not for themselves but, presumably, because they were both large men, or fat ones.

In my next letter I will tell of the fate of the divided kingdoms—of a divided nation.

No. 20

Dearest Auntie Fori,

This letter tells of conflict between Jews: not for the first or last time. Following the division of the Kingdom of Israel into two rival and often hostile kingdoms, those who lived in the Kingdom of Israel continued to be called Israelites. Those dwelling in the Kingdom of Judah were given the name 'Judah-ites', in Hebrew *yehudim*. From this came the name 'Jew'.

Rehoboam remained on the throne of Judah for seventeen years. During that time his eighteen wives and sixty concubines bore him twenty-eight sons and sixty daughters. He also, in the words of the Bible, in the fifth year of his reign, 'forsook the law of the Lord'. To punish him, God sent an Egyptian army, with Ethiopian and other allies in its ranks, against Jerusalem.

Sensing disaster, the Jews of Jerusalem 'humbled themselves' before God, even as the Egyptian troops were approaching. God accepted their contrition, promising: 'I will not destroy them, but I will grant them some deliverance'.

The Egyptians reached the outskirts of Jerusalem. To pay them tribute and send them on their way, Rehoboam was forced to give them the treasures of the Temple and of the King's house, including the two hundred shields of gold which Solomon had made. Rehoboam replaced the shields of gold with shields of brass. Among the cities that the Egyptians destroyed before they were stopped outside Jerusalem was Etzion-Geber, the port through which Solomon had traded with Africa and Arabia.

As fighting continued between Rehoboam and Jeroboam, those nearby kingdoms which had given their allegiance to Solomon—seeing the divisions and resultant military weakness of the Jews—reasserted their independence. The Philistines, Moabites, Edomites and Ammonites each threw off the overlordship that they had earlier accepted (Rehoboam's mother was an Ammonite). Damascus had already been lost during a rebellion in Solomon's reign: it became the chief city of a new kingdom, Aram, the area later to be known as Syria. To protect his diminished kingdom, Rehoboam was forced to build a series of fortified cities. 'And there was war between Rehoboam and Jeroboam in all their days.'

Rehoboam died in 917 BC. He was succeeded as king by his son Abijah. He set as his aim the restoration of a single Jewish kingdom, and launched a strong military attack on the north by proclaiming that there was no other legitimate dynasty than that of the House of David—his own. The attack was successful only in that Abijah gained several towns in the borderlands, including Bethel, but he failed to defeat the northern kingdom.

Jeroboam, who remained on the northern throne for another ten years, was determined to weaken the Israelite allegiance to Jerusalem. He therefore gave royal status to sanctuaries which he set up at Dan, in the far north of the country, around which the tribe of Dan had tilled the soil since the conquest of Canaan, and at Bethel, where Abraham had once lived. In both these sanctuaries he placed the golden image of a calf, an echo of Aaron's rebellion against Moses after the Exodus from Egypt.

Jeroboam also dispensed with the services of the Levites, the priests who carried out religious duties for all the tribes, and whom he considered too closely linked to Jerusalem. The priests whom he appointed at Dan and Bethel were drawn from other tribes. On Jeroboam's death in 912 BC, his son Nadab succeeded to the northern throne, but was killed within the year by an army officer, Baasha, from the tribe of Issachar. Baasha, having seized the throne, then put all Jeroboam's male descendants to death. Internecine Jewish killings had replaced the wisdom of Solomon.

While Baasha was King of Israel, a descendant of David—Abijah's son Asa—ruled over the Kingdom of Judah. In an action designed to restore the purity of Jewish worship, Asa 'removed all the idols that his fathers had made'. Even his family was not spared. He not only took away the title of Queen from his grandmother—the widow of Rehoboam—because she had made an idol to a pagan fertility goddess, but 'destroyed her idol, and burnt it'. Idols were destroyed throughout his kingdom, and prostitution banned.

A twentieth-century historian, Joan Comay (who once drove me in her car through the hills of Samaria, enthusiastically expounding her zeal for Biblical history) has commented: 'Asa is one of the few Hebrew kings who is commended in the Bible for his piety.'

Asa also took up arms against the northern kingdom. 'And there was war between Asa and Baasha all their days.' In the early days of that war, Baasha, advancing southward, came to within five miles of Jerusalem. Lacking sufficient troops to halt the advance, Asa turned to the King of Damascus, Ben-Hadad, for help, sending him gold and silver from

Solomon's Temple, and from his own royal palace. Seeing a chance for Syrian advantage in the warring Jewish kingdoms, Ben-Hadad agreed to help.

Marching across the Golan Heights—which in 1967 modern Israel captured from Syria—Ben-Hadad and his army reached the shore of the Sea of Galilee—the very shore which President Assad of Syria claimed almost three thousand years later, in the year 2000 AD, as an integral part of his dominions.

Baasha was forced to withdraw from the Jerusalem front in order to push back the Syrians in the north. But once he had withdrawn, Asa found himself confronted by another and more powerful enemy, a joint Egyptian and Libyan army, led by an Ethiopian general. This new enemy attacked from the south, but again Asa defeated those who sought to defeat him.

Baasha died in 888 BC after reigning over the northern kingdom for twenty-four years. Asa died thirteen years later, having ruled the southern kingdom for forty-one years. With all the care and precision of a modern historical study, the Bible sets out the lengths of each reign, establishing for the Jews a narrative from which they could feel linked to the struggles, aspirations and achievements of their forebears.

No. 21

Dearest Auntie Fori,

We are deep in the saga of the Hebrew kings. Asa's son Jehoshaphat was among the most successful of them. He ruled for twenty-five years, and brought a period of peace between the two Jewish kingdoms. His eldest son and heir, Jehoram, married Athaliah, a princess from the Kingdom of Judah. The two kingdoms even joined forces militarily, twice carrying out armed attacks across the River Jordan, first against the Moabites, who had rebelled against Jewish overlordship, and then against the king of Damascus, who had overrun the territory of some of the Jewish tribes who were settled on the eastern bank of the river.

Jehoshaphat continued with his father's work in rooting out idol worship. He also encouraged education in the religious laws and traditions. But he could do nothing to unite the divided Jewish land, and, accepting that the division was likely to be permanent, set up an effective military structure, based on five military districts. Existing fortifications were strengthened. Tax districts were re-organized on a more efficient basis. Judges were established in every fortified city, and given strict rules with regard to their judgments. Jehoshaphat himself told the judges: 'Take heed what ye do: for ye judge not for man, but for the Lord, who is with you in judgment.' He went on to warn them not to take gifts.

Jehoshaphat pursued good relations with the northern kingdom, accepting that it was by a virtual alliance, rather than by perpetual war-fare, that the two kingdoms could at last retain their strength with regard to the hostile world around them.

Having ruled the Kingdom of Judah for twenty-five years, Jeho-shaphat died in 851 BC. His stature as a wise and effective ruler was in stark contrast with that of his son Jehoram, whose eight-year rule in Jerusalem was marked by renewed war with the northern kingdom of Israel, the break away of the Edomites from Jewish overlordship, and the tendency of inhabitants of Jerusalem and all Judah 'to commit fornica-tion'. God took drastic action. The Philistines and Arabians attacked the Kingdom of Judah 'and brake into it, and carried away all the substance that was found in the king's house, and his sons also, and his wives'—all but his youngest son. Jehoram's tribulations were not yet ended. 'And then God smote him in the bowels with an incurable disease.' After two years he died, 'of sore diseases'. He was buried in Jerusalem, 'but not in the sepulchre of the kings'.

Fighting between the rival Jewish kingdoms was renewed. Within each kingdom violence could also be savage. In the northern kingdom of Israel, Baasha's son Ela was killed less than two years after succeeding his father, by Zimri, the commander of his chariot troops. Zimri's rule lasted a mere week: he was attacked in his turn by another army general, Omri, who was besieging a Philistine city but marched back to Zimri's capital, Tirzah, which he besieged and captured.

Zimri, trapped in the citadel, set it on fire, and was killed in the con-flagration. Only after Omri beat off the challenge of another would-be king, an army officer by the name of Tibni, was his rule firmly secured. With his new-found confidence he once more subjected Moab to Israelite overlordship. At the same time, through the establishment of good relations with the Phoenicians, who lived on the Mediterranean coast further north—with their capital at the port of Sidon—he opened up trade throughout the eastern Mediterranean. The Kingdom of Israel was then able to export grain and olive oil, and to import wood, minerals and sophisticated ornaments. Omri married his son Ahab to a Phoenician princess, Jezebel: an important dynastic alliance between the two kingdoms. These were times of peace and prosperity.

It is interesting that the first contemporary literary references we have from outside the Bible to the events recounted in the Bible date from the reign of Omri (only a hundred years after Solomon and David). From then on, stone tablets—the 'letters' and chronicles of the ancient world—bear increasing reference to the Israelites, their kings and their wars. An Assyrian chronicle refers to Omri as the name of the Israelite kings in general.

No. 22

Dearest Auntie Fori,

During the reign of King Omri over the northern kingdom, trade and commerce flourished. But Omri was ambitious to build a city to rival Jerusalem. He chose a site high in the hills, eight miles north of Shechem. He called it Samaria—in Hebrew, Shomron—and crowned it with a magnificent citadel. From it, in the distance far below, could be seen the Mediterranean Sea, twenty miles to the west.

Omri was not guided by religious values. The Bible says of him that he 'wrought evil in the eyes of the Lord, and did worse than all that were before him'. When he died in 869 BC, after twelve years in power, he was buried in his new capital.

When Omri's son Ahab succeeded as King, he brought further prosperity to the northern kingdom. But his wife Jezebel offended Jewish religious sensitivities by her worship of pagan gods. Not only that, she tried to replace the worship of the one God by two gods worshipped by her people: Baal, the chief god, and Asherah the goddess of fertility. Jezebel built a temple to Baal in the courtyard of the royal palace, and brought in 450 priests of Baal, and 400 of Asherah, whom she established and maintained as part of her royal household.

Ahab deferred to his wife's religious allegiances, going so far as to build an altar to Baal in Samaria itself. However irreligious his father Omri had been, Ahab did more to provoke God's anger 'than all the kings of Israel that were before him'. God's anger took a specific form, the arrival of the Prophet Elijah, who told Ahab that there would be neither dew nor rain in the land until the idol worship ceased. Ahab ignored the warning. As Elijah had predicted on God's behalf, a two-year drought began.

Urged to do so by God, Elijah, to save his own life from royal vengeance, sought refuge by an isolated brook east of the river Jordan. He drank the water of the brook, and was brought food by ravens. When the brook dried up, and still fearful of arrest, he fled to Phoenicia, and went to Sidon, the centre of Baal worship. Near Sidon he saw a widow gathering firewood. Elijah asked the widow, who was from the town of Zarephath, for food and drink. But she had none to spare, telling him: 'I have not a cake, but an handful of meal in a barrel, and a little oil in a cruse: and behold, I am gathering two sticks, that I may go in and dress it for me and my son, that we may eat it and die.' Once she and her son had eaten the cake, they had no more food to sustain them, and expected to die.

Elijah then told the widow, whose name the Bible does not tell us: 'Fear not; go and do as thou hast said: but make me thereof a little cake first, and bring it unto me, and after make for thee and for thy son. For thus saith the Lord the God of Israel, The barrel of meal shall not waste, neither shall the cruse of oil fail, until the day that the Lord sendeth rain upon the earth.' The widow did as Elijah instructed. And his prophecy was fulfilled. Her meagre stock of food was continually replenished.

The widow gave Elijah sanctuary in her loft. But then her son fell sick and died. Elijah took the dead boy from her, and carried him up into the loft where he had his bed:

And he stretched himself upon the child three times, and cried unto the Lord, and said, 'O Lord my God, I pray thee, let this child's soul come into him again.'

*And the Lord heard the voice of Elijah; and the soul of the child came
unto him again, and he revived.*

*And Elijah took the child, and brought him down out of the chamber
into the house, and delivered him unto the mother: and Elijah said, 'See,
thy son liveth.'*

Eight hundred years later another Jew, Jesus of Nazareth, was also to
perform miracles, including the miracle of the loaves and fishes, where
food was replenished as it had been for the widow of Zarephath and her
son; and the raising of Lazarus from the dead. Indeed, in later Jewish tradition Elijah was regarded as the precursor of the Messiah, for whose
arrival pious Jews still wait, twenty-nine centuries later. Every Passover,
when celebrating the Exodus from Egypt, Jewish families at the Passover
celebration place a cup of wine on the table for him, and keep the door
open, just in case Elijah returns, as it is hoped he will, to announce the
imminent arrival of the Messianic age.

The two miracles in Sidon were only a start. After three years in hiding, Elijah returned to the northern kingdom and confronted Ahab
again. 'Art thou he that troubleth Israel?' Ahab asked him, to which the
prophet replied: 'I have not troubled Israel; but thou, and thy father's
house, in that ye have forsaken the commandments of the Lord, and
thou has followed Baalim'—the idols erected to the god Baal.

Elijah asked Ahab to summon 'all Israel' on Mount Carmel, by the
Mediterranean shore—near the modern port city of Haifa. He also
asked Ahab to bring the 450 priests of Baal, and the 400 priestesses of
Asherah. Pointing out that 'I, even I only, remain a prophet', while the
priests of Baal amounted to 450 men, Elijah challenged them to 'call on
the name of your gods' to produce fire for the sacrifice of a bullock. This
they did from morning until noon, without result, whereupon Elijah
mocked them with sardonic humour: 'Cry aloud: for he is a god; either
he is talking, or he is pursuing, or he is in a journey, or peradventure he
sleepeth, and must be awaked.'

The priests continued to call upon Baal until the evening, but to no
avail. Elijah then built an altar, poured water on it, and called on God to
set it on fire. His call was answered. 'And when all the people saw it, they

fell on their faces: and they said, The LORD, he is the God; the LORD, he is the God.'

Elijah had triumphed. He told the people to take the 450 priests of Baal to the Kidron brook, where they were killed. 'Let not one of them escape' was Elijah's instruction. This was done, but he had then to flee the wrath of Jezebel, and went southward, into the Sinai desert, as far as Mount Horeb. There God spoke to him in 'a still small voice', telling him to return to the Kingdom of Israel, to anoint his own disciple, Elisha, as his successor as prophet, and to anoint Jehu as Ahab's eventual successor.

Back in the kingdom, Elijah found that Jezebel—by means of letters which she wrote, pretending that they were from Ahab—had caused the death, by stoning, of an innocent man, Naboth. Her aim was that Ahab could gain possession of Naboth's vineyard. Elijah went to see Ahab yet again. 'Hast thou killed, and also taken possession?' he asked the king, whereupon he forecast the end of Ahab's dynasty, and the early death of his successor.

Elijah's death was spectacular. He was walking with his successor Elisha, the two men talking together, when 'there appeared a chariot of fire, and horses of fire, and parted them both asunder; and Elijah went up in a whirlwind into heaven.'

In Jewish religious lore, Elijah returns in disguise, to rescue the righteous in their hour of need, and to ensure that justice is done. If the required *minyan*—the quorum of ten men—is one short at the start of a synagogue service, the stranger who appears, thus enabling the service to begin, will be Elijah in disguise.

In Jewish law, if a problem is presented which appears insoluble, it is set aside until Elijah's return—a moment when much else will be in the air, as he is expected to make his return as the herald of the Messiah.

No. 23

Dearest Auntie Fori,

We now come to a time of troubles and disaster for the Jews in their promised and much fought-over land. During the reign of Ahab over the

Kingdom of Israel, a new power was growing in the east: the Kingdom of Assyria.

In 853 BC the Assyrian king, Shalmanezer III, from his capital at Nineveh, led a strong army against the many kingdoms—including the two Jewish kingdoms—along the Mediterranean shore. Ahab and Ben-Hadad of Syria, having been mortal enemies, became allies, part of a larger coalition that sought to bar Shalmanezer's path. Battle was joined at Karkar, on the River Orontes, in northern Syria, more than two hundred miles north of Samaria and Jerusalem. The Assyrians were halted, but only for five years.

The region, in which small nations had fought each other, won over-lordships, and even, as in the case of Israel and Judah, divided in civil war, was now a wider battleground. One result of the external threat was that, for the first time since the Jewish kingdoms were divided, the King of Judah, Jehoshaphat, made a royal visit to Samaria, where he and Ahab held talks to devise common strategy. But in the first of their joint battles, against a traditional enemy, Ben-Hadad of Syria, Ahab was killed. After the battle, as the sun was setting, a proclamation went throughout the two Jewish armies, 'Every man to his city, and every man to his own country.' Jehoshaphat returned to Jerusalem, and Ahab's body was taken back to his capital, Samaria.

Ahab was succeeded by Jehu. In the bloody events that led to his succession, and his destruction of the House of Ahab—as forecast by Elijah—Jehu told King Jehoram that there could be no peace while Jehoram's mother, Jezebel, was alive, whose 'witchcrafts are so many'. He then shot an arrow through Jehoram's heart, before marching to Jezebel's palace in Jezreel.

Standing at her window, having 'painted her face', Jezebel taunted Jehu, who had just killed her son. Looking up at the window, Jehu asked,

'Who is on my side? Who?'

Two or three eunuchs then looked out, and Jehu called out to them: 'Throw her down', which they did: 'some of her blood was sprinkled on the wall, and on the horses: and he trod her under foot.'

Having trampled on the dead Jezebel, Jehu then went into her palace to 'eat and drink', sending his servants to go and bury Jezebel. 'And they went to bury her: but they found no more of her than the skull, and the feet, and the palms of her hands.' Then they remembered the words of Elijah, that 'the carcass of Jezebel shall be as dung upon the face of the field in the portion of Jezreel; so that they shall not say, This is Jezebel.'

Jehu was determined to allow no royal claimants to stand in his way in either kingdom. Learning that forty-two people, relatives of the late King Ahaziah of Judah, whom he had also defeated in battle, were on their way to Jezreel to give condolences to the family of Jezebel, he had them seized and killed. In Samaria, he had all Ahab's surviving relatives put to death. Then he entered Samaria and destroyed the temple of Baal.

Following this drastic action, Jehu ruled the Kingdom of Israel for twenty-eight years, until 816 BC. In his second year, the Assyrian army under Shalmanezer III returned, sweeping through Phoenicia and reaching Mount Carmel. Jehu, kneeling at the conqueror's feet, paid tribute to him: not only obeisance, but gold and silver. Shalmanezer then returned to Assyria. But the King of Aram (modern Syria), Hazael, seeing Jehu's weakened condition, seized the Israelite territory in what is today the Kingdom of Jordan, as well as Israelite territory in part of Galilee.

For Jehu's successor Jehoahaz, who reigned from 816 to 800 BC, the Kingdom of Israel was both reduced in size as a result of Hazael's conquests, and also became, in effect, a vassal of Aram, ruled from its capital, Damascus. Meanwhile, in Judah, another member of the House of David, Jehoash, had become king at the age of seven. Ruling first through his mother, and then alone, he reigned in Jerusalem for forty years. He too paid tribute to Hazael, sending him all the Temple treasures which the earlier kings of Judah had accumulated 'and his own hallowed things, and all the gold that was found in the treasures of the House of the Lord, and in the King's house'.

Relief came for both Judah and Israel when the Assyrians themselves re-conquered Damascus, marched to the coast, collected tribute from the local kings—as far south as Philistia—and then allowed both Judah and Israel to rule themselves, unimpeded by any external threats. For eighty years there was external peace. But within the Kingdom of Israel, fierce fighting frequently erupted among rival claimants to the throne.

The new king of Israel, Menachem, who came to the throne in 743 BC, brutally destroyed a Jewish town within his kingdom—Tappuah—which had refused to accept him as king. But he was forced to pay a massive tribute to the Assyrian king Tiglath-pileser. The money was raised from all the prosperous families of the kingdom. Menachem's son Pekahia remained subservient to the Assyrians, until he himself was overthrown in a palace coup by a soldier, Pekah, who then came to the throne in 736 BC.

King Pekah joined with the king of Aram to fight off another attack by Tiglath-pileser. He appealed to the king of Judah to join them also, thus forming a more effective alliance, but the king of Judah, Ahaz, declined. He did not want to risk defeat at the hands of the all-powerful Assyrians. Angered by this refusal, Pekah invaded Judah. King Ahaz then appealed to the Assyrians for help, sending them such gold as he could find from the Temple and the palace as an inducement. The prophet Isaiah tried to dissuade Ahaz from allying himself with the Assyrians, but Ahaz was not to be deflected from his course.

Tiglath-pileser attacked Syria and Israel, capturing both, and occupying almost all of the northern kingdom, including Galilee, the Jezreel valley and the plain of Sharon on the coast. The fortresses of Hazor and Megiddo were destroyed. Only the city of Samaria and the surrounding hills were still under Pekah's rule. The rest of the northern kingdom became an Assyrian province.

In 732 BC Pekah was assassinated, and Hoshea became king. For eight years he paid a tax—known as a 'tribute'—to the Assyrians, but then he led the remnant of the northern kingdom in a revolt against Assyria. The symbol of the revolt was the refusal to pay any more tribute. The Assyrians attacked, and within a year they had conquered. Hoshea was captured, and disappeared.

According to a legend much prized by Iraqi Jews—the twentieth-century inheritors of the first Jewish exiles—Hoshea did not remain in the Assyrian kingdom, but was deported further east, as far as Japan. There (so the legend continues) he became the first Japanese emperor, Ose—the father of the Imperial royal family.

The city of Samaria held out against the Assyrians for two more years. But, as you will see in my next letter, it had no real chance of surviving the continuing onslaught.

No. 24

Dearest Auntie Fori,

In my last letter, the northern Israelite capital, Samaria, high on its mountain ridge—with a view of the distant Mediterranean—was holding out against the Assyrian king Tiglath-pileser and his army. It was not captured for another two years, by his successor Sargon II.

Samaria was no longer a Jewish capital but a captive city, the whole of the northern kingdom being annexed to Assyria. Worse, the Assyrians rounded up a large number of the Jews of the northern kingdom, including all the important citizens, and deported them to a region just west of the river Tigris, and to Medea, further east—part of modern Iran.

An inscription of King Sargon, set up in his palace at Nineveh, is rather precise: it gives the number of Jewish deportees as 27,290. This was the first Jewish Diaspora—the dispersal of a people to the most distant corners of the known world. It would be followed in due course by a similar Diaspora of the Jews of the Kingdom of Judah. These two dispersals would, during the next two and a half thousand years, take the Jews to virtually every country on the face of the earth, and lead all sorts of peoples to claim to be one of the lost tribes—including one of the hill tribes in your own Indian North East Frontier Agency—of which Uncle Bijju was governor two decades ago.

The State of Israel has been reconstituted: as I write this letter it has just celebrated its 52nd anniversary. As many as five million Jews are living there now. But the majority of Jews in the world still live in the Diaspora: you and I are only two of some ten million of them. Even those several million Diaspora Jews who recite, every Passover, the final prayer, 'Next Year in Jerusalem', will almost certainly still be in the Diaspora a year later, when they will recite that prayer again, even though they are free to travel to Israel, and indeed to live there, if they wish.

A Law of Return, passed by the Israeli parliament in 1950, gives every Jew, wherever he or she might live, the right to Israeli citizenship once arrived at the country's shores (or its airport). Included in this right are the 196,000 Jews of London, where I am writing this letter, the 165,000 Jews of Washington, D.C., where you were once an ambassador's wife, and the 200-300 Jews in New Delhi—where you asked me about the history of the Jews, and where I promised to try to set one down for you!

No. 25

Dearest Auntie Fori,

With the dispersal of the Jews of the northern kingdom to a region far to the east of their homeland, a phase of Jewish history began that ended only with the creation of a Jewish State in 1948—2,670 years after the Assyrian victory. But the Assyrian conquest was not the end of Jewish sovereignty. Indeed, the southern kingdom, the Kingdom of Judah, survived for another 136 years. It was fortunate in the character of its greatest king, Hezekiah, who came to the throne in 720 BC, and ruled for twenty-eight years.

Hezekiah, while paying an annual tribute to the Assyrians to keep them at bay, was determined to make his kingdom strong enough, spiritually as well as militarily, to survive. The enormous power of Assyria to the north, and the cruel captivity of the former northern kingdom of Israel, were warnings of what could happen with weakness: either the spiritual weakness of those Jews who had begun yet again to drift towards pagan gods, or physical weakness as a result of lack of military preparedness.

Hezekiah was helped in his reforms by the most remarkable of the Hebrew prophets, Isaiah. It was Isaiah's firm belief—which he expressed in powerful language—that salvation could come only through God. His denunciations of religious backsliding were outspoken, to say the least. 'Ah sinful nation,' he declared, 'a people laden with iniquity, a seed of evildoers, children that are corrupters; for they have forsaken the Lord, they have provoked the Holy One of Israel, unto anger, they are gone away backward.'

The language of Isaiah was poetic but also poignant:

. . . the whole head is sick, and the whole heart faint.

From the sole of the foot even unto the head there is no soundness in it; but wounds, bruises, and putrefying sores: they have not been closed, neither bound up, neither mollified with ointment.

Your country is desolate, your cities are burned with fire: your land, strangers devour it in your presence, and it is desolate, as overthrown by strangers.

And the daughter of Zion is left as a cottage in a vineyard, as a lodge in a garden of cucumbers, as a besieged city.

Except the Lord of hosts had left us a very small remnant we should have been as Sodom, and we should have been like unto Gomorrah.

It was in the time of Abraham that God had destroyed the cities of Sodom and Gomorrah—by the Dead Sea—for their iniquities. It was only through a return to God, Isaiah told his fellow Jews, 'Thou shalt no more be termed Forsaken; neither shall thy land any more be termed Desolate.'

The work that Hezekiah did in conjunction with Isaiah was impressive. The Temple was restored—its doors and lamps repaired—and funds were acquired for its future maintenance from public gifts. In an attempt to revive religious worship, and strike at the growing pagan tendencies that had begun to spread among the Jews, Hezekiah decided to hold a special Passover celebration in Jerusalem. He sent out invitations, not only to the many leading figures and notables in his own kingdom, but, by special messengers, to the remnants of the Jews then living under Assyrian rule in the northern kingdom.

The letters of invitation, in the drafting of which Isaiah no doubt had a part, contained a strong element of rebuke:

Ye children of Israel, turn again unto the Lord God of Abraham, Isaac and Israel, and he will return to the remnant of you, that are escaped out of the hands of the king of Assyria.

And be not like your fathers, and like your brethren, which trespassed against the Lord God of their fathers, who therefore gave them up to desolation, as you see.

Now be ye not stiffnecked, as your fathers were, but yield yourselves
unto the Lord, and enter into his sanctuary, which he hath sanctified for
ever: and serve the Lord your God, that the fierceness of his wrath may
turn away from you.

Not everyone welcomed this formidable invitation. The Bible records that as the messengers passed from city to city in the former northern kingdom, the Jews to whom they went 'laughed them to scorn, and mocked them'. Nevertheless, some of the recipients 'humbled themselves, and came to Jerusalem'.

A great feast was held, and, at Hezekiah's request, God pardoned those who had hitherto neglected the religious precepts. As the celebrations continued, the Levites and the priests 'praised the Lord by day, singing with loud instruments unto the Lord'. A vast quantity of food was consumed, two thousand bullocks and seventeen thousand sheep. The festivities went on for seven days, and were then extended for another seven days, 'and they did eat throughout the feast'. No wonder there was 'great joy in Jerusalem'—as great, the Bible tells us, as any seen since the time of King Solomon five hundred years earlier.

That seems such a happy moment that I will end this letter here.

No. 26

Dearest Auntie Fori,

We left Jerusalem in the last letter with much jollity. But Hezekiah still had some strong decisions to make, once the eating and singing were over. Hardly had the feasting ended than the many hilltop shrines that could be found throughout the kingdom, which had drifted into pagan worship, were closed down. Also closed down were the many street shrines that had appeared in Jerusalem itself, which had likewise become a focal point of aspects of pagan worship. All that now changed, with Isaiah the prophet warning of dire consequences if there was any back-sliding.

Jerusalem would be 'ruined', Isaiah warned. God himself had said, in the words used by Isaiah, that 'Because the daughters of Zion are haughty, and walk with stretched forth necks and wanton eyes, walking and mincing as they go, and making a tinkling with their feet: Therefore the Lord will smite with a scab the crown of the head of the daughters of Zion. . . .' and much more besides, so that in due course 'instead of sweet smell there shall be stink', instead of hair, baldness, and 'burning instead of beauty'. So much for the women. As for the men, 'Thy men shall fall by the sword, and thy mighty in the war', and the gates of Jerusalem 'shall lament and mourn; and she being desolate shall sit upon the ground'.

Still, redemption was always at hand, once repentance and decent behaviour returned. 'For the Lord will have mercy on Jacob, and will yet choose Israel, and set them in their own land. . . .' The defence of that land depended, in the immediate present at least, on the king. Hezekiah realized that a strong army and good defences were essential. He built new and stronger towers around Jerusalem, and perfected a water supply system that brought water through an 1,800-foot underground tunnel cut deep through the rock from the Kidron brook into the very centre of the city. This would enable the citizens to have an ample supply of water in the event of a prolonged siege.

It was not only in defensive mood that Hezekiah strengthened his capital and his army. In 705 BC he took part in a revolt by a number of small nations against Assyrian domination of the region. Among the rebellious peoples were the Babylonians, who lived just south of Assyria, on the Tigris and Euphrates rivers. The Egyptian Pharaoh, always keen to see a powerful rival humbled, gave the rebellion his support. The King of Babylonia, Baladan, who had heard that Hezekiah had been sick, sent gifts and ambassadors. Hezekiah showed the ambassadors all the treasures of his household—'the silver, the gold, and the spices, and the precious ointment, and all the house of his armour', as well as treasures elsewhere in the Kingdom of Judah. But Isaiah strongly advised Hezekiah not to join with the Babylonians, warning the king—with a prophet's stern forecast—and in God's words: 'Behold, the days come, that all that is in thine house, and that which thy fathers have laid up in store unto this day, shall be carried into Babylon: nothing shall be left. . . .'

Hezekiah decided to go ahead with the new alliance, and with the rebellion, replying to Isaiah's warning with a question (a typically Jewish form of altercation): 'Is it not good, if peace and truth be in my days?'

The rebellion against Assyria went ahead. As a first step, Hezekiah halted the payment of the annual tribute, a definite act of defiance. Two city-states on the Mediterranean coast joined the revolt, the Phoenician city of Tyre (now part of Lebanon), and the Philistine city of Ashkelon (now a large coastal town in Israel). Babylonia, which took part in the revolt, was eventually crushed by the Assyrians, led by a formidable warrior-king, Sennacherib.

In 701 BC, having crushed Babylonia, Sennacherib turned his attention to the western rebels. The King of Tyre was deposed. An Egyptian army that tried to halt the Assyrian advance was defeated. Ashkelon was captured. Then Sennacherib advanced through the foothills of the Judaean mountains towards Jerusalem. Forty-two villages were captured, and most of their inhabitants deported to Assyria. In the lowlands lay the fortified city of Lachish: Hezekiah gave orders for it to be defended, but after a long siege, Sennacherib captured it.

A few years ago I wandered around the ruins of Lachish, a massive mound, subjected to archaeological diggings and discoveries, imposing in its height and antiquity. Its ruins are more than 2,700 years old. During the excavations, the remains of 1,500 bodies were found. At the time of their deaths, they had been placed in a large pit.

The Assyrian capture of Lachish was recorded by Sennacherib on a triumphant wall carving. This he had made at his palace in Nineveh, to show Assyria's powers and his own royal prowess. In the nineteenth century a British archaeologist found it, and brought it back to Britain. Today it is one of the treasures of the British Museum. Thus, when the mood takes me, I can take a twenty-minute bus ride into town and gaze on a graphic depiction of Hezekiah's loss. It is as vivid as any modern historical document.

From Lachish, Sennacherib turned his army towards Jerusalem, which he besieged. 'I imprisoned him in Jerusalem, his residence, like a bird in a cage,' the triumphant Sennacherib recorded in his account of the war. Hezekiah capitulated. He would pay whatever was needed to persuade Sennacherib to return to Assyria. His message to Sennacherib was abject, brief and unequivocal: 'I have offended; return from me: that which thou puttest on me will I bear.'

So much gold and silver did Sennacherib demand that Hezekiah had to strip both his royal palace and the Temple of their treasures. Even the gold on the Temple doors and pillars—decorations which Hezekiah had put on—had to be stripped off as part of the payment.

Sennacherib was not satisfied. Sending three senior officials, headed by the head of the Assyrian royal court, Rab-shakeh, to the walls of Jerusalem, he demanded the surrender of the city. The demand was made by Rab-shakeh, not in Assyrian, but in Hebrew—all the more humiliating, as the official diplomatic language of the time was Aramaic. So contemptuous was he of Hezekiah's ability to resist that he offered the Jewish king 2,000 horses—'if thou be able on thy part to set riders upon them'.

It was Isaiah who urged Hezekiah not to give in further, and not to surrender the city. Reporting God's words, the prophet told the king not to fear Sennacherib: 'I will send a blast upon him, and he shall hear a rumour, and shall return to his own land; and I will cause him to fall by the sword in his own land.'

That very night many Assyrian troops died. The Jews ascribed this to Divine intervention. Later commentators have suggested that bubonic plague swept through the Assyrian camp. Sennacherib's forces withdrew. Jerusalem remained the capital of the Kingdom of Judah, which itself remained independent. Jewish sovereignty, repeatedly threatened, had survived another crisis, though Assyrian sources show that Hezekiah subsequently returned to vassalage and paid a huge tribute.

No. 27

Dearest Auntie Fori,

As you saw in my last letter, the Assyrians, having threatened Jerusalem itself, had returned to their own land, and the Kingdom of Judah had survived. In due course, Hezekiah was succeeded by his twelve-year-old son Manasseh, who reigned for forty-five years. To continue to keep Assyria at bay, he paid the annual tribute which his father had. He even joined Assyria, during the reign of the Assyrian king Asshurbanipal, in an attack on Egypt.

Many elements of paganism resurfaced. Astrology and witchcraft, imported from Assyria, became popular. Jewish religious worship was challenged by other forms of worship that were anathema to pious Jews. The Bible says of Manasseh: 'He reared up altars for Baal . . . and worshipped all the hosts of heaven, and served them', building altars for the pagan gods inside the Temple courtyards.

According to one tradition, even child sacrifice was re-introduced in the Valley of Hinnom, a few hundred yards from the Temple Mount, and a shrine set up in the Hinnom valley at the low cliff where the child sacrifice took place. Manasseh himself was said to have sacrificed one of his sons there. The Bible recounts; 'And he made his son pass through the fire, and observed times, and used enchantments, and dealt with familiar spirits and wizards: he wrought much wickedness in the sight of the Lord, to provoke him to anger.'

God's anger was expressed in fearful words, as recorded in the Book of Kings: 'I will wipe Jerusalem as a man wipeth a dish, wiping it, and turning it upside down.' Menasseh's rule came to an end in ignominy. He offended the Assyrians, who took him to Assyria in chains. He was succeeded by his son Amon, who set up statues of horses and chariots in the Temple, in honour of the Assyrian sun-god.

After only two years Amon was murdered by his own palace officials, who were themselves then captured and killed. The new king was Amon's eight-year-old son, Josiah. Ironically, but not perhaps surprisingly after his grandfather's idolatrous reign, and his father's continuation of idolatrous practices, Josiah was to gain the reputation, during his thirty-one-year reign, of being the most righteous of all the Hebrew kings, including his great-grandfather Hezekiah.

No. 28

Dearest Auntie Fori,

As this letter begins, the saga of the Hebrew kings nears its end. When Josiah was eighteen, in 627 BC, he began to repair and to purify the Temple, much as his great-grandfather Hezekiah had done eighty years earlier. He demolished the shrine in the Hinnom valley where child sacrifice had been renewed, and pulled down the pagan statues which his grandfather and father had worshipped, and broke them into pieces. He then 'cast the dust' of these statues in the Kidron valley.

Most importantly during the reign of Josiah, in the course of renovating Solomon's Temple ancient texts and laws were said to have been found and transcribed—essentially commandments over and above the 125 in the Book of Exodus. They form the basis of the Book of Deuteronomy—a Greek name given to the third of the Five Books of Moses and meaning 'the Second Law', that is to say, the rest of the 613 commandments which have guided Jews to this day—and of the Book of Leviticus (the name means 'the priestly book'). It is here that is found for the first time the concept of the Jews as the 'chosen people'—about which I have written in an earlier letter and also the first reference to the location of the Temple in Jerusalem as the exclusive site for sacrifices, to stop rival sites being established.

Although the Kingdom of Judah ended not long after Josiah's reign, the texts of Deuteronomy and Leviticus were kept alive by the scribes in exile in Babylon, and then brought back by Ezra to Jerusalem in 458 BC to regulate the lives of observant Jews: I will write to you about Ezra in one of my later letters.

A woman prophet, Hulda, warned Josiah that Jerusalem would be destroyed by God because of its wickedness. It would not, however, she said, be in his lifetime. What did happen while Josiah was on the throne was the death of Asshurbanipal, and the rapid disintegration of Assyrian power. It was Babylonia that now rose to prominence, much as Isaiah had warned almost a century earlier.

The days of the Kingdom of Judah, which once Hezekiah had so powerfully strengthened, and whose religious piety Josiah had struggled so hard to restore, were numbered. The weakened Assyrians made an alliance with Egypt. An invading Egyptian force was challenged by Josiah in a battle at Megiddo (the Biblical Armageddon). The army of the Kingdom of Judah was defeated and Josiah killed by an arrow.

The Kingdom of Judah was in deepest danger. It became a vassal of Egypt. Josiah's son Jehoahaz, whom the Egyptians allowed at first to be King, was taken into captivity after only three months. His younger brother Jehoiakim was allowed to succeed him as king, but was forced to raise large sums of money to pay the Egyptian tribute. Meanwhile, a new power was arising on the River Euphrates—the Kingdom of Babylon. In 605 BC, at the city of Carchemish on the upper Euphrates, the Babylonian king, Nebuchadnezzar, defeated an Egyptian–Assyrian army that had tried to push into Babylonia. Counter-attacking with vigour, Nebuchadnezzar conquered the whole eastern Mediterranean coastline as far south as Gaza.

Whether the Kingdom of Judah should take up arms against any direct Babylonian attack was much debated. The chief voice calling for nothing to be done was that of the prophet Jeremiah. His view was that the Babylonians were God's instrument, propelled forward by God to punish the Jews for their religious laxity. In great anger, King Jehoiakim had Jeremiah's book of prophecies burned in the royal palace. Jeremiah dictated them again, to the scribe Baruch, who read the prophecies aloud in front of the Temple.

The Babylonians extended their control over three nations bordering the Kingdom of Judah: Moab, Ammon and Syria. In 600 BC they began to attack from the north and east. Two years later King Nebuchadnezzar was ready—having quelled some internal unrest—to join the attack himself. As his forces drew near, Jehoiakim died, and was succeeded by his eighteen-year-old son Jehoiachin. An Egyptian promise to send Judah military help against the Babylonians failed to materialize.

After a three months' siege, the Jews were forced to surrender. The new king was taken to Babylon as a prisoner. With him, the Babylonians took away his mother, the rest of his family, and his officials. All were imprisoned.

In the flush of their victory the Babylonians pillaged Jerusalem and destroyed the Temple of Solomon itself. The Bible gives a graphic account of the triumph of Nebuchadnezzar over Jerusalem:

And he carried out thence all the treasures of the house of the Lord, and the treasures of the king's house, and cut in pieces all the vessels of gold which Solomon king of Israel had made in the temple of the Lord, as the Lord has said.

And he carried away all Jerusalem, and all the princes, and all the mighty men of valour, even ten thousand captives, and all the craftsmen and smiths: none remained, save the poorest sort of the people of the land.

There was worse to come. Nebuchadnezzar had set up a new king—Zedekiah, Jehoiachin's uncle—in Jerusalem. But after four years on the throne as Nebuchadnezzar's vassal, paying a heavy tribute to Babylon, Zedekiah decided to rebel. He found allies in this risky enterprise in the rulers of Tyre and Sidon on the coast, and Moab and Edom inland. Only the prophet Jeremiah spoke out against rebellion. Walking about Jerusalem with a wooden yoke on his neck, he addressed Zedekiah and the people of Judah, speaking in God's name:

> *Bring your necks under the yoke of the king of Babylon, and serve him and his people, and live.*
>
> *Why will ye die, thou and thy people, by the sword, by the famine, and by the pestilence. . . .*
>
> *Serve the king of Babylon, and live: wherefore should this city be laid waste?*

Zedekiah set aside his plans for the revolt, and sent ambassadors to Babylon to assure Nebuchadnezzar of his loyalty. But five years later, in the year 589 BC, the king changed his mind, and, in alliance with Tyre and Egypt, raised the flag of revolt. It was to no avail. Nebuchadnezzar returned in force, and Jerusalem was again besieged. At the same time the Edomites, Zedekiah's former potential allies, took advantage of the Babylonian attack to launch their own attack on Judah from the south.

For two years Nebuchadnezzar and his forces cut off Jerusalem from any help, until 'famine prevailed in the city, and there was no bread for the people of the land'. Babylonian 'siege engines'—massive catapults that hurled huge stones high into the air, and heavy battering rams, made a breach in the city walls. Going from house to house, Babylonian soldiers looted and destroyed everything in their path. On the night of the invasion Zedekiah managed to slip out of the city. Accompanied by a few soldiers, palace officials, and his family, he made his way down to the plain of Jericho, more than a thousand feet below sea level. There the Babylonians caught up with him, and defeated his troops, and captured both the king and his sons.

Zedekiah and his sons were taken to northern Syria, to Nebuchadnezzar's campaign headquarters at Riblah. There a terrible fate awaited him. 'And they slew the sons of Zedekiah before his eyes, and put out the eyes of Zedekiah, and bound him with fetters of brass, and carried him to Babylon.'

The captain of Nebuchadnezzar's guard, Nebuzar-adan, then travelled to Jerusalem, where he burned down the Temple, the royal palace, 'and all the houses of Jerusalem, and every great man's house he burnt with fire'. He then destroyed the walls of the city. Sixty Jewish soldiers who had been found in Jerusalem, as well as the leading scribe, and five of Zedekiah's courtiers, were taken to Nebuchadnezzar at Riblah, and killed there. Nebuzar-adan then took all the Jews still living in Jerusalem, 4,600 in all, to Babylon. 'Thus Judah was carried away captive out of his own land.'

Once more, only the poor were left behind, to work the land and maintain the vineyards for the use of the conqueror. Jewish nationhood had come to an abrupt and violent end.

No. 29

Dearest Auntie Fori,

Following the destruction of the Kingdom of Judah—the only one of the two Jewish kingdoms to survive into the seventh century BC—the Bible records the agony of those in the southern kingdom who, after more than a hundred years of independence, had been conquered and subjected to the full rigour of alien rule:

> *Our inheritance is turned to strangers,*
> *Our houses to aliens,*
> *We are orphans and fatherless,*
> *Our mothers are as widows,*
> *Our necks are under persecution,*
> *We labour and have no rest.*

The second dispersal was also lamented by the captives in a plaintive song, Psalm 137, sung in the centres of the new Diaspora, to which they had been deported:

By the rivers of Babylon, there we sat down, yea, we wept, when we remembered Zion.

We hanged our harps upon the willows in the midst thereof.

For there, they that carried us away captive required of us a song: and they that wasted of us required of us mirth, saying, 'sing us one of the songs of Zion.'

How shall we sing the song of the Lord in a strange land?

If I forget thee, O Jerusalem, let my right hand forget her cunning.

If I do not remember thee, let my tongue cleave to the roof of my mouth; if I prefer not Jerusalem above my chief joy.

The last independent King of Judah, Jehoiachin, was kept in prison in Babylon for thirty-seven years. He was released from prison— together with his five sons—by Nebuchadnezzar's successor, who set Jehoiachin's throne 'above the kings that were with him in Babylon'— presumably royal captives from other conquered nations—and enabled him to eat bread 'all the days of his life . . . a continual diet . . . every day a portion until the day of his death, all the days of his life.'

The Assyrian and Babylonian conquests had both led to dispersal and exile. Some Jews fled back into Egypt, many of them settling in the port city of Alexandria. Jeremiah himself, together with a small group of sol-diers from Zedekiah's army who had tried in vain to maintain armed resistance, were given sanctuary at Tahpanhes, on the eastern edge of the Nile Delta, in Egypt. Even in exile, Jeremiah urged adherence to God's laws. Accompanied by his faithful scribe, Baruch, he uttered dire warn-ings against those Jews in the Diaspora whom he saw in Egypt worship-ping an ancient fertility goddess.

In exile in Egypt, Jeremiah also sang a powerful lament for Jerusalem:

How doth the city sit solitary, that was full of people! how is she become a widow! She that was great among the nations, and princess among the provinces, how is she become a tributary!

She weepeth sore in the night, and her tears are on her cheeks: among all her lovers she hath none to comfort her: all her friends have dealt treacherously with her, they are become her enemies.

Judah has gone into captivity. . . .

Jeremiah lived his last years in Egypt, and died there. Other exiles went northward into what is now Turkey. But the largest dispersion was back to Mesopotamia, Abraham's birthplace, and to the cities of the Euphrates and Tigris valleys.

The dispersions left the Jews a fragmented people, scattered throughout the eastern Mediterranean, and into Persia. It was in Persia that the courage of a Jewish queen, Esther, prevented the mass murder of the Jews by the head of the royal court, Haman. That story, which is at the centre of the Jewish festival of Purim, will be one of my later letters, when I tell you about Jewish fasts and festivals.

Despite persecution and danger—and danger averted, as in the story of Esther—no matter where the Jews were forced to go, often made to live in a particular part of a city, they rebuilt their lives and livelihoods as best they could. Maintaining family life and religious worship, they followed their traditions, retained faith in their one God, and sustained a sense of unity and belonging with their fellow-Jews everywhere. The more the dispersals continued, the further apart they became geographically: there were Jews whom they might never meet, and whose region of the Diaspora they might never visit.

Wherever Jews lived, Judaism had become a linking and unifying force of the strongest power, able to survive the pressures of war, conquest, occupation, tyranny, separation and dispersal. As Jewish scribes in what had been the Kingdom of Judah recorded the past history of Jewish nationhood—the Books of Joshua, Judges, Samuel, Kings—other scribes, living under Persian rule, recorded the Books of Chronicles, Ezra and Nehemiah. Wherever they might live, Jews had their history, and with it their national identity, in books which were their daily study, and inspiration. At the same time the custom was introduced of including Biblical texts in the tefillin (phylacteries) worn on the forehead and forearm, and in the mezuzah—a small box—affixed to all doorposts of every Jewish household. Moments in the annual calendar that had originally been agricultural festivals—Passover, Shavuot and Sukkot, about each of which I will be writing to you—were turned into Pilgrim Festivals that commemorated Jewish history, during which Jews travelled to Jerusalem and to the Temple. Yom Kippur—the Day of Atonement—about which I will also write, was introduced into the yearly cycle of worship. Above all, the Jewish God ceased to be 'merely' the only tribal God of the Jews among peoples who worshipped many gods, but became, in the Jewish perspective, the only God.

Having conquered Babylon in 539 BC, the Persians allowed the Jews to return to Jerusalem and Judaea from their Babylonian captivity. Although Judaea was still under Persian overlordship, the Persians allowed it wide-ranging autonomy. The walls of Jerusalem were rebuilt under Nehemiah, himself a Jewish Persian official, the former drink steward to King Artaxerxes I, whom Artaxerxes had appointed governor of Judaea. Tradition asserts that the task of rebuilding the walls was completed in fifty-two days. To re-populate the city, Nehemiah arranged for a tenth of the Jewish population of Judaea to take up residence there. He also cancelled the debts of the poor. At the same time, Ezra, who had returned to Jerusalem from the Babylonian exile, persuaded the Jews to make a new Covenant, this one not with God but among themselves, in order to strengthen their Jewish identity by separating themselves from foreign nations.

Ezra, known as 'Ezra the Scribe', has a book of the Bible to himself. Rabbinic sources rate him with Moses; had the Torah not been given to Moses, they said, it would have been given to Ezra. The seventeenth-century Jewish philosopher Spinoza, a pioneer of Biblical criticism, went so far as to suggest that Ezra was the actual compiler of the Five Books of Moses.

As is clear from the Book of Ezra, on return from the Babylonian exile, Ezra was determined that the Jews conduct their lives as an exclusive people. He fought against the marriage of Jewish men with non-Jewish women: indeed, he evicted such men and their children from the community. His words to the congregation, as recorded in the Bible, are uncompromising: 'Ye have transgressed, and have taken strange wives, to increase the trespass of Israel. Now therefore make confession, unto the Lord God of your fathers, and do his pleasure: and separate yourselves from the people of the land, and from the strange wives. Then all the congregation answered and said with a loud voice, As thou hast said, so must we do.'

Nehemiah also acted as a purifier of Jewish tradition, especially in regard to Temple practices, which had clearly lapsed over the years. 'Thus cleansed I them from all strangers,' records the Book of Nehemiah (which follows the Book of Ezra) 'and appointed the wards of the priests and the Levite, every one in his business; And for the wood offerings, at times appointed, and for the first fruits. Remember me, O my God, for good.'

Nehemiah's prayer, asking God to remember a person for the good deeds he has done, and to be the recipient of good treatment, has entered Jewish phraseology, as a universal Jewish greeting on the New Year: 'May you be remembered for a good year.'

No. 30

Dearest Auntie Fori,

Despite their dispersal over vast regions, the Jews never gave up their physical or spiritual connection with the Land of Israel. Even when the land itself was under the domination of the Assyrians and the Babylonians, or of the empires such as that of Persia that succeeded theirs, Jewish communities survived in Palestine. Jerusalem was always a centre of Jewish activity: especially bustling during the Pilgrim Festivals, during which Jews made their way up to the city, and to the Temple—or, when the Temple was destroyed, to whatever remained of its structure. Galilee, with its rolling hills and fertile valleys, was an area of particularly full Jewish settlement.

In the Diaspora, as in the Land of Israel itself, an attempt was made to preserve the balance between obedience and subservience, between accepting alien rule, and rejecting harshness and humiliation. In 338 BC, in Persia, there was a Jewish uprising against what had become the severity of Persian rule. The revolt was crushed, and the Jews moved eastward again, seeking refuge and a new place to live by the shores of the Caspian Sea, and along the western coast of India. As Jewish communities were established further and further away from Jerusalem, Jews recalled the words of the prophet Jeremiah: 'Seek the peace of the city whither I have caused you to be carried away captives, and pray unto the Lord for it: for in the peace thereof shall you have peace.'

Jerusalem itself saw several conquerors, and became a provincial city of several large empires: first the Babylonian, followed by the Persian, then the Empire of Alexander the Great—who conquered Jerusalem while on his way to India. Alexander was the only conqueror of Jerusalem in a thousand years who did not order the city to be destroyed: in recognition of this, some Jews name their third son Alexander.

After Alexander's death in 323 BC his empire was divided between his generals. One of them, Ptolemy, established a dynasty in Egypt. Another, Seleucus, ruled the area now known as Syria. The tiny land of Judaea, located on the highway that linked their two capitals, became a battleground between them, changing hands seven times between 332 and 302. For the next hundred years it was governed by Egypt. Then, in 198 BC, Antiochus III reconquered it for the Seleucid Empire. The Jews had become pawns in an imperial struggle.

No. 31

Dearest Auntie Fori,

Alexander the Great, and after him the Ptolemies and the Seleucids—the rulers of Judaea—were carriers and propagators of late Greek (Hellenistic) culture. In Judaea, as in Syria and Egypt, Greek became the language of administration and literature.

Greek names, Greek clothes and Greek manners affected many Jews. In Egypt, during the third century BC, the Hebrew Bible was translated into Greek—known as the Septuagint—for use by Greek-speaking Jewish communities. Times were good. Peace was secured. First the Egyptians, and then the first Seleucid emperor, Antiochus III, granted the Jews freedom to worship their own God. The Temple in Jerusalem, which Alexander the Great had allowed to stand, remained the focal point of Jewish worship.

When, in 175 BC, Antiochus III was succeeded by his son Antiochus IV, all tolerance ended. For the new ruler Hellenism was not merely one way of life, but the only way. In Jerusalem, a minority of Jewish Hellenists, assimilated and well-to-do, supported him. The Jewish world, not for the first time or the last, was divided. The Hellenist Jews encouraged the new king to remove the deeply religious High Priest, Onias III, a member of one of the great priestly families, and to replace him with his brother—the Greek name by which he wished to be known was Jason, his Hebrew name was Joshua.

Less observant than Onias, the High Priest Jason made no effort to challenge the Hellenization and assimilation of the Jews in Judaea, or even in Jerusalem. But even he fell victim to Jewish intrigue, being replaced as High Priest by the lay leader of the Jewish Hellenists, Menelaus, who gave Antiochus some of the golden vessels from the Temple, and, in a desperate attempt to assert his own legitimacy, murdered the former High Priest, Onias.

Observant Jews began to leave Jerusalem, among them a priest, Mattathias. His story and that of his family, the Hasmoneans, was to transform the situation in Judaea, and restore Jewish self-esteem. With him we leave Biblical times behind us. 'Ancient times' still lie ahead, a strange thought! Henceforth, we learn about our forebears, not from the Bible, but from a growing number of written records containing information, debate and ideas set down by rabbis, travellers and scribes in every generation.

Part Two

THE HISTORICAL ERA

No. 32

Dearest Auntie Fori,

As we enter the historical era, we come to a time of defiance and revolt—and of the re-emergence of Jewish nationhood. The Seleucid ruler of Judaea, Antiochus IV, decided to challenge the new power that was gaining strength each decade—that of Rome. Attacking the recently established Roman military garrisons in Egypt, he was, however, driven back. Humiliated by this defeat, he took his vengeance on Jerusalem. His adversary there was the former High Priest, Jason, who had led a revolt against the excesses of Hellenism, denouncing paganism and the Greek way of life as undermining Jewish unity.

Antiochus won control of Jerusalem, and then moved to suppress Jewish religious worship, ordering the Jews to make sacrifices to the Greek gods and to profane the Sabbath. Circumcision of new-born sons was forbidden: two women who defied this order were arrested, paraded through the streets of Jerusalem, and then thrown to their deaths—with their children—from the city wall.

Jewish defiance continued. When a leading sage and teacher, Eleazar—the name of one of the Biblical Aaron's pious sons—was ordered to eat the flesh of a pig which had been sacrificed to Zeus, the father of the Greek gods, he refused to do so. Antiochus IV himself tried to persuade the much respected old man to do so, to give a lead, and thus help undermine Jewish resistance. The King told Eleazar, in front of a group of religious Jews who had been brought to witness the scene:

Before I begin inflicting torture upon you, greybeard, I would give you this counsel; eat of the swine's flesh and save yourself. I respect your age and your hoary head; but I cannot think you a philosopher when you

have so long been an old man and still cling to the religion of the Jews.
Why do you abominate eating the excellent meat of this animal which
nature has so freely bestowed upon us?

Eleazar replied without hesitation that he would not transgress the
laws of his religion even if it seemed a small thing, telling the King:
'Transgression is of equal weight in small matters as in large, for in either
case the Law is equally despised.' Terrible tortures were then inflicted on
him. When a royal courtier suggested that he should eat meat that was
permissible, but pretend it was pig, to save his life and enable the king to
say that it was pig, he refused. He was in his ninetieth year, he said, how
could he deceive the faithful? He was then tortured again until he died.

Among those who were forced to witness this terrible scene was a
Jewish woman, Hannah, and her seven sons. After Eleazar's death, they
too were given a choice between sacrificing a pig to Zeus and then eating it, or death. One of the sons replied at once that if the venerable
Eleazer, their teacher, could die for his faith, so could they. He was
seized, his tongue cut out, and his hands and feet cut off. He was then
thrown into the fire. In turn each of his brothers was then given the
choice between violating their religious laws or death. Each, in his turn,
chose death. Their mother then submitted to the same fate.

So powerful an impact did this story of defiance and martyrdom
have, that mediaeval Christian Europe celebrated these seven 'Maccabean Martyrs'—though they were not members of the Maccabee
family—as heroes, canonized them, and made them the symbol of the
Church Militant. Their Seleucid persecutor was made the symbol of
the Antichrist. In the French town of Lyon a Church of the Seven
Holy Maccabees was consecrated; and in Geneva, in the Cathedral of
St Pierre, there is to this day a chapel to their memory, where pious
Roman Catholics light votive candles. In mediaeval paintings their
mother, Hannah, appears at the side of the Virgin Mary, her sons being
depicted with severed hands, and with seven swords.

The Hasmonean family—led by Mattathias—had, as I wrote in my
last letter, left Jerusalem to escape the Hellenization. Known also as the
Maccabeans—because Judah, the son of Mattathias, would be nicknamed 'Maccabee', which means hammer—they had gone to live and

carry out their priestly duties in the town of Modi'in, on the border of the former kingdoms of Israel and Judah. In the last ten years of the twentieth century, modern Modi'in has been transformed from a small Israeli village into a thriving metropolis. Then, as now, from the hilly ground of the town can be seen the thin line of yellow coastal sand dunes and the often sparkling waters of the Mediterranean, only fifteen miles to the west.

Mattathias was determined to resist Antiochus IV's continuing efforts to repress Jewish worship. In 166 BC a royal officer, reaching Modi'in with a group of Seleucid soldiers, gave the order, which was being repeated in all the Jewish towns and villages, for the Jews to sacrifice a pig to Zeus. They would then have to eat a piece of its flesh—forbidden under the Jewish dietary laws. As the villagers listened in horror—and Jewish tradition asserts that the Seleucid officer was himself deeply unhappy at having to give the order—Mattathias and his five sons stood defiantly at the head of the assembled villagers, and refused to move towards the altar which the officer had set up. The officer, recognizing the priest as a man of determination and authority, said to him:

> *You are a leader, honoured and great in this city, and supported by sons and brothers. Now be the first to come and do what the king demands, as all the Gentiles and the men of Judah and those that are left in Jerusalem have done. Then you and your sons will be numbered among the friends of the kingdom and you and your sons will be honoured with silver and gold and many gifts.*

Mattathias replied, without hesitation: 'We will not obey the king's words by turning aside from our religion to the right hand or to the left.' But one of the villagers, frightened of Seleucid anger, decided to obey the royal command. As he pushed forward towards the altar, Mattathias himself seized the sacrificial knife and stabbed him. He then turned on the Seleucid officer and stabbed him to death. Kicking the altar to the ground, Mattathias and his sons then seized the soldiers: the revolt had begun. Fleeing to the hills, the defiant Maccabees called on all Jews to join them and to take up arms against their rulers.

Mattathias was killed in a battle later that year. His five sons survived.

The eldest, Judah Maccabee, became the leader of the revolt in his father's stead. It was he who first defeated the Seleucids in battle, captured Jerusalem, and began to restore the Temple. In a bold diplomatic and military move he formed an alliance with Rome, at that time the growing power in the central Mediterranean region. But as he continued to try to push the Seleucids back into Syria he was killed in battle, as his father had been five years before him. One of his brothers, Eleazar, was also killed in battle, crushed by the body of an elephant he had just slain.

During the continuing period of Hasmonean rule, which lasted from 166 BC until 37 BC—two of Judah Maccabee's brothers, Jonathan and Simeon, much enlarged the area under Jewish control. They succeeded in taking over Lydda, in the coastal plain (where later, Crusaders knights from England were to discover the legend of St George and his dragon and make St George the English national emblem). Jonathan and Simeon reached and captured the port of Jaffa, one of the few places along the coast where ships could find a natural refuge, if not a natural harbour, between the off-shore rocks and the shore.

Under the Hasmoneans the authority of the priests, and of the High Priest, was re-established. Jonathan became High Priest. He was succeeded by his brother Simeon and then by Simeon's son, John Hyrcanus I, who—in the seventh year of the the Jewish kingdom's independence—began to extend its borders yet further. Samaria, the region conquered six hundred years earlier from the Israelites by the Assyrians, was regained. Idumaea (formerly Edom), an independent kingdom south of Judaea, was overrun and its inhabitants converted to Judaism—by force. Among the converts was the Antipater family, one of whose descendants, Herod, was to be among the greatest, and most controversial, of Jewish rulers.

John Hyrcanus was almost certainly the first of the Hasmonean dynasty to mint coins of his own, an important mark of independence in the ancient world. The Romano-Jewish historian Josephus calls his reign a 'happy' one, and there was economic prosperity. But it was military prowess which made the Hasmonean story one which Jewish children many hundreds, even a thousand years later, learned and admired. One moment of pride was when a joint Jewish and Egyptian army successfully defended the Hasmonean kingdom from an attack by Roman troops led by Ptolemy. Two Jewish generals were among the commanders of the Egyptian forces.

No. 33

Dearest Auntie Fori,

The Hasmonean dynasty ruled for 129 years. In the centuries ahead, when life in the Diaspora hit difficult times, those 129 years served as an increasingly remote yet ever notable reminder that Jews had once been sovereign in their own land, even after the Babylonians had destroyed the Biblical Kingdom of Judah. The Hasmonean kingdom also ensured that monotheism would survive in a world of growing national powers and defined borders. In 139 BC, twenty-six years after the establishment of the new Jewish kingdom, the Roman Senate recognized Jewish independence. At the same time the Hasmoneans sought even greater powers than those bestowed upon them through the High Priesthood. John Hyrcanus's son and heir, Aristobulus, declared himself King, the first Hasmonean to seek, and to use, the royal title.

Aristobulus also continued the policy of territorial expansion, and of the conversion of neighbouring peoples. During his reign, the Ituraeans to the north were conquered and then forced to convert to Judaism. Further territorial conquests were made by Aristobulus's brother, Alexander Yannai, who succeeded Aristobulus as King in 103 BC, and ruled for twenty-seven years. Under Alexander Yannai the Hasmonean kingdom reached its largest extent: covering a greater area than modern Israel today. His conquests included the northern Sinai coast as far as Rhinoconara—the modern Egyptian port and fresh-water oasis of El Arish. The imposing Mount Carmel range of hills, overlooking the modern city of Haifa, was also conquered.

Once again, however, as on the eve of the Assyrian conquest six hundred years earlier, the Jews began to quarrel among themselves, and lurched into civil war. Religious differences had opened up between the Hasmoneans and the Pharisees. Four main issues divided them. Alexander Yannai was attracted to aspects of Hellenistic culture, which the

Pharisees resisted. The Pharisees challenged the combination in one person of the High Priesthood and the monarchy, especially as the Hasmoneans, though of a priestly family, were not of a High Priestly one. The Pharisees opposed the Hasmonean policy of extending the national borders, forcing Yannai to abandon compulsory military service and rely on mercenaries. In matters of religious worship, the Pharisees had evolved the Oral Law—a mass of traditional interpretations that were associated with individual scholars—which they considered as binding, while Alexander Yannai and the priesthood regarded only the Written Law—as set down in the Five Books of Moses—as binding (and considered that it gave them a degree of flexibility in Hellenization).

In his capacity as High Priest, Alexander Yannai found himself opposed by the Pharisees. Violence flared; and it was only under the rule of Alexander's wife, Salome Alexandra, who came to the throne in 76 BC, that a compromise was reached. But it did not last long. When she died, her two sons fell out over the succession. Antipater, one of her former ministers, called in the Romans to adjudicate. Antipater sided with the elder brother, Hyrcanus II, sent an army to drive out the younger brother, Aristobulus, and then abolished the Hasmonean monarchy, Hyrcanus II then being recognized merely as 'ethnarch' (representative) of the Jews throughout the Roman Empire. Antipater was rewarded by the Romans by being made Regent of Judaea.

Earlier in this letter I mentioned how the 'Maccabean Martyrs' became a focal point of Christian tradition. But it was to the Jews that the Maccabees meant the most. The 'Maccabean Martyrs' also entered the Jewish liturgy, the Story of Hannah being traditionally sung by Jewish women throughout the Middle East and North Africa, and as far east as Persia, on the annual anniversary of the destruction of the Temple by the Romans—an event that took place two centuries after the Maccabean saga.

Until today Jewish authors, painters and composers have portrayed the story of the Hasmonean dynasty in historical works, literature, art and music. In the late nineteenth century Eastern European Jewry found inspiration in Anton Rubinstein's opera *Die Makkabaeer,* which had its premiere in Berlin in 1875. In the year of Israel's restored independence—1948—the American author Howard Fast published a novel, *My Glorious Brothers*. In the sixth year of the existence of the new State of Israel—1954—the Israeli writer Moshe Shamir published *The King of Flesh and Blood,* a novel based on the life of Alexander Yannai.

Twenty-five years after the Roman conquest of the Hasmonean kingdom, the flag of revolt was raised again. It was led by one of Alexander Yannai's grandsons, Antigonus Mattathias, who had become High Priest in 40 BC. Persuading the Parthians—to the east—to join him, he took on the might of the Roman army, and was defeated. With his defeat, in 37 BC, the Hasmonean dynasty came to an end, both in its royal and priestly aspects, though Mariamne—the niece of Antigonus Mattathias—was later to marry King Herod—a Jew who came to the throne as a Roman-appointed ruler in 37 BC, after the defeat of the last Hasmonean High Priest.

That, however, is another story, and certainly another letter.

No. 34

Dearest Auntie Fori,

With the emergence of Herod as ruler of Judaea we meet one of the most remarkable characters in the Jewish story. In 44 BC, seven years before he came to the throne, he had already been marked out as someone who would not hesitate to take harsh action. That year, having been appointed by the Hasmoneans to be Governor of Galilee, he took up arms against rebel forces there and defeated them. He then executed the rebel leaders without trial.

Brought to account for this act by the religious court in Jerusalem—the Sanhedrin—and facing the death penalty if found guilty of carrying out the executions solely on his own secular authority, Herod arrived at the court with his soldiers, all heavily armed, and tried to intimidate the judges. At that point the Hasmonean king, Hyrcanus II, stopped the proceedings and enabled Herod to escape from the city. He made his way northward, to Syria, which was at that time a Roman province. There, the Roman ruler appointed him governor of a small but important province, Coele Syria, with his capital at Samaria—once the capital of the Kingdom of Israel which the Assyrians had conquered and destroyed.

Herod was a Jew. His grandfather was an Edomite who had been forcibly converted to Judaism a century earlier, and his father was Antipater, who had called in the Romans and been rewarded by being made Regent of Judaea. Herod threw in his lot completely with Rome. When the Hasmonean king Aristobulus II invaded Galilee, it was Herod's forces that defeated him, preventing the extension of Jewish rule further north.

Ambitious to rule Judaea, Herod befriended the Roman general Mark Antony, and also gave him money. He was appointed king in 40 BC, but it took three years before he could finally drive out the Hasmoneans and their supporters, and establish himself in Jerusalem. Two large delegations of Jews went to Mark Antony to urge him not to appoint Herod as King; Mark Antony imprisoned them, and then put them to death. In 37 BC Herod's forces, with support from the Roman army, reached Jerusalem, and, after a five months' siege, captured it.

Herod ruled Judaea unchallenged from 37 BC until his death thirty-three years later. To maintain his rule, he ensured that no rival, not even any member of his family, could oust him. Among those whom he killed was his wife Mariamne—a member of the Hasmonean royal house—his mother-in-law (also a Hasmonean), his two sons, and many other blood relations. Roman officials participated in the trial in which his two sons were condemned to death. He also gave orders, which were obeyed, for the heir to the Hasmonean throne, Aristobulus—his wife's brother—to be drowned in a swimming pool in Jericho. He also put to death the last Hasmonean king, Hyrcanus II, the man who had earlier enabled him to escape the justice of the Sanhedrin, and he ordered the execution of forty-five members of the Sanhedrin—the religious court that had been trying him for murder when he escaped their jurisdiction. From that moment the Sanhedrin, which had supported the Hasmoneans as a legislative body, lost all its influence.

When Herod's patron, Mark Antony, fell from power, Herod immediately switched his allegiance to Antony's rival Octavian. He entertained Octavian at Ptolemais (now the port-city of Acre) and travelled specially to Egypt to congratulate Octavian on the death of Antony. When Octavian became Roman Emperor, taking the imperial name of Augustus, he rewarded Herod for his change of allegiance, and for his power in Judaea, by giving him further territory to the north of Judaea. For his part, Herod supported the military activities of Augustus's son-in-law Agrippa, leading a naval expedition on Agrippa's behalf into the Black Sea.

In return for his support of the Roman Empire, and for keeping the Jews, Greeks and Syrians within his borders loyal to Rome, Herod was given the title 'the Great', and the official designation: 'A King who is the ally and friend of the Roman people.' Although having no right to conduct an independent foreign policy, and while paying an annual tribute to Rome, he was allowed unfettered authority over the administrative, financial and religious affairs of Judaea: a kingdom that included Samaria (the former northern Kingdom of Israel in Biblical times), Idumaea (formerly Edom, his family's homeland) to the south, Gaulanitis (now the Golan Heights), Banias (given to him by Octavian), and Jericho (which had formerly been given to Cleopatra by Mark Antony).

Even before he murdered his Hasmonean wife, Mariamne, and their two sons, Herod had taken a second wife, a Jerusalemite called Doris, by whom he had a son. After Mariamne's murder he married eight more times, and fathered fourteen further sons and daughters. All of them survived, as did his brothers, for whom he appears to have had some affection.

Herod built up his army carefully, using few Jews, but bringing in mercenaries from as far away as Thrace and even Gaul. His rule was also buttressed by a wide-ranging system of informers: his was very much what in a future millennium became known as a 'Police State'. High Priests were appointed at his whim, and equally arbitrarily dismissed. All Jewish autonomous institutions—so prized under the Hasmoneans— were abolished. His notorious ruthlessness and cruelty are expressed in the New Testament story of the Massacre of the Innocents. But he did make strenuous and successful efforts to find food for the people in time of famine; he enabled landless Jewish farmers to work the soil; he constructed irrigation works around Jericho which made it an agricultural haven in the desert; twice he reduced the burden of taxation—albeit taxation that he had imposed; and he took effective action against one of the curses of his day, highway robbery, which was particularly prevalent in Trachonitis, the desert area east of the Golan Heights, on the road to Damascus.

Another of the acts of Herod which made him praiseworthy in Jewish eyes concerned those who lived beyond Judaea. On several occasions, when Jewish communities in the Diaspora were harassed by their rulers, he would intervene on their behalf. When the Greek cities of Asia Minor deprived the Jews in their midst of the privileges of citizenship, Herod successfully intervened to have those privileges restored.

Although he was himself Jewish, Herod made great efforts to encourage Greek culture. The Hellenization of the Jews, the first effective assimilation—which in the United States today leads to almost half of all Jewish marriages being mixed marriages—began in earnest with Herod's reign. Among the Greek cultural institutions that he established in Jerusalem were a theatre and a hippodrome. He even gave substantial sums of money to Greece, to help the Greeks finance the Olympic Games, of which he was made honorary life president. Herod also instituted sports in honour of Augustus, and sent his many (surviving) sons to Rome to be educated.

It was as a builder of great structures that Herod made his most visible and lasting mark. Cities were founded, and cities were expanded, under his close scrutiny and enthusiasm. The two most impressive examples of his urban planning were Caesarea, on the Mediterranean coast, and Sebaste in the hills of Samaria. Even today, after two thousand years, their ruins are impressive. Other buildings testified both to his love of impressive structures, and his desire to be as secure from attack as any previous ruler of Judaea had been: the Antonia Fortress in Jerusalem, the fortress and palace of Herodium, on a hilltop in the Judaean desert (only a few miles from Jerusalem), and the fortress and palace of Cypros, near Jericho, were three of his enterprises. His most remarkable building achievement was the palace and fortress of Masada, high on a cliff spur, overlooking the southern end of the Dead Sea. Its water conduits, reservoirs and hanging palaces are a marvel of construction.

Herod was also a successful entrepreneur. After renting the copper mines of Cyprus from Augustus, he made a considerable personal profit from his royalties—half of the mines' output. For religious Jews, Herod's greatest achievement was the rebuilding of the Temple in Jerusalem. He extended its base and built monumental retaining walls, and created a building the beauty of which was praised by all who saw it. Ten thousand labourers and a thousand priests worked nine years to complete it. The new Temple was known as 'The Second Temple of Herod'; it was said that a person who had not seen it 'has never beheld a beautiful building in his life'. But Herod offended Jewish religious sensitivities by placing a large and imposing ornamental Roman eagle on the facade of the Temple. The massive Herodian blocks of stone that characterized his building works were a remarkable feature of the Temple, especially the high western retaining wall of the Temple Mount. That wall survives as today's much-visited 'Wailing Wall'.

A recent visitor was Pope John Paul II, who on 26 March 2000 left a message between two of the large Herodian stones: 'God of our fathers, you chose Abraham and his descendants to bring your Name to the Nations: we are deeply saddened by the behaviour of those who in the course of history caused these children of yours to suffer, and asking your forgiveness we wish to commit ourselves to genuine brotherhood with the people of the Covenant.' Thus, two thousand years after the Herodian era, a Catholic leader held out the hand of reconciliation to those Children of the Covenant—the Jews.

No. 35

Dearest Auntie Fori,

We are still in the reign of King Herod. At the very the end of his life he uncovered a plot by Antipater, his son by Doris, who was scheming to succeed him. A court was convened in the presence of the Roman governor of Syria, and Antipater was sentenced to death. All that was then required for the sentence to be carried out was the approval—from Rome—of the Emperor Augustus himself. Augustus gave his approval, but commented: 'I would rather be Herod's pig than his son.'

Herod died five days after his son was executed. During those five days he ordered two further executions. After two Pharisee scholars had incited a number of Jews to pull down the Roman eagle which Herod had set up on the facade of the Temple, he ordered it to be put back in place, and the perpetrators of the deed arrested, and burned to death. It may well have been his last command.

The Second Temple survived Herod, and was one of the wonders of its time. Among the sages who taught there was one of the great figures of Jewish history, Hillel. He was said to have been a descendant of the House of David. Like many of the rabbis who taught in Jerusalem, he had been born in Babylon, a descendant of exiles of more than three hundred years earlier, and as a young man had made the journey to Jerusalem—had 'gone up' to Jerusalem, *aliyah* in Hebrew, for the city is built high in the Judaean Hills, some 2,000 feet above sea-level, with views from its very highest points of both the Mediterranean and the Dead Seas. To 'go up' was the aim of all Jewish pilgrims during the Pilgrim Festivals.

Hillel was appointed ha-Nasi, the President, of the Sanhedrin—the spiritual leader of the Jews—in 30 BC, seven years after Herod came to the throne, and held office for forty years, until 10 AD. He and his colleague Shammai, the vice-president of the Sanhedrin, were in continual debate, with six specific controversies attributed to them, and more than three hundred controversies to their followers, the 'Houses' of Hillel and Shammai. In later years there was some simplification of their differences, which were almost certainly exaggerated, with Hillel and those who supported him being identified with the poor, Shammai with the prosperous. Hillel's interpretations of Jewish law were seen as in the main more lenient than those of Shammai. It was said, for example, that when Shammai wanted to restrict entry to the religious schools to the more affluent, upper-class students, Hillel insisted they should be open to all, whatever their social background.

One of the supposed differences between Hillel and Shammai gave rise to a story, and a saying, that has been placed at the centre of Jewish religious practice. A non-Jew was said to have gone to see Shammai, and told him that he wanted to learn all about Judaism while standing on one leg. Shammai shooed him away; how could the whole vast compendium of Jewish laws—the Torah—be explained in such a short time? But when this same person went to Hillel with the same request, Hillel is said to have replied simply: 'What is hateful to you, do not unto your neighbour; this is the entire Torah, all the rest is commentary.'

'What is hateful to you, do not do unto your neighbour. . . .' How one wishes that this rule could be followed, even today, by those all over the world who torment and persecute their fellow human beings. Incidentally, although Shammai had a reputation for severity, he did advise his pupils: 'Make your Torah study regular; say little and do much; and receive everyone with a cheerful countenance.' This last injunction is certainly something you, Auntie Fori, have always done. Hillel also asked, with what has become a central piece of Jewish philosophy: 'If I am not for myself, who will be for me? But if I am for myself alone, what am I? And if not now, when?'

No. 36

Dearest Auntie Fori,

While Herod was still king, a Jew—Jesus—was born, most probably in 12 BC. That was the year of a Roman census that had forced his parents to travel from Galilee where they were living, to Bethlehem, their home town, where Jesus was born. His name was the common Greek form of the Hebrew name Joshua. His mother Mary's name was Miriam in Hebrew. Christian tradition asserts that, through his mother, he was a direct descendant of King David; in Jewish tradition, the Messiah was to be a descendant of David.

Jesus spent his youth and early manhood in Judaea. Like all Jewish male children he was circumcised when he was eight days old. Brought up in Nazareth, he was about eight years old when Herod died. On a visit to Jerusalem as a young man he is said to have been so engrossed in the worship in the Temple that it was only with difficulty he was brought away.

Jesus became a preacher—the concept of rabbi did not exist in those days—preaching mostly in Galilee. He then embarked upon what was, for a Jew, a revolutionary path, being baptized in the River Jordan by his cousin John the Baptist—who was prophesying the end of days and the coming of the Messiah—performing miracles, speaking in parables—

stories of ordinary life with a moral—and being proclaimed as the Messiah by his followers: the name 'Jesus Christ' means 'Jesus the Messiah'. He appeared to call himself the 'Son of Man', a term used at that time for the Messiah, though Jesus himself always used the term in the third person—someone who was expected soon, but not necessarily him.

In the Book of Daniel (in the Hebrew Bible), the Son of Man is the man-like judge of the Last Days whom Daniel saw in a dream, '. . . and behold, one like the Son of Man came with the clouds of heaven. . . . And there was given him dominion and glory, and a kingdom, that all people, nations, and languages, should serve him: his dominion is an everlasting dominion, which shall not pass away, and his kingdom that which shall not be destroyed.'

Jesus regarded poverty as a virtue, condemned violence, and was essentially a pacifist, telling his followers: 'Do not resist one who is evil'. When he broke with Jewish tradition on the Sabbath and healed a woman who had been crippled for eighteen years, the Gospel of St Luke tells us that 'the ruler of the synagogue answered with indignation, because that Jesus had healed on the Sabbath day', insisting that those wanting to be healed should come during the six working days, 'and not on the Sabbath day'. Jesus answered: 'Thou hypocrite, doth not each one of you on the Sabbath loose his ox or his ass from the stall, and lead him away to watering? And ought not this woman, being a daughter of Abraham, whom Satan hath bound, lo, these eighteen years, be loosed from this bond on the Sabbath day?'

Travelling to Jerusalem in what were to be the final days of his life, he criticized those who used the precincts of the Temple for buying and selling, and predicted the destruction of the Temple. He then took part in what some scholars believe was the Passover meal, telling his twelve apostles: 'With all my heart I have longed to eat this pascal lamb with you before I die'.

According to the Christian account in the New Testament, Jesus was then betrayed by Judas, one of the apostles, arrested by the Temple guard, and taken to the High Priest, Caiaphas. The Council of the Sanhedrin, presided over by Caiaphas, may then have examined him and tried to trap him into making blasphemous statements—such as that he had proclaimed himself the Son of God. It then handed him over to the

Roman Governor, Pontius Pilate. The Romans crucified him, putting on his cross the letters 'INRI'—the mocking abbreviation for 'Jesus of Nazareth, King of the Jews'.

The accepted date for the crucifixion is between 30 and 35 AD (Pilate was governor from 27 to 36 AD). According to Christian belief, after the crucifixion Jesus ascended to heaven—as both the Son of God and the Messiah. But in Jewish tradition, the Messiah was not a Divine incarnation, nor was he expected to rise from the dead. It was these two new beliefs that set the new religion, Christianity, apart from Judaism.

While he was on the cross, Jesus, a pious Jew, called out in his agony words which many Jews recite in times of grave personal danger, words from Psalm 22: 'My God, my God why hast thou foresaken me?', and, a few moments before he died, the words from Psalm 31: 'Into thine hand I commit my spirit.'

In Jerusalem, Jesus's brother James—in Hebrew, Jacob—became head of the Christian congregation. In 62 AD, some thirty years after his brother's crucifixion, he was stoned to death, it is said on the orders of a Jewish High Priest, for continuing to preach that his brother was divine. After James's death the leadership of the Christian church in Jerusalem devolved upon Simon, a cousin of Jesus. Another brother of Jesus, Judah, had grandsons who lived until the reign of the Emperor Trajan (who came to the imperial throne in 98 AD): they were leaders of the Christian church in Galilee.

The first great Christian preacher after the crucifixion was a Diaspora Jew, Saul—who later took the name of Paul—a member of the tribe of Benjamin (as had been Saul, the first Israelite king). He had been born in Tarsus, in what is now southern Turkey. According to the New Testament, the future Christian leader Paul had been a pupil of the Jewish sage Rabban Gamaliel the Elder.

After a vision on the road to Damascus, Paul travelled throughout the eastern Mediterranean, preaching from synagogue to synagogue, extolling Jesus and largely creating the Christian faith. Before Paul's time it was possible to be a 'Jewish Christian'—someone who regarded Jesus as a great teacher and prophet, an observant Jew but not divine.

Many conversions took place during Paul's ten-year journey, which took him to Cyprus, to Asia Minor and to the Greek cities of Salonika and Corinth, all places with large Jewish populations. His last journey was to Rome, where the Romans arrested him, and where he died, possibly during the anti-Christian persecutions of the Emperor Nero in 64 AD.

Also martyred in Rome was Simon, who had been given the Greek and Hebrew names for 'rock': Cephas in Hebrew, Peter in Greek. A Jewish fisherman from Galilee, he was not only one of the Twelve Apostles but the 'rock' on whom Jesus chose to build his church: 'You are Peter, and on this rock will I build my church . . .'.

At first, Peter exercised authority over the converted Jews in Jerusalem. Then he set out, not unlike Paul, on missionary journeys to Judaea and Syria. One Jewish tradition has it that Peter was a devout Jew, a Pharisee who took it on himself to preach to the Gentiles in order to take the pressure off the Jews to convert, and that he was the author of one of the main prayers in the Jewish liturgy, *nishmat kol hai* ('the soul of everything that lives'), the prayer of thanksgiving recited during morning prayers on Sabbath and Festivals, extolling God's greatness and man's inadequacy to praise him.

What is certain is that, after some apparent hesitation, Peter supported Paul's campaign to extend Christianity to non-Jews—to the Gentiles—without first obliging them to become circumcised. It was Cornelius, a Roman soldier stationed in the port city of Caesarea, who was the first non-Jew to be baptised by Peter and become a Christian. Peter's burial place in Rome, now St Peter's, became the centre of Roman Catholicism and of the Papacy.

By 300 AD tens of thousands of Jews and Gentiles had been converted to Christianity in Jerusalem, Judaea, Syria, Asia Minor and Greece, on the islands of Crete, Rhodes and Cyprus, and in North Africa. The Jews who did not convert were confronted with hostility which was to intensify 1,000 years after the crucifixion, as they became portrayed as the 'Christ killers'.

Pope John XXIII—who during the Second World War, while Papal Nuncio in Turkey, successfully interceded with the Bulgarian government not to deport its Jews to the death camps in German-occupied Poland—gave orders in 1959 for the anti-Jewish passages in the Good Friday prayer, including the description of the Jews as *perfidi*—perfidious—to be deleted, and to be replaced by a prayer for the Jews. Thus Christian anti-Semitism found one of its staunchest opponents at the highest rank of the Roman Catholic church hierarchy, the Pope of Rome, the lineal successor of St Peter.

No. 37

Dearest Auntie Fori,

Under Herod, Judaea had been careful not to offend Rome, and was able to preserve only those autonomics—albeit wide ones—that Rome would permit. With Herod's death in 4 BC the imposition of full Roman rule returned. The Jews were to remain subjects of Imperial Rome for several centuries, until the power of Rome itself disintegrated. Starting in 4 BC such self-government as the Jews were able to secure was dependent on the policy or whim of the Roman Emperor.

In 40 AD a Jewish ruler, and subject of Rome, King Agrippa I, wrote to the Roman Emperor Caligula, setting out what were to be the main themes of Jewish identity in the centuries to come. Caligula had issued an imperial decree, ordering statues of himself to be placed in all temples within the area of Roman jurisdiction, including the Temple in Jerusalem. The Jews rioted because this decree was against their religion, declaring that they would rather die than submit to such an order. Agrippa, who was in Rome at the time, wrote to Caligula to explain the Jewish standpoint in its widest aspect: 'In all men, O Emperor, a love of their country is innate, as is an eager fondness for their national customs and laws.'

The Jewish King went on to explain to the Roman Emperor: 'I am, as you know, a Jew, and Jerusalem is my country,' and he declared, with courage as well as pride: 'My nation is inferior to none whatever in Asia or in Europe, whether it be in respect of prayers, or of the supply of sacred offerings.' Agrippa went on to point out to Caligula that Jerusalem was not merely the Holy City of a single country, Judaea, but also of the 'ten thousand' cities, towns and villages in which the Jews lived, throughout the Roman world, and beyond it. 'And not only are the continents full of Jewish colonies,' he wrote, 'but also all the most celebrated islands'—among them Crete, Cyprus, Rhodes, Malta, Sicily and Sardinia.

Agrippa's appeal succeeded, although Caligula ordered the rioters to be punished. But before that order could be put into effect he was assassinated. In Jerusalem, Agrippa moved the Jews to deep affection by presenting the golden chain given to him by Caligula as a votive gift to the Temple, and by reading in the Temple the Biblical injunction: 'Thou mayest not put a foreigner as a King over thee, who is not thy brother.'

Under Roman rule, the Jews, like all Roman subjects, could accommodate themselves to a life of subservience but relative calm, and even prosperity. Even so, national instincts remained strong, accentuated by any act of Roman unfairness or tyranny. In 66 AD a Jewish revolt broke out, led by the Zealots. Many Jews opposed the revolt. But the Zealots seized control of Jerusalem, of much of the Galilee, and of parts of the coast. Within a year the Romans had regained Galilee, following the siege of the Zealot fortress of Gamla, on the Golan Heights. But it was not for another four years that, in 70 AD, under the generalship of Titus, the son of the Roman Emperor, the Romans conquered Jerusalem, destroying the Second Temple, and taking many captives away to Rome. Also taken to Rome were the holy vessels of the Temple, including the great menorah. In Jerusalem 12,000 Jews were massacred and the rabbis, refusing to interrupt the service in the Temple, were killed at the altar. The city was reduced to rubble, and an exultant Rome struck coins inscribed *Judaea capta,* 'Judea enslaved'.

On the Arch of Titus, which stands today at the edge of the modern city of Rome, the treasures of the Temple are seen being brought in triumph to the Imperial capital. I took my son David—whom you so enjoyed meeting in Delhi not so long after your ninetieth birthday—to see them a few months ago.

No. 38

Dearest Auntie Fori,

The revolt against Rome lasted for another three years after the destruction of the Temple. It revealed a spirit of its independence that marked the Jews out as somewhat different from the normal 'client' peoples of Rome. Docility had never been a noted feature of the Jewish character. Neither the Jewish sense of unity as a people, nor the inner strength of their religious life, allowed them to merge completely into the pattern and morality of Roman life, with its many gods and altars, and its pagan morality. The universal Roman sentiment, 'I am a citizen of Rome', which brought security and pride to those under Roman rule as widely scattered as Hadrian's Wall in the north of Britain, the plains of the Danube, and the Nile Delta, brought no such sense of citizenship to the Jew.

Jewish resistance did not rely solely on local forces. In their revolts against Rome, the Jews had been supported by Jews outside the bounds of Roman rule, in Persia and in Babylon. There was a sense of universal responsibility by Jews towards their fellow Jews.

The last of the Zealots held out against the Romans in the desert fortress of Masada, overlooking the Dead Sea. It was not until 73 AD that Jewish resistance on Masada was crushed, when the last of the defenders killed their wives and children, and then themselves, to escape capture.

The last days and hours of the Jews on Masada were most powerfully described by Josephus, the Jewish general who transferred his allegiance from the rebels to the Romans, and whose history of those times, *The Jewish War,* is one of the great narrative histories of all time: he is truly the first Jewish historian. Much of his detailed account of the struggle for Masada was confirmed 1,890 years later by the archaeological excavations of Yigael Yadin, who found twenty-five skeletons of men, women and children thrown in a heap in a small cave on the southern cliff of the fortress. He also found eleven small ostraca—pieces of specially broken pottery—each inscribed with a single name, and all written by the same person. These were almost certainly the lots described by Josephus which the last ten survivors of the Roman siege drew to choose who would kill the other nine and then himself.

One aspect of Roman rule after the revolt was to disperse the Jews inside Palestine itself, denuding Jerusalem and forcing the Jews to live in coastal cities whose predominant population was non-Jewish, cities such as Ashdod and Yavne. Yet even this act of hostility led to a positive and decisive result, when one of the great Jewish sages at the time of the Second Temple, Johanan ben Zakkai, persuaded the Romans not to destroy the school at Yavne, so that the sages there could continue to teach there, and 'to observe the mitzvot and to study the Torah'. Of these 'mitzvot'— Divine Commandments—I will write to you in a future letter.

Because the Romans allowed the school at Yavne to continue, the central function of Jewish spiritual life was preserved in the Land of Israel itself, despite the loss of the Temple.

At Yavne, where Rabban Gamaliel II was the leading teacher, a theological system was created that replaced the sacrificial system of the Temple, and reduced the hitherto central role of the priests. New sages were ordained there, and given the title of 'rabbi'—the first time this title was used. Those bearing it were members of the reconstituted Sanhedrin— the highest judicial body of Judaism—and could act in its name. In the days of the Temple, the sins of the people had been expiated by animal sacrifice. Now, with the Temple destroyed, there was another means of expiation of sins. 'What is it?', Johanan ben Zakkai was asked, and he answered: 'It is deeds of lovingkindness.'

Not all the Jewish sages supported the experiment at Yavne. But Gamaliel, who presided there from 80 to 110 AD, travelled both to Syria and to Rome itself in search of greater support for Yavne, which flourished. Religious questions were submitted to it, and missions were sent out, some led by Gamaliel himself, to ask for money from the Jews of the Diaspora for the strengthening of Jewish religious life in the Land of Israel. These missions were successful. The Diaspora paid, the Jewish institutions grew—both in size and authority—and links were forged which ensured that the problems of the Jews in their own land would continue to be of concern to the Jews outside.

Gamaliel made changes to the ritual that were to affect Jewish worship to this day: The Passover seder night ritual was reformulated (I will write to you about this in the special 'Passover' letter I promised you earlier); the Amidah prayer was made a central and daily part of the synagogue service; and burial rites which stressed social distinctions were abolished. Above all, Gamaliel brought the different schools of interpretation (sometimes characterized as the rigorous and the liberal, though that is a simplification) under one spiritual roof.

No. 39

Dearest Auntie Fori,

In 115 AD, forty-five years after the revolt of the Zealots in Palestine, the Jews in Egypt and Cyrenaica (modern Libya) turned against their Roman rulers. They were described by a Roman writer 'as though carried by some wild and riotous spirit'. It took two years before the revolt was crushed. News of it spread throughout the Jewish world. On Cyprus, the Jews rose up against the ruling Greeks, but were defeated by a Roman army, and then expelled from the island. In Mesopotamia, a Jewish uprising led to the expulsion of the local Roman administrators, but soon the power of Rome was reasserted. Seventeen years later, in 132 AD, the Jews of Judaea rose up in one last revolt, under the leadership of Simon Bar Kochba. The story of that revolt was to inspire Jews through the centuries.

In the early months of the revolt, Simon Bar Kochba drove the Romans from Jerusalem, where he minted coins with the inscription 'Jerusalem's liberation' and 'Israel's redemption', dating those of 132 AD as 'Year One'. If Roman rule had been harsh, that of Bar Kochba was far from mild. He insisted on the most unquestioning obedience: according to one legend, everyone joining his army had to cut off a finger first, as a sign of determination. According to the Christian Saint Jerome, Bar Kochba would hold a lighted blade of straw between his teeth, to give the impression that flames were coming out of his mouth.

Bar Kochba's self-confidence was considerable. When greeted with the customary phrase, 'God will help', he would reply: 'God will neither help nor hinder.' The Emperor Hadrian sent a Roman army of 35,000 men against the rebels. Tens of thousands of Jews were killed—some accounts say hundreds of thousands. Bar Kochba was driven out of Jerusalem, and then died, in 135 AD, in defence of his last redoubt, the stronghold at Betar, in the Jerusalem Hills. The date was the 9th of Av, *Tisha b'Av* in Hebrew, the date already mourned as the anniversary of the destruction of the First and Second Temples. Today the Tel Aviv-to-Jerusalem railway line, built by the Ottoman Turks in 1892 and widened

by the British in the 1920s, runs in the deep valley below the Betar battlefield.

As punishment for the Jewish rebellion, Hadrian imposed severe
penalties against the practice of the Jewish religion, turning Jerusalem
into a heathen city, and re-naming it Aelia Capitolina. Yavne was closed
down, and Hadrian expelled almost all the Jews from Judaea, which had
been their historic homeland since the death of Moses. Even the name
'Judaea' was expunged, and the region given a new designation, 'Syria-
Palaestina', thus reducing it to a part of Syria.

No. 40

Dearest Auntie Fori,

This letter is about a remarkable man. His name was Rabbi Akiva
ben Joseph, known popularly as Rabbi Akiva. He was said to have been a
descendant of a convert to Judaism many generations before his birth—
one rabbinic tradition says he was a descendant of no less than Sennacherib, the conqueror of Judaea, an attempt to show that even the
worst enemies of the Israelites could not prevent their descendants from
becoming Jews. Another distinguished rabbi, Akiva's pupil Meir, was said
to have been descended from Nero.

A shepherd boy in his youth, Akiva married the daughter of the
wealthy landowner for whom he worked. He is said to have left his wife
and children to study in the academies of the leading rabbis of his day,
and to have returned to her—after twenty-four years—in the company
of thousands of those who had become his disciples. His own religious
academy, at Bnei Brak—today an ultra-Orthodox suburb on the outskirts of Tel Aviv—became a centre of learning, where a whole generation of rabbis were trained.

In 95 AD, Akiva went to Rome, where he prevailed upon the Emperor to annul anti-Jewish legislation. At Bnei Brak he promulgated a
written code of religious and personal conduct, based upon hitherto oral
traditions. In the words of one Jewish saying, 'What was not revealed to
Moses was discovered by Akiva.'

According to legend, almost certainly fanciful, when the Bar Kochba revolt broke out, Akiva, then in his early nineties—as old, Auntie Fori, as you are—hailed Bar Kochba as the Messiah. He is also said to have put the weight of his authority behind the revolt, saying, of Bar Kochba, 'A star has stepped out of Jacob', to link Bar Kochba's name, 'Son of a star', with the phrase in the Book of Numbers: 'There shall step forth a star out of Jacob'. Letters that survive from that period, hidden in caves, show that he was originally Ben, or Bar, Koseva.

Following the defeat of Bar Kochba's revolt, Akiva is said to have refused to follow the Roman ban on all Jewish religious practice and study. He was imprisoned, but managed to smuggle out messages to his pupils and followers. The Romans sentenced him to be executed. As a terrible preliminary to execution, Roman soldiers tore away pieces of his flesh with iron combs. He continued to pray, reciting the Shema, the prayer 'Hear, O Israel!' which enjoins every Jew to pray to God 'with all my heart and all my soul and all my might'. He was asked how, while in such an agony of pain, he could continue to pray. He replied: 'All my life I have sought to serve God with all my heart, all my soul, and all my might. Now I realize the meaning of serving God "with all my soul", that is, even though he is taking away my life.'

Akiva died under torture. Ever since, the recitation of the Shema has been the traditional final confession of faith of every Jew on his or her deathbed. During the Holocaust—almost a thousand years after Akiva's death—the words 'Hear O Israel!' and the prayer's opening confession of faith to serve God were spoken by possibly millions of Jews in the final moments before they were murdered. The faith of Akiva the Martyr was their inspiration.

A rabbinic story set down two thousand years ago tells of Moses being miraculously transported to one of Akiva's classes. Listening to the discussion between the students and their master, he was upset not to be able to understand what Akiva was teaching. Then one of the students asked Akiva how he knew a certain thing he had just told them, and Akiva replied, 'It is tradition from Moses our Teacher.' At that Moses' mind was set at rest.

No. 41

Dearest Auntie Fori,

Despite the attractions and missionary efforts of the early Christians—almost all of whom were Jews, like Jesus and his disciples—Jews in the lands where Christianity became the dominant religion tenaciously maintained their links to their Bible and its language, even as they adopted the languages, dress and customs of the lands in which they lived. Throughout the Diaspora, and throughout the growing Christian world, Biblical Hebrew remained the language in which Jews prayed and read the weekly portion of the Bible in their synagogues.

As each new Jewish generation grew to adulthood, its experiences and memories became increasingly those of their particular region of the dispersal, often very far indeed from the Land of Israel, its landscape and its climate, its fruits and seasons. But their Bible story and its language, their prayers and their religious songs, their traditions and festivals, told them of that land, of its physical beauty, its mountains and rivers, of its patriarchs and its prophets, of its judges and its kings, of its heroes and sages, and of God's promise that it was there, to the Land of Israel, that they were destined to return.

The vision of the return was held out to the scattered Jews not only in their Bible, but in their daily prayers. Long after it became impossible for all but a handful of Jews to take part in the Pilgrim Festivals, and go up each year to Jerusalem, the hope, 'Next Year in Jerusalem,' remained, as it remains to this day, the concluding prayer of the Passover meal, spoken by all present as the festivities come to an end. Hope and expectation became powerful factors in maintaining Jewish identity, as did the belief that the Messiah would eventually come. In a prayer, dating from mediaeval times—a prayer which was often spoken during the Holocaust by those about to be killed—Jews declare: 'I believe in perfect faith in the coming of the Messiah.'

Another, equally powerful factor in the survival of the Jewish heritage was the actual Jewish presence in the Land of Israel. Despite the worst excesses of Roman persecution, including the total destruction of Jerusalem itself, the Jews were never totally driven out of their land. Between the Roman conquest and modern times Jewish communities, families and individuals maintained an unbroken link between the 'chosen people'—chosen, not to rule over others, but to carry out God's commandments—and their promised land.

Before the Temple had been destroyed by the Romans, twenty-four priestly families had been responsible for the Temple services. After the destruction of the Temple these twenty-four families remained in the Land of Israel, living in the towns and villages of the Galilee. Other Jewish families lived east of the Galilee, in the sheltered uplands of what are now known as the Golan Heights, far from the Roman legions encamped at Jerusalem or Caesarea.

In the aftermath of the destruction of Bar Kochba's revolt in 135 AD, the Jews held together as a community. About five years after the revolt had been crushed, the Romans allowed the re-opening of an Academy, or Bet Din (House of Law), not at Yavne, where it had been at the time of the revolt, but at Bet Shearim in the Jezreel Valley. From there it moved some seventy years later to Sepphoris in the Galilee, and finally to Tiberias in about 240 AD. The northern hills of Galilee replaced the coastal plain as the focus of Jewish life, both spiritual and temporal. Farming was revived. Synagogues were built. Religious sayings were collected and annotated. Even the rabbinical leaders in Babylonia—at that time the main centre of religion in the Diaspora—were persuaded to submit to the spiritual authority of the sages in the Land of Israel.

The Jews, although part of the Roman province 'Syria-Palaestina' and completely under Roman sovereignty, were allowed since the year 200 AD a community leader, known officially as *ha-Nasi,* the President, whose authority covered both religious and civil aspects of Jewish life. Jews even regained the right to own their own land. More important still, their religious life flourished. The central figure in this religious development was Judah ha-Nasi, known because of the extreme piety and probity of his private life as *Rabbenu ha-Kadosh,* Our Holy Teacher—known simply as Rabbi, the teacher. He was the grandson of Rabban Gamaliel of Yavne, a former President of the Sanhedrin, and was much influenced by his grandfather's teachings. Coming to prominence in Galilee in 200 AD, Judah ha-Nasi made one of his chief aims the maintenance and unity among the Jews of the Land of Israel. This he achieved by encouraging the widespread study of the Torah, and the fulfillment of the religious and social code by all classes of people. Above all, he strove to preserve the unity of Judaism and to prevent the fragmentation of world Jewry.

It was Judah ha-Nasi who ensured that Hebrew was preserved as the language of prayer. Indeed, although Aramaic was the daily language throughout the region, he insisted on speaking only Hebrew with his family and friends. It was said by his contemporaries: 'From the time of Moses to the time of Rabbi, Torah and greatness were never so concentrated in one person.' The Mishnah—a remarkable compilation of the oral law—served as the basic Jewish code of conduct and the foundation for future generations of interpretation and development. It was the written discussion of each section of the Mishnah—itself a vast work—that would later form part of the Talmud, the many-volume centrepiece of daily learning and discussion among devout and observant Jews.

Hitherto it had been thought impious to write down interpretations of the Torah, because this might put human interpretation on the same level as the divine text. Interpretation was therefore committed to memory. By Judah ha-Nasi's time there had been so much persecution of Jewish scholars that it was felt necessary to write down interpretations, lest they be forgotten. From that moment, the Oral Law ceased to be oral.

Another change had also taken place in the Jewish religion: until the time of the Mishnah, Judaism was primarily a religion centred on the Temple and the wisdom of the High Priest. From the time of Judah ha-Nasi the evolution and inner debates of Judaism centred on Jewish law as written down in the Mishnah, and as discussed in the Talmud.

Judah ha-Nasi was buried in Bet Shearim. His wisdom was proverbial. One of his sayings was: 'I have learned much from my teachers, more from my colleagues, but most from my pupils.' He also said—in an echo of Eleazar, a martyr of Seleucid vengeance almost four hundred years earlier: 'Be as punctilious in observing a light as a weighty commandment, for you do not know their relative reward.'

No. 42

Dearest Auntie Fori,

During the 1920s, when you were about to leave Budapest for London, and to enter into the Indian orbit, a group of Jewish farmers from a kibbutz in the Jezreel valley—one of the most beautiful valleys in Palestine—arrived in Jerusalem. Theirs was a strange mission. They had come from their kibbutz, Bet Alfa, to see the distinguished archaeologist, Professor Sukenik (the father of another distinguished archaeologist—and general—Yigael Yadin). Seated in Sukenik's study the farmers told him how, in the course of digging the foundations for a new cowshed, they had dug into what seemed to be an ancient mosaic.

The farmers' first thought on exposing the mosaic had been to cover it up again and to tell nobody. After all, their task was to expand their kibbutz, to cultivate the valley, to feed the growing number of Jews in Mandate Palestine. An archaeological find in their midst could only impinge on their restricted land area and close it off from cultivation.

Yet the farmers had realized at once that there was something special about this mosaic. It must, they knew, be important. Hence their journey to Jerusalem. And indeed it was not only a fascinating ancient relic but, as Professor Sukenik quickly realized, proof of a Jewish presence in the Jezreel valley in the 'dark ages' of Jewish life; those 'forgotten' centuries which followed the Roman destruction of the Temple, and the crushing of Jewish political life.

Professor Sukenik hurried northwards to view the mosaic for himself. It proved to be the central floor of an ancient synagogue, much of the foundation of which could still be traced. As excavations proceeded an inscription was discovered, dating the mosaic itself to the reign of the Emperor Justin I, who ruled from 518 to 527 AD. The simple but strong style of the mosaic, archaeologists concluded, represented a folk art which had developed at that time among the many Jewish villages of Galilee.

So it was, through the accident of a farmer's spade, that one more piece of evidence emerged of the continuity and the richness of Jewish life in the Land of Israel in the eighteen centuries between the fall of Masada and the nineteenth-century 'return to the land', of which kib-butz Bet Alfa—founded in 1922 by pioneers from Poland—was itself a part.

The story of those eighteen centuries is one of struggle and survival against a succession of enemies. By destroying the Temple, the Romans cut the head from the Jewish spiritual and political life in the Land of Israel. By seeking out and killing Jewish families descended from the House of David, they sought to make it physically impossible for the Kingdom of David to be restored. Jewish farms were confiscated and, as at the village of Motza just outside Jerusalem, Roman soldiers were given these farms as a reward for their zeal. Throughout the conquered province, the Roman Tenth Legion, whose soldiers had been in the fore-front of the war against the Jews, remained as a permanent feature of Roman control. One of their camps was recently uncovered at the very entrance to modern Jerusalem, during building works at the Convention Centre—scene of innumerable modern events, including the Jerusalem Book Fair and the Eurovision Song Contest.

Despite the deliberate severity of Roman rule, the Jews remained in their land, enduring the hardships, and the departure of tens of thousands of their relatives, some of whom were taken as captives to Rome, others dispersed throughout the vast territories of the Roman world, from Spain to the Crimea.

Many of those who remained, like the dispossessed farmers of Motza, were allowed to go on cultivating their own land, no longer as owners, but as tenant farmers, faced with the constant danger of sudden and arbitrary eviction if for some reason they failed to please their Roman masters.

Taxation on the Jews of 'Palaestina' was more severe than in almost any other part of the Roman Empire. For the Jews, a double tax system was introduced, both for individuals—a poll tax—and for their produce. Forced labour was also brought in, whereby Jews were compelled to build the roads along which the Roman conquerors could more easily reach the distant outposts of the province.

Despite the difficult time, with Roman rule an apparently per-manent feature of Jewish life, the links which bound the Jews of the

Diaspora to the Land of Israel remained strong. Indeed there was a movement back even in those early days, and in every generation individuals and groups can be found for whom the return was a central feature of their lives. Thus Rabbi Nathan, the son of a leading Babylonian scholar, returned to the Land of Israel to serve under Gamaliel's son Simeon, and built up a reputation as a teacher and an interpreter of the law, inspired, according to legend, by the Prophet Elijah himself.

It was Rabbi Nathan who laid down that the surplus of money collected for a burial service should be used 'to build a monument over the grave'. And as one of the earliest of those who had returned from the Diaspora, he declared: 'There is no greater love than love of the Torah; there is no wisdom like the wisdom of the Land of Israel; and there is no beauty like the beauty of Jerusalem.'

The Jews of Galilee still looked to Jerusalem as their ultimate spiritual centre. Nor were the earlier restrictions on their return to Jerusalem maintained. Gamaliel's grandson, Judah ha-Nasi, whose work, as I wrote in my last letter, was dominated by the completion of the Mishnah—the vast body of Jewish oral law—supported the Roman general Septimus Severus at the time of his struggle with Pescennius Niger, the Jew-hating governor of Syria. With Niger's defeat, Severus relaxed the restrictions on the Jews. One of his successors, Alexander Severus—who became Emperor in 222 AD—allowed the Jews to govern themselves in all matters of religious law.

During this Severan 'golden age' the spiritual leader of the Jews, the Nasi, was allowed to levy taxes on the Jewish community for its internal administration, to try both civil and criminal cases, and to enforce judgments against the guilty party. Judah ha-Nasi himself was said to have obtained many favours from the Romans, including land in the Jezreel Valley and on the uplands east of the Sea of Galilee—in the area now known as the Golan Heights.

The new favour in which the Jews found themselves, affected even their access to Jerusalem. The official Roman ban on Jews living in the city remained in force. But it was ignored and a resident Jewish community, 'the holy community in Jerusalem', came into being. Elsewhere the Jews were encouraged to live in the growing cities, such as Bet Guvrin and Lydda. More synagogues were built—the ruins of those at Baram and Kfar Nahum (the Capernaum of the New Testament and the teach-ings of Jesus) are visible and striking even in the twenty-first century. Not only individual Jews but whole families and groups of Jews emi-grated from Babylon, and from elsewhere in the Diaspora. The court of the Nasi became one of opulence and regal pomp, and the Emperor Alexander Severus, who had shown such favour to the Jews, was called derisively by his enemies *archi-synagogus*—the 'head of the synagogue'.

The severities of Roman rule intensified under the rule of Emperor Diocletian, who reigned for twenty years beginning in 284 AD, and was responsible for the 'Great Persecution' of both Jews and Christians, both of whom refused to worship the Emperor. In Palestine, Jewish wor-ship and learning struggled to survive. At the same time, Roman sol-diers attacked Jewish farmers for food and loot. When the Emperor Constantine began to promote Christianity from 313 AD new perils opened up for the Jews in the renamed provinces of 'Palaestina Prima' and 'Palaestina Secunda'. Of these perils—the Christian shadow that was to hang over so much of Jewish history in the centuries ahead like a black cloud—I will write in later letters.

No. 43

Dearest Auntie Fori,

It was clear, despite the failures of national revolt and regional upris-ing against Rome, that the Jews would not easily disappear. Indeed, they not only multiplied and flourished under Roman rule, but repeatedly showed themselves capable of a blend of proud independence and reli-gious piety, amid the often harsh routine of daily life. From Cádiz, on the Atlantic coast of Spain, to the shores of the Black Sea, and beyond, into the mountains of the Caucasus, the Jews considered themselves, and were considered by those among whom they lived, to be a single people. They had acquired, in the process of defeat and dispersal, a great inner strength. Their belief in their one God and his commandments served to unify, inspire and preserve them. Their festivals, including Passover, their festival of liberty, and the pattern of their daily prayers, linked communi-ties that had no physical contact.

Many aspects of Jewish life in Roman times were to set the pattern for the next two thousand years. The Jewish peasant and shepherd of the Biblical era proved, under the rule of Rome, to be a person fitted equally well for city life, for sea-borne trade, for commerce and for the rigours of a competitive existence. In Spain and North Africa, Jews adapted to the economy of the olive-growing, wine-making world. In Italy, contemporary records show Jews working as weavers, garment makers, bakers, shipping merchants and actors—a versatile foretaste, two thousand years in advance, of life in London or New York.

As Roman rule advanced northwards and eastwards against the tribes living along the Rhine and the Danube, or westwards to the French towns of Marseille, Bordeaux, Toulouse, Lyon and Orléans, so too were Jewish merchants to be found, plying their trades. Even beyond the regions controlled by Rome, the Jews survived, multiplied and worked in the local trades, as farmers and cattle raisers along the Tigris and the Euphrates, as wine-growers in the Caucasus or as traders in the distant ports of the Black Sea.

Not every decade was one of suffering or persecution. Even under Roman rule there were times when Jewish life was one of normality and of opportunity. By 300 AD the Jews of the Roman Empire had been guaranteed freedom of religion, were exempt from military service, and allowed to practice Jewish law in disputes between Jews. Recognized as a separate people, they were able to preserve their own religious traditions while at the same time participating in the daily life around them.

No. 44

Dearest Auntie Fori,

One reason for the survival of the Jews as a people was their ability, while living in exile, to reconstruct, preserve and advance their religious life. This was particularly the case at the great Babylonian religious academies of Sura and Pumbeditha, on the River Euphrates. At a time when the mighty Roman Empire was itself in a slow but irreversible decline, Jewish rabbinical study flourished in Babylonia, culminating in the completion of the Babylonian Talmud in about 500 AD: some thirty volumes of commentary and reflection on the Biblical narrative—about two and a half million words, 5,900 pages in all—material for a lifetime of study, discussion, learning and, above all, daily religious practice.

The Babylonian Talmud—and its Jerusalem counterpart, produced about a hundred years earlier—provided a bedrock of exposition, bringing the same debates and interpretations to every Jewish community, wherever in the Diaspora it might be.

The academies of Sura and Pumbeditha became (in the words of *The Encyclopedia of Judaism*), 'the centre of world Jewry'. Their importance continued in Muslim times. It has been argued that, had it not been for the Jews of Babylonia, Judaism would not have survived, for even while they flourished, to the west, in the Roman Empire under Theodosius I (379–395), Christianity was finally proclaimed throughout the Empire as the only permitted religion, and when the Roman Empire fell to the barbarians in 410, the Eastern (Byzantine) Empire, which ruled Palestine, continued to harass the Jews. This persecution came to a climax in 425, during the reign of the the Emperor Theodosius II. From then on, the Babylonian academies had to carry the torch of Jewish religious teaching.

No. 45

Dearest Auntie Fori,

As Christianity spread more and more widely during the fourth century, the Jews of the Land of Israel found that both their Holy City—Jerusalem—and their principal area of settlement—Galilee—had become objects of Christian desire. In towns such as Tiberias, Capernaum and Nazareth, where the Jews had remained the principal inhabitants, Christians built churches and monasteries, and catered for a growing number of Christian pilgrims who made their way to their Holy Land from Greece, Italy and the Balkans. As well as pilgrims who settled permanently, many local non-Jews, with no tradition of monotheism, were converted to Christianity. There is evidence that a number of Jews also accepted conversion.

Christian violence against the Jews of Palestine broke out from time to time with great severity. At the beginning of the fifth century a Christian monk from northern Syria, Bar Sauma, led a band of like-minded fanatics through Palestine, destroying synagogues. On another occasion Jews were attacked in more than twenty towns throughout the country. But despite these setbacks the authority of the Nasi was preserved, and by some emperors even enhanced.

For several decades, while the Christian world was itself in spiritual turmoil and violent division, the Jews of Palestine were left unmolested. Under the Emperor Justinian there was a further revival of synagogue building, including synagogues in Jericho, Gaza, Ashkelon and at the hot springs of Hammath-Gader, in the gorge of the River Yarmuk, under the shadow of the Golan Heights. But with Justinian there also came a renewed religious persecution, as Christianity itself expanded, as new churches were built, and as the Church found it increasingly convenient to single out 'the Jews' as the enemy of the true faith. Even synagogue building was suddenly prohibited, and the Jewish courts were deprived of more and more of their autonomy.

However much hampered or persecuted, the Jews of Palestine remained, in the coastal plain, in Judaea and Samaria, in the Jordan valley, and above all in the Galilee. They held on with tenacity to their ancient land, and to their Jerusalem-oriented faith. Neither the severity of Roman rule nor the new zeal of Christian faith had dislodged them. Jewish religious writings grew, and Jewish prayers continued to centre on the land of their fathers; the land they called *Eretz Yisrael,* the Land of Israel, a land where they themselves still farmed and traded, worshipped—and looked forward to the day when the Messiah would come.

No. 46

Dearest Auntie Fori,

As the Persian armies, the enemies of the Byzantine Empire, approached the Land of Israel in 614 AD they were helped in their conquest of Roman rule by the Jews. Hastily assembled, Jewish troops joined the Persian army in its entry into Jerusalem, where the Persians established a Jewish leader, Nehemiah ben Hushiel, as ruler. Many Christians were forced to leave the city and their churches were closed. But this period of Jewish autonomy was brief. Three years later, the Persians, siding with the Christians, turned against Nehemiah and killed him.

After five more years of Persian rule, hope again seemed to open up for the Jews of Palestine. A Byzantine army, led by the Emperor Heraclitus, reconquered the land. As the Byzantines advanced a wealthy Jewish leader, Benjamin of Tiberias, put Heraclitus up in his Galilee home, paid for the feeding of his army, and even went with him on the march to Jerusalem. For his part, the Emperor promised to overlook the Jews' previous support for his Persian enemies.

These favours and pledges were in vain. Hardly had Heraclitus entered Jerusalem than the pressure of local Christian interests prevailed. An imperial decree was issued expelling the Jews from the city. Many who resisted the decree were killed. Others were put on trial. Hundreds—perhaps thousands—of Jews were forcibly converted to Christianity.

With the re-establishment of militant Christianity in Jerusalem, as in much of the Mediterranean region, more than five hundred years had passed since the destruction of the Second—Herodian—Temple by the Romans. The next thousand years were to see new rulers, and a new religion, in the Land of Israel. The new rulers would be the Arabs, and the new religion, Islam.

No. 47

Dearest Auntie Fori,

It was in 622 AD that the fifty-year-old Mohammed was forced out of Mecca, by Arabs who resented his insistence that Allah was not one god among several hundred—albeit the chief god—but a single deity. He fled to the town of Yathrib, which had been founded by Jewish date-growers and which had a flourishing Jewish community. The Jews knew the town by its Hebrew name, Medina—the City, or State—and this was the name Mohammed used in the Koran, Islam's holy book, a compilation of his sermons.

During his first two years in Medina, Mohammed won over the Arab tribes of the area to monotheism. The Jews were, of course, already believers in one God. One of Mohammed's achievements during those two years was to make a covenant between the Jews and the Arabs of the region to form 'one community, to the exclusion of all other men'—that is, to the exclusion of those who still worshipped many gods. In a Pact of War, the members of this community agreed to help and protect each other. Judaism and Islam seemed destined for amicable coexistence, as allies.

Mohammed based many of the precepts of Islam (the word means submission—to God) on Judaism. The dietary laws of Islam were a version of the laws of kashrut—about which I will write to you in a later letter. The Muslims of that time fasted on Yom Kippur, prayed facing Jerusalem, and were allowed to marry Jews. The reason why Mohammed instituted Friday prayers was, according to several authorities, to avoid conflict with the Jewish Sabbath.

It seems that Mohammed was prepared to convert to Judaism, his basic religious beliefs being so similar, provided the Jews recognized him as the last of the Jewish Prophets. This they would not do: the last previous Prophet, Malachi, had lived about a thousand years before Mohammed, shortly after which the Tanakh—the three divisions of the Jewish Bible: Pentateuch, Prophets and Hagiographia—had been finalized. In addition, the stories in the Koran that derived from the Hebrew Bible also varied from it in many particulars: such variants were unacceptable to the Jews, for whom the Biblical record constituted *Torah Min-Hashamayim*—the Teaching from Heaven—that is, from God.

It was also unacceptable to the Jews that while Mohammed rejected the Christian claim that Jesus was divine, he saw Jesus as one of the Prophets, as he aspired to be. It was also hard—if not impossible—for the Jews, whose Biblical language was Hebrew, to accept the Koran, which was written in Arabic, as a holy book, although, in the centuries to come, in lands which fell under the rule of Islam, many Jewish religious leaders were to speak and write—and think—in Arabic.

Mohammed began to criticize Judaism. He began to describe Jewish—and Christian—worship as containing many additions that were not part of the simple faith of Abraham, whom Muslims saw as the father of their faith—the father of Ishmael, from whom they believed they were descended. In 624 Mohammed instructed his followers to face Mecca, not Jerusalem, when they prayed. A year later he changed the fasting of Yom Kippur, which took place in the autumn, to another fast, that of Ramadan, in the spring. References to the Jews in his sermons— the 114 chapters which make up the Koran—became more hostile, often intensely so. Then, when Mohammed was attacked by pagan tribes outside Medina, the Jews remained neutral, failing to observe the alliance of the Pact of War.

Militarily, Mohammed went from strength to strength. In 630 he and his followers conquered Mecca, from which he had been been chased out eight years earlier. Islam had a new centre, and the Jews a new adversary. Two years later, in 632, Mohammed died. Within four years his followers had conquered Palestine and Syria. Within a decade they were masters of Egypt, Mesopotamia and Persia. From Egypt they advanced across North Africa, to the Atlantic Ocean, and in 711 they entered Spain. Everywhere they conquered, Jews were among their new subjects.

The Jews and Islam will be the theme of my next letter.

No. 48

Dearest Auntie Fori,

No clear divide marks Ancient and Mediaeval times. For the Jews of Palestine, the watershed was the coming of Islam in 636 AD. Jerusalem was captured two years later. Roman rule and Christian predominance in Palestine were both at an end.

No generalization can characterize the life of the Jews in Palestine under Islam. Each century saw some new turn or twist in their affairs. For the first fifty years they prospered. The last Byzantine ruler of Jerusalem, the Christian Emperor Heraclius I, had expelled the Jews from the city nine years earlier. The first Muslim ruler, the Caliph Omar I, allowed them to return and granted them—as he granted the Christians in the city—the unimpeded right of their religious worship. But Omar did expel all non-Muslims, including Jews, from the coastal region of the Hejaz—today part of Saudi Arabia—including Mecca and Medina.

Under Omar II (717–720) severe restrictions against non-Muslims were introduced throughout the Muslim world, from the Persian Gulf to the Atlantic Coast of what is now Morocco. The Jews—like the Christians—became *dhimmis*—'protected', but with disabilities and obligations which marked them out as second-class citizens. Above all, they had to pay a special tax, often when doing so, being obliged to bow their heads lower than the tax-collector's head, as an act of submission, and at the same time to submit to a symbolic—but sometimes more than symbolic—slap in the face.

Humiliation was frequent. Jewish (and Christian) shops had to be lower than the street, so that Muslims always stood at a higher level than non-Muslims. No dhimmi building could be taller than a corresponding Muslim one. And dhimmi-owned land was heavily taxed. But whereas in Christian Europe, Jews were not allowed to own land at all, or to be members of the merchant guilds, the Muslims allowed both. Even commercial partnerships between Jews and Muslims were permitted, something inconceivable at that time in Christian Europe.

In Mesopotamia, the Muslim rulers respected the authority of the leaders of the Jewish Babylonian community—the Exilarchs, hereditary rulers claiming descent from King David who lived in princely style, collecting taxes and appointing judges. Nor did they do anything to impede the work and authority of the Jewish religious teachers—the Geonim—who were preserving the traditions and scholarship of the four-hundred-year-old Babylonian religious academies of Sura and Pumbeditha.

When, in 762, the Caliphate moved the capital of the vast Islamic empire to Baghdad on the River Tigris, the authority of the Jewish religious academies near the city was enhanced. Rav Amram, the head of the Academy of Sura, who died in 874, produced the *siddur*—the prayer book which became standard throughout the Jewish world, and about which I will write to you in my letters on Jewish worship. It was the first work to supply a logical arrangement of the prayers for every occasion in the year, as well as the rule for Sabbath observance and the Festivals. Ironically, it was originally written as a guide for the distant Jewish community of Barcelona. It was to become the standard for the Babylonian (later Sephardi) rite, and, from the eleventh century at least, a model for European (Ashkenazi) ritual.

Saadiah Gaon, who was born in Egypt in 882, emigrated to Palestine as a young man, and then settled in Babylonia. He and his colleagues in the Babylonian academies introduced written vowels into Hebrew, in order to fix the pronunciation. They also fixed the division between words, sentences and paragraphs in the Bible.

Saadiah Gaon himself produced the first Hebrew grammar, as well as a Hebrew rhyming dictionary, and an explanation of words that appear only once in the Bible, whose meaning cannot thus be tested against any other usage. So outstanding was his communal and intellectual leadership that he was given the title *aluf*—prince: today in Israel, in modern Hebrew, aluf is the title for general. His Arabic translation of the Bible is in use to this day by Yemenite Jews in both Yemen and Israel. In the twelfth century, Maimonides—of whom I will write later—said of him: 'If it were not for Saadiah, the Torah could well have disappeared from among the Jewish people.'

In the year 930, in a move which divided the Babylonian Jews, Saadiah Gaon attacked the lifestyle of the incumbent Exilarch, David ben-Zakkai, accusing him of failing to observe the Halakhah (religious law) properly, and of exploiting his office for personal gain. It took seven years, and much communal bitterness, before the two men were reconciled: the Muslim Caliph presided over the reconciliation ceremony.

On the coast of Palestine, the Jews of the Romano-Byzantine city of Caesarea had opened the gates to the Muslim liberator. The rule of Islam enabled them and Jews throughout Palestine to recover from the hardships of Byzantine rule, and to flourish for several centuries in the local economy as weavers, fishermen and farmers, reviving long-neglected wheat fields. Under this period of benevolent Islamic rule there was not only a revival of the Jewish communities of the Galilee, Jerusalem and the Jordan Valley, but a return of Jews to Palestine from other lands under Muslim rule.

One of the leading Jewish families in tenth-century Jerusalem, living within sight of the newly-built Dome of the Rock, had come from Fez in Morocco, at the western extremity of Muslim rule. A member of this family, Solomon ben-Judah, was head of the rabbinical academies of Jerusalem and Ramla, whose emissaries travelled as far afield as Seville in Spain and Aleppo in Syria.

In some decades, Jews in Palestine and elsewhere in the Muslim world had to be recognizable on sight by their compulsory yellow turbans. Christians had to wear blue turbans. Under the Caliph Al-Hakim (996–1021), in both Palestine and Egypt there was a brief but widespread destruction of synagogues and churches, while the imposition of severe land taxes on all non-Muslims forced more and more Jews to give up their centuries-old farming in Galilee.

Forced from the land, the Jews of Muslim 'Filastin' (Palestine) and 'Urdunn' (Jordan) moved into the towns. There, often as traders, leather-tanners and dyers, they rebuilt their livelihoods, and clung tenaciously to their faith, permitted—as they had not been for much of the period of Roman rule—to travel freely to Jerusalem. Above all, the Muslims had none of the intense hatred of Jews which arose in the Christian world from the accusation of 'Christ killers'. Jews under Islam were not confined in ghettos, as they were in Christian Europe, and physical attacks on Jews were far less frequent.

Reaching Spain, Islam was backed, as were the Christian kingdoms, by armies and the sword. But for the Jews, Islam came not as an enemy, but as a liberator. The Jews of Toledo—like the Jews of Caesarea—opened the gates of the city to welcome the Muslim horsemen. These were memorable years in Jewish history. Jewish writers, doctors, financiers and diplomats were held in high esteem. Religious learning flourished. A Jewish general commanded the Muslim army of Granada. Jewish poets developed new and beautiful styles. It was a golden age.

No. 49

Dearest Auntie Fori,

According to a Jewish legend, the Babylonian academies had sent four distinguished scholars to the communities in the Diaspora, to raise funds for the work of the academies. While crossing the Mediterranean by boat they were captured by pirates, and then ransomed to the different Diaspora communities. One founded a scholarly centre at Fustat (Old Cairo). Another established a centre for religious study in Kairouan, in Tunisia—one of the holy cities of Islam. Another set up an academy at Narbonne, in southern France. The fourth, Moses ben Chanoch, became head of the Jewish Academy in Cordoba, in Muslim Spain. As the influence of Sura and Pumbeditha declined, these four western centres gained in authority, the most flourishing being that in Spain, where Islam provided a tolerant backdrop to Jewish creativity and prosperity.

The golden age of Spanish Jewry began with the Muslim conquest and the establishment of the Umayyad kingdom in 755, with its capital at Cordoba. Throughout Umayyad rule, Jews were active in medicine, agriculture, commerce and crafts. A Jewish religious academy, at Lucena south of Cordoba, flourished from the ninth to the twelfth century. Lucena, Granada and Tarragona were known by Arab geographers as 'Jewish' cities. A Jewish court physician, Hisdai ibn Shaprut, became chief of customs and foreign trade: he also negotiated on behalf of the Umayyad Caliphate with the Christian rulers to the north. Jewish literature flourished. The tenth-century linguist and Hebrew poet Dunash ben Labrat (who had studied under Saadiah Gaon in Baghdad) introduced Arabic meter into Hebrew poetry, laying the foundations for mediaeval Jewish poetry: one of his songs is today part of the special Grace After Meals which is said after a wedding.

Jews also made a leading contribution to geographic understanding: prominent among tenth-century Spanish geographers was a Jew, Ibrahim ibn Yaqub, who undertook a substantial journey through central and eastern Europe, reaching the court of the German Emperor Otto I in 966. Among his descriptions is one of a salt mine in Germany worked by Jews. Another distinguished Jew from the Spanish golden age was Isaac ibn Yashush (who died in 1056), the court physician to the Muslim ruler of the coastal town of Denia. Ibn Yashush was a brilliant grammarian who wrote a Hebrew-language study of the inflection of Hebrew verbs, and a Bible commentary based on critical—and surprisingly modern—methods.

The golden age of Spanish Jewry was shattered by the Berber conquests of 1086 and 1146. Ironically, some aspects of that golden age were to return after the Christian conquest of southern Spain, at a time when elsewhere in Christian Europe the expulsion and persecution of Jews were rife. The crown of Spain tried to protect the Jews against anti-Jewish agitation by the Church, and by the Spanish merchants. Royal protection and patronage were effective in Castile from 1080 to 1370, and until 1412 in Aragon, where Jews were invited to settle on the newly conquered lands, and did so. The leading astronomer in Christian Spain in the second half of the thirteenth century was a Jew, Isaac ibn Sa'id, who prepared a remarkable sphere of the heavenly movements. Jewish courtiers rose to positions of administrative and financial prominence. But Jewish courtiers, if they fell from favour—or became too rich— could lose their lives, and such royal protection as existed came to an end well before the mass expulsion of 1492.

No. 50

Dearest Auntie Fori,

It was not only travel, trade and religious practice that flourished in the tolerant years of Islamic rule. Jews even rose to positions of great political importance. The Caucasus was ruled at one time in the early Muslim era, not by Muslims, but by Jewish governors. For several years the port of Siraf, on the Persian Gulf, was under a Jewish administrator. In Egypt, Jews filled the posts of Minister of Taxation and Minister of Finance as well as the important office of Inspector of the Affairs of State.

Whenever the local Jews were protected by such powerful co-religionists, their communities and their livelihood were unmolested. In return for being allowed to lead a normal daily life, free from persecution, they brought skills, energy and prosperity to the towns in which they lived, and in which they sought to be loyal and productive citizens.

But even under Islam the balance of tolerance could quickly overturn, and with horrifying results. Even in tolerant times the Jew remained, in Muslim eyes, a dhimmi: a second-class citizen never really accepted as an equal, however successful or helpful—or even indispensable—his services might be. When tolerance turned to intolerance, the dhimmi status became a burden and a curse, inviting anti-Jewish violence against individuals and whole communities.

It was the emergence of the more fanatical Muslim sects that turned hope to despair overnight. One such sect, the Almohades, came to prominence in Morocco in 1033—at a time when England was ruled by King Canute—and among their first acts of fanaticism was the massacre of more than six thousand Jews at Fez. Three decades later, in the year of the Norman Conquest of England—1066—a further five thousand Jews were killed by Muslim fanatics in the city of Granada, in Muslim Spain.

Persecution of the Jews broke out at different times in all the lands of Islam. Punitive taxation, restrictions on where Jews might live, robberies, looting, expulsion and even forcible conversion are recorded in each century, in a wide area from the Atlantic Ocean to the Persian Gulf.

Seldom as prolonged as the persecution of the Jews in Christian lands, but often as intense, the Muslim acts of violence against the Jews reinforced the lowly dhimmi status, reducing many of the Jewish communities to weakened, impoverished, frightened and subdued shadows of their former pride and prosperity of the pre-Muslim years. Indeed, the Jews of Arab lands had no choice but to accept their lower status in return for the right to lead humbler lives relatively unmolested for long periods.

No. 51

Dearest Auntie Fori,

By the year 1000 AD the Jews of Germany lived securely within the confines of the German Empire, which at that time stretched from Avignon to Prague, and from Cologne to Rome. Jewish scholarship flourished, most remarkably in the career of Gershom ben Judah, who lived most of his life in Mainz. Known as Rabbenu Gershom—Our Master Gershom—he had no illusions about the travails confronting Jews at that time. 'From day to day my suffering increases', he wrote, 'the next day is harder than the one that passed.' Through his Talmudic Academy, he made known to the Jewish students of the Rhineland the works of the Babylonian and Jerusalem sages, established a reliable version of the Talmud, and copied out in a clear text the whole of the Mishnah and the Talmud, basing himself on the best manuscript sources he could find.

The fierce anti-Jewish riots which broke out in Mainz in 1012—when Gershom was forty-seven—did not deter his work. Patiently he gave his judgment on myriad issues of daily life through a series of replies to questions—the method of instruction favoured by the rabbis, and known as *responsa*. Gershom's responsa were noted for their broad-mindedness. The view of a majority in any community must be accepted by the minority. No man could divorce his wife against her will. Polygamy—which still existed in some Jewish communities—was no longer acceptable. A person who had returned to Judaism after lapsing from it must not be reminded of his former apostasy. No individual could read another's private correspondence. Prohibitions on Jewish business relations with non-Jews could be relaxed. So impressed were the Jews by Gershom's wisdom that many subsequent decisions on which he had not ruled were ascribed to him, in order to give them greater authority.

In 1096 anti-Jewish violence spread throughout the Rhineland. The Crusades were to accentuate the isolation of the Jews of Germany: thousands died at the hands of fanatical 'men of God', for whom the Jews were 'Christ killers', deserving only death. Fleeing from their homes, the Jews crowded the roads with their wagons in search of some other town elsewhere in Germany or even further eastward, in which they could once more set up their shops and synagogues. With them they took the language of the German towns in which they had lived—Yiddish, the language which they had made their own, reserving Hebrew for their religious worship and ceremonies.

Slowly, during a period of four hundred years, these Yiddish speakers moved eastwards, driven in each generation closer and closer to the flat dark forests and bleak bogland of the Pripet marshes. The hatreds against them grew as Christian revival spread.

No. 52

Dearest Auntie Fori,

In the early Middle Ages the Jews flourished in two particular regions of western Europe, the Rhineland and Provence. The great Jewish scholar Rashi, born at Troyes, in northern France, in 1040 AD, studied as a young man in the Rhineland town of Worms, returning to Troyes when he was twenty-five. His influence as a Biblical and Talmudic commentator had spread throughout western Europe by the time of his death in 1105. The name Rashi was an acronym of his actual name: **R**abbi **Sh**lomo **Y**itzhaki. As a religious judge he was, according to the custom of the time, unpaid: it is said that he earned his living from vineyards he owned. Jewish wine-growing was to be one of the Rothschild-sponsored activities in Palestine from the 1880s.

Rashi's commentary on the Bible—a classical Hebrew text for religious students ever since—was translated into Latin in the the thirteenth century, much influencing Christian translations of the Bible, and was the first Hebrew book to be printed with a known date, 1475. His replies to those who asked him about points of Jewish law—his *responsa*—like those of Rabbenu Gershom before him, were noted for their liberal approach. Thus Rashi ruled that a man could interrupt Grace After Meals to feed his animals, based on the scriptural injunction to feed one's animals before oneself. Humility was also a noted aspect of his replies. How many writers or teachers (myself included) are willing to answer an enquiry, as Rashi once did: 'I was asked this question before, but I realize that my answer then was wrong, and I welcome the opportunity to correct my mistake.' Two of Rashi's sayings—both of them essentially Talmudic—have a particularly universal and humanistic aspect, 'Do not rebuke your fellow-man so as to shame him in public' and 'To obey out of love is better than to obey out of fear.'

Rashi's commentary on the Babylonian Talmud, which in its original Aramaic had become obscure, made that essential exposition of Jewish Oral Law accessible once more to the Jewish masses in the Ashkenazi world. *Ashkenaz* is the Hebrew for Germany: later Ashkenazi Jews spread throughout Eastern Europe, then Western Europe, and in due course to the Americas.

When Rashi died, his commentary was unfinished: it was completed by his grandson, Samuel ben Meir—known by his acronymn as the Rashbam—who had been his student. While Rashi was alive he admitted that he sometimes changed his own commentary in favour of his grandson's. Like Rashi, Samuel ben Meir was a wine-grower, and also a sheep farmer.

The spread of Jewish learning stimulated the jealousy of some Christian scholars, whose influence went far beyond scholarly debate or rivalry. In France, the Jews were repeatedly subjected to attack and expulsion. In 1240 all Hebrew books were burned in Paris, the Jews driven out of the city, and their schools and synagogues destroyed or converted to Christian use. And in 1306 the Jews were expelled from the whole of northern France.

As so often happened in Jewish history misfortune in one region led to good fortune in another. With the expulsions from Paris and northern France, the Jewish community in Provence gained in both numbers and achievement. In more than a hundred towns and villages throughout southern France Jewish communities flourished: there were three synagogues in Marseille alone.

In 1348, at the height of their prosperity, as many as 15,000 Jews lived in Provence. Some followed the by then traditional Jewish role of money-lending, although in Provence their rate of interest was considerably lower than elsewhere during that period. Other Provençal Jews were traders in grain and wine. But many were to be found cultivating their own fields, market gardens and vineyards. As at Charlemagne's court five hundred years earlier, in Provence Jews were among the principal doctors of the region, serving the Christian as well as the Jewish community.

Although harassed by the Church, the Jews of Provence were protected by the king, who refused a number of ecclesiastical pleas for their expulsion. Nevertheless, from 1341 all Jews had to live in a separate quarter in each town, were forbidden to employ Christians, and were forced to wear a distinctive badge.

There were also anti-Jewish riots, some encouraged by the Church, and the most violent of all in 1348, by the spread of the Black Death. It was easy, and politic, to blame this horrendous plague on the Jews, even though such relief as could be provided was often only possible through the local Jewish doctor. As the Black Death claimed tens of thousands of victims, the survivors turned savagely on the Jews: in Toulon the Jewish community was almost completely massacred.

For one more century, Jews lived on in Provence, and for several decades were protected by the rulers, especially Queen Yolande, who refused to allow the arbitrary arrest of Jews, and 'Good King' René, who allowed Jews to enter every branch of commerce, trade and craft. The Jewish badge remained: but René allowed it to be a smaller one. There was another feature of mediaeval Jewish life in western Europe to which King René was opposed: the frequent forcible baptism of Jews.

In 1481 Provence was united with France, and in the next twenty years anti-Jewish violence led to widespread distress. Then, in 1501, the Jews were expelled from Provence, and a community which could date its origins back for more than a thousand years was uprooted and scattered, except for those who accepted, as many did, conversion to Christianity.

No. 53

Dearest Auntie Fori,

One of the longest-lasting Jewish communities was that on the island of Majorca, in the Balearic Islands, today best known to northern Europeans as a sunny Mediterranean holiday destination.

Jews are recorded in the Balearics, on the island of Minorca in the fifth century, at a time when the Vandals ruled there. It seems the Vandals, despite their name, had no animus against the Jews. But when a Byzantine general, a devout Christian, overran Majorca in 534 AD, the Jews there were killed. Six hundred years later, in 1135, under benevolent Muslim rule, Jews were again recorded living on Majorca.

Under the rule of the Christian kings of Aragon, which began in 1229, Jews fared much better than during the previous Christian dispensation. They could own land on Majorca, including in the principal town, Palma. King James I of Aragon, who conquered the Balearics, had several Jews in his retinue.

Such was the settled and indeed prized nature of Jewish life on the Islands under Christian rule that Jews emigrated to Majorca from Marseille and other southern French towns, from North Africa, and from Alexandria in Egypt. The Jews on the Islands, including those of Ibiza, Minorca and Formentera, were given permission to trade with the local Christians, using credit, for commerce in textiles, cereals, oil, linen and saffron.

In 1269 the Jews of Palma were granted the right to own vineyards and town houses, although they could not live next to Christians. In 1290, a 'Jewish Street' was established in Palma, protected with a wall and with entrance gates.

Jews expelled from France in 1306 found refuge on the Islands, among them Rabbi Aaron ha-Kohen, a leading scholar. Three years later the first Blood Libel occurred on Majorca. The Jews were accused of murdering a Christian child in order to use his blood to bake the Passover bread. They were attacked, but the King ordered the attackers to be punished, and protected the Jews against further Christian violence. In 1331 King James III ordered his viceroy on the island to help the Jews build a synagogue, despite the opposition of Pope John XXII in Rome.

A Jewish alchemist, known only by his first name, Menachem, served as physician and astrologer to King Pedro IV, who conquered the Islands in 1343. In the 1340s Judah Mosconi, a Jewish physician, emigrated from Greece and went to live on Majorca.

Jewish astronomers and cartographers—crucial figures in an age of maritime trade and exploration—flourished on the Islands. One of these cartographers, Abraham Cresques, and his son Judah, were pioneers of accurate mapping (you have asked me, Auntie Fori, to draw you some maps to go with these letters; I hope I may do so in the spirit of the Cresques father and son).

When, in 1351, sailors took a number of Jews captive, King Pedro ordered them to be freed on payment of a modest ransom. Twenty years later, in the aftermath of the Black Death—a time when hundreds of communities throughout Christian Europe accused the Jews of poisoning the wells and turned savagely against them—Pedro protected the

Jews on the Islands from attack. In 1381 he granted a Jew, Solomon Benallell, the right to manufacture soap on Majorca. That year, a map of the world by Abraham Cresques was sent by the King of Aragon as a gift to the King of France.

The peace and prosperity of the Jews of the Balearics came to an abrupt end in 1391, as anti-Jewish feeling swept through Spain, unstoppable in its venom. On each of the Islands, whole communities were wiped out. The synagogue in Palma was closed down and Jews were forced to attend sermons at which the Christian priests urged them to convert.

Refusing to accept baptism, many Jews died as martyrs, among them a leading rabbi, Vital Ephraim Gerondi. Other leading Jews accepted baptism, including Judah Cresques, who changed his name to Jaime Ribes, and later made maps for Henry the Navigator of Portugal.

Some Jews managed to flee to North Africa, among them one of the most senior members of the community, Simeon ben Zemah Duran, who settled in Algiers, as did a family of converts, the Najjars, who then returned to Judaism.

As the anti-Jewish fury subsided, efforts were made to revive Jewish life on the Islands. Jews from Portugal were encouraged to settle there. The synagogue in Palma was renewed, and Jews were exempted from attending Christian sermons. But within a decade the anti-Jewish zeal of Roman Catholicism was renewed. A Blood Libel accusation in 1432 led to severe riots throughout Majorca, and three years later the Jewish community ceased to exist: two hundred were forcibly converted, the rest fled to North Africa,

The converted Jews, known in Spain as *conversos,* and on Majorca as *chuetas,* lived on as Christians, mostly as silversmiths, secretly practising their Judaism century after century. The Spanish Inquisition, reaching the islands in 1488, continued to seek them out.

As late as 1675, 1677 and 1691, large numbers of such 'secret' Jews were brought to trial and executed. Only in 1782 did it become an offence to attack or persecute conversos, although there were serious riots against them in 1856. Just over a hundred years later, in 1966, a number of Majorcan secret Jews emigrated to Israel, hoping to return to the faith whose tenets they had largely lost, but the experiment was short-lived: unable to make the transition to the Jewish State, they returned to Majorca.

Today there are at least 300 'secret' Jewish families on Majorca—no longer forced to live in secret—1,500 years since their ancestors first arrived there.

No. 54

Dearest Auntie Fori,

This letter will be about the greatest Jewish thinker of the mediaeval period, Moses Maimonides, who was born in the Spanish city of Cordoba in 1135.

Maimonides is known to Jews as 'the Rambam', from the acronym of his Hebrew name, **M**oses **b**en **M**aimon. Fleeing a fanatical Muslim sect that captured Cordoba when he was thirteen, he made his way to Fez, in Morocco, where he studied both theology and medicine. When Islamic fundamentalism grew in Fez, he and his family fled to Palestine, which was then—in 1165—under Christian rule. They lived first in the port of Acre, then in Jerusalem, and finally in Hebron—where Abraham, Isaac and Jacob are buried. But Christian oppression was even more harsh than that of Islam, and his family soon made their way to Cairo. There, Maimonides spent the rest of his life.

There is an Indian aspect which will interest you, Auntie Fori. Maimonides and his brother David went into business as traders. But David was drowned in the Indian Ocean while on a trading journey, and the family's wealth—the goods he was taking to India—was lost with him. As a result, Maimonides gave up his career as a trader, and became a physician. In due course he was appointed personal physician to the Egyptian Grand Vizier. At the same time, he became the spiritual leader of the Jewish community in Egypt, spending each Sabbath dealing with communal affairs. He also wrote a masterful synthesis of Jewish law as set out and scattered through the Five Books of Moses, and compiled commentaries on the Mishnah which included the principles of the Jewish faith—the earliest known attempt to formulate a Jewish creed. He wrote several medical treatises; made the most systematic list of all 613 commandments; and set out codes of law for business, and for worship in synagogue. His *Guide for the Perplexed,* which he finished in 1190, is a remarkable compilation of philosophical and religious wisdom. Translated into Latin, it greatly influenced Christian thinking at that time.

Maimonides wrote his *Guide for the Perplexed* and his commentaries in Arabic, which was later translated into Hebrew. His most important work, however, *Mishne Torah* ('Review of the Law'), the first attempt to organize the laws of the Talmud in a comprehensive and logical code, he wrote in Hebrew. Indeed, his use of the Hebrew language had a strong influence on the development of the language. His Review aimed at putting aside the abstract discussions and story-telling of the Torah and concentrating on the laws.

'I have undertaken,' Maimonides wrote in his preface, 'to write a book making plain what is forbidden and allowed, impure and pure, and all the other laws of the Torah; all in clear language and a brief style'. In this he succeeded—in five heavy volumes. Herman Wouk's *This Is My God,* first published in 1959, is a masterpiece of inspiration for all those interested in Judaism. My own father, Peter Gilbert, was much influenced by it and introduced me to it. Wouk notes that Maimonides 'took the encyclopaedic work of hundreds of sages over a thousand years and recast it in a single book, omitting nothing of consequence. And he did it while practising medicine and rising to become one of the busiest and best doctors in the Moorish world, eventually court physician to the Sultan in Egypt.'

In one of his most important pastoral letters, which he wrote in Arabic, to the Jews of Yemen, Maimonides warned against false messiahs, and a tendency to messianism which created expectations that could only be unsatisfied, and disturbing. The first of his Thirteen Principles of Faith was the existence of God, 'which is perfect and sufficient unto itself, and which is the cause of the existence of all other beings'.

When Maimonides died in Fustat (Old Cairo) in 1204 his loss was mourned throughout the Jewish world. Muslims as well as Jews mourned for three days in the city. His body was taken for burial from Fustat to Tiberias, on the Sea of Galilee. To this day it is a place of pilgrimage. He was often compared with the Biblical Moses. On his tombstone are the words: 'From Moses to Moses, there never arose another like Moses.'

Knowing the Indian emphasis on wise eating, you will be interested to know, dearest Auntie Fori, that among the medical and dietary advice which Maimonides gave was the insistence that we chew each mouthful of food at least twenty-four times. I tried it at lunch today, just before I set down to write this letter. A curious sensation—but no doubt beneficial.

No. 55

Dearest Auntie Fori,

It was not Islam but Christianity which, with the coming of the Crusades, posed the most serious threat to the Jews of that whole area. From Christian Europe, starting in 1095 and continuing at intervals until 1250, tens of thousands of soldiers set off with zeal, under the banner of the Cross, to try to wrest the Holy Land from the Muslim 'infidel'. They succeeded, holding Jerusalem for a hundred years, but were then driven away by the Muslim warrior Saladdin. On their way through the Christian towns of the Rhineland and Central Europe they often turned aside from their religious quest to attack Jews. Particularly savage killings were recorded in Speyer, Worms, Trier, Cologne, Regensburg, Metz and Prague. Many of Cologne's Jews were hidden by the local bishop in eight villages near the city, but the Crusaders hunted them down and killed them. In all, the Crusaders killed about 5,000 Jews.

Reaching Beirut, the Crusaders showed what would be the fate of the Jews of Palestine when all thirty-five Jewish families living in the city were massacred. At Haifa the Jews joined the Muslims in the port's defence. But the Crusaders swept all before them. Thousands of Jews were murdered in the Galilee, on the coastal plain, in Samaria and in Judaea. Many of those who were not murdered were either sold into slavery in Europe or ransomed by the Jewish community in Egypt.

The Crusaders ruled in Jerusalem from 1099 to 1187. They drove the Jews from the Jewish Quarter of the city and brought in Christian Arab tribes from east of the River Jordan to settle in the Jewish homes and alleyways which they had so brutally cleared out. But the Jewish love of the Land of Israel could not be blotted out. In 1210, after Crusader rule had ended, more than three hundred rabbis from Flanders and Provence travelled to Palestine to help rebuild the Jewish communities which had been decimated by Crusader massacres and expulsions.

Even during the harsh years of Crusader rule the Jews looked to the Land of Israel with a special longing. The Spanish-born Judah Halevi expressed this longing when he wrote of Jerusalem:

> *Beautiful heights,*
> *Joy of the world,*
> *City of a great king,*
> *For you my soul yearns,*
> *From the lands of the west.*
>
> *My pity collects and is roused*
> *When I remember the past:*
> *Your story in exile,*
> *Your temple destroyed.*
>
> *I shall cherish your stones and kiss them,*
> *And your earth will be sweeter,*
> *Than honey to my taste.*

In 1140 Judah Halevi himself set out from Spain for the Land of Israel. According to legend he was approaching the walls of Jerusalem when an Arab horseman—or, some said, a Crusader horseman—trampled him to death. As he lay dying he is said to have recited his most famous poem: 'Zion, shall I not seek thee?'

No. 56

Dearest Auntie Fori,

Jews have always welcomed debate, even if they do not always win it. In 1263, in Christian Spain, the sixty-nine-year-old scholar and philosopher Moses Nahmanides engaged in a four-day disputation with a Christian theologian, Pablo Christiani—himself a Jewish convert to

Christianity. The debate was held in Barcelona in the presence of the King of Spain, who guaranteed Nahmanides freedom of speech. Christiani insisted that the Talmud contained blasphemies against Jesus, the traditional charge. He also claimed that within the Talmud was proof of Christianity. In reply, Nahmanides challenged the Christian view that Jesus was the 'Prince of Peace', insisting: 'From the time of Jesus until the present the world has been filled with violence and injustice and the Christians have shed more blood than all other peoples.'

The debate was broken off by the Church without any conclusions being reached: they had not liked the way Nahmanides argued his case. The King told the Ramban—the acronym by which Nahmanides was known: 'I have never seen a man defend a wrong cause so well.' A week later the king himself attended synagogue, and spoke, after which a Christian friar gave a sermon urging the Jews to convert to Christianity, a sermon to which Nahmanides was allowed to reply. As a reward for his skill in debate, the King gave Nahmanides a gift of money. He returned to his home town, Gerona, but two years later, in 1265, was forced to leave Spain after the Dominicans brought a charge against him for blaspheming Jesus.

Travelling to Palestine, Nahmanides arrived there in 1267, seven years after the Tartar invasion from central Asia, when thousands of Jews and Christians had been murdered, and Jerusalem devastated yet again. 'I am banished from my table,' he wrote, 'far removed from friend and kinsman, and too long is the distance to meet again. But the loss of all else which delighted my eyes is compensated by my present joy in a day passed within thy courts, O Jerusalem, where it is granted me to caress your stones, fondle your dust, and to weep over your ruins. I weep bitterly but I find joy in my heart. I rend my garments but I find solace in so doing.'

From Jerusalem, Nahmanides wrote to one of his sons, who had remained in Spain, that the city 'has no master, and he that wishes may take possession of its ruins'. He set to work to help restore the shattered communities, explaining to his son: 'We have procured from Shechem'—today's Nablus—'Scrolls of the Law which had been carried thither from Jerusalem at the time of the Tartar invasion. Thus we shall organize a synagogue and shall be able to pray here. Men flock from Damascus,

Aleppo, and from all parts to Jerusalem to behold the Place of the Sanctuary, and to mourn over it. May you, my son and your brothers, and the
whole of our family, see the salvation of Jerusalem.'

No. 57

Dearest Auntie Fori,

For the Muslim world, the Christian expulsion of the Jews from
Spain in 1492—and from Portugal five years later—led to an influx of
talented, resourceful people. Isaac Abrabanel, one of Spain's most distinguished rabbinical scholars, who was also financial adviser to King Ferdi-
nand and Queen Isabella, was among those who fled, in his case to
Naples (where he completed his commentary on the Book of Kings).
Even his privileged position at court had been unable to protect him
from expulsion.

More than 160,000 Jews were forced to leave Spain in 1492. These
'Sephardi' Jews—the Hebrew word for Spain being *sepharad*—were scattered throughout the known world, which was itself expanding. More
than 25,000 reached Holland; 20,000 found a home in Morocco; 10,000
in France and 10,000 in Italy. As many as 5,000 made the perilous journey across the Atlantic Ocean to the Dutch possessions along the coast
of South America, in the Caribbean, and in North America.

The largest single group of exiles from Spain, 90,000 in all, went to
the thriving cities and towns of the Ottoman Empire. The Muslim ruler
Mohammed II (1451–1481) had already liberated the Jews from Byzantine oppression in Constantinople, which he captured in 1453. His successor, Bayazid II (1481–1512) welcomed the Jewish refugees from Spain
to all the cities of his empire: to Constantinople itself (known as Istanbul
to the Turks), to Algiers, Alexandria, Damascus, Smyrna and Salonika, as
well as to the towns of Palestine, following the Ottoman conquest in
1512. Many Jews who went to Palestine settled in the Galilee: already in
1498 they were reported in Safed trading in fruit and vegetables, cheese,
oil, and spices. Within a century Safed had become a centre of Jewish
mysticism and rabbinical learning.

The Jews of Spain who reached Palestine after 1512 found a small but vigorous Jewish community which had maintained itself there despite many difficulties since the defeat of the Crusaders and the Muslim conquest. It was under the rule of the Mamluk sultans of Egypt, a hundred and seventy years before the expulsion from Spain, that the return of the Jews had gathered momentum, despite moments of persecution. In 1322 a Jewish geographer from Florence, Ashtory Ha-Pari, had settled in the Jezreel valley, where he wrote a book on the topography of Palestine. The Jews of Safed, Ramla and Gaza were recommended by Christian travellers as ideal guides. Thus Jacques of Verona, a Christian monk who visited the Holy Land in 1335, not only noted the long-established Jewish community at the foot of Mount Zion, in Jerusalem, but wrote: 'A pilgrim who wished to visit ancient forts and towns in the Holy Land would have been unable to locate these without a good guide who knew the Land well or without one of the Jews who lived there. The Jews were able to recount the history of these places since this knowledge had been handed down from their forefathers and wise men. So when I journeyed overseas I often requested and managed to obtain an excellent guide among the Jews who lived there.'

But Muslim rule had become harsh and intolerant. In 1491, the year before the expulsion of the Jews from Spain, a Christian pilgrim from Bohemia, Martin Kabtanik, recorded in his book *Journey to Jerusalem* how 'there are not many Christians but there are many Jews, and these the Moslems persecute in various ways. Christians and Jews go about in Jerusalem in clothes considered fit only for wandering beggars. The Moslems know that the Jews think and even say that this is the Holy Land which has been promised to them and that those Jews who dwell there are regarded as holy by Jews elsewhere, because, in spite of all the troubles and sorrows inflicted on them by the Moslems, they refuse to leave the Land.'

The conquest of Palestine by the Ottoman Turks in 1512 provided a new tolerance and a new impetus to Jewish life. Jews from Christian Spain were drawn by the new tolerance, which opened up many opportunities for them. Jews traded in fruits and vegetables, cheeses, spices and olive oil. Others were prominent in the weaving trade. In Jerusalem the

Jewish community built four fine synagogues, which were to see 400 years of continuous worship, until their destruction by Arab Legion artillery during the Israeli War of Independence in 1948.

In Galilee, Jewish communities flourished in both Tiberias and Safed. After the collapse of the Jewish scholarly centres in Spain, Safed had become the new centre of Jewish learning—just as Spain had earlier replaced the Mesopotamian centres. Above all, Safed saw a flourishing of Jewish mysticism.

The fifteenth century saw no diminution of the Jewish presence in Palestine. Jews continued to return, typified by Elijah of Ferrara, an Italian rabbi who became spiritual head of the Jerusalem Jewish community in 1438, and by another Italian Jew, Obadiah of Bertinoro, also a famous rabbinical scholar, who settled in Jerusalem in 1488. As for Christian observers, they continued to be impressed by the Jews of the Holy Land. In 1486 a distinguished pilgrim, the Dean of Mainz Cathedral, Bernhard von Briedenbach, noted that the Jews of Jerusalem and Hebron 'will treat you in full fidelity—more so than anyone else in those countries of the unbelievers'.

Christian visitors to the Holy Land noted the desolation of Galilee. But this was no deterrent to those Jews, especially in Eastern Europe, whose situation in the Diaspora satisfied neither their social nor spiritual needs, and for whom Palestine was a distant and yet—with perseverance—an accessible land.

The Jews in Galilee not only preserved and enhanced the traditions of Jewish mysticism and rabbinical learning, they also renewed the Jewish link with the soil. In 1574 a French doctor wrote in his account of his travels: 'We look around Lake Tiberias and see the villages of Beth Saida and Korazim. Today Jews are living in these villages and they have built up again all the places around the lake, starting fishing industries, and have once again made the earth fruitful, where once it was desolate.'

The Jews under Islam knew no such intensity of hatred as they faced in many Christian lands. Indeed the lowly status of dhimmi which Islam accorded them served as a protection. While allowing individual Jews to succeed in Islamic society, it prevented their communities from assimilating. Many Jewish communities, because of the geographic vastness and disunity of the Muslim world, became cut off from their fellow-Jews in distant lands. But they preserved their own Jewishness with tenacity, even in remote 'lost' areas such as the mountain villages of the Sahara and the stony deserts of Yemen.

No. 58

Dearest Auntie Fori,

Seventy years ago, when you first went to India, the boast of the British Empire—of which India was the great jewel—was that it was an Empire on which the sun never set. This was indeed true, but it was true for less than a hundred years. The same boast could be made for the Jewish Diaspora, and has been true for more than a thousand years.

Of all the ancient Jewish communities scattered around this globe, and making possible this imperial-style boast, the two most unusual were those of India and of China. Both were in existence more than a thousand years ago, when Charlemagne ruled Europe.

The first Jewish families probably reached China less than two hundred years after the destruction of the Second Temple by the Romans. Their descendants remained in China, preserving the knowledge that they were indeed Jews, until the twentieth century. Their origins are obscure. The first of them most probably reached China as silk merchants with the caravans from Samarkand and central Asia, or even by sea from the Persian Gulf.

With the rise of the new religion, Islam, which had conquered the lands from Spain to Samarkand by 750 AD, and had planted the symbol of the Crescent—as the successor to the Menorah and the Cross—at Jerusalem, the Jewish traders found a new strength. For it was at this troubled time of intense Christian–Muslim conflict that they were able, as Jews, to maintain the threatened trade routes along which goods valued in both extremes of Asia had to travel.

It is from Arab and Muslim writers in the ninth century that we know the extent to which Jewish traders, and Jewish-operated trade routes, linked the Kingdom of the Franks—ruled by Charlemagne's descendants—with the Chinese kingdom in the distant east.

These Jewish traders brought to Europe the silk and spices of China,

and took to China the dyed clothes and glassware of Europe. A graphic
description of their work and wares is given by the ninth-century Arab
writer, Ibn Khurdadhbih, who wrote:

> *The routes of the Jewish merchants called Radanites, these merchants*
> *speak Arabic, Persian, Roman, the language of the Franks, Andalusians*
> *and Slavs. They journey from west to east, partly on land, partly by sea.*
> *They transport from the west eunuchs. They take ship in the Land of the*
> *Franks, on the western sea, and steer for Fatama. There they load their*
> *goods on the backs of camels and go by land to Kolzum, where they*
> *embark again, and sail for Jeddah: then they go to Sind, India and*
> *China. . . .*

Fatama was at what is now the northern end of the Suez Canal, Kolzum
at the head of the Gulf of Suez: a journey I took in reverse on my return
from India by sea in 1958.

Another Muslim writer, Ibn Al-Faqth, noted at this same period—
more than a thousand years ago—that the Jews took from Europe to
China 'brocade, and a superior sort of beaver skin,' and that they came
back from China with 'all sorts' of goods.

It was a third Muslim writer, Abu Zaid, who has left us the first, tan-
talizing reference to Jews who must actually have been living in China
in the tenth century, at some time between 877 and 878 AD. Describing
the revolt of Banshu, the Chinese bandit, or rebel, Abu Zaid recorded,
some thirty years later, how when Banshu captured the Chinese city
of Khanfu after a long siege '. . . he put its inhabitants to the sword.
And men experienced in their affairs have mentioned that he killed
120,000 Muslims, Jews, Christians and Magians, who lived in this city
and became merchants in it, apart from those killed among the Chinese
inhabitants.'

Abu Zaid added that the number of the four sects killed in Khanfu
was known because the Chinese had taxed them according to their size.
No specific number of Jews is given, but it must certainly have been a
noticeable community, if not a large one.

Whenever it actually took place, the transformation from trade to
settlement had certainly taken place more than a thousand years ago in

the distant cities of Imperial China. A Jesuit writer, Father Ricci, writing in 1605, has recorded the oral tradition of the 750-strong Jewish community in the Chinese town of Kaifeng, that their ancestors had reached China before 1127 from Persia. Their daily language was Persian. Henceforth, until modern times, Jews survived in China, and guarded their Jewish writings and traditions. At the same time, by the slow but inevitable process of intermarriage—for they were cut off entirely for more than eight hundred years from all contact with the Mediterranean and Europe—they gradually acquired Chinese features. Their physique and appearance, and their clothes, became increasingly Chinese. By the beginning of the nineteenth century they spoke only the Chinese dialects of the towns in which they lived.

But this complete absorption into the world around them did not prevent them from preserving their sense of being Jews, nor did it stop them from trying to maintain their Jewish mode of life—as they saw it—or their Jewish worship.

Thus it was that when the Jesuits reached China in the early 1600s, they discovered the Chinese Jews, were fascinated by them, and kept copious records of what they found. And it is to these Jesuit missionaries that we owe our knowledge of the daily life and habits of the Jewish communities of China.

The Jesuit archives in Paris contain a rich collection of material brought back by these early missionaries from China, including a detailed plan of the synagogue at Kaifeng, first built in 1163, and restored in 1279. Also in the archive in Paris are many examples of Hebrew script found in Kaifeng: script that had survived eight hundred years of complete isolation from the outside Jewish world. In addition, the Jesuits brought back a series of Chinese words which represented the whole spectrum of Jewish life, thought and worship, including 'Scroll of the Law, with cover', 'Festival for Perambulating the Law', 'Elder of the synagogue', 'the Twelve Tribes', 'Rabbi', 'ritual slaughterer', 'Temple for the Veneration of the Law', and 'Israel'—this latter rendered in Chinese as *yi-tz'u-lo-yeh*.

The Jesuit reports on the Jews of China are full and fascinating. Despite eight centuries of Chinese influence, the Jews still retained the vestiges of their origins, and were recognizably Jews. In the letter sent from Peking on 26 July 1605, Father Ricci writes: 'We learned about the Christians in Kaifeng through a Jew by profession of his faith, nationality and features, who came to visit me during the past days. . . . His two brothers studied Hebrew and are, apparently, rabbis in the Jewish community. . . . This man did not know the word Jew, but called himself only Israelite.'

Father Ricci had in his house an image of the Madonna and Child, and St John the Baptist. His letter continued: 'When this man saw the image, he thought it represented the two children, Jacob and Esau, with Rebecca. He therefore said: "Although I do not worship images, I want to offer reverence to my earliest ancestors." Therefore he knelt and worshipped.'

Father Ricci and the Jew of Kaifeng then discussed the life of the Jews of the town: '. . . he admitted to me that they were unable to keep their law in China, owing to the fact that the circumcision, the purification, the non-eating of pork, and other things impeded their relationship with others, especially for those who wanted to become officials.' As for the Jewish religion, and the Old Testament, Ricci noted that the Jew '. . . did not know much, although he told many stories from the Old Testament, of the Twelve Tribes, of Moses, down to the story of Abraham, of Judith, of Mordecai, of Esther and others, although the sound of the proper names was quite different.'

Another Jesuit, Father Matteo, copied down the text of the Hebrew books which he found in the Kaifeng synagogue. Father Matteo was told by the rabbi, 'the Messiah would come ten thousand years hence.' In 1621 another Jesuit missionary noted: 'Their religion is mixed with paganism . . . but they are less esteemed than the Mohammedans.'

In 1642 a flood struck the city of Kaifeng. Hundreds of thousands of Chinese were drowned. The Jewish community also suffered greatly, but managed to save most of their scrolls of the law, and twenty-six different Hebrew texts. A new synagogue was built and the scrolls copied. Various historical narratives were prepared, and also a Memorial Book of the dead of the community, and of their ancestors. These narratives survive, as does the Memorial Book. Their testimony is substantial, saved for posterity by Jesuit missionaries in the early eighteenth century.

The Memorial Book traces back the Jewish family trees to 1400 AD.

The names from that time are clearly Jewish: Abraham, Isaac, Samuel, Obadiah, Ezra, Elkanah and David. In the fifteenth century the Jewish names still predominate, among them Moses, Joseph, Hayyim, Judah, Manasseh, Adonijah, Daniel and Zebulun. But by 1600 the names have become mixed, with Chinese in the ascendancy, thus: Meir, Eliezer, Mattithiah, Ithamar, Chung-te, Chung-kuei, Shih-kuei, Chin, Shih, Shih-ying, Yung-kuang, Yi-fan, Hsien-yi and Rabbi Akibah.

With the departure of the last of the Jesuits, the records of the Jews of China recede into darkness. It is almost certain that no Europeans visited them between 1723—the last Jesuit visit—and 1850, by which time their Jewishness, and their knowledge of Judaism, had almost entirely vanished.

It was a British missionary organisation that sought, in 1850, to remake contact with the Jews of Kaifeng, and which procured more than fifty Hebrew manuscripts. The Jews of Kaifeng asked the missionaries to help them to relearn Hebrew, and to send them religious texts. Their request, dated 20 August 1850, read:

'. . . during the past forty or fifty years, our religion has been but imperfectly transmitted, and although its canonical writings are still extant, there is none who understands so much as one word of them. It happens that there yet survives an aged female of more than seventy years, who retains in her recollection the principal tenets of the faith.'

The letter continued: 'Our synagogue in this place has long been without ministers. The four walls of its principal hall are greatly dilapidated.'

The Jews of Kaifeng had now been 'discovered' by Europe. Dozens of visitors flocked to see them. Their way of life became the subject of curiosity and comment. But it was too late to help them. Intermarriage had become widespread. The ability to read their own Hebrew texts had disappeared. Their physical appearance had become completely 'Chinese'. They no longer even kept the Sabbath.

By 1900 there were only some fifty Jews in Kaifeng who still had the surname which had been acquired by their forefathers, and who still considered themselves in some way different from their neighbours. An American visitor in 1923 noted disparagingly: 'All those I saw looked less Jewish than do some of the Chinese.' Nine years later another American

Jewish visitor noted: 'They know they are Jews, but know nothing of Judaism. They realize they are Chinese, completely assimilated, yet there is pride in the knowledge that they spring from an ancient people who are different from the other Chinese in Kaifeng.'

The Jews of Kaifeng were the one Chinese Jewish community of whom a virtually continuous record has been preserved since the Jesuit visits. But other ancient communities, more than twenty from Peking in the north to Canton in the south, are known to have existed in the Middle Ages, descendants in all probability of the silk traders of the ninth century, and surviving in fragments until modern times. In the Chinese labour force, imported into California in the early 1860s, seven 'Jews' are recorded. In 1854 a Chinese Jew of one of the mediaeval communities— Hangkow—was sent to Bombay, and circumcised there: his photograph, taken in 1906, shows that he was of Chinese features, like the Chinese Jews of Kaifeng.

No. 59

Dearest Auntie Fori,

This letter comes closer home to you—in the geographic sense— than that of any of my earlier ones. I want to write this week about the Jews of India. They were, as far as history tells us, of an equally ancient origin to the Jews of China. They too, in all probability, had reached India in the two centuries following the destruction of the Second Temple in the year 70 AD. They too had been traders, and refugees, seeking a permanent haven. They too absorbed in part the physical features and lifestyle of their surrounds.

And yet the Jews of India, unlike those of China, did not become a forgotten people, nor did they lose their knowledge of basic Judaism. Instead, in each generation, they retained sufficient elements of Judaism to enable them, in this century, to constitute one of the more important Jewish communities of the world. Numbering more than 30,000, they formed one of the more vigorous of the Jewish groups which, after 1948, contributed to the 'ingathering of the exiles' in the newly formed State of Israel.

The two principal Jewish groups in India, dating back to the immediate post-Temple era, were the Cochin Jews and the Bene Israel, who
originally lived in the villages of the Konkan along the coast south of
today's Bombay. The Cochin Jews possessed an ancient charter, dating to
between 974 and 1020 AD, which the local Rajas granted to Joseph Rabban and seventy-two families with him, giving them such substantial
protection that they not only survived, but flourished, 'far away'—one
historian has written—'from the bigots, the robber kings, the conver-
sionists, the Inquisitors, and the crusaders' and therefore able to survive
in one place, and with their faith unchallenged.

The Portuguese took control of Cochin in 1502 and of Goa in 1510.
In Cochin, the local Rajas were able to protect the Jews for a hundred
and fifty years, until 1662, when, during the Portuguese–Dutch war, the
Portuguese massacred many Jews, and drove others to flight. When Vasco
da Gama reached Kerala he told the local ruler, the Zamarin: 'The Jews
killed our Saviour, so get rid of them'. The Zamarin gave the Jews a
nominal thrashing and sent them away, telling them: 'When this plague
disappears you can come back.'

In Portuguese Goa the Jews found no protection from militant
Roman Catholicism, other than conversion to Christianity, but in 1560
the Portuguese imposed the full rigours of the Inquisition there, which
duly began to burn Jews who had converted. Seventeen years earlier, the
Muslims in the port of Cranganore had joined with the Portuguese to
massacre the Jewish community there—an offshoot of the Cochin one.

Fortunately for the Jews of Cochin, help was at hand. In 1663 the
Dutch drove the Portuguese from Cochin, and offered the Jews the protection of their civilized way of life, and religious tolerance. Just over a
hundred years later, in 1795, the British became the paramount power,
and they too respected the Jewish community, leaving it unmolested.

In one respect, the Cochin Jews had become influenced by a funda-
mental tenet of the Hindu world around them: the caste system. In time,
the Jews of Cochin were clearly and permanently divided into two
castes, the 'black' Jews and the 'white' Jews, with segregated synagogues,
and a definite sense of 'white' superiority over 'black'. And yet even in
respect of the caste system, these Jews had not entirely succumbed to the
pressures and customs of the society around them. A report by Elkan N.

Adler, published in the *Jewish Chronicle* on 11 May 1906, noted that 'although the White Jews are fair, some of them are certainly not quite white, nor are the Black Jews quite black.'

The Bene Israel had known similar challenges to their basic Jewish way of life. Believing themselves to be the descendants of Jews who had left Galilee at the time of Antiochus IV (175–163 BC), they preserved the rudiments of Judaism intact, but, like the Jews of Kaifeng, they had suffered considerably from their thousand-year isolation, cut off from any other Jewish community, or from the mass migrations and wide travels of the Jews of Europe, north Africa and the Middle East.

In 1680 a Bene Israel leader, Jacob Semah, established a small Jewish colony at Surat, which had become an English East India Company trading station in 1613. In the second half of the eighteenth century the colony moved to the even more important East India Company trading station at Bombay. There they flourished, not only under the protection of European rule, but also with the renewed contact with world Jewry which the European traders brought them. While the Jews of Kaifeng finally lost the link which had survived tenuously for so many generations, the Jews of Bombay re-entered the mainstream of Jewish life, rescued by the steady eastward advance of the European powers, and of the British Empire.

A Cochin Jew, David Rahabi, visited the Bene Israel in the the mid-eighteenth century—Bene Israel legends transposed his visit to 'about the year 1000'! He reported that a single Jewish prayer—the Shema, with its powerful opening words, 'Hear, O Israel!'—was the only Hebrew they knew. All the Jewish festivals were still celebrated at the time of his visit, but under other, Indian-style names: the Day of Atonement being known, not as Yom Kippur, but as the 'Fast of Door Closing'. The Jewish dietary laws, and circumcision, had both survived.

David Rahabi set himself the task of re-teaching the Bene Israel the details of the Jewish faith, and introduced them to the Sephardi ritual of prayer. He also provided them with a prayer book in their own language, Mahratti, and trained successors to continue with his work.

In the British war against Tipu Sultan in 1783, five Bene Israel brothers fought in the British army. One of them, Samuel Ezekiel Divekar, rose to the rank of Native Commandant (Subedar Major). Captured by Tipu Sultan, he was released after the intervention of Tipu Sultan's mother, who pleaded with her son that the Bene Israel were mentioned with favour in the Koran. Divekar vowed that as soon as he could he would build a synagogue as a thank-offering. He carried out his vow, constructing and endowing the first Bene Israel synagogue, in 1796, in Bombay.

During the nineteenth century the Bene Israel Jews acquired surnames drawn from the villages in which they lived. These ended mostly in the suffix '-kar'—thus, 'Jhiradkar'. But with the renewed contact with most westerly Jewry, they began to take on Biblical surnames, thus, Mr Abraham, Mr Moses, or Mr Elias.

As their Jewishness revived, they retained, however, their own 'caste' system, and for those who were considered 'white' intermarriage with their 'black' fellow-Jews was frowned upon, and frequently forbidden.

Despite this tentative bowing to the caste system of their Hindu neighbours, the Bene Israel had no real identity of faith or custom with the Indian world around them. Rabbi Hugo Gryn, who was their rabbi in the Byculla suburb of Bombay from 1957 to 1960, has commented: 'They were not discriminated against, but they were not helped.' And so it was that in 1948 the establishment of the State of Israel gave them, as Jews, a focus and a territorial identity, which they had earlier lacked. Indeed, Israel provided them with a bridge whereby they could cross their hitherto nearest Jewish world, that of the Baghdadi Jews, who regarded them with little-disguised contempt.

In Israel they found different problems, including the problem of colour, but they also benefitted from the basic 'oneness' of the ingathering Jewish communities from many different regions. They were no longer freaks or outcasts, and of the 24,000 Bene Israel in India at the end of the Second World War, as many as half settled in Israel. Others went to Britain, Canada and Australia.

In 1947, after Indian independence, many Indian Jews reached high positions in Indian public life. Hannah Sen—whom you, Auntie Fori, knew well—was President of the All-India Women's Conference and a courageous fighter for the rights of women in India. Joshua M.

Benjamin was Chief Architect of the Government of India, responsible for the imposing Parliamentary Annex building in New Delhi. Ezra Kolet—who once worked under Uncle Bijju at the Ministry of Finance—served as Secretary of the Ministry of Shipping and Transport, responsible for chartering ships to bring food to India. A co-founder of the Jewish Welfare Association in New Delhi, Kolet was also a keen musician, and set up the Delhi Symphony Society.

I have three personal links with the Jews of India. The first dates back to 1958, when you and I first met, and I also met a brother and sister, David and Jean Jhirad. They were the new generation of an old and distinguished Indian–Jewish family. Their father, Elijah Ephraim Jhirad, born in Quetta, was active in Jewish affairs in Delhi. A lawyer by profession, he had joined the Royal Indian Navy when war broke out in 1939. After independence he became the navy's Judge-Advocate-General. My diary of those far-off days records several long talks with David and Jean long into the night, about the issues of those days: caste and class, wealth and poverty, imperialism and communism: the intense discussions of idealistic youth. Jean won my heart. I have often wondered what happened to her. Only when I was writing these letters did I learn that she had died in London, after a long illness, almost twenty years ago, while still in her forties. David lives and works in Washington.

My second link with the Jews of India came through the friendship of Samuel Solomon, whom I knew as a British Jew living in Hampstead (his daughter Emma Klein became a writer on Anglo-Jewish themes). Samuel Solomon was in fact an Indian Jew, born in Calcutta in 1904, four years before you, Auntie Fori, were born in Budapest. His mother's father, Elias Moses Duveck-Cohen—the family came originally from Syria—owned the largest theatre in Calcutta. His brother (Samuel's great uncle), Sir David Ezra, was Sheriff of Calcutta, related by marriage to the Sassoon family, Indian Jews, one of whose number, Sir Victor Sassoon, became a member of the Indian Legislative Assembly in 1922.

After schooling in India, Samuel Solomon was educated in Britain, then returned to India as a member of the Indian Civil Service. He took up his first post, as an Assistant Magistrate and Collector, in 1927. Following periods as an Assistant Settlement Officer, a District and Sessions

Judge, and Publicity Officer of the Government of Bihar, in 1942, as Director of Development to the Government of Orissa, he was responsible for the reception of thousands of refugees fleeing the Japanese invasion of Burma: many were cast ashore naked on the coast of Orissa after the Japanese had bombed their frail craft.

After taking up residence in Britain in 1947, Samuel Solomon helped raise funds for the new State of Israel. When I knew him, in the 1960s, it was his tales of his life and career in India that fascinated me. Such is the nature of Jewish history (on which I once lectured as 'Jews on the move'), that six of his seven grandchildren were born in Israel, and live there today.

My third link with India is more recent, dating back to 1974: my friendship with Hugo Gryn, then a Reform rabbi in London—as senior rabbi of the West London Synagogue. A decade and a half earlier, while based in Bombay, he had travelled extensively through India, lecturing on Judaism and Jewish history in many Indian universities. During the course of his travels he met Indian Jews in many cities—including Poona, Cochin, Delhi and Ahmedabad (where he became a friend of Uncle Bijju's cousin Raja Hathisingh, the Governor of Gujarat, with whom I once spent an amusing day).

Although Hugo was initially sent to minister to the Bene Israel Jews in Bombay, he extended his work to include the Baghdadi Jews—nineteenth-century immigrants from Iraq—as well as Jews from Europe, among them refugees from Nazi Germany. He became a respected leader among them all, and encouraged many to emigrate to Israel. To this day he is remembered with affection among the Jews of Bombay, and also among the Jews of Cochin. His experience of the different faiths of India stimulated his own inter-faith interests, which were later to be such a prominent aspect of his influence in Britain. His death in 1996, while in his sixties, is still greatly mourned. He was a survivor of the Holocaust: in 1944 he was deported from Hungarian-occupied Ruthenia—from the town of Beregszasz—to Auschwitz, where his younger brother Gabi was murdered. Gabi was then ten years old.

No. 60

Dearest Auntie Fori,

When I came to see you in India in 1958, one of my grandparents—my mother's mother, Golda Green—was still alive. She, like the grandparents or great-grandparents of a majority of British Jews, was born in Russia, more than a thousand miles to the east of London, in the remote region of which the Pripet Marshes are the centre.

A hundred years ago there were more than seven million Jews living in that far-off region, the Jewish 'Pale of Settlement' of what was then Tsarist Russia. Although the most educated among them spoke Russian, their daily language was the flourishing language of Yiddish. It was the language of their joy and woe, of their business activities and literature, and of their closely-knit family life.

Where had they come from, these Jews of the Pripet Marshes—of Warsaw to the west, of Vilna to the north, of Kiev to the east, and of hundreds of villages and hamlets all round—the Jews of the shtetl, all speaking the guttural Germanic tones of their Yiddish in such contrast to the Slav tones of the Russian, Polish and Ukrainian languages around them? In 1917 one of these 'Pripet Marsh' Jews, Chaim Weizmann, was to persuade the British Government to support the idea of a Jewish National Home in Palestine.

The Jews of Russia had reached their crowded, settled, shtetl life by two quite different routes. Several thousand, perhaps tens of thousands, had undoubtedly come, at the very beginning of the Middle Ages, from the area of the Black Sea and the Caspian Sea, from the vast kingdom of the Khazars. These once nomadic people were a central Asian tribe, with Mongoloid features, whose kings had converted to Judaism in about 700 AD. After this conversion, the land under their control had become a region of refuge for thousands of 'real' Jews who were being persecuted at that time throughout Byzantium, in the Balkans, and in southern Persia.

These Jews of Greece and Persia came to the Khazar kingdom two hundred years before the Norman Conquest of England, and lived for those two hundred years in relative peace and prosperity, growing rice and cereals, honey and vineyards. They were also shepherds and some—along the shores of the Caspian Sea—fishermen. They traded with fellow-Jews in far-off Spain and North Africa. They corresponded with the Jews of Spain. They helped another central Asian tribe, the Magyars, to conquer what is now Hungary—your original homeland—and some of them even settled with the Magyars along the Danube.

When, in 1016, fifty years before the Norman Conquest of England, a joint Russian and Byzantine army defeated the already much weakened Khazar army, these 'Khazar' Jews were forced to flee once more: Jews on the move, the frequent fate of some Jews in every generation. These Jews were no longer simply the descendants of Jewish refugees from Greece and Persia. Intermarriage with original Khazars who had been converted to Judaism had introduced central Asian features, high cheek-bones and oriental eyes. I remember my own shock, a decade ago in Toronto, on being introduced, in an all-Jewish gathering, to a 'Mr Khazar', and, on turning to shake his hand, finding in front of me a person who was my personal vision of someone from the remotest steppes of central Asia.

These Jews of the Caspian—Khazars, or Mongols—were, with the first defeat of the Khazars by the Kievan Russians in 965 AD and the final destruction of the Khazar kingdom in 1016, dispersed and homeless. Already in 986, as the *Russian Chronicle* records, some Khazar Jews had gone to see the Russian ruler, Vladimir, at Kiev, and had even invited him to accept Judaism.

With the destruction of Khazaria some of the Jews found their way back to Greece and the Mediterranean, exiles once more. But many must have been taken back with their Russian conquerors to the lands of southern Russia—to Kiev and Kharkov—areas which had themselves only recently become part of the slowly expanding area of Russian control.

The Khazar Jews who settled in Russia were not particularly liked or welcomed: such historical records as survive show, for example, that a hundred years after their arrival anti-Jewish riots broke out in Kiev itself, and many were killed. But still they sought to lead a normal life, to preserve their Judaism, to trade, to raise families, and to survive.

Surviving fragments of evidence from this distant period tell of another, extraordinary development, affecting those Khazar Jews who had somehow managed to remain in the Caspian region, despite the destruction of the Khazar kingdom. Among the documents found in the Cairo Genizah—a vast repository of ancient Jewish letters and documents—was one, first published in 1920, and dated from the twelfth century, in which appear the sentences:

> *In the mountains which are in the land of Khazaria there arose a Jew whose name was Solomon ben-Dugi.*
>
> *The name of his son was Menachem, and with them was an eloquent man whose name was Ephraim ben-Azariah of Jerusalem.*
>
> *They wrote letters to all the Jews, near and far, in all the lands round them. They said that the time had come in which God would gather his people Israel from all the lands to Jerusalem, the Holy City—and that Solomon ben-Dugi was Elijah, and his son the Messiah.*

It is almost certain that this false-messiah, Menachem ben-Solomon ben-Dugi, is the very same Menachem ben-Solomon ben-Ruhi, better known as David El-Roi, who was killed in 1160 at the height of his messianic aspirations, after leading an uprising in Kurdistan. One scholar, A. N. Poliak, is convinced that this David El-Roi was a Khazar Jew, one of the survivors of the dispersed community, who was in the process of leading his followers from Khazaria to Jerusalem when he was killed.

Meanwhile, in the very same years that the defeated Jewish Khazars—and there was a second Khazar Diaspora followed the Mongol invasion of the area in the thirteenth century—were finding new homes in southern Russia, another group of Jews, numerically much larger, were being driven out of their homes, along the river Rhine. These Jews had in the days of the Roman Empire travelled from the Mediterranean, and even from Palestine, to settle as traders in all the outposts under Roman control.

It was two thousand years ago that Jews first came to western Europe, with the Roman legions. Along the great rivers, the Ebro in Spain, the Rhône and Seine in France, the Rhine and Elbe in Germany, they established small trading posts from which they could supply the

Roman forces and the local inhabitants. In Italy itself, the Roman heart-land, they were numerous and active. And with the disintegration of the Roman Empire, the triumph of the barbarian tribes, and the coming of the Dark Ages, they still somehow survived.

In the many small towns and forts along the rivers of 'Germania' the Jews found it possible to earn a living, and when the rule of Rome was replaced by that of the 'barbarians' they remained as traders and middle-men, spreading slowly throughout the territory of what was to become the unifying, protecting power of Charlemagne and his Franks. In the European empire which Charlemagne created, the Jews had been given complete freedom in their commercial transactions. But on his death in 814 AD not only his empire, but the tolerance with which it had been associated, was cast into turmoil. The Jewish struggle for fair dealing and equality began, a struggle which was to last for more than a thousand years.

No. 61

Dearest Auntie Fori,

The history of the Jews and Poland has been bedevilled, especially in the last hundred years, by a deep Jewish perception of Polish anti-Semitism, exemplified most recently in the revelation (at the very end of the twentieth century) of the massacre of the Jews of the village of Jed-wabne in 1941, perpetrated not by the German occupiers but by their own fellow Polish villagers. Yet the early years of Polish–Jewish history had many positive aspects, not least because it was on Polish soil that the Jews fleeing from Germany were allowed to settle, even encouraged to do so.

As early as 1170 AD, a hundred years after the first expulsions from Germany, Jews were found administering the Polish mint, and striking coins with Hebrew inscriptions. Forty years later, Jews were allowed to own land in Galicia. In the fourteenth century the Jews of Cracow received a charter which decreed that 'if the Jew enters the house of a Christian, no one has the right to cause him any injury or unpleas-antness'. Within a few years, similar privileges had been granted to the

Jews of Lithuania. Jewish communities emerged in town after town. An inscription from about 1234 mentions 'Rabbi Jacob Savra of Cracow . . . a great scholar and fluent in the entire Talmud'.

A turning point for the good came in 1264, when King Boleslaw V of Kalisz issued a charter giving the Jews his protection. Poland had suffered terribly during an incursion by the Mongol hordes from central Asia, and Boleslaw recognized the Jewish ability to help restore his country's trading and commercial prosperity. A century later, in 1385, when the Grand Duchy of Lithuania was joined with Poland, the Charter was extended to Lithuania.

But, as so often in Jewish history, the right to settle and the right to be unmolested were frequently challenged by local mobs, and by Christian fanaticism stirred up by those who felt the need for a scapegoat. During the European-wide Black Death, Jews were everywhere blamed for the spread of the plague which had no other explanation for the people of that time, and Poland was no exception: a Polish chronicle of the year 1349 states: 'All Jews . . . almost throughout Poland, were massacred'.

In western Poland, in 1399, a rabbi and thirteen elders were accused of destroying Church property, tortured, and then burnt alive. In 1407, there were anti-Jewish riots in Cracow, and a Jewish money-lender was publicly tortured and burnt to death. Further east, in Moscow, the Jewish court physician, Master Leon, was put to death in 1490 for failing to cure the son of the Grand Duke. In 1495 the Jews were expelled from Lithuania, which for more than two hundred years had given them sanctuary.

Individual Jews reached positions of prominence in every walk of Polish Jewish life. Polish Jews traded in cloth, dyes, horses and cattle, trading their wares as far away as Venice and the Crimea. A decree of King Ladislaus II, dated 1425, referring to a remote area in Polish Galicia, states: 'As we have great confidence in the wisdom, carefulness and foresight of our Lvov customs-holder, the Jew Volchko . . . after the above-mentioned Jew Volchko has turned the above-mentioned wilderness into a human settlement in the village, it shall remain in his hands till his death.' Another Jew, Natko, was granted the salt mines of Drohobycz by King Casimir Jagello.

But the security of the Jews of Poland seemed assured. King Boleslaw's charter was renewed several times, most forcefully by King

Casimir IV, of the Jagellonian dynasty, in 1453. In the sixteenth century, Rabbi Moses Isserles—known by the acronym Rema—stated that it was 'better to live on dry bread and peace in Poland' than in lands elsewhere that were more dangerous for Jews. Isserles coined a pun on the Hebrew form of Poland, Polin, saying that it derived from the two Hebrew words *po lin* ('here, he shall rest'). Isserles himself founded a *yeshiva*—rabbinical college—in Cracow, supporting its students at his own expense, and became head of the rabbinical court in the city. Among his books was one on the laws of forbidden and permitted foods. Isserles died in 1572. His fame as a scholar was such that it was said of him, and is inscribed on his tombstone, which still stands in the Cracow cemetery: 'From Moses to Moses there has arisen no one like Moses': that is, from Moses Maimonides to Moses Isserles there has arisen no one like the Biblical Moses.

In 1569 Poland conquered the Ukraine, adding considerably to the number of Jews under Polish rule. Jewish bailiffs were often put in charge of the large estates which the Polish nobility acquired in the Ukraine. Jews would lease the estates, paying large sums of money for them for a number of years, and then have unlimited rights over the peasants. The Jews were doubly detested by the Ukrainian peasants: first as absentee landlords, and second as the instruments of foreign—that is Polish—rule.

Jewish learning and culture flourished, a sixteenth-century Polish chronicler noting that 'the Jews use Hebrew books and study science and arts, astronomy and medicine'. Jewish scholars and teachers abounded. Jewish internal administration was centralized and regularized by the Council of the Lands, a focal point of Jewish communal activity. Magnificent synagogues were constructed, including the Rema Synagogue in Cracow and the Great Synagogue in Lvov.

No. 62

Dearest Auntie Fori,

In central and western Europe the situation of the Jews continued, throughout the sixteenth century, to be such as to encourage continual flight, and emigration eastward, chiefly to Poland. In 1500 the Jews were expelled from the Rhineland, in 1541 from Prague, and in 1571 from Berlin. The eastward migration was continuous.

Anti-Jewish hatreds in Christian Europe reached a cruel climax in the sixteenth century, during the Protestant revolution, when Martin Luther, who had launched that revolution, published in 1543 his letter *Of the Jews and Their Lies.* In this letter, Luther gave what he called his 'honest advice' to his fellow-Christians. Originally his letter was friendly towards the Jews, in the hope that if they were no longer persecuted they would convert to Christianity. When the Jews did not convert, Luther's rage knew no bounds. His advice to his fellow-Christians was in seven sections. Each section was as forceful, and as full of furious hatred, as Luther could devise.

The first section bluntly declared that the synagogues of the Jews 'should be set on fire, and whatever does not burn up should be covered or spread over with dirt so that no one may ever be able to see a cinder or stone of it. And this ought to be done for the honour of God and of Christianity in order that God may see that we are Christians, and that we have not wittingly tolerated or approved of such public lying, cursing and blaspheming of His Son and His Christians.'

Luther had no shortage of suggestions. The pamphlet's advice continued:

> *Secondly, their homes should likewise be broken down and destroyed. For they perpetrate the same things there that they do in their synagogues. For this reason they ought to be put under one roof or in a stable, like gypsies, in order that they may realize that they are not masters in our land, as they boast, but miserable captives, as they complain of us.*
>
> *Thirdly they should be deprived of their prayerbooks and Talmuds in which such idolatry, lies, cursing, and blasphemy are taught.*
>
> *Fourthly, their rabbis must be forbidden under threat of death to teach any more.*
>
> *Fifthly, passport and travelling privileges should be absolutely forbidden to the Jews. For they have no business in the rural districts since they are not nobles, nor officials, nor merchants, nor the like. Let them stay at home.*

Sixthly, they ought to be stopped from usury. All their cash and valu-
ables of silver and gold ought to be taken from them and put aside for
safekeeping. For this reason, as said before, everything that they possess
they stole and robbed from us through their usury, for they have no other
means of support.

This was not the end of Martin Luther's threats and fulminations.
There was more 'honest advice; to come. Section seven dealt with Jewish
youth:

Let the young and strong Jews and Jewesses be given the flail, the ax, the
hoe, the spade, the distaff, and spindle, and let them earn their bread by
the sweat of their noses as is enjoined upon Adam's children. For it is not
proper that they should want us cursed Goyyim to work in the sweat of
our brow and that they, pious crew, idle away their days at the fireside in
laziness, feasting and display. And in addition to this, they boast impi-
ously that they have become masters of the Christians at our expense. We
ought to drive the rascally lazybones out of our system.

If, however, we are afraid that they might harm us personally, or
our wives, children, servants, cattle, etc. when they serve us or work for
us—since it is surely to be presumed that such noble lords of the world
and poisonous bitter worms are not accustomed to any work and would
very unwillingly humble themselves to such a degree among the cursed
Goyyim—then let us apply the same cleverness 'expulsion'—as the
other nations, such as France, Spain, Bohemia, etc., and settle with them
for that which they have extorted usuriously from us, and after having
divided it up fairly let us drive them out of the country for all time.

Luther's pamphlet ended with an appeal to all princes and nobles
with Jews in their domains to act 'so that you and we may all be free of
the insufferable devilish burden—the Jews'.

In face of such bigotry, and the violence which it encouraged, the
Jews had little alternative but to flee. Again and again they were driven
out with fire and sword. They also cast about for some mystic force that
might help them. Elijah, Rabbi of Chelm (a city later synonymous with
Jewish fools, the butt of endless jokes), who died in 1583, believed in a

man-made creature—a *golem*—that would be capable of great destruction. On his forehead would be the three Hebrew letters AMT (for *emet*, 'truth'). Only when the A was removed, leaving MT (for *met*, 'death') would the golem be subdued. Rabbi Elijah and his descendants had many discussions about the golem. Would it, for example, be allowed to join the minyan, the quorum required for collective prayers? Their answer was no. Many years later, another Elijah, the great Gaon of Vilna, told a disciple that as a boy he had tried to make a golem but had seen a vision which told him to stop.

By 1760, and throughout the second half of the eighteenth century, the legend was transferred to the distinguished Rabbi Judah Loew of Prague (who had died in 1609), but it had no historical basis either in Loew's life or in his era. Nevertheless, once associated, albeit quite wrongly, with the saintly rabbi, the golem legend—specifically that Loew created the golem to serve him but was forced to restore him to dust when the golem began to go wild and endanger the lives of Prague's citizens—became a basis for innumerable scary tales and rumours, as well as novels, plays, an orchestral suite, an opera, a ballet, and several films, including a 1920 German silent film which was remade in France as a talking film in 1936, and a post–Second World War Czech film.

No. 63

Dearest Auntie Fori,

In 1648—just over three hundred and fifty years ago—the Jews of Poland, Lithuania, and the Ukraine were attacked by the Cossack leader Bogdan Chmielnicki, whose followers brought destruction and death to several hundred Jewish communities over a period of eight years, murdering more than 100,000 Jews, torturing hundreds of thousands more, and driving many out of the region altogether, to Holland, Germany, Bohemia, and to the Balkans; back to the very lands from which they had been driven by persecution two, three, four and five centuries before.

More than three hundred communities were destroyed by 'Chmiel the Wicked', as the Jews named their tormentor—it is a Jewish custom to say, after mentioning his name, as with any hated enemy of the Jewish people, 'May his name be blotted out'. But despite the terrible slaughter, Jewish life in the region was not destroyed, and slowly the communities were restored.

One repercussion of the Chmielnicki massacres was a remarkable messianic upsurge. The central figure was not from Poland, but from the Ottoman Empire—Shabbetai Zvi. When he was twenty-two years old, at the time of the Chmielnicki massacres, he claimed to have experienced a heavenly voice telling him he was the redeemer. In synagogue in Smyrna, his home town (today's Izmir) he pronounced the name of God—YHVH—the four Hebrew letters which appear 6,823 times in the text of the Hebrew Bible, but the pronunciation of which is forbidden by Jewish tradition—except for the High Priest (in ancient times) on the Day of Atonement. Shabbetai Zvi also 'cancelled' the fast of the Ninth of Av, commemorating the destruction of the Temple, and announced that the birthday of the Messiah was the same day as his own. The rabbis in Smyrna put him under a *herem*—a ban of excommunication.

Moving to Salonika, he celebrated his messiahship by 'marrying' the Torah in a mystical ceremony. Expelled by the Salonika rabbis, he travelled throughout Greece and Turkey, after which, accompanied by growing numbers of followers, he sailed to Palestine, where he was crowned 'King-Messiah' by a well-known mystic and faith healer, Nathan of Gaza. Nathan became his prophet, announcing that Shabbetai would depose the Sultan of Turkey and lead the Jews back to the Promised Land. In alarm, the rabbis of Jerusalem arrested him, had him flogged to extract a recantation—which he refused—and then excommunicated him. Returning to Smyrna in 1665—fifteen years after his expulsion— he announced that the year 1666 would be the year of redemption, when he would ride into Jerusalem on a lion. Abolishing the separation of men and women at synagogue services, repeatedly pronouncing the forbidden name of God, and turning all fast days into feast days, he announced the establishment of twenty-five 'territories', each with a king, and with his brother as 'King of Kings'.

Sailing from Smyrna to Constantinople to depose the Sultan, Shabbetai was arrested, imprisoned, and offered the choice between conversion to Islam or death. He chose conversion, put on a turban, and was given the Muslim name Mehmet Effendi. The Sultan granted him the honorary title of Royal Doorkeeper and gave him a pension.

Some of Shabbetai's followers likewise accepted Islam. They and their descendants, known as the *Donmeh,* retained their Jewish identity in secret, intermarried, and survived as a recognised group until today. Djavid Bey, a leader of the Young Turk Revolution in 1908, was a Donmeh; in the Second World War the Donmeh were treated as non-Muslims and had to pay a special tax.

Other of Shabbetai's followers believed that his conversion was part of the trials and tribulations that must inevitably precede his triumphal appearance as Messiah. After a few years the Sultan banished him to the port of Dulcigno, in Albania (now Dulcinj, in Montenegro). From there he still kept in touch with those who believed he was the Messiah. He died in Dulcigno in 1676.

It was among the Jews of Poland, reeling from the Chmielnicki massacres, that the Shabbataean movement had its biggest impact. Many were eager, even desperate, for Divine intervention to alleviate their harsh lot. But with his conversion to Islam, the new-found zeal soon faded, leaving only suppressed hopes of redemption.

Shabbetai, incidentally, is the Hebrew for the planet Saturn. There were two other well-known Jews with the same name. One was Shabbetai ben Meir Ha-Kohen, a Lithuanian rabbi who at the time of the persecution of Lithuanian Jews in 1655 fled to Bohemia. One of his published writings was an important historical account of the fate of the Jews of Poland during the Chmielnicki massacres. There was also an early Hasidic leader, Shabbetai of Raszkow, who edited a prayer book and also a collection of kabbalistic writings. He died in 1745, at the age of ninety.

In Poland, after the Chmielnicki massacres, thousands of Jews who had been forcibly converted to Christianity were permitted by the Polish king to return to Judaism. The pattern of daily life was restored, precarious as always, but with an opportunity for peace and quiet, a livelihood from which families could be raised, and education of the children—the Jewish imperative—continued.

No. 64

Dearest Auntie Fori,

In the eighteenth century, in three separate years, 1734, 1750 and 1768, the pattern of Jewish daily life was again shattered by massacres in the Ukraine. In 1768, during these 'Haidamak' massacres, as they were known, the Jews of the town of Uman defended themselves tenaciously. Even so, most of them, including their women and children, were brutally murdered in the synagogue. Some, agreeing to pay a ransom, were brutally murdered after they had paid it.

Yet these slaughters of innocents, the destruction of synagogues, the burning of homes, not only failed to shame, but strengthened, the deep Jewish sense of community and spirituality. For in the wake of the Haidamak massacres, eastern European Jewry was swept by a deep, lasting, and spiritually uplifting revolution, Hasidism. Once more, Jewish creativity had found a remarkable focus.

Hasidism was a religious movement that appealed to the Jewish masses. The Hasidim believed that joy—*simcha*—religious fervour—was the prime factor in Jewish life, and the key element in divine worship. As 'the whole earth is full of His glory', how can anyone on earth be miserable?

Love of the Land of Israel also played a part in the Hasidic philosophy, so much so that in 1777 a group of several hundred adherents, old and young, set off from Russia for Palestine, then under Turkish rule. Two years earlier the Turks had imposed a heavy 'head-tax' on all Jews, while in 1720 the Ashkenazi synagogue in Jerusalem had been seized by local Arabs and the scrolls of the law destroyed. But the Hasidim were undeterred, and, together with many non-Hasidic Jews, made the hazardous journey, led by one of their best-known learned men, the forty-three-year-old Menahem Mendel of Vitebsk. They settled in the Galilee, joining the thriving Jewish community of those whose ancestors had come from Spain and Portugal more than 250 years earlier.

The year 1788 saw another Jewish exodus: the arrival of the first Jews in Australia. They were Jews from Britain, convicts who had been sentenced to transportation for life. There were thirteen in all; one of them, Esther Abraham, had been transported for stealing a bundle of lace. She was pregnant at the time. Her daughter, Rosanna, was the first Jewish child to be born in Australia.

The Hasidic movement was founded in the first half of the eighteenth century by Ba'al Shem Tov ('Master of the Good Name')—Israel ben Eliezer—known to his followers, by the acronym of his name, as the Besht.

The Hebrew word *hasidut* means saintliness. The Besht, who died in 1760, and those who followed his spiritual path, brought a sense of heightened joy and religious enthusiasm to the practice of Judaism. It also brought a hierarchical concept that had been absent in the earlier Judaism of the rabbis and sages: the belief that it was through the Hasidic leader—the Tsaddik, or righteous man—that Divine grace flowed: that only through his Tsaddik could the ordinary Hasid learn how God was to be worshipped, and approach God.

For the Hasid, God is ever-present in the world. 'At every step,' writes the historian of Judaism, Geoffrey Wigoder—a friend of mine who died recently, and who was a font of earthly as well as historical wisdom—'the true Hasid sees the Divine energy pervading the material universe. Provided he uses the world in a spirit of holiness, he worships his Creator even when eating, drinking, and attending to his other physical needs.'

The Yiddish word for rabbi—*reb,* or *rebbe*—is often applied to a Hasidic leader, as well as to a teacher.

The Hasids were opposed from the outset by religious Jews of the older, traditional worship, the Mitnagdim (the Hebrew word for 'opponents'). They were distressed to see how the Hasids separated themselves from the existing communities and synagogues, forming separate circles of life and worship, always glad to make recruits to their movement, but seeming to regard the regular stream of Orthodoxy with disdain. Above all, the Mitnagdim considered the concept of the Hasidic Tsaddik as an intermediary between man and God to be offensive to the religion, and the total, almost mystical devotion to the Tsaddik by his followers to verge on idolatry.

In the nineteenth century the ideals and practice of Hasidism were opposed by the *Haskalah* movement—the Jewish Enlightenment—about which I will write to you next week. Followers of the Enlightenment, who believed that the Jewish religion must change to adapt to the modern world, were strongly opposed to what they saw as the mystical obscurantism in Hasidism, as well as to the Hasidic rejection of secular learning, and of the need—seen as a crucial element of modernity by the Enlightenment—to be educated on the language of the society around them.

Still, despite the opposition of mainstream Orthodoxy and of the Enlightenment, Hasidism flourished, and flourishes today. Among the Hasids, Yiddish is widely spoken, and the use of Hebrew in daily life is shunned on the grounds that it is exclusively the language of the holy books and of prayer. Zionism is opposed by some Hasidic dynasties as the false intervention by man into God's realm of authority. Others, including the Lubavitcher Rebbe—who died recently at the age of ninety-two—encouraged his followers to take an active part in the politics of the Jewish State, often from a politically right-wing perspective.

In their dress, the Hasids of today still wear the costume favoured by Polish Catholic noblemen in the eighteenth century: the time of their own foundation. But they have vested in it the mystical qualities of their own aspect of Judaism. Thus the wide-brimmed fur hat, the *shtraymel,* with its thirteen sable tails, is believed by many Hasidic groups to represent the thirteen qualities of Divine mercy.

At his table, on Sabbaths and festivals, the Rebbe (as the Tsaddik has become known), tastes small amounts of the food that is put before him, and then distributes the bulk of it to his followers, who have gathered to be with him. They believe that eating food that their Rebbe has tasted is a path to holiness. When the meal is over, they listen to the Rebbe expound that week's portion of the Torah, and then break into song and dance, in accordance with the words of Psalm 100: 'Serve the Lord with gladness: come before his presence with singing.'

Each Hasidic group, or 'dynasty', has its own variety of belief. Among the most influential Hasidic groups today is the Lubavitch Habad movement. The word Habad is an acronym of the three Hebrew words *hokhmah, binah, da'at*—wisdom, understanding, knowledge. The group was founded by Shneur Zalman of Lyady. Born in 1745, he worked for many years on a new codification of Jewish law, part of which was accidentally destroyed in a fire. He gained a large following throughout White Russia and Lithuania. In Vilna, the 'Jerusalem of Lithuania', he was opposed by one of the great leaders of traditional Orthodoxy, the Gaon of Vilna, who refused even to meet him, or his fellow Hasidic leader, Menahem Mendel of Vitebsk: indeed, as a result of the influence of the Gaon of Vilna, a rabbinical ban (*herem*) was pronounced on Hasidism, and a volume in honour of the Ba'al Shem Tov was publicly burnt. The Gaon of Vilna was equally critical of the Jewish Enlightenment, about which I shall write to you in my next letter. The Gaon, incidentally, is said to have given his first public homily, in synagogue, at the age of six, and astounded the rabbis present by his wisdom.

In 1798, as Shneur Zalman's following spread throughout northern Russia, he was arrested by the Tsarist authorities and accused of being a religious heretic, as well as a political danger to the authority of the Tsar. He was imprisoned in St Petersburg for more than a year. His release is, to this day, celebrated by his followers as a festival of joy, and a triumph of the legitimacy of his Lubavitch dynasty. Among his sayings was: 'The only way of converting darkness into light is by giving to the poor.' On his death in 1813 the dynastic succession passed through his son-in-law, Dov Ber Schneersohn, who set up his 'court' in the White Russian town of Lubavitch; the succession remained in his family through six generations, each one known as the Lubavitcher Rebbe. The last of the line, Menahem Mendel Schneersohn, was born in Russia in 1902. When, in 1994, he died in New York City at the age of ninety-two, some of his followers were convinced—and remain convinced—that he will return as the Messiah, and soon.

No. 65

Dearest Auntie Fori,

In the 1770s a new cast of thought began to grip the Jewish imagination in Europe, *Haskalah*—the Hebrew term for Enlightenment, which I mentioned in my last letter as opposing what it saw as the backward-looking beliefs of the ultra-Orthodox Hasidic movement.

The Enlightenment was to influence Jewish thought and behaviour for more than a hundred years, and, indeed, to have an impact until today. One of its principal attractions, to many Jews, first in Germany and then spreading south into Italy and east into Poland and Russia, was the argument that secular studies should be recognized as a legitimate part of the education of every Jew. Torah study would continue, but the new world of science would also be embraced, as well as the pursuits of the 'modern' world: agriculture, crafts, engineering, the arts.

Israel Zamosc, a Galician-born Talmudist and mathematician, had published in 1741 one of the earliest attempts to use modern secular knowledge to interpret Biblical and Talmudic literature. In 1765 he published a book on the importance of the sciences in Jewish education. The German-Jewish playwright and philosopher Gotthold Ephraim Lessing challenged the claim of any religion to represent absolute truth.

The Jewish Enlightenment was not afraid of assimilation. Indeed, in many aspects it embraced it, turning with enthusiasm to the language, manners and dress of the people among whom Jews lived. The German-born son of a Torah scribe, Moses Mendelssohn—to whom Israel Zamosc had taught astronomy and mathematics—argued that a Jewish translation of the Bible into German was 'a first step towards culture' for the Jews of Germany, and helped complete it in 1783.

An observant Jew throughout his life, Mendelssohn's impact on the Enlightenment, and on Jewish emancipation, was considerable. He was the first Jew who published in German. His philosophical writings led him to be called 'the German Socrates'. For him, Judaism was not in conflict with the rational spirit of the age. 'We have no doctrines that are contrary to reason,' he insisted. 'We added nothing to natural religion save commandments and statutes.' In his book *Jerusalem,* published in 1783, he urged the separation of Church and State. Religion should be a matter of individual decision and conscience, not coercion. The study of Talmud was not included in the Jewish Free School founded on his initiative in Berlin in 1778. 'We were not all created to become Talmudists', were the defiant words of the poet and linguist Naphtali Herz Wessely.

One powerful influence on the Enlightenment was the work of those known as 'Court Jews': wealthy and influential Jewish individuals—many of them bankers—who worked with and often sustained the

power of the local rulers, and who engaged in a wide range of commercial transactions with non-Jewish leaders and traders. They and their
families brought the wealthier and more prominent Jewish circles into
frequent and close contact with the non-Jewish world, and were influenced by the secular culture of the world around them. In both Germany and Alsace-Lorraine, wealthy Jews were teaching their children
German and French, so that they could move easily in non-Jewish
circles, both for business and social life.

This 'linguistic assimilation' became central to the Jewish Enlightenment. Today it is the norm. Your 'native tongue', Auntie Fori, was Hungarian, mine English. In many Jewish communities, Yiddish was set
aside—pushed aside and cast off. Indeed, one of the charges against Jews
had been that by using Yiddish in their business transactions among
themselves, they had been able to deceive their non-Jewish interlocu-
tors. Moses Mendelssohn was influenced by this: he also regarded Yiddish as 'ridiculous, ungrammatical, and a cause of moral corruption'.
When the Austrian ruler, Joseph II, put restrictions of the use of Yiddish, Naphtali Wessely approved.

David Friedlaender, a pioneer in the theory and practice of assimilation—who was married to the daughter of the Prussian banker and
Court Jew David Itzig (Israel Zamosc's patron)—was so convinced that
Yiddish was responsible for 'unethical conduct' and the 'corruption' of
religion that he translated the daily prayers into German. One of the
arguments he put forward in 1810 in favour of the emancipation of the
Jews of Prussia was the 'wave of baptisms' there, a sign of the degree of
assimilation.

Linguistic assimilation was in evidence in many lands. In 1806 in
Holland, a Jewish weekly newspaper began to appear in the Dutch language. By the 1840s, Hungarian had replaced Yiddish in 'your' Hungary
as the language of instruction in Jewish schools, and rabbis had begun to
give their sermons in Hungarian.

One aspect of the Enlightenment that at first sight seems contradictory was the encouragement of modern Hebrew. Mendelssohn regarded
the Hebrew language as 'a national treasure'. Jonathan Eybescheutz (who
in 1725 had been one of the Prague rabbis who excommunicated the
Shabbatean sect, but whose younger son later presented himself as a

Shabbatean prophet) wanted all Jews to speak fluent Hebrew. Wessely, who had studied under Eybescheutz, pioneered the revival of Biblical Hebrew, and of Hebrew-language poetry. A Hebrew-language monthly began publication in 1783 in the East Prussian city of Königsberg—as a vehicle of the Enlightenment. Its publishers, 'Friends of the Hebrew Language', changed their (Hebrew) name in 1786 to 'Seekers of Good and Wisdom and Friends of the Hebrew Language'. Its articles were published in Hebrew—and in German.

No. 66

Dearest Auntie Fori,

For the Jews of western Europe the nineteenth century opened hopefully. Under the influence of the French Revolution and of Napoleon Bonaparte, the Jews of Frankfurt, Mainz, Venice and Rome found the restrictions on their dwelling places lifted, and the gates of the ghetto torn down. The Italian Jews, whose emancipation he procured, called him, in Hebrew, *Helek Tov:* Good Part, or Bona-Parte. In 1807 the Jews of Westphalia were granted full emancipation by his brother Jerome. Four years later the Jews of Hamburg, Mecklenburg, Lübeck and Bremen were all granted full civil rights.

Napoleon himself sought to deflect Jewish national consciousness into the nation states of which the Jews were a part. Religious freedom was to be unimpaired, but any sense of wider Jewish identity was to be abandoned, except with regard to Palestine. As he had made his way northward from Egypt in 1799, to confront at Acre a combined British and Turkish army at Acre (which defeated him) he passed on the coastal plain within twenty miles of Jerusalem and, in an attempt to rally the Jews of Palestine to his cause, announced—while at Ramla—that it was his aim, if victorious over the Turks, to 'return to the Jews their Jerusalem' ('rendre aux juifs leur Jérusalem').

Individual Jews certainly served Napoleon well. Berek Joselewicz joined Napoleon's Polish Legion in 1807, won the Légion d'Honneur, and died fighting the Austrians two years later, having reached the rank of Colonel. But Jewish aspirations—national, social or economic—were far from Napoleon's mind, despite his proclamation at Ramla. In 1808 he issued a decree restricting the economic activity and freedom of movement of the Jews in France's eastern provinces—where the Jews were most numerous—for a period of ten years. It was known to the Jews as the 'Infamous Decree'. Only his defeat in 1815 brought its restrictive provisions to an end.

In the century that followed Napoleon's defeat, much of his emancipatory ideal was to be realized, as the spread of civil rights to Jews throughout western Europe opened up hitherto undreamed-of opportunities, while at the same time blunting the edge of isolation. Above all, the Jewish Enlightenment (Haskalah), of which I wrote in my last letter, continued to gain in influence. In 1813 a school was founded at Tarnopol, in the Orthodox heartland of Galicia, where, in addition to Biblical studies, arithmetic, history and geography were also taught, and the language of instruction was German. In Warsaw a Jewish school where the instruction was in Polish was opened in 1819.

A Jewish school where secular studies were an integral part of the curriculum was founded in the Russian Black Sea port of Odessa in 1826: pupils were encouraged to speak 'the pure German or Russian language'. In the Italian city of Padua, a rabbinical seminary was opened in 1829 which obliged those training for the rabbinate to study secular subjects: its rules and regulations were printed in Italian. Seminaries for the teachers of the Enlightenment opened in Amsterdam in 1836, and Budapest in 1857.

The secular education of Jews went side by side with the ending of many of the disabilities imposed on Jews since the Middle Ages. Jews entered local schools and universities, national parliaments, governments, the landowning classes, and the highest ranks of society—as Barons, Counts and Lords. Many converted to Christianity. Some had to convert in order to reach the ranks of the nobility. Even for those who retained their Judaism, beards and the outward trappings of Jewish Orthodoxy became a thing of the past. Jewish clothes were abandoned, Jewish hats set aside. Jewish names were replaced by names more in keeping with the local scene: as your family name Friedmann became Forbach, and mine—Fichtencwajg—was transmogrified to Goldberg and then to Gilbert.

No. 67

Dearest Auntie Fori,

By the time of Napoleon, the number of Jews in the east—Poland, Lithuania, western Russia—had reached several millions. Their lives were being changed dramatically—not by Napoleon—but by the persistent westward expansion of Tsarist Russia. Between 1772 and 1815 the whole of central and eastern Poland, and all Lithuania, was annexed by Russia.

The Jews were fortunate to find a friend and ally at the highest level of Russian society and power—the statesman-soldier Prince Potemkin. He encouraged Jews to settle in southern Russia, especially in the Cossack regions which he was annexing. One of the beneficiaries of Potemkin's scheme was the ancestor of Taya Zinkin, who served with you, Auntie Fori, in the work of helping Muslim refugees in Delhi in 1947, and was for many years *Manchester Guardian* correspondent in India. Her family was originally a Hungarian Jewish one like yours. After being given lands by Potemkin, near the town of Uman, they later established sugar beet plantations and sugar beet factories. The Bolshevik Revolution drove the family to France, where they lived until Hitler forced them yet further afield.

Potemkin's biographer Simon Sebag-Montefiore (a member of a distinguished Anglo-Jewish family) tells us that two previously Cossack—and Greek—towns, Kherson and Ekaterinoslav, became 'at least partly Jewish towns' as a result of this Jewish settlement. He also relates how Joshua Zeitlin, a Jewish merchant and scholar, travelled with Potemkin, managed his landed estates, arranged financial deals to supply his armies—as the Rothschilds were doing for other rulers in central and western Europe—and was given by Potemkin the status of 'Court adviser'. This allowed Zeitlin to own both land and serfs. Russian Jews called Zeitlin, in Hebrew, *ha-sar*—the lord.

In the south, Russian policy was dominated by two long-drawn-out wars with Turkey, the first from 1768 to 1774, the second from 1787 to 1792. Potemkin encouraged the Jews to fight for his tsar, Catherine II—

Catherine the Great. Indeed, he created a specifically Jewish force—the first entirely Jewish military force since the time of Bar Kochba's rebellion against Rome more than 1,600 years earlier.

Potemkin's Jewish regiment was called the Izraelovsky—a verbal echo of Peter the Great's magnificent Izmailovsky Guards. It was half infantry and half cavalry, and it fought in battle against the Turks. The Jewish mother, anxious that her soldier son should not exert himself too much—even for Potemkin—would urge him (in emphatic Yiddish): 'Kill a Turk—and rest.' This became a popular exhortation for not overdoing things in any walk of life.

Successive Tsars had different attitudes to the Jews under their rule. In 1742 the Empress Elizabeth had banned all these 'enemies of Christ' from her kingdom. In 1791 Catherine the Great established the 'Pale of Settlement', effectively restricting Jewish settlement to the Lithuanian and Polish provinces where most Jews lived, having come under Russian rule as a result of the westward annexations of the previous twenty years. After 1812 the Pale was extended to include the newly conquered region of Bessarabia.

Within the Pale, the 'Jewish Statute' of Tsar Alexander I, promulgated in 1804, gave Jews the right to attend Russian schools, and also authorized the Jews to set up their own schools, provided the language of instruction was Russian, Polish or German (as opposed to Yiddish, the Jewish lingua franca, which was not too far removed from German). In 1817 Alexander outlawed the blood libel which had brought fear and suffering to the Jews of Russia during the previous two centuries. But in 1822 he began the systematic expulsion of Jews from many Russian villages, particularly in Byelorussia—also known as White Russia—and since 1991, Belarus.

Alexander I's successor, Nicholas I, who came to the throne in 1825, introduced two years later the much-hated Cantonist System: the conscription of Jews between the ages of twelve and twenty-five for a twenty-five-year term of service in the army once they were eighteen. Those under eighteen were sent to special military schools. Christian communities had to provide seven recruits per 1,000 inhabitants, Jews ten. Heavy fines were imposed on any Jewish community that did not provide its quota of recruits, so much so that the communities employed *khapers* (catchers) to seize people. Many of the Jews who served fought in battle. In the Crimean War, 500 Jewish soldiers and sailors died in the defence of Sebastopol against the Anglo-French forces. As part of his anti-Jewish policies, Nicholas I expelled the Jews from the city of Kiev, a vibrant Jewish centre, and removed all Jews from within twenty miles of Russia's western border. His son Alexander II (1855–1881) pursued more liberal policies, abolishing the Cantonist System and extending the rights of professional association and practice to Jewish merchants, intellectuals, craftsmen, physicians and pharmacists. Jews took a leading part in railroad building, the development of coal mining, the textile industry, the sugar and tea trades, the export of timber and grain, and banking. Some Jews were among the wealthiest people in Russia, and took a lead in working for the rights of all Russian Jews.

Jews incurred the anger of Alexander II when they played a prominent part in the Polish insurrection of 1863. To keep the Jews clear of Polish national ferment, the Tsar had granted Polish Jews full civil emancipation, something unheard-of elsewhere in the Russian Empire. Jewish quarters were abolished. Jews could buy landed estates, and join the merchant and artisan guilds. A hated Russian tax on kosher meat was abolished. But many Jews still rallied to the cause of an independent Poland. Many Jews fought in, and even organized, partisan detachments: one such detachment was commanded by an Austrian Jew, Major Julian Rozenbach, who was killed in action. Several hundreds Jewish soldiers were among those executed by the Russians after they had been captured. One of them, Wladislaw Rawicz, had commanded the insurgents in the whole Podlasie region.

Through good times and bad, the Jewish population of Russia grew, from just over two million in 1850 to more than five million at the end of the nineteenth century. But with the start of systematic anti-Jewish violence—the pogroms—in 1881, following the assassination of Alexander II, Jews again became scapegoats and victims and turned increasingly to emigration. The 'May Laws' of 1882, one of the first pieces of legislation of Tsar Alexander III (1881-1894) prohibited Jews from living in villages, restricting them to towns and townlets—the latter, as I have written earlier, known to the Jews as 'shtetls'.

From 1887 the number of Jewish students in schools and universities was strictly limited. Many went abroad to study. In 1891 most Jews were expelled from Moscow. In the reign of the last Tsar, Nicholas II (1894–1917), Konstantin Pobedonostsev—Russian statesman and Supreme Prosecutor of the governing body of the Russian Orthodox Church, the Holy Synod—supported a project of the German Jewish philanthropist Baron Maurice de Hirsch for the emigration of three million Jews from Russia within twenty-five years: Hirsch was buying land for such settlement in Canada, Argentina and Palestine. Pobedonostsev is said to have expressed his hope, and that of many in the government, when he remarked: 'One-third of the Jews will convert, one-third will die, and one-third will flee the country.'

With the abdication of the Tsar in 1917, and the start of Russia's revolutionary era, all Jewish disabilities were abolished, as was the Pale of Settlement. Thousands of Jews who had converted to Christianity in previous decades, in order to avoid discrimination, returned to Judaism. But there were tens of thousands of descendants of converted Jews who no longer felt Jewish in any way, and saw no need to return to the fold. On Simeonovskaya Street in St Petersburg is a church in which a Jewish doctor, Asher Blank, was baptized, changing his first name to Alexander on his baptismal certificate. This otherwise obscure Jewish convert to Christianity—he became a medical doctor—was the grandfather of Lenin: his daughter married Lenin's father. Under Hitler's definition of a Jew—one Jewish grandparent—Lenin was a Jew.

No. 68

Dearest Auntie Fori,

In western Europe the nineteenth century brought a new dimension to Jewish history. With the spread of liberalism and democracy, the Jew was increasingly able to play a positive, and an equal, part in political, economic and even social life. As early as 1848 a Jew had entered the French Cabinet, and with each succeeding decade individual Jews reached ministerial office elsewhere in western Europe; in Holland in 1860, in Italy in 1870, in Britain in 1909 (the year after you were born, Auntie Fori), in Denmark in 1911. A baptized Jew, Benjamin Disraeli, had already, in 1868, become Prime Minister of Britain. For Englishmen brought up on caricature portraits of Jews, above all Shakespeare's Shylock and Dickens's Fagin, Disraeli might seem exotic, even alien, but he upheld and extended the British Empire in a way that even the most bigotted patriot could admire.

After the Congress of Berlin in 1878, Bismarck said of Disraeli, admiringly: 'The Jew, now there is man.' Disraeli's father came from a distinguished line of Italian Jews who had been forced to leave Spain in 1492: in Italy their surname was 'Israeli'. When his grandfather Isaac came to Britain from Ferrara in 1748 he took the somewhat aristocratic prefix D', becoming D'Israeli. His son Isaac married a Jewess from Italy, Maria Basevi, from an even more distinguished family. Their son Benjamin was born in Britain in 1804. At school he received instruction in Hebrew from a rabbi who visited the school once a week.

Isaac D'Israeli was a member of the Bevis Marks synagogue in London, but he quarrelled with the synagogue management when they wanted to make him Warden, an honour that would have involved him making a serious financial contribution to the community. Isaac D'Israeli never became a Christian, but a Christian friend persuaded him to have his children baptized, including Benjamin, who changed his name to Disraeli and wrote novels before rising through the parliamentary ranks to become Prime Minister. Had there been no baptism, under the rules then in force the young man could not have entered Parliament, let alone emerged as Prime Minister. To this day no other Jew, whether converted or not, has governed Britain, though no religious barrier exists any longer.

By 1870 almost all the universities of western Europe had opened their doors to Jewish students. The medical professions admitted Jewish doctors. Jewish lawyers and journalists worked on equal terms with their non-Jewish colleagues. Jews even found themselves granted the social honours and titles previously reserved for the old aristocracies. In 1885 a Jew received a peerage in Britain; this first Jewish Lord was Nathaniel Rothschild, a great-grandson of the Frankfurt founder of the dynasty, Mayer Amschel Rothschild.

Meanwhile, in Germany many Jews argued following the defeat of Napoleon in 1815 that their true future as German citizens lay in assimilation, and even in Christianity. Among the growing number of Jewish converts were to be found some of Germany's most famous Jews, including Heinrich Heine and Karl Marx (I will write to you about converts in a later letter). But in 1819 an outbreak of mob violence, the 'Hep! Hep!' riots, showed the depth of popular German anti-Semitism, which was never far from the surface of daily life, stimulated by hatred of successful Jews, and suspicion of assimilated Jews, whose patriotism to Germany was still doubted. Anti-Semitic remarks and writings came openly from philosophers and historians, politicians and pamphleteers.

As the nineteenth century brought increasing emancipation and progress to the Jews of western Europe, so they found themselves more and more involved in the sufferings of Jews elsewhere, both in Arab lands and under Tsarist oppression. And when, from 1881, the Russian pogroms grew in intensity, it was towards the havens of western Europe, as well as to the United States, that the Jews of Russia emigrated, bringing with them new skills, dynamic energies, restless ambition, poverty, and the challenge of different manners and traditions.

In western Europe this influx of 'aliens', as they were so often called, provoked new and more intense anti-Semitic activities. Intellectuals as well as thugs argued in public about the Jewish 'evil'. And it was the impact of this new anti-Semitism on the Viennese journalist Theodor Herzl which led him to campaign in favour of a Jewish State. Of Herzl—and his Zionism—I will write to you in a later letter.

No. 69

Dearest Auntie Fori,

By 1870 there were more than eight million Jews within the Russian borders. The assassination of Alexander II a decade later led to anti-Jewish pogroms and in severe restrictions on Jewish rights, including a *numerus clausus* (the Latin phrase means 'closed numbers') which drastically reduced the number of Jewish youngsters who could go to Russian schools—a feature of the Enlightenment which was thereby reversed. You yourself, Auntie Fori, were the victim of a numerus clausus when you wanted to go to university in Budapest in the 1920s.

In 1880—when each of my four grandparents was young, and living in the Jewish Pale of Settlement in western Russia—with the start of the widespread pogroms, the geographic unity and richness of Jewish–Yiddish life in Tsarist Russia began to dissolve. In thirty years, more than three million Jews left Russia. As many as one million went to Western Europe, including Britain. Of them, 50,000 went to Palestine, then ruled by the Ottoman Turks. Nearly 3,000,000 crossed the Atlantic to the United States, the country known to the Jewish–Yiddish world of Eastern Europe as the *Goldene Medina*—the 'Golden Realm'.

The pogroms in Russia led some Jews to join the revolutionary movements calling for the overthrow of the Tsar and his autocracy. Others turned to the Lovers of Zion movement, which advocated the settlement of Jews in Palestine. In 1892 the Russian-born Chaim Weizmann, then aged seventeen, left his Pripet Marsh shtetl, the village of Motol, for the journey that was to take him to Germany, Britain and Palestine: he became the first President of the State of Israel in 1948. Another Jew born under the rule of the Russian Tsar, David Ben-Gurion, left his birthplace, Plonsk, a small town forty miles north-west of Warsaw, in 1906, when he was twenty. Forty-two years later he became Israel's first Prime Minister.

The Jews were on the move, still with their Yiddish links and language. However much more and more Jews, under the influence of the Enlightenment and modernity, went to Russian, Polish, German and Hungarian language schools—and entered the life of the country they lived in speaking its language—Yiddish remained the largest single language spoken by Jews.

That Yiddish world was destroyed during the Second World War. Of the six million Jews who were murdered in the Holocaust, as many as four million came from Yiddish-speaking areas. Of course, Jews being Jews, indefatigable even when confronted by apparently impossible odds, they made repeated efforts after the Second World War to revive the Yiddish language, which was still spoken by hundreds of thousands of increasingly elderly immigrants. At some American universities, Yiddish classes and courses, begun with only slender expectations, flourished. One such course was also begun in London, and another in Oxford. Most recently, the Lithuanian capital, Vilnius—freed from Communist rule in 1991—has seen the teaching of Yiddish started up again—by a Yiddish teacher, Dovid Katz, who had formerly taught at Oxford. But the hundred-year-old New York Yiddish newspaper, *Forward,* founded in 1897, had to abandon its Yiddish version and go into an entirely English edition.

I'm checking on this! It seems there may be a Yiddish—and even, most recently, a Russian—version of *Forward* still being published in New York.

There are!

No. 70

Dearest Auntie Fori,

You spent several years in the United States, from 1961 to 1968, when Uncle Bijju (your husband now for almost seventy years) was Indian Ambassador there. Indeed, I stayed at your home in Washington once. Then, as now, the Jews of the United States formed the largest mass of Jews within a single sovereignty: nearly twice as many as in Israel today. American Jews represent every facet of Jewish experience, from the most rigorous orthodoxy to the most complete assimilation. They contain among their number speakers of both the Hebrew and Yiddish languages, both precious guardians of the Jewish heritage.

Within the United States, Jews can aspire to every area of work and achievement. In a land almost unique in the opportunities available to its citizens, they have risen to the top of every profession. Their mark on commerce is substantial. Their contribution to Hollywood is legend. They have been important beneficiaries of a tolerant society—not needing persecution to show the range of their talents.

These Jews of the United States have a long and varied history, going back more than three hundred years. Indeed, at the very moment when Oliver Cromwell was inviting the Jews back to Britain, the Dutch rulers of two American towns, New Amsterdam and Newport, Rhode Island, were welcoming Jewish victims of Catholic persecution from Brazil.

The Jews in Brazil had lived at first under tolerant Dutch rule. But with the conquest of Brazil by the Portuguese in 1654, they found themselves once more the victims of religious bigotry, even across the Atlantic, an ocean which they had crossed following their brutal expulsion from Spain and Portugal. Now they were wandering again in search of security. And it was the Dutch in North America who gave them haven.

Jews forcibly converted to Christianity by the Inquisition yet still remaining Jews in secret were called Marranos; they too had lived in Brazil since the Portuguese conquest in 1500. One of those who accompanied the first Portuguese settlers that year was Gaspar de Gama, a Jew from India—your India, Auntie Fori—who three years earlier had been captured by the Portuguese in India and forcibly baptised. Marranos in Brazil who were betrayed to the Inquisition were sent to Lisbon for trial. Isaac de Castro, who reached Brazil from Holland, was arrested for teaching Judaism to the Marranos, sent to Lisbon and burnt at the stake during a collective burning of 'heretics'—most of them former secret Jews—in 1647.

More tolerant Dutch rule in part of Brazil from 1624 enabled the secret Jews to emerge. By 1636 there was a synagogue in Recife, but no rabbi. By 1642 a second congregation had been set up, led by a distinguished rabbi from Amsterdam, Isaac Aboab de Fonseca, himself a former Marrano from Portugal. He thus became the first 'American' rabbi. But with the reconquest of Brazil by the Portuguese in 1654, Aboab returned to Amsterdam.

Beginning in 1654, the first twenty-three Jewish refugees in New Amsterdam constituted the cradle of American Jewry. But as so often happened in Jewish history, the haven was not always as welcoming as it seemed on the surface. The Director General of the New Netherlands, Peter Stuyvesant, protested to the Dutch West India Company about the settlement of a 'deceitful race' who practiced an 'abominable religion'. Above all, Stuyvesant feared that Jewish financial acumen—their worship at the 'feet of Mammon' as he put it—would capture the trade and limit the profits of the Dutch West India Company.

The Jews challenged Stuyvesant's hostility, writing direct to fellow-Jews in the Dutch West India Company. As a result, after a three-year struggle they were given formal permission to live, trade and travel throughout the Dutch dominions. But because of Stuyvesant's persistence, they were not allowed to build a synagogue, or to be elected to public office.

In 1664 the Dutch territories were taken over by Britain. New Amsterdam became New York. The earlier restrictions were lifted. Jewish merchants took a leading part in the Colony's overseas trade, helped by their links with Jewish traders in the Caribbean, Italy, the Near East, and even India.

Meanwhile, Jewish refugees from persecution in central Europe turned increasingly to the hazardous journey across the Atlantic. As British control spread, so too did Jewish settlement. After the Spaniards were driven from the southern state of Georgia in 1733, European Jews began to settle in the Georgian seaport of Savannah. Jews were among the German immigrants who made their homes in Pennsylvania. After the partition of Poland in 1772, and the first destruction of Polish independence, Polish Jews joined the trans-Atlantic exodus. Among these Polish Jews was Haym Salomon, a leading financier, and one of the pioneers of Wall Street.

American Jews played their part in the War of Independence. A group of forty Jewish soldiers who fought in a company of sixty men against the British in South Carolina were nicknamed 'the Jews' Company.' Salomon was arrested by the British as a spy, and then succeeded in spreading dissension among the German officers who were a part of the British force, and in persuading many of them to resign from the army.

The rulers of the newly independent United States looked with favour on their Jewish citizens. George Washington himself told the Jews of Newport, Rhode Island, in Biblical language, in 1790: 'May the children of the Stock of Abraham who dwell in this land continue to merit and enjoy the goodwill of the other inhabitants, in which every one shall sit in safety under his own vine and fig-tree, and there shall be none to make him afraid.'

In the war between Britain and the United States in 1812, Jews again fought to defend the Republic. Indeed it was a Jewish officer, Captain Mordecai Myers, who led the one successful charge against the British at Crysler's Farm on 11 November 1813, although the Americans—suffering from cold and hunger, and ravaged by disease—lost the battle, and with it failed to conquer Canada.

With every upheaval in Europe, more Jews came to the United States. The havoc following the Napoleonic wars in southern Germany brought several thousand German Jews across the Atlantic in the 1820s, and the first specifically German Jewish congregation was established in New York in 1825.

The failure of the European revolutions of 1848 led to yet another wave of Jewish immigration, raising the total New York Jewish population from some 6,000 in 1826 to more than 50,000 in 1850. Jews had taken a prominent part in the European revolutions. In Paris, in 1848, Captain Moise (his first name is not known) won praise for his capture of the police headquarters. In Hungary, in 1849, several thousand Jews fought in the ranks of those struggling for Hungarian independence. When the revolution was defeated, heavy fines were imposed on several Hungarian Jewish communities. In Italy, Rabbi Shmuel David Luzzato— known by his acronym of Shadal—was an active supporter of the Italian Risorgimento, which sought an end to all foreign rule in Italy. In 1860, on Garibaldi's 'March of the One Thousand', eleven of the marchers were Jews. In the Polish insurrection of 1863 at least a hundred Jews took part as armed volunteers. One of them, Rafal Kraushaar, was praised by his fellow-Polish revolutionaries as 'a learned Jew in poverty'. He was among the first to be wounded in the fighting.

Once in the United States, many Jews worked their way inland, helping to open up new trading posts and new territories to American control. As early as 1792, a Jew, Jacob Franks, had begun trading with the Indians in what is now Wisconsin. During more than a decade of trading he established a reputation for integrity, fair-dealing and hospitality, and in 1805 he built the first saw-mill in that remote region.

As the American frontier moved westward, the Jewish traders moved with it. The first synagogue services on the Mississippi were held at St Louis in 1836. In 1842 the Jewish Colonization Society of New York sent an emissary, Henry Meyer, to buy farming land near Chicago for a Jewish colony. When he did, a considerable number of Jews made the journey westwards, although only a few remained as farmers. The rest turned to the commercial prospects of Chicago itself, where the first Jewish congregation was organized in 1847.

In the 1850s Lazarus Straus opened a small general store in the interior of Georgia: his business later grew into the Macy's emporium in New York. In the same decade, not far from the banks of the Mississippi, Adam Gimbel, an itinerant peddler, laid the foundations of what was to become one of the largest department store empires in the United States. Gimbel, from Bavaria, had reached New Orleans in 1835. He opened his first store in Vincennes, Indiana in 1842. In the 1880s his sons Jacob and Isaac founded Gimbel Brothers in Milwaukee, Wisconsin. In 1894 their brothers Charles and Ellis opened a department store in Philadelphia. New York followed in 1910. By 1961 there were fifty-three Gimbel department stores throughout the United States.

Jewish Orthodoxy found itself challenged by less rigid forms of Jewish worship, which flourished. So also did Jewish self-help, characterized by the Hebrew Benevolent Society founded in 1822, the B'nai B'rith in 1843 and the Hebrew Orphan Asylum in 1859. The first Jewish-endowed hospital was founded in New York in 1852. In it, poor patients were given free treatment, and non-Jews were admitted equally with Jews.

It was in 1840 that the United States emerged as a defender of Jewish rights outside America. This was a turning point for American Jewry, who now found themselves in a position to help their fellow-Jews in both Europe and Asia. This first intervention came during the persecution and torture of Jews in Damascus, when the United States Consul in Egypt was instructed 'to display the active sympathy of the United States.' At the same time, a direct appeal was made to the Ottoman rulers in Constantinople to alleviate the condition of Syrian Jewry.

The United States' diplomatic intervention of 1840 was remarkable in one particular respect: no American citizen was involved as a victim. But in its message to Constantinople the American Government explained that the United States had a special right to intervene, because its own institutions made no distinction between citizens on the basis either of race or religion.

Further interventions followed in successive decades. Beginning in 1853, the State Department was active in putting pressure on the Swiss Government to abandon its discrimination against Jews. The pressure was continued for more than twenty years, when full civil rights were finally granted to all Jews by the new Swiss Constitution of 1874.

Meanwhile official American diplomatic initiatives were taken on behalf of Jews in Serbia, Morocco, Roumania, Russia and even Palestine.

With the coming of the Civil War, the Jews shared in the social divisions, and in the fighting. Like the society of which they were an integral part, their ranks were split. In Baltimore, in 1855, Rabbi Einhorn had preached against slavery. 'Break the bonds of oppression,' he declared, 'let the oppressed people go free, and tear every yoke.' But in New York, Rabbi Raphall preached that human bondage was a 'divine institution.'

In the Civil War itself the division was uneven: some 3,000 Jews volunteered for service in the Confederate army, 7,000 in the Northern (Union) army. More than five hundred of these Jewish soldiers were killed in the fighting. There were other hardships also for the Jews. In 1861 Rabbi Einhorn had been forced to flee to New York after threats to his safety, and an assault by a pro-slavery mob. Later, as the Confederate States began to face defeat, anti-Semitic accusations were made against the Secretary of State, Judah P. Benjamin, who was accused of treason and profiteering. In the North, General Grant had roused Jewish fears by his order expelling all Jewish cotton traders behind his line, an order which was, however, quickly revoked by President Lincoln himself.

Thus both George Washington and Abraham Lincoln had shown themselves well-disposed towards the Jews of the Republic.

No. 71

Dearest Auntie Fori,

Following the American Civil War, Jewish life in America prospered. Even those who had supported the Confederacy were able to recover their former positions. Raphael J. Moses, who had served as a major in the war, became chairman of the Georgia Judiciary Committee. He became famous throughout America in 1878, when he was campaigning (unsuccessfully as it happened) for Congress. His opponent having taunted him with being a Jew, Moses answered, in a letter which was to serve as a clarion call for American Jewry:

'I feel it an honour to be one of a race whom persecution cannot crush, whom prejudice has endeavoured in vain to pursue, who after nearly nineteen centuries of persecution still survive as a nation and assert their manhood and intelligence.

'Would you honour me? Call me Jew.'

By the time Raphael Moses wrote this letter, there were more than a quarter of a million Jews living in the United States. New congregations were being founded every year. Nor was Jewish education neglected— in 1864 a Hebrew Free School Association had been founded in New York. Fine synagogues were being built, while Reform Judaism, ever spreading, reached a peak of influence with the founding of the Hebrew Union College in Cincinnati in 1875. Charitable institutions prolifer- ated, sustained by fraternal orders such as the B'nai B'rith and the Sons of Benjamin.

In 1880 all this activity, all these large congregations, the settled life of a quarter-of-a-million Jews, was to change overnight. The cause was the start of the great exodus of Jews from Russia.

For the next thirty years a vast mass of Jews, despairing of any liberal policy in Russia, sought out the liberties of the United States. Between 1880 and 1915 more than two-and-a-half million Jews reached the United States, most of them from the Polish provinces of Russia, many from elsewhere in Russia, and some from Russia's equally intolerant neighbour, Roumania.

American Jewish life was transformed. The Russian immigrants' birthrate was high. Exclusively Jewish districts grew up in all major cities. In those districts Yiddish became the dominant language, while Yiddish newspapers and theatres flourished. As labour conditions wors- ened, Jewish workers took a lead in organizing strikes for better condi- tions and better wages: strikes which were stimulated by the Triangle Shirtwaist fire in New York in 1911, when 146 Italian and Jewish female workers lost their lives. By an extraordinary coincidence, the last sur- vivor of that fire, a woman of one hundred and five, died while I was writing this letter. The strikes culminated later in 1911 in a three-month strike of 60,000 cloakmakers, who demanded that their union should be recognized as the sole bargaining agent with their employers. The 'Pro- tocol of Permanent Peace' with which this strike was settled was worked out by Louis Brandeis, later the first Jew to be appointed to the United States Supreme Court.

By 1925 the Jewish population had risen to four-and-a-half million. There were Jewish communities in every State, from more than a million and a half in New York to a thousand in Arizona and five hundred in Nevada. These Jews had become a rigorous and integral part of American life, preserving their own traditions, drawn now so predominantly from Russia, but at the same time adapting with consummate success to the style and demands of their new world. In the First World War, a quarter-of-a-million Jews served in the American armed forces, and 3,500 were killed.

In 1925 the rush of immigration ended. The influx of eastern European Jewry, which in the previous forty years created a base of American Jewry as we now know it, was abruptly halted. Under the Quota Act of 1925, only 5,962 immigrants could be allowed in from Poland in any one year, a further 2,148 from Russia, and 749 from Roumania. At this rate, it would have taken more than 250 years to reach the numbers of the previous forty years. But by the time the door closed, American Jewry was already a powerful force, on the threshold of entering its most active period as a truly American, unpersecuted, and vibrant people.

No. 72

Dearest Auntie Fori,

It was in the nineteenth century that the Jewish situation in Muslim lands, which had reached its own golden age in Muslim Spain more than seven hundred years earlier, began to worsen. In 1839, in the eastern Persian town of Meshed, a Muslim Holy City—through which I travelled in 1958 on my way to you!—a fanatical Muslim mob, incited by a false rumour, burst into the Jewish Quarter, burnt the synagogue and destroyed the Scrolls of the Law. A massacre of Jews seemed imminent. It was, however, averted, but only by recourse to one of the curses of mediaeval Christianity, forcible conversion. This time the whole Jewish community was forced to accept the Muslim creed.

The converted Jews of Meshed did not give up their Judaism. Even while making the pilgrimage to Mecca and Medina, in order to give the appearance of true Muslims, they nevertheless were able, in secret, and at great risk, to maintain intact the basic tenets of Judaism.

The Meshed 'Jews' migrated in small groups to central Asia, to India, to Britain and to Palestine. But this was a slow and difficult process. It was only a century later, after the creation of the State of Israel in 1948, that the majority of Meshed's secret Jews were able to abandon Islam and to go as a restored Jewish community to the Jewish State. One such secret Jew was Mordechai Zar. Born in Meshed in 1914, he had managed to reach Palestine at the age of twenty-two, just before the Second World War. In 1969 he became deputy Speaker of the Israeli Parliament.

The forcible conversion to Islam of the Jews of Meshed was but a first taste of the bitter sufferings to come throughout the Muslim lands. In the very next year, 1840, the Jews of Damascus—then ruled by the Turkish Sultan—were falsely accused of murdering a Christian monk and his Muslim servant. According to the accusation—one which had been common in mediaeval Christendom—the Jews were said to have used the blood of their victims in the baking of the Passover bread. This 'blood libel', which the Nazis were to revive, roused the local Arab population to a fever of hatred. A Jewish barber, arrested at random, was tortured until he 'confessed'. The names he gave led to more arrests. Two of those arrested died under torture. A third converted to Islam to save his life. More Jews were arrested, including children, and the torture continued.

The fate of the Jews of Damascus led to worldwide protests. Not only Jews but non-Jews in London, Paris and New York demanded justice for those who had been falsely accused, and for the whole Jewish community of Damascus. The protests were successful. The Sultan agreed to drop the blood libel charges and all the surviving prisoners were released.

The Damascus Affair, as it was known at the time, was a grim reminder of how tolerance and acceptability could dissolve rapidly, transforming itself into fanatical hatred and persecution. Throughout the 1860s the Jews of Libya were subjected to punitive taxation. In 1864 as many as five hundred Jews were killed in the Moroccan cities of Marrakech and Fez. In 1869 a further eighteen Jews were killed in Tunis. On Jerba Island, an Arab mob looted Jewish homes and shops, burning synagogues and striking fear into the whole community.

A new life elsewhere was now sought. Many went to France, others to Ottoman-ruled Palestine. In November 1843 a British Christian missionary, then in Jerusalem, had recorded the arrival in the city of 150 Jews from Algiers, and he noted: 'There is now a large number of Jews here from the coast of Africa, who are about to form themselves into a separate congregation.' Other Jews from Muslim lands, including re-mote towns in Yemen and the Muslim-ruled central Asia principality of Bukhara, also managed to reach the greater tolerance of Jerusalem. There, they helped revive Jewish life in the Holy City, and by 1870 to bring about a Jewish majority in Jerusalem's amalgam of Jews, Muslims and Christians.

The continuing disabilities of Jews in Arab and Muslim lands con-trasted increasingly as the nineteenth century progressed, with the grow-ing emancipation of Jews elsewhere, especially in the United States and Western Europe. Jews elsewhere began to feel a renewed sympathy with the plight of their less fortunate brethren. Based in Paris, the Alliance Israélite Universelle founded in 1860 organized the co-operation of Jews all over the world to help those whose rights were incomplete, and to spread Jewish education to those lands where Judaism was under pres-sure or attack. The Alliance was particularly active in Morocco and its archive, carefully examined in the 1970s by the writer David Littman, a good friend of mine, shows just how restricted and at risk were the lives of the Jews of Muslim North Africa.

In 1875 twenty Jews were murdered by the Muslim mob at Demnat, in Morocco. The Jewish communities' newspapers in Europe, still indig-nant at the persecution of the Jews in Christian Russia, gave prominence to this new example of Muslim bigotry.

Life for the Jews under Islam continued to be a harsh one as the nineteenth century advanced. In Morocco Jews continued to be set upon in the streets and murdered, often in broad daylight. In Tripolitania in 1897 synagogues were plundered, and individual Jews murdered. Nor did the coming of the twentieth century bring an improvement. In 1903 forty Jews were murdered in the Moroccan town of Taza. In Yemen in 1905 old laws were revived, whereby Jews were forbidden to raise voices in front of Muslims, to build their houses higher than Muslims, or to engage in any traditional Muslim trade or occupation.

Even those Jews who managed to travel from North Africa, central Asia or Yemen to Palestine found that the local tolerance had begun to decline. Indeed, as early as 1891 the leading Muslims of Jerusalem had telegraphed to the Ottoman authorities in Constantinople, about Jews coming from Russia, 'praying that the entry of such Jews should be prohibited', and with this protest there began a general mood of suspicion of Jewish immigration, which was to turn even before the First World War to violence and killing.

No. 73

Dearest Auntie Fori,

The forcible conversion of the Jews of Meshed in 1839, and the blood-libel accusation in Damascus in 1840—both of which I wrote about in my last letter—reinforced the long-standing Jewish ideal that the Jews should have somewhere to go where they could be their own masters, free from the whims and tyrannies of those who had a hatred of the Jewish faith and culture. Among those who had protested against the Damascus tortures was a British Jew, Sir Moses Montefiore, who after a successful business career had come to devote his life—and he lived to the age a hundred—to the cause of his persecuted fellow-Jews wherever they might be.

On 11 June 1842 a grandson of the Duke of Marlborough, Colonel Charles Churchill—a member of the family of which Winston Churchill was to be the most famous member—wrote to Montefiore that in his view the Jews ought to promote the regeneration of Palestine and the eastern Mediterranean region. Were they to do so, the Colonel believed, they would 'end by obtaining the sovereignty of at least Palestine.'

Charles Churchill felt strongly that the Jews should resume what he described to Montefiore as their 'existence as a people'. Four years after his letter, a fellow-Englishman, George Gawler, published a pamphlet urging the establishment of Jewish colonies in Palestine as 'the most sober and sensible remedy for the miseries of Asiatic Turkey'. Gawler, who had fought in 1815 at the Battle of Waterloo and had later become the first British Governor of South Australia, published a second pamphlet in 1847, stressing the need for the emancipation of the Jews. Two years later he accompanied Montefiore to Palestine.

It was Gawler who pressed Montefiore to set up Jewish agricultural villages in Palestine. Nor were he and Charles Churchill alone among British non-Jews in advocating a Jewish return to the Land of Israel. In 1847 a British peer, Lord Lindsay, on his return from Palestine wrote in his account of his travels: 'The Jewish race, so wonderfully preserved, may yet have another stage of national existence opened to them, may once more obtain possession of their native land. . . . The soil of Palestine still enjoys her Sabbaths, and only waits for the return of her banished children, and the application of industry, commensurate with her agricultural capabilities, to burst once more into universal luxuriance, and be all that she ever was in the days of Solomon.'

The efforts of Sir Moses Montefiore to encourage Jewish villages in Palestine were rewarded with success in 1856, when he received an edict from the Turkish Sultan allowing the Jews to buy land there. Montefiore took immediate advantage of this, purchasing agricultural land both at Jaffa and Jerusalem. Later he extended his land purchases to the Galilee, Tiberias and Safed. George Gawler continued to support Montefiore's efforts, and remained a firm advocate of the right of the Jews to be masters in their own house.

On 10 August 1860 Gawler wrote in the *Jewish Chronicle:* 'I should be truly rejoiced to see in Palestine a strong guard of Jews established in flourishing agricultural settlements and ready to hold their own upon the mountains of Israel against all aggressors. I can wish for nothing more glorious in this life than to have my share in helping them to do so.'

In western Europe assimilation and participation seemed increasingly, as the nineteenth century advanced, to be the Jewish answer to prejudice and persecution. But one voice was raised against this apparent panacea by a German Jew, Rabbi Hirsch Kalischer, who denied that there was safety in assimilation. Kalischer argued that spiritual redemption could only come for the Jews after their physical return to the Land of Israel.

Pointing out that all European nations were struggling to achieve independence, Kalischer rebuked his fellow-Jews for failing to have a similar objective. In 1860 he supported a society set up that year in Frankfurt-on-Oder with the aim of promoting a return of the Jews to Jerusalem. The society published his book, *Derishat Ziyon* (Zion's Greetings), in which he urged as the essential first stage of Jewish redemption a return of the Jews to the land of their fathers, not to live on charity, but through manual work and agriculture; not dependent for security on the Turks, but defending themselves by their own Jewish guards, specially trained for the task.

No. 74

Dearest Auntie Fori,

The vision which Rabbi Kalischer expounded with such fervour—the return of the Jews to work the soil of Palestine—did not perish. Among the first to turn it into practical reality was a Jew from Strasbourg, Charles Netter, who was one of the founders of the Alliance Israélite Universelle, set up to provide work and training for Jews in distress anywhere in the world. Netter was attracted to the idea of extending the work of the Alliance to Palestine, and in 1867 he suggested helping Jews from Persia to escape their life of poverty and persecution by setting up agricultural settlements in Palestine. After a visit there in 1868 Netter wrote with enthusiasm of Palestine as a place where Jews could go in order to escape from hostility elsewhere, and be trained in agricultural pursuits.

Netter's enthusiasm had a practical result; in 1869 he went to Constantinople where, like Moses Montefiore before him, he obtained the approval of the Turkish Sultan for his scheme. A year later, in 1870, as a result of Netter's efforts, a Jewish agricultural school was founded near Jaffa. It was known as Mikveh Israel ('Israel's Hope', a phase taken from the Book of Jeremiah) and its 650 acres were an important step on the road to fulfilling Kalischer's vision of Jewish agricultural self-sufficiency. Kalischer himself thought of leaving Germany to settle there but, at the age of seventy-five, was unable to make the journey.

Elsewhere in Palestine Sir Moses Montefiore had continued his philanthropic and constructive work year by year, and in 1860 the Montefiore Houses, the first residential houses to be built outside Jerusalem's city walls, had been opened as a shelter for poor Jews. There, complete with their own windmill, they were able to be less dependent on outside charity. Four years later a girls' school was founded inside the Old City by a member of the Rothschild family, Evelina de Rothschild, and by 1870 there were 9,000 Jews in Jerusalem, amounting to half the city's population.

The idea of a return of the Jews to Palestine found a spiritual mentor in Rabbi Judah Alkalai, a Sephardi Jew. Born near Belgrade, Rabbi Alkalai had, like so many Jews in Europe, been deeply disturbed by the Damascus Affair, and argued that Jewish redemption could come in the wake of human action. Even the growing controversy between Orthodox and Reform Judaism could be resolved, Alkalai believed, through Jewish 'national' unity. But God would wait for man to take the first steps. Such was Alkalai's message, and in 1874 he himself, aged seventy-six, travelled to Jerusalem, where he remained until his death, a vigorous advocate of spoken Hebrew as the Jewish language of everyday life, and of the organization of world Jewry as a national force.

In the same year as Rabbi Alkalai's move to Jerusalem a British explorer, Charles Warren, published a book entitled, boldly, *The Land of Promise.* In his book he envisaged a Palestine with as many as fifteen million inhabitants. In order to reach this goal Warren advocated widespread Jewish rural settlement. In a second book, *Underground Jerusalem,* published a year later, Warren wrote that for the time being Palestine would have to be governed on behalf of the Jews by someone else, 'allowing the Jew gradually to find his way into its army, its law, and its diplomatic service, and gradually to superintend the farming operations, and work himself on the farms.' But after only twenty years of such activity, Warren believed, the Jewish principality 'might stand by itself, as a separate kingdom guaranteed by the Great Powers.'

The stage was set for a new revolution. Some Jews had managed to remain in their land for nearly two thousand years of struggle and isolation. They had not only survived, they had grown and flourished. They had preserved their links with the Diaspora, and been fortified by the Diaspora, numerically and spiritually.

Then in 1881, thousands of Russian Jews became victims of a

renewed upsurge of persecution and violence. Several hundred were killed. Others were beaten up in the streets, or had their homes and shops looted. This period of pogroms was paralleled by similar discrimination and unrest in Roumania. One result was a mass exodus to America and western Europe. But there was another result, much smaller in scale, but substantial in its impact on Jewish history.

'The Jews', a Roumanian law had laid down in the 1870s, 'do not have a country of their own, and therefore do not belong to any State'. And so it was that on 20 December 1881 the representatives of thirty-two local Roumanian Jewish groups met at the Roumanian town of Focsani, and for three days discussed the Jewish need to 'regain national honour'. It was essential, they argued, to re-awaken in Jewish hearts those 'holy feelings which the sheer weight of pain, want and poverty had put to sleep for thousands of years.' These Jews concluded that as a first step a hundred families should leave for Palestine in the following year. Thus was born the first positive step of what was to become a great movement of Jews from both Roumania and Russia, the *Hovevei Zion*—the Lovers of Zion movement—the precursor of the Zionist Movement, about which I will write to you soon.

It was in Russia, not Roumania, that the Lovers of Zion gained its most numerous adherents. But even from Russia the movement had small beginnings. By the end of 1881 two groups of families, in all no more than fourteen people, gathered in Kremenchug and Kharkov, and pledged themselves to leave for Palestine as soon as possible. Their leader, Zalman David Levontin, was only twenty-six years old. But, as he wrote to a friend before setting out in January 1882 to study the problems with which the immigrants would be faced: 'I have found it necessary to move from words to deeds.'

Even as he was travelling from Russia to Palestine, the young Levontin appealed for funds in the Jewish press in south Russia. His appeal was answered by one of his own uncles, an answer with sufficient magnanimity for members of the Lovers of Zion movement to purchase a plot of land on the coastal plain. They called the plot Rishon le-Zion ('The First in Zion'). In August 1882 the two groups set off from Russia to till the soil there. As they sailed across the Black Sea southwards towards

Constantinople the first group of Roumanian Jews, more than 200 people, were likewise embarking for land which they had purchased at Samarin, just south of Haifa.

These two boatloads of pioneers represented the first steps of the emerging Zionist imperative which was to have so powerful an impact on the life of world Jewry in the century to come.

No. 75

Dearest Auntie Fori,

A hundred years ago Zionism was a romantic dream, a hope shared by a small number of idealists. For despite two thousand years of prayer and 'longing' for the Land of Israel, it was not Palestine, but America, that beckoned the millions of Jews who lived in Russia and eastern Europe. For these millions, the overriding need was to escape from poverty and persecution. It was the streets of New York, not those of Jerusalem, which were said to be paved with gold—or at least with golden opportunity. But idealism has a force which defies statistics, and those few for whom the Land of Israel was a dream—the Lovers of Zion and the like-minded Bilu group inside Russia—clung to their dream with a tenacity which none could dislodge not even the German rabbi who declared with solemn emphasis: 'Frankfurt is my Jerusalem.'

The first Bilu and Lovers of Zion pioneers who went to Palestine in 1882, from both Roumania and Russia, numbered less than three hundred. But what they lacked in numbers they made up for in zeal. One of them, Zeev Dubnow, expressed this zeal in lyrical language when he declared, on the eve of his departure for Palestine:

> *The aim of our journey is rich in plans. We want to conquer Palestine and return to the Jews the political independence stolen from them two thousand years ago. And if it is willed, it is no dream. We must establish agricultural settlements, factories and industry. We must develop industry and put it into Jewish hands. And above all, we must give young people military training and provide them with weapons.*

> *Then will the glorious day come, as prophesied by Isaiah in his promise of the restoration of Israel. With their weapons in their hands, the Jews will declare that they are the masters of their ancient homeland.*

In July 1882 Zeev Dubnow and his group of Bilu pioneers reached Jaffa from Odessa. They were welcomed to Palestine by Charles Netter, who gave them work at the Mikveh Israel agricultural school, which he had founded twelve years earlier. Netter, however, died later that same year, and the Bilu pioneers found themselves without a patron, forced to hire themselves out as labourers, and lacking the resources to set up their own community. Nevertheless, by persevering, they did manage to purchase land in the Judaean foothills, and in December 1884, less than three years after their first dream of action, they began to build up their own settlement, Gederah.

Meanwhile, in Russia, the anti-Jewish violence continued, and in November 1884 the Lovers of Zion met in conference in Germany, at Kattowitz in Upper Silesia (now the Polish city of Katowice). Of the thirty-two delegates, twenty-two were from Russia, six from Germany, two from England, and one each from France and Roumania. The Russian-born writer and journalist Nahum Sokolow put forward specific proposals for industrial development in Palestine. A British Jew, Zerah Barnett, who had twice been to Palestine—first in 1871 to help found the Mea Shearim (Hundred Gates) quarter outside the walls of Jerusalem, and again in 1878 to help found the Jewish village of Petah Tikvah (Gateway of Hope)—spoke as the delegate from London of the hardships facing the settlers.

The Kattowitz Conference allocated money for two projects already existing in Palestine, for Petah Tikvah itself and for the newly established settlement of Yesud ha-Ma'alah, struggling to survive in the desolate swamplands of the Huleh marsh.

Zionism even in its early days was not an appeal only to the Jews of Europe, or a response to the evils of Russian anti-Semitism. In May 1885 it became a further imperative as a result of a savage anti-Jewish outbreak in the Moroccan town of Demnat. The Jewish press in Europe gave wide coverage to this pogrom within the Muslim world. Sir Moses Montefiore, who from his home in Britain, and on his many travels, had been vigilant in the cause of Jewish rights for more than fifty years, made a strong public protest.

Following the Demnat massacre, a young Russian Jewish boy, not yet eleven years old, wrote to his schoolteacher of the need to 'rescue our exiled, oppressed brethren who are scattered in all corners of the world and have no place to put up their tents.' For the sake of these Jews, the schoolboy added, it was essential 'to establish a place to which we can flee for help.' In America, he believed, although it was a land 'where enlightenment prevails,' the Jews would be 'beaten'. They would be beaten also in Africa, and particularly in Morocco. The letter ended:

'Let us carry our banner to Zion and return to our first mother upon whose knees we were born. For why should we look to the Kings of Europe for compassion that they should take pity upon us and give us a resting place? In vain! All have decided: The Jew must die but England will nevertheless have mercy upon us. In conclusion to Zion!—The Jews—to Zion! Let us go.'

The writer of this letter was Chaim Weizmann. His youthful anguish and aspirations foreshadowed a lifetime devoted to the cause of Zion, and to a Jewish homeland in Palestine. In 1917 he was at the centre of the evolution of Britain's Balfour Declaration, which offered the Jews a 'National Home' in Palestine. In the 1920s and 1930s he was the leading advocate, in Britain and on the world diplomatic stage, of Jewish statehood. In 1948 he became the first President of the State of Israel (a position held half a century later by his nephew Ezer Weizman).

No. 76

Dearest Auntie Fori,

This letter will be a short one: it is almost midnight, and I want to get something off to you in the post tomorrow morning. I hope you will like the special stamps I have chosen for it.

Sir Moses Montefiore, that strong supporter of Jewish causes and of Jewish settlement in Palestine, died in July 1885, three months before his 101st birthday. Since his first visit to Jerusalem in 1827 he had been regarded by persecuted Jews throughout the world as their 'champion'.

In the two decades following his death, steady progress was made in Palestine towards the realization of his ideal.

The pioneers who reached Palestine in the last quarter of the nineteenth century faced terrible hardships: disease, swampland, a primitive local agriculture, brigands, isolation and poverty. But two years before Montefiore's death, a thirty-six-year-old philanthropist, Baron Edmond de Rothschild, born in Paris, had been drawn actively into the task of giving financial help to all the struggling settlements in Palestine. He set about buying substantial acres of land throughout Palestine for Jewish agricultural development. Money was no object; the problem was to get men and women willing to till the often barren and inhospitable soil. 'The Baron', as he was known, did his best, financing the planting of vineyards, and setting up the wineries needed to turn grapes into tasty—and saleable—wine.

By 1890 more than 50,000 Russian-born Jews had settled in Palestine. In Jerusalem, the Jews numbered more than 25,000, out of a total population in the city of 40,000. The Arabs, a majority in the sparsely populated countryside, watched this influx of newcomers from Russia with alarm, and in June 1891 the leading Muslims of Jerusalem telegraphed to the Turkish authorities in Constantinople, asking that the entry of Jews 'should be prohibited'. One of the reasons that they gave was that as the European Jews were 'skilled in all different kinds of trades, the Muslims could not compete against them'.

As a result of this protest all Jewish immigration was forbidden by the Turks. But after a short time the ban was not enforced. That same year a Christian priest, Hugh Callan, asked in his *History of Jerusalem:* 'What is to be her future? Shall the Russians rule through their Greek Church (as they like to), or shall the Jews possess her? This at least is sure: while, the rest are strangers, the Jews are still the only patriots there.'

One of these 'patriots' was a strange, stern, visionary young man who had come from Russia with a single aim: to make Hebrew the daily language of the Jews of the Land of Israel. He was born Eliezer Yitzhak Perlman in 1858, in Lithuania. In 1880, while in Paris, he published his first article advocating that Hebrew rather than any 'foreign' language should be the language of instruction in the Jewish schools in Palestine—where some taught in French, others in German. For this article he used the pen-name was Ben-Yehuda—Son of Judah—which became the name by which he is best known. Settling in Palestine in 1881, he informed his wife that henceforth they would converse only in Hebrew. At first he faced fierce local Jewish hostility to his idea, but he persevered, determined to develop a truly 'modern' spoken Hebrew, and to make it the language of daily life.

Ben-Yehuda's story is a reflection of Zionism's early struggles, not only against the 'outer' world Turks and Arabs, but against the 'inner' world of counter-pressures in the life of the Jews themselves: from Orthodoxy, with its stress on the realm of worship, to assimilation. When his vision was mocked, Ben-Yehuda persevered. In 1890, with a like-minded group of friends, most of them Russian-born immigrants like himself, he founded a Language Association in Jerusalem which was a prelude to the emergence of Hebrew as the everyday language of the Jewish State. He also began work on a Hebrew dictionary: after his death in 1922 it was continued by his son Ehud, the seventeenth and final volume appearing in 1959—eleven years after the establishment of the State of Israel with Hebrew the language of daily life, as Ben-Yehuda had dreamed, and to which he had devoted his life's work.

No. 77

Dearest Auntie Fori,

In 1891 there was severe criticism of the activities of the Lovers of Zion from one of the most brilliant Russian Jewish writers of his time, Asher Ginsberg, who took the nom-de-plume of Ahad Ha-am (Hebrew for 'One of the People'). After his first visit to Palestine in 1889, he argued that the country must become more than a series of agricultural settlements. What was needed, he wrote, was a 'spiritual centre'. High moral standards were therefore essential. Work and modesty, the frugal and humble life, were an indispensable part of any return to Zion.

Ahad Ha-am wrote of the difficulties which he believed were being ignored by those who advocated mass Jewish emigration to Palestine: the barrenness of much of the soil, the hostility of the local Arabs who could not be expected to 'yield their place easily', and the power of the

Turkish authorities to obstruct settlement. Yet he wrote also of the old vision, infused with a new spiritual element. While emigration to America was still, he believed, the only way to provide the solution to the Jews' economic problem, there was in addition 'the need to create for ourselves a fixed centre through the settlement of a great mass of our people in one territory on an agricultural basis, so that both the Jews and their enemies may know that there is somewhere in the world a place where, though it may be too small to contain the whole people, a Jew can lift up his head like a man, can get his living from the soil by the sweat of his brow, and can create his own conditions of life in his own national spirit.'

If there was to be any hope of solving that aspect of the question, Ahad Ha-am added, 'it is to be found only in Palestine.'

In 1893 Ahad Ha-am travelled to Paris and London, in search of funds and pioneers. 'As for the English Jews', he wrote in his diary, 'and the hopes I had that they would do something for the Jewish cause—I blush for shame and will say nothing.' While in England, Ahad Ha-am was overcome with doubts about the Jewish fate. 'Is there really a bright future in store for us?' he wrote in his diary. 'Or is this the last ray of light?'

In September 1893—while Ahad Ha-am was in London, worrying about the Jewish future—a young Jewish journalist was on holiday near his home in Vienna. His name was Theodor Herzl, and he was arguing at a friend's house in favour of assimilation. 'Ever heard of Charles Darwin?' Herzl asked his friend. 'He puts forward the theory that the species adapts itself. We shall do the same. By living with the Gentiles, by imitating their ways, by being forced into the political and economic currents and influences which determine their lives, we shall become like them.' Once the Jews were like the Gentiles, Herzl believed, they would be free of anti-Semitism. 'Here is our Fatherland,' Herzl's friend concluded. Yes, Herzl agreed: 'In our Austrian Fatherland.'

Leaving his friend's house that evening, Herzl passed a group of hooligans who shouted at him, 'Pig-Jew'. Herzl was shaken. It was certainly not him personally they were abusing, he thought. 'They don't know me at all. It was my Jewish nose and my Jewish beard they were sneering at. So much for all my fine thoughts about time and liberalism solving this problem.'

Herzl's subsequent awakening was swift and dramatic. While in Paris to report the trial of Captain Alfred Dreyfus—falsely accused of passing secrets to Germany—he was shaken by the strength of French hostility, not merely towards one Jewish army officer, but towards all Jews. In June 1895 he went to see the wealthy if eccentric Jewish philanthropist, Baron Maurice de Hirsch, to unfold a new scheme: the need for all Jews, even the wealthy and the contented, to work towards the goal of a Jewish state in Palestine. 'I had no intention of becoming involved in Jewish affairs', Herzl told Hirsch, 'but the alarming growth of anti-Semitism has made me change my mind', and he went on: 'For nearly two thousand years we have been dispersed all over the world and without a State of our own. This has led to much tragedy and degradation. If we had our own political centre again we could begin to solve our problem.'

Hirsch listened politely, but replied sceptically to Herzl's vision: 'The rich Jews will give you nothing. They're hard. They harden their hearts to the sufferings of the poor.'

In September 1895, in Vienna, Karl Lueger's anti-Semitic Christian Social Party triumphed in the municipal elections. Watching this alarming rise of publicly proclaimed anti-Semitism, Herzl noted in his diary: 'The mood among the Jews is one of despair.' Herzl persevered, however, in his belief that he could persuade both Jews and Gentiles to support the idea of a Jewish State of Palestine. Some of those to whom Herzl had expounded his ideas considered him insane. One Jewish friend advised him to see a psychiatrist. But he found one distinguished and respected ally in Max Nordau, another Jewish newspaper correspondent living in Paris in the 1890s, who told him: 'If you are insane, we are insane together. Count on me!'

In February 1896 Herzl published his book *The Jewish State*. In it he declared bluntly: 'Palestine is our ever-memorable historic home. The very name of Palestine would attract our people with a force of marvellous potency.'

In his book Herzl pointed to the part played by anti-Semitism in bringing the Jews to their existing desperate situation. 'We have honestly

endeavoured,' he wrote, 'to merge ourselves in the social life of surrounding communities and to preserve only the faith of our fathers. We
are not permitted to do so. In vain we are loyal patriots . . .' And yet,
Herzl added, 'we are strong enough to form a State and, indeed, a model
State. We possess all human and material resources necessary for the purpose.'

Much of Herzl's book dealt with the specific details of immigration,
land-purchase, house-building, labour laws, manual work, commerce,
industry, education, welfare and social life in the new State. 'The Maccabeans will rise again,' he proclaimed in his closing sentences. 'We shall
live at last as free men on our own soil, and die peacefully in our own
homes.'

Following the publication of Herzl's book, a ferment of argument
and anticipation was unleashed among the Jews of Europe. Many were
totally opposed to the idea of a Jewish State, fearing that if it came into
being, those who did not like Jews would insist that they went there
('Jew, go to Palestine!' was a frequent cry among anti-Semites in Poland
in the 1930s). But Herzl was an optimist, and he persevered until, on the
morning of Sunday, 29 August 1897, the first Zionist Congress opened in
Basle. This was a turning point in modern Jewish history, which was to
make the twentieth century a turning point in modern Jewish history,
the moment from which so many of today's realities came: the State of
Israel, founded half a century later, and the Arab-Israel conflict, which
was still unresolved more than a hundred years after that first Zionist
Congress had launched the vision of Jewish sovereignty in the Holy
Land.

By air mail
Par avion

Part Three

THE TWENTIETH CENTURY

No. 78

Dearest Auntie Fori,

More than two hundred delegates gathered in Basle for the first Zionist Congress. More than a third of them (70 out of 197) had come from Russia. The scepticism of the Lovers of Zion had been overcome. Even Ahad Ha-am, although not a delegate, was present at the Congress, and agreed to be included in the official photograph. There were Jews from Palestine, Jews from Arab lands, Jews from Britain, and even a Jewish woman from New York, Rosa Sonnenschein, the editor of the *American Jewess.*

Herzl, as President of the Congress, spoke with fervour to an audience which, however sceptical some of them might have been in the months leading up to the meeting, was caught up in the future which he envisaged. 'We have met here,' he said, 'to lay the foundation stone of the house that will some day shelter the Jewish people.' It was not to be a secretive or chance affair. 'We have to aim,' he insisted, 'at securing legal, international guarantees for our work.' Nor would the delegates merely disperse once their deliberations were over. 'At this Congress,' Herzl declared, 'we bring to the Jewish people an organisation it did not possess before.'

Herzl's aim was to enable an outcast people to act with dignity. The Jews, he explained, were no longer to 'steal into the land of their future'. Instead they would negotiate their return openly, by legal agreement with the Great Powers. That agreement, Herzl insisted, 'must be based on rights and not on toleration'. Once the negotiations were successfully completed, he envisaged, not the existing pace of piecemeal settlement—'infiltration' he called it—but 'the settlement of Jewish masses on a large scale'.

Speaking after Herzl, Max Nordau, the Congress Vice-President, stressed Zionism's importance as a reaction to the material and moral misery of the Jews in the Diaspora. In Eastern Europe, North Africa and Asia, he said, where as many as nine-tenths of world Jewry were living, 'the misery of the Jews is to be understood literally. It is a daily distress of the body, anxious for every day that follows, a tortured fight for bare existence.' But there was also, Nordau said, the misery of the western Jew, the emancipated, half-assimilated Jew, a misery that took the form 'of perpetual injury to self-respect and honour, and of a brutal suppression of the striving for spiritual satisfaction'.

As soon as the Zionist Congress was over, Herzl and his newly-formed Zionist Organisation set about the raising of funds, negotiating with the Great Powers, and seeking wider Jewish support. Herzl was elated by what had been achieved. On 3 September 1897, on his return to Vienna, he wrote in his diary:

> Were I to sum up the Basle Congress in a word—which I shall guard against pronouncing publicly—it would be this: At Basle I founded the Jewish State.
> If I said this out loud today, I would be answered by universal laughter. Perhaps in five years, and certainly in fifty, everyone will know it.
> The foundation of a State lies in the will of a people for a State. . . .

Those who shared this 'will' strove to follow Herzl's example. After his death in 1904, the leadership and focus of Zionism moved first to Germany, and then to Britain. It was in Britain that, in November 1917, Chaim Weizmann was able to persuade a harassed war-time Government to issue the Balfour Declaration, in which the British Government stated that it viewed with favour 'the establishment of a Jewish National Home' in Palestine, once Turkey had been defeated, and Turkish rule over Palestine ended.

Commanded by General Allenby, British forces—including Australian and Indian troops—advancing from Egypt, were at that very moment preparing to drive the Turks from Jerusalem.

While Zionist Jews dreamed of Palestine and—after the defeat of the Turks and the establishment by Britain of the Jewish National Home—

went there and worked for the creation of a Jewish State, other Jews, in their millions, were content to be part of the primarily Christian societies in which they lived, looking for countries other than Palestine where they could fulfil their personal ambitions and potential. Many left the restrictive confines of the Russian Empire for western Europe and the United States, where they flourished. Lithuanian-born Sidney Hillman was one of the leaders of a labour union strike in Chicago in 1910 which closed down the city's clothing factories. That same year St Petersburg–born Lev Samoylovich Rosenberg—who changed his name to Leon Bakst—took Paris by storm with his theatrical designs for the Ballets Russes. Warsaw-born Casimir Funk, while doing research in London in 1912, discovered vitamins.

When the First World War broke out in August 1914, Zionists dreamed of the defeat or the winning over of Turkey and the achievement of nationhood in Palestine. Other Jews prepared to serve whatever country they lived in, even if they would be fighting against countries which also had large—and equally patriotic—Jewish populations.

No. 79

Dearest Auntie Fori,

The First World War was a remarkable one in the Jewish story. Jews fought in all the warring armies, often facing each other, and killing each other, across the trench lines. Jewish soldiers in the German, Austro-Hungarian, Turkish and Bulgarian armies (the Central Powers) faced Jewish soldiers in the British, British Commonwealth, French, Belgian, Italian, Serb, Greek, Roumanian, Russian and in due course American armies (the Entente Powers, also known as the Allied and Associated Powers). In many ways the First World War was the climax of Jewish patriotic endeavour on behalf of the nations among which Jews lived.

The philosopher Ludwig Wittgenstein fought as an Austro-Hungarian officer on the Russian front. René Cassin, who was later to be the first president—with Eleanor Roosevelt—of the United Nations Commission on Human Rights—fought in the French army and was badly wounded, winning the Médaille Militaire. Ludwik Hirszfeld, while serving as a German army doctor in Serbia, discovered the bacteria of paratyphoid C (now known as *Salmonella hirszfeldi*). In 1917 Fernand Widal, professor of pathology at the University of Paris since 1900, discovered a vaccine against typhoid that enormously reduced the risk of typhoid contagion. A young British officer, Leslie Howard—the grand-son of a Hungarian rabbi—was badly wounded on the Western Front in 1917. He later became a leading actor of stage and screen, starring in 1939 in *Gone With the Wind,* and was killed in the Second World War when the passenger plane in which he was flying from Lisbon to London was shot down by the Germans.

Among the German-Jewish war dead in the First World War was the astronomer Karl Schwarzchild, who pioneered the study of 'black holes' in the stellar system: he died from an illness contracted while he was on active service on the Russian front.

Some Jews held high military rank. Louis Bernheim, a Belgian Staff Officer, commanded the troops that held up the German advance to Antwerp in 1914, long enough to enable Britain and France to protect the Channel ports. Although later badly wounded, he rose to the rank of General while on active service, and in 1918 commanded three Belgian divisions in the liberation of Flanders.

The highest ranking Jewish officer in the First World War was Lieutenant-General Sir John Monash—the first military commander in more than two hundred years to be knighted by a British monarch on the battlefield. Monash was an Australian who in civilian life had been an engineer, specializing in reinforced concrete construction. In 1915 he commanded one of the Australian brigades that landed on the Gallipoli Peninsula. In 1918, when in command of the Australian and New Zealand troops in France, he was a pioneer in the use of tanks—which had been prepared for their very first use in combat by a British Jew, Colonel Alfred Stern.

The first helicopter capable of flight was developed by a Jew, Budapest-born (as you, Auntie Fori) Theodore von Karman, a member of the Aviation Corps of the Austro-Hungarian forces. In Italy, the Jewish mathematician Vito Volterra helped design and build airships that were used by the Entente Powers in the war: he was the first to use helium rather than hydrogen as the far safer fuel.

In Germany, the chemist and later Nobel Prize winner Fritz Haber took a leading part in the development of mustard gas as a weapon of war: it was first used in battle by the German army on 22 April 1915 (the British used their own gas on the battlefield soon afterwards). Another German Jew, Walther Rathenau—who was assassinated in 1922 by German anti-Semites—ensured that Germany had the raw materials needed to maintain its war-making powers.

Bravery on the battlefield saw five Jewish winners of the Victoria Cross in the British army. The first to receive this highest of awards for bravery was Lieutenant Frank Alexander De Pass—a Londoner and a Sephardi—who was killed in action in 1915 leading his Indian troops on the Western Front. He was awarded the Victoria Cross for an action on the day before he was killed, rescuing under heavy fire an Indian soldier who was lying wounded in open ground. The largest number of Jews killed in action in the First World War were Russian Jews, 100,000 in all, one-seventh of all who served. More than 40,000 Jews were killed fighting in the Austro-Hungarian forces. The next largest Jewish death toll was in the German army, 12,000 in all. The Nazis were later to erase their names from the war memorials in a dozen German cities. In the French army, 9,500 Jews gave their lives in the military struggle.

In the British army, 8,600 Jews were killed. On a recent visit to the Western Front, I paid my respects (laying a small stone, as is the Jewish custom, on the tombstone) to several of those whose distinctive Star of David is carved on their tombstones in the Commonwealth War Graves cemeteries. Among the Jewish war dead in the British army was the painter and poet Isaac Rosenberg, whose 'Trench Poems' were a powerful evocation of the horrors of war. He was killed in action seven months before the war ended.

As I wrote in one of my earlier letters, about American Jewry, a quarter-of-a-million Jews served in the American armed forces, of whom 3,500 were killed in action. Among the other Jewish war dead were a thousand Jews who fought in the Turkish army, and a thousand in the Bulgarian army (both allies of Germany). Roumanian Jews lost 900 soldiers in action and Serbian Jews 250, fighting for the Entente Powers. Fighting for two other Entente countries, 500 Jews were killed in the Italian army and 125 in the Belgian army. Among the Australian soldiers killed in action, 300 were Jews. Among the Australian soldiers who survived was Private Leonard Keysor, who won the Victoria Cross on the Gallipoli Peninsula in 1915.

Harvey Sarner, in his book *The Jews of Gallipoli,* recounts the story of how Private Keysor had already established a reputation as a 'bomb thrower', hurling a simple type of hand grenade—made from jam tins, and filled with explosives and metal scraps, and dangerous to handle as well as to receive. Private Keysor 'was at his best', writes Sarner, 'when picking up and returning the bombs thrown by the Turks'. Their response to his action was to cut the fuse on their bombs, thus reducing the time before they exploded. Knowing he could not wait for the bombs with such short fuses to actually fall into his trench, Keysor caught them in the air, like cricket balls, and tossed them back to the Turks, astonishing his comrades in the process. In the course of this catching and bomb throwing he was twice wounded and ordered to go to the hospital, but he refused to leave the trench. When another company suffered the loss of all its bomb throwers, he volunteered to throw bombs for them, catching and throwing bombs for an incredible fifty hours. His efforts were effective in maintaining control over a section of trenches when it was imperative they be held.

Jews who were subjects of King George V fought in many different British Imperial and Commonwealth armies: with the Australians, Canadians, New Zealanders, South Africans, British West Indians (including Jamaicans), and Indians; in every branch of warfare—including the Machine Gun Corps, the Rifle Brigade, the Royal Air Force, the Royal Navy, the Royal Field Artillery, the Cavalry, the Tank Corps, the Guards—and on all the battlefronts, on land, at sea and in the air.

One group of Jews fought as a specifically Jewish unit: the Zion Mule Corps, responsible for taking munitions and supplies from the beaches to the front-line trenches at Gallipoli. These Jews were volunteers, from Egypt: many of them had been expelled from Palestine by the Turks on the outbreak of war. A citation for a Distinguished Conduct Medal tells of how one member of the Zion Mule Corps, Corporal Grouchkowsky, 'although wounded in both arms . . . delivered the ammunition'.

A recent visitor to the Gallipoli Peninsula, the First World War historian Lyn MacDonald, recently sent me a photograph she took of a gravestone in one of the forty Commonwealth cemeteries on the Peninsula. The inscription, headed by a Star of David, reads: 'Believed to be buried in this cemetery, Jacob Rotman, Zion Mule Corps, 3 June 1915. Their glory shall not be blotted out.' According to the *British Jewry Book of Honour,* published in 1922, Rotman was a private soldier, recruited in Cairo. He might well have been one of the thousands of Jews expelled from Palestine by the Turks. Ironically, his grave is on Turkish soil.

In 1918 the British government authorized the setting up of three battalions of Royal Fusiliers—some five thousand men in all—of entirely Jewish soldiers, to fight against the Turks in Palestine. One of the men recruiting for the Fusiliers in the United States was David Ben-Gurion, later Israel's first Prime Minister. Among those who joined in America was Nehemia Rubichov, whose son Yitzhak, born on Jerusalem in 1922, was twice Prime Minister of Israel: as a young man he took the Hebrew surname Rabin.

The man who helped set up both the Zion Mule Corps and the Jewish battalions of the Royal Fusiliers, Russian-born Vladimir Jabotinsky—later a pioneer of Jewish self-defence in Palestine, and the founder of the Revisionist Zionist movement—wrote: 'The Jewish people may be proud of its five hundred mule drivers and of its five thousand fusiliers—all of them—from Whitechapel, from Tel Aviv, New York, Montreal, Buenos Aires and Alexandria. They came from four continents, and one of them from the fifth, Australia. And they did their duty conscientiously and nobly, for the Jewish future.'

It was only when the Russian Bolsheviks, on the eve of their revolution, threatened to pull Russia out of the war that the British Government took immediate action. Desperate to find a means of encouraging Russian Jews to call on their government to remain at war, and to fight it more vigorously, Britain finally issued a declaration—which Zionist Jews had been urging for more than two years—promising the Jews a National Home in Palestine if the Entente Powers were victorious. An Entente victory would mean the defeat of Turkey, enabling Britain—should she conquer Palestine—to establish Jewish autonomous institutions. Turkish rule would give way to British rule, and the Zionist cause would have a patron with power at its elbow and territory at its disposal.

The British pledge, known to history as the Balfour Declaration—after the Foreign Secretary, A. J. Balfour, who signed it—thrilled Zionist Jews throughout the world. But it came too late to influence the Jews of Russia in favour of a greater Russian war effort. Even while, as part of the circumstances of the declaration, Britain was arranging to send leading Zionists, among them Chaim Weizmann himself, to Russia, by sea, to rally support for the war, the Bolshevik revolution took place, and Lenin, as virtually his very first act, announced the withdrawal of Russia from all hostilities.

Ironically, the British army reached Jerusalem at that very moment. Had Russia still been at war, the Jews of Russia would have seen that a Jewish National Home in Palestine was not a mere hope, but a potential reality.

Thus the prospect of a Jewish State—however far distant that might be—was born of a British wartime pledge, when the Jews were needed.

No. 80

Dearest Auntie Fori,

No account of the Jews in modern times can avoid the vexed question of Jews who convert to Christianity—converted 'out', as Jews describe it. One of the most influential First World War poets, Siegfried Sassoon, was a Christian—a grandson of David Sassoon, a distinguished Indian Jew, born in Bombay in 1832, who had emigrated from India to make a new life in Britain (David Sassoon's grandfather Sheikh Sassoon ben Salah had been the President of the Jewish community in Baghdad for forty years, and Chief Treasurer of the Ottoman Pashas of Baghdad). Raised as an Anglican, Siegfried Sassoon converted to Roman Catholicism in his early seventies.

Almost two hundred years ago, Moses Schneersohn, the son of the first Lubavicher Rebbe—the charismatic leader of an ultra-Orthodox Hasidic sect—converted to Christianity, as did the daughters of the Jewish philosopher Moses Mendelssohn: hence Moses Mendelssohn's grandson, the composer Felix Mendelssohn-Bartholdy, was a Christian. Despite this, Felix Mendelssohn appears in one of the basic works of 'Jewish' reference, the *Dictionary of Jewish Biography* edited by Geoffrey Wigoder.

Jews will always debate whether a convert, or a Christian of Jewish descent, is or is not a Jew. According to Jewish religious law a Jew is defined as anyone with a Jewish-born mother (as in Felix Mendelssohn's case).

In the nineteenth century—as I wrote to you—Benjamin Disraeli's father converted to Christianity—as did the composer Gustav Mahler, whose works Hitler was to ban as 'degenerate Jewish music', and the great-great-grandfather of Raoul Wallenberg, who, as a Swedish diplomat, was to issue protective documents to several thousand Jewish families in Budapest in 1944. The German poet Heinrich Heine was a convert, as were the grandparents of the United States Presidential candidate Barry Goldwater (who sought election in 1964—when you and Uncle Bijju were in Washington).

Among Jews who converted to Christianity was Theodor Herzl's son. Another convert was the Polish born Jean-Marie Lustiger, who is today the Cardinal Archbishop of Paris. Anton Zolli, the Chief Rabbi of Rome in 1945, converted to Christianity after the war.

In Britain, a number of politicians who are thought of, by some, as Jewish, are converts who have no wish to return to their Jewish roots. One, Edwina Currie, was an active Conservative politician in Margaret Thatcher's era. Another, Nigel Lawson, held Cabinet office in the Thatcher government. The Bishop of Birmingham in the Thatcher era, the Right Reverend Hugh Montefiore, is a member of a prominent Jewish family, the Sebag-Montefiores, and a kinsman of the nineteenth-century Jewish philanthropist Sir Moses Montefiore, about whom I have written to you.

Jews often take pride in the 'Jewishness' of individuals who came to regard themselves as Christian, and felt no sense of Jewishness. The author of *Doctor Zhivago,* Boris Pasternak, was a convert—and also a Nobel Prize winner. He appears in the *Encyclopaedia Judaica* list of Jewish Nobel Prize winners.

The most controversial Jew of recent times, Karl Marx, whose works were the inspiration for great social upheavals, revolution and—in a perverted form—tyranny, did not consider himself a Jew. His father, Heinrich Marx, the son of a rabbi in Germany, was a convert to Christianity whose original name was Hirschel Halevy Marx. His mother was descended from a Dutch rabbi of the seventeenth century. When Karl Marx was six years old his father became a Lutheran. The young Karl went to a Lutheran school, but evolved into a fierce atheist, denouncing all religion as 'the opium of the masses'. As to the Jews, Marx was distinctly hostile, asking in one of his writings: 'What is the world cult of the Jew? Huckstering. What is his world God? Money.'

As Jews say when confronted with unpleasantness, *Oy Vey!*—'Oh dear!' But Marx too appears in both Wigoder's *Dictionary of Jewish Biography* and Israel Levine's *Faithful Rebels,* subtitled 'A Study in Jewish Speculative Thought'.

Emancipation brought to Western European Jewry, for the first time in more than a thousand years, the myriad opportunities of equal rights and full citizenship. It made the Jews feel less alien, encouraging their participation, and even assimilation, into the societies of the West. Many Jewish families abandoned their Jewish identity and, by intermarriage, brought their Jewish heritage to an end. Others turned to a secular lifestyle and beliefs, or converted to Christianity.

As well as Jewish converts to Christianity, who may not consider themselves or still be considered Jewish, there are many people who have one Jewish parent, who may move towards Judaism, or have some residual Jewish feelings. Among such 'half-Jews' is the actress Gwyneth Paltrow, who is descended on her father's side from a dynasty of Russian rabbis. Another 'half-Jew', General Wesley Clark, who commanded the NATO forces in Yugoslavia last year, only discovered his half-Jewish status late in his life, and warmly embraced it. Today, in the United States, where almost half of American Jews marry non-Jews, the number of half-Jews under the age of eleven already exceeds the number of full Jews under that age. This poses many problems for Jewish demography in the twenty-first century.

No. 81

Dearest Auntie Fori,

A dark and terrible era began in 1933, when Hitler came to power in Germany. From the first days of his Nazi regime, Jews were singled out for isolation, harassment and persecution. Between 30 January 1933, the day he became Chancellor, and 1 September 1939, the day he launched his armies against Poland, it was upon the Jews of Germany that the brunt of his hatred fell.

Jews had lived in Germany for 1,600 years. In the First World War 12,000 had been killed fighting for the Fatherland. Hitler's hatred transcended any such patriotism. German schoolchildren were taught that 'the Jew' was a pest, the carrier of disease, a corrupter of 'pure' German youth. Adults were told that Jews must be removed from Germany in order to preserve the 'Aryan race', a biological fiction skilfully promoted by strident propagandists, which stirred up the most vicious racism. The fate of the Jews was not left only to popular prejudice or mob violence. Two main instruments of Nazi power, the Gestapo (secret police) and SS (black-uniformed 'Protection Squads') could arrest without warrant, imprison without trial, torture without restraint, and murder without repercussion.

Half of Germany's 500,000 Jews were able to find refuge outside Germany before the outbreak of war. But as soon as war came the German Government sealed its borders. Many of those who had found refuge elsewhere had found it in countries such as France, Belgium and Holland which were later overrun by Germany. These refugees then became captives. Anne Frank and her family were German refugees from Frankfurt who found sanctuary in Holland. Later, after being betrayed while in hiding, they were deported to Auschwitz, the concentration camp where as many as a million Jews were murdered.

The six years during which Hitler consolidated his power, before the outbreak of war, saw the imposition of restrictions on every aspect of Jewish participation in German life. These Jews were Germans, yet they were systematically removed from German schools, colleges and universities, and not allowed to practise in their professions. Jewish members of associations for the deaf, the blind and the disabled were thrown out of those associations. Under the Nuremberg Laws of 1935 Jews were relegated to second-class citizenship—they became the Untouchables of Germany. The definition of a Jew was anyone with even a single Jewish grandparent. Hitler himself signed the Nuremberg Laws, which put the full power of his totalitarian police state behind racial isolation and segregation, including discrimination against those who might be even 'one-quarter' Jewish.

In the concentration camps in which tens of thousands of Communists, Socialists, trade unionists, liberals and all critics and opponents of the regime were incarcerated, and many killed, several hundred Jews had been murdered in the first five years of Nazi rule over Germany. In March 1938 Hitler annexed Austria and a further 183,000 Jews came under German rule. They were at once subjected to all the cruel rigours of Nazism.

In November 1938, in a single night of terror—known as Kristallnacht, the 'Night of Broken Glass'—more than ninety Jews were killed in the streets, and several hundred synagogues set on fire. That night, thousands of Jewish shop windows were smashed (hence the name 'broken glass') and Jewish apartments ransacked in virtually every town in Germany and Austria. In the months that followed, as many as five hundred Jews were killed as a result of ill-treatment and sadism in the camps inside Germany to which they had been deported.

One result of the Kristallnacht was an intense revulsion, especially in Britain, against the anti-Jewish campaigns of the Nazi regime. The British government, which had already taken in 40,000 German and Austrian Jews, immediately offered to take in 10,000 Jewish children. Known as the Kinder (and their journey to safety by train and boat as the Kindertransport), they were brought to Britain from Germany and Austria, first to reception centres, and then to non-Jewish families who looked after them: Margaret Thatcher's parents were among several thousand families who took in a Jewish child. Almost all the Kinder last saw their own parents when they waved goodbye to them at railway stations throughout Hitler's Reich. In 1943 most of those parents were deported eastward by the Nazis and murdered.

No. 82

Dearest Auntie Fori,

In July 1936, while Hitler was consolidating his power in Germany, General Franco made his—ultimately successful—bid to defeat the Spanish Republic and impose a Fascist regime on Spain. Tens of thousands of volunteers hurried from abroad to support the Spanish Republic. More than two thousand of these were Jews, for whom the struggle in Spain was the first moment at which they could participate on the battlefield in the struggle against the forces of reaction and repression. Many were Jewish Communists, for whom the evils of Nazism and Fascism had to be fought, some under Moscow's direct command, others as part of the International Brigade.

One of the early organizers of American volunteers in New York was a Jew, Edward Bender. In Spain, among the members of the amateur vaudeville troupe that entertained the troops was Bernard Abramofsky—who sang his own songs, in both English and Yiddish. Not long after his cousin Harold Melofsky, a fellow-entertainer, was killed in action, Abramofsky was shot for desertion.

One of the most powerful books about the Spanish Civil War, *Spanish Testament,* was written by the Hungarian-born Arthur Koestler, a Jewish journalist who was at one point imprisoned by Franco; indeed, he was sentenced to death as a spy, but saved by the international outcry on his behalf. Churchill was among those who interceded for him. He was born in Budapest in 1905—only three years before you, Auntie Fori—and his book *Darkness at Noon,* written in 1941—a devastating critique of the Soviet purges of the 1930s—was an enormous influence on my generation.

Many of the Jews who fought in Spain were later leaders of post-war Communist regimes in eastern Europe. One of them, Budapest-born Erno Singer, who took the surname Gero, had been active in Bela Kun's

Communist revolution in 1919, and was First Secretary of the Hungarian Communist Party at the time of the anti-Communist uprising of 1956, which he tried to stop. It was he who called in the Soviet tanks which crushed the uprising.

The chief military adviser to the Republican army was a Jew, the Soviet general Grigori Shtern (who took the *nom de guerre* Grigorevich). Like his fellow Soviet volunteers he was sent to Spain by Stalin. In 1939 he commanded the Soviet forces in the Far Eastern battles with Japan, where he was awarded the coveted decoration Hero of the Soviet Union. Another Soviet general, who commanded the Republican Air Force in Spain, was Jacob Smushkevich, the son of a poor Lithuanian-Jewish tailor: three years later he returned to the Soviet Union to command the Red Air Force. On the eve of the German invasion of the Soviet Union in 1941, Smushkevich was Chief of the Air Defences of the Soviet Union. Within a short while, he, like Shtern, fell foul of Stalin. Both were executed. The *Ukrainian Encyclopaedia* gives the same day—28 October 1941—for their respective 'tragic' deaths—not explaining the nature of their demise.

A third Russian Jewish general who fought in Spain was Lazar Stern, who commanded the 11th International Brigade, in which the number of Jews was largest. Among the countries they came from were France, Austria, Poland and Hungary. Stern fought under the name Emile Kleber, leading the volunteer forces that helped prevent Franco from capturing Madrid in November 1936, and fighting with distinction at the battles of Jarama and Guadalajara in 1937. Accused of 'Internationalism' by the Soviet secret police, he was suddenly recalled from Spain and disappeared, one of the millions of victims of Stalin's purges.

At the battle of Guadalajara, General Stern had shared the battle honours with another Jewish commander, Hungarian-born Bela Frankel, who fought under the name General Lukacs. He had committed himself to the Soviet Union at the time of the Bolshevik Revolution, and a decade before the Spanish Civil War had been appointed deputy director of the Theatre of the Revolution in Moscow. Later he became head of the literary activities organization of the Red Army and the Red Navy. Commanding the 12th International Brigade, Lukacs led German anti-Nazi volunteers, Italian anti-Fascists, Franco-Belgian and Polish volunteers into battle: the largest single cohesive group in his Brigade were Jews. He was killed in action in Spain in 1937.

I must mention one more Soviet Jewish general, Simon Krivoshein, the son of a watchmaker. In 1931 he joined one of the very first Soviet mechanized formations. Stalin sent him to Spain with twenty-nine other Red Army officers, in command of fifty tanks. It was they who took a major part in the defeat of Franco's forces at the battle of Guadalajara in March 1937. Krivoshein later commanded a mechanized corps against the Germans in 1941, and was leading an army corps in the battle for Berlin in 1945.

British and American Jews—though not holding general's rank— volunteered for Spain and fought on all the war fronts. Several of the physicians sent to the republican side from the United States, by the American Medical Bureau to Aid Spanish Democracy, were Jews. Among them were Dr Irving Busch and Dr Edward Barsky, a surgeon at the Beth Israel Hospital in New York who put together a team that included four other doctors, eight nurses and two ambulance drivers.

Shortly before writing this letter, I was lecturing in a small town just north of New York. After my talk, I met a retired lawyer, Jay Greenfield, whose brother Hy had been mortally wounded during the fighting in Spain. Hy Greenfield had been tended by Dr Barsky. Jay Greenfield was five years old when his brother was killed—earlier this year he made a pilgrimage to Spain to his brother's grave in the small village cemetery of Segura.

No. 83

Dearest Auntie Fori,

This is the hardest letter to write. Between 1939 and 1945, as a result of Hitler's racist venom—I cannot bring myself to call it an ideology— six million Jews were murdered, and Jewish life was destroyed over much of Europe. Culture, humanity and the ongoing pulse of generations were all blotted out in conditions of extreme cruelty and barbarism. Like the word Holocaust, the Yiddish word *churban*—the destruction—and the Hebrew word *sho'ah*—the catastrophe—each try to encapsulate what was done. But no single word, or volumes of words, can fully express the horror.

It is not only a question of the name of this period of Jewish history. It is also a question of imagination. Can anyone who did not witness the event really understand its enormity? Will the depth of the evil perpetrated on the Jews of Europe ever be grasped, in all its range of horrors, by ordinary, decent people trying to lead normal lives? As one survivor wrote to a friend immediately after the war, in describing the murder of as many as a million and a half Jewish children: 'If you have a pathological imagination you may be able to picture this yourself, but if you are a normal person you will never be able to bring this chapter of horrors to life, in spite of all your imaginings.'

With the German invasion of Poland in September 1939 a new phase of brutality began: the deliberate murder, at random in their homes, synagogues, shops or streets, of more than five thousand Jews: men, women and children. Some were locked in synagogues and then the synagogues were set on fire. Others were driven to nearby woods or ravines and shot.

Following the German conquest of western Poland, hundreds more Jews were killed while they were being driven eastwards, across marsh and river, over the border into Soviet territory. Then a new policy came into being: forcing Jews out of their homes, and into several hundred specially designated ghettos. The ghettos were sealed. Disease and starvation were rife. Hundreds died, and thousands grew weak. Meanwhile, in April 1940 German rule spread to Denmark and Norway, in May 1940 to France, Belgium and Holland, and in April 1941 to Yugoslavia and Greece. Tens of thousands more Jews were caught in a trap, isolated, forced to wear a yellow star, and put on near-starvation, and then on starvation rations.

By the spring of 1941 more than two thousand Jews were dying of hunger every month in the Warsaw Ghetto, and a further seven to eight hundred a month in the Lodz Ghetto.

Although tens of thousands of Jews had now been murdered, the full intensity of the Holocaust had yet to be reached. In the spring of 1941, in the small German town of Pretzsch, on the River Elbe, Nazi killing squads were being prepared for a terrible task.

On 22 June 1941, the German army launched its invasion of the Soviet Union. These killing squads—known as Einsatzgruppen—moved eastwards in the wake of the army, slaughtering on a scale previously unknown in Jewish, or indeed in world, history. Within three weeks, more than fifty thousand Jewish men, women and children had been shot down without mercy. Many were dragged from their homes to the nearest ditch or pit. The old, the sick, the disabled and babies were shot in their homes, or in their beds. No one found was spared.

After this three-week orgy of killing, the killing squads continued their work week after week, and tens of thousands more Jews were murdered. The killing spread wider and wider, through Lithuania and Latvia to Estonia, through Volhynia and Ukraine, from the Baltic Sea to the Black Sea. Within eight months, as many as a million Jews had been murdered.

This enormous number was not enough for the Nazi plan, which aimed at the total destruction of every single Jew, and every vestige of Jewish life. On 8 December 1941 an experiment had been tried in a remote wood in German-occupied Poland. Four thousand Jews, brought from eight different villages, were forced into specially rein-forced trucks, driven into the wood, and gassed by the exhaust fumes. The experiment took four days. On one of the days a visitor came from Gestapo headquarters in Berlin. His name was Adolf Eichmann. Twenty years later he was to tell a court in Jerusalem that he had been sickened by what he saw. But at the time, he judged the experiment to have been a success.

The name of the wood was Chelmno. In the coming weeks, tens of thousands of Polish Jews were brought there, from an ever-widening region, and gassed. Eichmann, meanwhile, had returned to Berlin. On 20 January 1942, at a conference in a villa on the Wannsee, overlooking the lake, he listed, for the leading German civil servants present, the number of Jews still remaining in Europe. The list was compiled country-by-country. Every Jew on it was to be found, deported, and either worked to death or gassed. Even Britain and Eire appeared on the list. So too did neutral Switzerland and Sweden, Spain and Portugal.

What the Germans called 'the Final Solution of the Jewish Question' was about to be put into operation. The German army stood victorious from the Atlantic Ocean almost to the Caspian Sea, from the far north of Norway to North Africa. Throughout the German-occupied areas of Europe the rule of the Gestapo enforced obedience. Deliberate deception by the killers cloaked the true nature and scale of what was happening.

During the early spring of 1942 Chelmno death camp was expanded. At the same time, three more death camps were built by the Germans on Polish soil, at Belzec, Sobibor and Treblinka. Between them, these four camps took a terrible toll, as more than two million Jews were brought by train, most of them in cattle trucks, from all over Europe. Almost all of them were gassed within a few hours of reaching the camps. Only a tiny fragment were set aside for slave labour, mostly sorting the clothes and belongings of the victims—materials which became part of the German war economy—or being forced to dispose of the corpses. Two million Jews were murdered in these four death camps within a year. Then, as the Soviet Army began to advance towards Germany, the Gestapo ordered all the bodies to be dug up and burned, and the ashes scattered in the nearby forests.

In March 1942, while the four death camps were at the height of their operation, a fifth death camp was opened. It was a camp where hundreds of thousands of those who arrived were not gassed immediately—as at Chelmno, Belzec, Treblinka and Sobibor—but where hundreds of thousands more were kept alive in vast huts as a reserve of slave labour. The name of this fifth camp was Auschwitz. In May 1942 the first Jews were gassed there: they were women, children and old people judged by the Gestapo to be 'useless mouths'. In the next two and a half years, more than a million Jews were gassed there, or murdered with brutal savagery.

Long after Chelmno and the other three death camps had been levelled to the ground, Auschwitz was continuing with its evil work. Today, amid the stark remains of crematoria and gas chambers blown up by the Nazis—and row upon row of wooden huts—one feels helpless even to express emotion. The mud, squalor and stench of death have gone. But an eerie sense of evil remains.

No. 84

Dearest Auntie Fori,

This will be a short letter. It is about a group of Jews who have often been in my mind, the doctors and nurses who were murdered in the Holocaust. Their lives had been dedicated to healing, and to caring for the sick. But they were as much the 'vermin' in Nazi eyes as any other Jew. Some were venerable and distinguished when they were murdered. Others were at the start of careers that would have been devoted to saving life.

One of my treasured possessions is the photocopy of a book called *The Martyrdom of Jewish Physicians in Poland,* published in New York after the war, which gives the names and life stories of 2,500 Jewish doctors and nurses who were murdered in Poland alone. The number throughout Europe must be twice that.

The first of the Polish Jewish victims to appear in the book is Mateusz Aberdam, a gynecologist from Przemysl, an attractive town in what used to be the eastern region of the Austro-Hungarian Empire. He was active in Jewish social life in the town. His fate was to be deported to Auschwitz in 1943 and murdered there. He was forty-four years old.

Several of those in the book were born, dearest Auntie Fori, in 'your' year—1908. Izaak Mandel, a doctor in the East Galician town of Przemyslyany—born like you a citizen of the Austro-Hungarian Empire—was murdered by local Ukrainians while trying to take shelter in a nearby village. Jakub Taffet was a general practitioner in the present Pope's home town, Wadowice, near Cracow: he perished in Lvov during the German occupation, as did his younger brother Teofil, a member of the Jewish Council—set up by the Germans to regulate the running of the ghetto—who was hanged by the Gestapo. Naftali Lichtenbaum, a gynecologist and obstetrician, practised in Warsaw: he did not survive the war. A woman pediatrician, Francizka Hirsch-Rotkopf, who practised in Wieliczka, near Cracow, was deported to the death camp at Belzec in August 1942 with her husband, Julian, himself a doctor, and almost all the other 8,000 Jews of the town and nearby villages. There were no survivors of that deportation.

Another of those in the book, a Jewish woman doctor, Chaja Manusiewicz, was born three years after you, Auntie Fori—in 1911. She graduated from the University of Vilna, married a Christian, practised medicine in the small town of Wsielub, in Byelorussia, and, when the Germans invaded the Soviet Union in 1941, escaped to the forests and joined the partisans. She was killed fighting the Germans.

The last person in the book is Izaak Zyw. Between the wars he was a surgeon in the city of Lodz. During the early years of the war he worked in a dispensary in the Warsaw Ghetto. He was murdered, with his family, when the Germans raided his apartment. He was forty-one years old.

The *Martyrdom* book is 497 pages long: and all it does is to give names and a brief note of careers, usually four or five lines. Were the same amount of space—not very much for a human life—to be given to each Jew murdered in the Holocaust, including the million and a half children and youngsters under the age of sixteen, one would need more than 2,000 such books.

No. 85

Dearest Auntie Fori,

I would like to write now about Jewish resistance during the Holocaust. While the Germans continued to murder Jews in eastern Poland and western Russia, and to deport Jews to death camps from everywhere else in Europe that lay under their control, tens of thousands of Jews tried to revolt against the German grip. Some managed to flee the confines of the ghettos on the eve of the slaughter or deportation. A few, having been left for dead amid a mass of corpses, even managed to escape from the slaughter pits.

Within each ghetto, enormous efforts were made, despite hunger and hardships, to maintain morale, to educate the children, to hold concerts and theatrical performances, to make sure that the cultural life and sanity of pre-war Jewry did not disappear. In the Theresienstadt Ghetto, to which more than 140,000 Jews were deported (and where Theodor Herzl's daughter Trude was among the many thousands who died of hunger), a group of teenage boys produced, in greatest secrecy, a weekly magazine: each issue had to be copied out by hand in an attic. Younger children were encouraged to draw and paint: most of them were later deported to their deaths at Auschwitz, but the art classes and the stage plays and the musical compositions that marked their short, tormented lives in the ghetto were in themselves acts of resistance: the resistance of the human spirit, its refusal to allow itself to be reduced to the level of beasts or slaves.

In the Warsaw Ghetto, during Passover 1943, Jewish fighters took up such weapons as they could find, and fought against the heavily armed occupation forces. They fought for a whole month, until 7,000 had been killed and the Germans, using artillery, had reduced the ghetto to little more than a charred ruin. In Israel today, the anniversary of the start of the Warsaw Ghetto revolt has been designated Heroes and Martyrs Memorial Day. During the two-minute silence, drivers who are in their cars stop and get out, standing silently to attention in the road as the memorial sirens sound throughout the country.

When news of the Warsaw Ghetto revolt reached the Jews in the Vilna Ghetto, one of them, Hirsh Glik, wrote a song which quickly became the watchword of all Jewish resistance fighters and partisans. Its first stanza—still sung today at many Jewish memorial gatherings throughout the world, reads:

> *Never say that you have reached the very end*
> *Though leaden skies a bitter future may portend*
> *The hour for which we yearned will yet arrive*
> *And our marching step will thunder: 'We survive!'*

A year after writing this song, Hirsh Glik was among thousands of Jews deported from Vilna to a slave labour camp in Estonia. There all trace of him was lost.

In January 1942 the United Partisan Organization had been formed in Vilna. When the round-up of Vilna Jews began a year later, one of its leaders, Aba Kovner, led a group of Jewish partisans to the nearby forest, where they fought against the Germans. Three years later they entered Vilna with the Red Army on the day of liberation.

Armed revolts took place in at least two dozen ghettos: among them Cracow—the city where my grandmother had been a student at the end of the nineteenth century, before emigrating to Britain. Among the fighters in the Cracow Ghetto were two young women, Gole Mire, who was killed, and Rivka Liebeskind, who survived. Both were members of the Jewish Fighting Organization, which linked the fighters in many ghettos, by means of couriers, and at great personal risk. Most of them were killed: some fighting, some ambushed, some betrayed by non-Jews.

During the ghetto revolts, all of which were courageous if doomed acts of hopeless resistance—the Germans always being able to bring in overwhelming military power—some Jews managed to escape to the forests and join partisan units, including entirely Jewish partisan units. Jews fought against the Germans in woods and marshes throughout Europe. Deep in one of the forests of Byelorussia, three brothers, Tuvia, Zus and Asael Bielski, not only led a group of partisan fighters, but built and protected a hiding place for 1,200 women and children who had escaped from the ghettos of the region. Asael was killed in action against the Germans. Tuvia and Zus survived.

Jews carried out acts of resistance even in the death camps. At Treblinka, inmates rose up in unison against their guards. At Sobibor, a Jewish prisoner-of-war, Alexander Pechersky, an officer in the Soviet Army—with whom I later corresponded—led a revolt of the slave labourers there. He survived the war; but his fellow resistance leader, Leon Felhendler, a Pole, was murdered by anti-Semitic Poles within a year of liberation (as were some 1,500 other Jews who had returned to their pre-war homes).

Even in Auschwitz, Jewish slave labourers in the Birkenau section of the camp—where most Jews were kept, and murdered—rose up in revolt. They succeeded in destroying two of the four gas chambers there, before being hunted down and killed. One of those caught and killed was Roza Robota, from the Polish town of Sosnowiec, who helped smuggle explosives into the camp. She was executed in front of all the women inmates of Birkenau. Even under terrible torture, she would not reveal the names of others who had been in the plot.

It is inspiring to dwell on the many acts of courage and defiance, on the bravery and the decency, of those who were marked out as victims by the Nazis, but who refused to succumb without protest: who strove, however terrible the circumstances, to retain their humanity. The words of God which Moses passed on to the Israelites—'Choose life'—were the guide of Jews during the Holocaust even when their lives were being threatened and destroyed by evil forces that had massive military power on their side, and a terrifying desire to kill.

One survivor of the Holocaust, Monick Goldberg, now living in the United States—he was only fifteen when the war ended—wrote to me while I was preparing a book about 732 teenage survivors who were brought to Britain in 1945: 'Fifty years on, I reflect that I could tell my father that I have not forgotten what I learned as a boy. I helped my fellow man when I could. I am proud to be a Jew, for I have seen man behave worse than beasts, but the Jews remembered Rabbi Hillel who taught us, "If you find yourself in a place where there are no men, you must strive to be a man." We were among beasts, and I am proud to declare that we upheld the dignity of man.'

As well as the story of Jewish resistance during the Holocaust, of collective resistance, and of individual acts of courage and defiance, there is the story of the many thousands of non-Jews who risked their own lives—and often the lives of their families—in order to save Jewish life. More than 16,000 non-Jews are known to have hidden Jews and fed them, and to have protected them from deportation and death. Several thousand Jewish children were hidden by non-Jews—particularly in Holland, Belgium and France. More than three hundred Germans helped save Jews inside Germany itself; several German factory owners in German-occupied lands—men such as Oskar Schindler, about whom Steven Spielberg made his film *Schindler's List*—also saved Jews from deportation and death.

In the city of Lvov—part of Poland between the wars, of Austria–Hungary before 1914—a leading churchman, Archbishop Sheptitski, who in the early 1920s had supported the anti-Jewish movement of

Simon Petlura—hid Jews from the very first days of the German occupation. Those whom he thus saved included the Chief Rabbi of Lvov and his family. Sheptitski also encouraged other churchmen, as well as his own sister, a leading nun, to do likewise.

The Italian and Hungarian governments both rejected German pressure to deport Jews: it was only with the German military occupations of Italy in 1943, and of Hungary in 1944, that deportations began. The Hungarian Regent, Admiral Horthy, had twice refused Hitler's personal demands for the deportation of Hungary's Jews.

Several European governments saved Jews. The Bulgarian King and parliament refused to deport any of Bulgaria's 48,000 Jews: indeed, the Jewish population of Bulgaria was larger at the end of the war than at the beginning. Finland agreed to deport all its 2,300 Jews, most of them refugees from Germany and Austria, but when the first eleven deportees were murdered by the Gestapo, the Finnish government refused to allow any more to be taken away, and the rest of Finland's Jews survived the war. The Danish people smuggled almost all Denmark's 6,500 Jews to safety in Sweden—in a single night.

The deeds of those who helped are truly heroic. Most of them were ordinary citizens who reacted instinctively—as Christians and as human beings—against the madness and barbarity of anti-Semitic violence, by riskng their own lives to help Jews. In Israel, where they are known as 'Righteous Gentiles', a national law ensures they are recognized and honoured.

No. 86

Dearest Auntie Fori,

Jewish soldiers fought in all the Allied armies. From the first days of the German invasion of Poland in September 1939, Jewish soldiers fought alongside the Poles in defence of their country, and 3,000 were killed in action. When Hitler invaded France, Belgium and Holland in May 1940, Jewish soldiers were to be found in all the defending forces. When he struck at Yugoslavia and Greece in April 1941, the same was true. And when he invaded the Soviet Union in June 1941, Russian

Jewish soldiers were in action. In the early weeks of the war a Jewish general, Jacob Kreiser, held up a German tank attack for two days.

The first Soviet writer to be killed in action was a Jew, Lev Kantorovich, as was the first woman pilot to be shot down and killed—Lydia Litwak.

Jews also fought as partisans and resistance fighters in every land under German occupation. During the first six months of 1941 more than 130 Jews, mostly Polish-born, were shot in Paris for acts of resistance against the German occupation forces. The Chief Rabbi of Athens, Elias Barzilai, joined the Greek partisans, one of hundreds of Greek Jews to do so. In Italy, among the partisan leaders, was a young Jewish woman, Rita Rosani. She was caught and killed while fighting far behind the German lines, near Verona.

When Hitler declared war on the United States in December 1941, yet more Jews found themselves as part of the Allied armies, fighting on land, at sea and in the air until the defeat of Nazism in May 1945. American Jews served with distinction in all the war zones, as soldiers, sailors and airmen. They were also among the liberators of the concentration camps.

On 9 December 1941, two days after Pearl Harbour, an American Jew, Sergeant Meyer Levin, launched the bombs which sank a Japanese battleship from a Flying Fortress. He died later in the war trying to save fellow crew members when their plane crashed into the Pacific. Another Jewish airman, Sergeant Albert Garshowitz, from Canada, a wireless operator, was among those shot down and killed in the Dambusters Raid over Germany in 1943.

More than 30,000 Palestinian Jews volunteered to fight, and served with the British forces in all the war zones. A Palestinian Jewish pilot, George Ernest Goodman, was among those who took part in the Battle of Britain in 1940. Born in Haifa, he was twenty years old at the time of the battle. For his courage in a series of actions in shooting down at least six attacking German aircraft, he was awarded the Distinguished Flying Cross. In 1941, while on active service in North Africa, he was shot down and killed. Palestinian Jews fought alongside British and French troops in the battle to wrest Syria from Vichy France. It was in this struggle that Moshe Dayan—later Israeli Chief of Staff, Minister of Defence, and Foreign Minister—lost his eye.

At Passover 1943, in Tripoli, some of these 'Palestinians', as they were then known, met for the first time American, British and South African Jewish soldiers. Their singing together of 'Hatikvah'—Hope—the 'Jewish' national anthem, was a moving experience for all who were present.

Palestinian Jews served as stevedores, working in ports that had been badly bombed by the Germans and Italians. One such group, No. 462 Company, was on board ship crossing the Mediterranean to Malta—then under siege—when their ship was torpedoed, and 148 of them killed. When I was in Jerusalem earlier this year I saw the memorial on Mount Herzl that lists their names.

In the summer of 1944 a Jewish Brigade Group was set up, mostly of Jews from Palestine, who fought in Italy. Its words of command were in Hebrew. Instead of shouting out 'one-two!, one-two!' as they marched the men called out the Hebrew equivalent, *alef-bet!, alef-bet!* ('a–b'). In all, 83 members of the Brigade Group were killed in action; a further 651 Palestinian Jews lost their lives in action elsewhere.

Gerald Smith, a Londoner who was a member of the Brigade, remembered how, after serving as a stretcher bearer in Italy, he became an army driver. 'I'll never forget driving through Austria and Germany,' he recalled. 'The deeper into Germany the more silent we all became. There was utter devastation everywhere. People stared at our Jewish flags with incredulity. We pitied the people of ruined Cologne until we encountered that indescribable smell and realized that we were close to the Bergen-Belsen concentration camp.'

Jews fought on all the battlefronts, in Europe and in Asia. They were killed in action on the most remote Pacific islands, in the cruel seas of the Atlantic, and in the fiercest battles of the war. This was brought home to me for the first time when I visited Normandy on the fiftieth anniversary of the landings of June 1944, and saw the Star of David engraved on tombstones in the graveyards that mark the ebb and flow of battle after the troops had gone ashore.

The second time that the Jewish contribution to the war effort made its impact on me was on the fiftieth anniversary of the defeat of Germany in May 1945. I was being shown round the new war memorial and museum in Moscow and, looking up at the walls of names of men and women who had been awarded the highest Soviet decoration for bravery, Hero of the Soviet Union—names inscribed in letters of gold on white marble—saw many Jewish names among them.

The third moment on which the Jewish contribution to the military struggle against Hitler made a strong impression was at the Special Forces Club in London. As I walked up the main stairway, on which were hung the photographs of Britons who had given their lives in German-occupied Europe, I found myself passing a photograph of Hanna Szenes—code-named 'Minnie' to the British—the Budapest-born immigrant to Palestine who, while working on a kibbutz, had volunteered to be parachuted behind German lines.

Hanna Szenes and thirty-one other Palestinian Jews volunteered for this task. Seven were captured and killed, among them Hanna Szenes. She was twenty-two years old. When I was last in Budapest, I found a small park named after her.

No. 87

Dearest Auntie Fori,

Outside the war zones Jews also made their contribution to the Allied war effort. Twelve military ambulances were presented to the South African army by Jewish refugees from Germany who had found shelter in South Africa during the war. A similar number of ambulances were presented to the British Army by the Jews of Palestine, who had raised the money for them.

Among the contributions made by individual Jews was that of J. Robert Oppenheimer, who led the atom bomb construction team at Los Alamos. Also working at Los Alamos were Richard Feynman, a future Nobel Prize winner, and James Franck, who opposed dropping the atom bomb on Japan. Theodore von Karman—whom I have already mentioned in an earlier letter—a Jew born in Budapest, co-ordinated American wartime jet propulsion research.

The ability of individual Jews to fight was matched by the ability of other Jews to narrate—to set down graphic accounts of the fighting around them. Among the war correspondents in the Allied armies during the Second World War were many Jews, for whom journalism

had always been a popular profession. One of the first journalists on
the American soldiers' newspaper *The Stars and Stripes* was Ralph G.
Martin, a graduate from the Missouri School of Journalism. At the age of
twenty-two he was sent to North Africa as a combat reporter.

In the Soviet Union, the filmmaker Sergei Eisenstein, whose father
was Jewish, joined with a number of leading Jewish intellectuals in the
Soviet Union—among them the brilliant actor-manager Solomon
Mikhoels, who had once played a masterly *King Lear* in Yiddish—to pro-
claim their pride in being Jews, and to raise international awareness of
the mass murder of the Jews on Soviet soil.

Ilya Ehrenburg, a Soviet Jewish writer and novelist who had been a
Russian war correspondent on the Eastern Front in the First World
War—and whom Uncle Bijju met, I believe, in the 1960s—was in Paris
at the time of the German invasion of France in 1940. His war reporting
and subsequent book *The Fall of Paris* won him the Stalin Prize. Among
the Jewish journalists from the West was Alexander Werth, *Sunday Times*
correspondent in Moscow. His account of the liberation of Majdanek
concentration camp in the summer of 1944 gave the world its first eye-
witness account of the horrors of the Nazi death camps.

In the Americas, South Africa and Australia, far from the European
war, Jewish life went on, in thousands of synagogues and millions of
homes. Jewish schools taught and celebrated the traditional festivals
and the Biblical story. Jewish creativity was not dimmed. Sometimes it
focused on the war. Lillian Hellman's play *Watch on the Rhine,* first performed in New York in 1941, told the story of a German who risked his
life to oppose the Nazi regime. Sometimes it was far removed from grim
reality. Also in 1941, the American comedian Danny Kaye (born David
Daniel Kaminsky, to Russian immigrant parents) came to prominence
in the film *Lady in the Dark,* displaying a formidable talent for witty
tongue-twisting by reeling off the names of fifty Russian composers in
thirty-nine seconds.

In 1943, Leonard Bernstein, the American-born son of immigrants
from the Ukraine, made his conducting debut with the New York Phil-
harmonic Orchestra. In 1944 Lauren Bacall (born Betty Joan Perske in
New York) starred in the film *To Have and Have Not.* In her memoirs,
written in 1979, she called herself 'just a nice Jewish girl from New

York', and added: 'Going back through my life now, the Jewish family feeling stands proud and strong, and at least I can say I am glad I sprang from that. I would not trade those roots—that identity.'

Jewish identity survived Hitler's attempt to destroy it. It survived even in Europe, where his executioners were almost entirely successful, and it survived beyond Europe where eight million Jews had lived and flourished. News of Hitler's attempt to destroy Jewish life created a renewed sense of Jewish solidarity, national identity and self-esteem.

Those Jews who had managed to escape from Europe on the eve of the Second World War, and even after war broke out, were the fortunate few. In the post-war world they constituted the remnant and the representatives of the millions who had been murdered. Among them was Joseph Isaac Schneersohn, the leader of the Habad Lubavitch Hasidic sect—about which I have already written to you—who reached New York from Poland in 1940. Under his leadership—and from 1950 to 1994 under that of his son-in-law, Menachem Mendel Schneersohn—the Lubavitch movement found a new base and a new strength in the United States, from which, during the half century which followed, it spread its influence worldwide, championing Orthodoxy and encouraging a return to Judaism by those who had lapsed.

Another of those who reached the United States in 1940 was the Roumanian-born Saul Steinberg, whose *New Yorker* cartoons came to be regarded as quintessentially American.

Jewish life in Palestine continued with vigour during the Second World War, with new kibbutzim set up every year. The first was set up a month after the outbreak of the war, on the northern shore of the Dead Sea. Its members were recent immigrants from Germany and Central Europe. Three other kibbutzim were set up in 1940 by immigrants from Czechoslovakia, Yugoslavia and Hungary. In 1942 kibbutz Kfar Blum was founded, on the edge of the Huleh swamp. It was named after the French Jewish politician Léon Blum—Prime Minister of the pre-war Popular Front—who was then being held in German detention. Many of its members were from the Baltic States and Britain, members of the Habonim youth movement. It was known as the 'Anglo-Baltic' kibbutz. Much of its funding came from the American Labour Zionist Organisation. The settlement of Kfar Etzion, ten miles south of Jerusalem, which had been abandoned after the Arab riots of 1936, was re-founded in 1943 by pre-war Orthodox Jewish immigrants from Poland. Eight miles north of the Palestinian Arab city of Gaza, other Polish Jews founded Yad Mordechai ('The Hand of Mordechai'), named after the leader of the Warsaw Ghetto revolt, Mordechai Anielewicz, news of whose death while leading the resistance had just became known in Palestine.

No. 88

Dearest Auntie Fori,

As a historian, I am always interested in the fate of the Jewish historians of the generation before mine.

The leading Warsaw Jewish historian, Emanuel Ringelblum, who in 1928 was one of the founders of the Circle of Young Historians, was murdered by the Nazis in Warsaw in 1944. Philip Friedman, another inter-war Polish Jewish historian, survived the Holocaust in hiding in Lvov, then emigrated to the United States and became a leading historian there. Another Jewish historian of the inter-war years, Jacob Shatzky, emigrated in 1927 from Poland to the United States, where he wrote a three-volume history of the Jews of Warsaw.

The leading Jewish historian of the pre– and post–First World War period was Simon Dubnow. In 1908 he began teaching at the Institute of Jewish Studies in St Petersburg, and from 1919, after the Bolshevik Revolution, at the Jewish People's University. In 1922 he left Russia, teaching first in Berlin, and then, after Hitler came to power, moving to the Latvian capital, Riga. It was there, on 8 December 1941—aged eighty-one—that he was shot down in the street—some say by a Gestapo officer who had been a former pupil of his—during the mass deportation of the Jews of Riga to a death camp.

Dubnow's pioneering publications included *An Outline of Jewish History*, in three volumes, and a three-volume *History of the Jews in Russia and Poland*. His last words, on being shot, were, in Yiddish: *'Schreibt und farschreibt!'*—'Write and record!'

To 'write and record' became the Jewish imperative during the Holocaust for thousands of people, including historians. One of those who kept detailed records of life in the ghettos of German-occupied Poland was Meir Balaban, whose first, prize-winning essay on Polish-Jewish bibliography had been published—in Polish—in 1903, when he was twenty-six. His first book, on the Jews of Lemberg (Lvov) at the turn of the seventeenth century, was published three years later. Balaban was a co-founder in 1927 of the Institute for Jewish Studies in Warsaw—which survives to this day. From 1928 he was a lecturer in Jewish history at the University of Warsaw. In 1942 he died in the Warsaw Ghetto, at the age of sixty five—only a year older than I am now.

In all, Balaban published seventy historical studies, including a history of the Jews of Lublin (in 1919) and a two-volume history of the Jews of Cracow (1931, 1936). On my last visit to Warsaw I visited his grave. The Jewish cemetery in Warsaw is the second largest in Europe. The largest is the Weissensee Jewish cemetery in Berlin. Both survived the Second World War virtually intact.

Another distinguished Polish Jewish pre-war historian, Max Weinreich, was a co-founder in Vilna of the Yiddish Scientific Institute—YIVO. He wanted the Yiddish-speaking world to have its archives and documents and history and intellectual power. Weinreich left Vilna for New York in 1932. When the YIVO headquarters moved there eight years later, he became its director. His book *Hitler's Professors*—to the recent reprint of which I wrote an introduction—showed the many links between German scholarship and the Holocaust.

Weinreich's greatest achievement was his four-volume *History of the Yiddish Language*. 'Even in the rapidly fragmenting milieu of Yiddish culture,' writes the historian Irving Howe, 'he could assume a role more deeply integrated, carrying greater communal responsibility and status, than most American scholars so much as aspire to.'

Writing of Weinreich reminds me of your comment—so prevalent among 'western' Jews half a century ago—when I asked you about Yiddish and you replied: 'Yiddish? We looked down on Yiddish.'

Weinreich's efforts certainly helped preserve the rich heritage of a language that had created a vibrant literature, poetry, song and humour.

The Austro-Hungarian born historian Salo Wittmayer Baron left his post at the Jewish Teachers' College in Vienna in 1926 and moved to New York. There, during the following sixty years, he published a remarkable eighteen-volume *Social and Religious History of the Jews*. It was Baron who, in 1961, was asked to set out the historical background to the Holocaust as the opening witness at the Eichmann Trial.

In his book on Russian and Soviet Jewry, written in 1964, Baron noted prophetically, about the Jews of the Soviet Union, that 'in some yet as unpredictable fashion, they will, before very long, recover their ancient vitality to find some unprecedented solutions to the novel, intrinsically contradictory challenges of discrimination by, and assimilation to, one of the great nations of history.'

Baron was an outspoken opponent of what he called 'the lachrymose conception' of Jewish history, in which the way the story of the Jews is told can be characterized as: 'They beat us and they beat us some more'.

Salo Baron died in 1989, at the age of ninety-four. Two years earlier a non-Jewish historian, Paul Johnson, in his pioneering one-volume book *A History of the Jews,* gave voice to Baron's concerns when he wrote of the Jews: 'No people has been more fertile in enriching poverty or humanizing wealth, or in turning misfortune to creative account.'

Paul Johnson concluded—as I would like to feel both Salo Baron and I would conclude: 'In continuing to give meaning to creation, the Jews will take comfort from the injunction, thrice repeated, in the noble first chapter of the Book of Joshua: "Be strong and of good courage; be not afraid, neither be thou dismayed: for the Lord thy God is with thee whithersoever thou goest." '

No. 89

Dearest Auntie Fori,

Your own grandfather—your father's father—came, as you have told me, from Miskolc, a town in north-east Hungary. You asked me to tell you something about the town.

When war came in 1939, five hundred Miskolc Jews with alleged 'irregularities' in their nationality were deported to German-occupied Poland, where almost all of them were killed. Several hundred more, young and old alike, were seized in 1941 and sent to Kamenets-Podolsk in the Ukraine, where almost all were killed. Following the German occupation of Hungary in 1944, the remaining 10,000 were deported to Auschwitz: only 105 survived.

Such was the typical and terrible fate of all Hungarian provincial towns. The Jews of Budapest, though confronted by great terror, never faced the wholesale deportation to Auschwitz and virtual total destruction of their community. Your own father, as you told me, was living in 1944—in an apartment at 3 Pozsonyi Street. I see from my researches that at the time of the Hungarian Fascist control of the city, that building was under the protection of the Swedish Embassy, one of more than forty apartment buildings to which the diplomat and 'Righteous Gentile' Raoul Wallenberg had affixed the seal of neutral Sweden. Some of these protected houses were raided by Hungarian Fascists and their occupants seized and killed, but most were successfully protected by the Swedish emblem.

To return to Miskolc. The first Jews to live there, at the start of the eighteenth century, earned their livelihood selling alcoholic beverages. In 1717 the local municipal authorities discussed expulsion, but allowed the Jews to stay, and eleven years later gave the town's Jews the right to sell at the local market. Within a hundred years, Jews in Miskolc owned houses and land, and the Jewish community had its own judicial authority, able to impose fines and even corporal punishment. The Great Synagogue, which your grandfather must have attended, was built in 1861.

The *Encyclopaedia Judaica* notes that the Jewish educational institutions in Miskolc 'were amongst the most developed and ramified throughout the country'. By 1910, two years after you were born in Budapest, the Jewish population of Miskolc numbered more than 10,000: it constituted the highest percentage of Jews of any town in Hungary—about 20 per cent.

After the Second World War a small Jewish community was reconstituted in Miskolc—some 2,300 Jews in all. They even had a Jewish elementary school, until it was closed down by the Communist regime. By 1990, when Communism came to an end in Hungary, there were less than a thousand Jews in the town.

No. 90

Dearest Auntie Fori,

I thought you would like a letter about the Jews of Hungary, the country where you were born just over ninety years ago, and where assimilation and conversion became commonplace in the early years of the nineteenth century. A few of these things I have touched on earlier, but 'your' Hungary deserves a letter of its own—just for you!

Modern Hungary traces its origins to the failed Hungarian revolution against Austria in 1848–1849. Many Jews took part in this as Hungarian patriots, and as a result felt the full weight of Austrian hostility, including a massive communal fine. The first emancipation came a decade later, in 1859, when in the 'new' Hungary, with its growing autonomy, Jews were allowed to engage in every profession and settle in all localities.

Formal emancipation came by act of the independent Budapest Parliament on 20 December 1867. By then there were more than half a million Jews in Hungary. Among them was a recently married couple, the Weiss family, who in 1874 decided to emigrate to the United States, the land of hope and opportunity for millions of European Jews. With them they took their baby son Ehrich, who was only a few weeks old. Later he was to become famous as Harry Houdini, one of the greatest escapologists of all time, billed as 'The World's Greatest Magician'.

For the Jews who remained in Hungary, emancipation and prejudice went hand in hand, as they did so often for Jews all over the world. In 1882 there was a blood libel accusation in the town of Tiszaeszlar, and anti-Jewish violence in several towns, leading to fears of an upsurge of persecution. But the blood libel was condemned by many Christian leaders, and in 1895 the Jewish religion was officially recognized as one of the religions accepted in Hungary.

Jews were able to do well: as merchants, craftsmen, landowners, writers, doctors and thinkers—even sportsmen. Hungarian Jews were among the leaders of the Zionist movement; the founder of political Zionism, Theodor Herzl, was born in Budapest. In north-eastern Hungary there was a flourishing of Hungarian-rooted Hasidism. Assimilation was also widespread, and conversion to Christianity. Anti-Semitism was a continual factor in Hungarian life, often only of spoken prejudice, but sometimes breaking out with violent results. Budapest, the capital which drew so many Jews to the opportunities it offered, was known derisively as 'Judapest' (in South Africa, at the same time and for the same reason, Johannesburg—or Jo'burg in the local parlance—was known as 'Jewburg.')

In the First World War, as I wrote to you, Auntie Fori, in my 'First World War' letter, 10,000 Hungarian Jews were killed in action fighting for Austria–Hungary. During the war, the Budapest-born playwright and novelist Ferenc Molnár (his original surname was Neumann) wrote such impressive newspaper reports from the Eastern Front that they were published by the *New York Times*—even though the United States and Hungary were on opposite sides.

After Bela Kun took power at the head of a Communist regime in 1919, several fellow-Jews were among his ruling commissars. He operated a 'Red Terror' against his opponents, even against the moderate elements in his own government. Banks, large businesses and country estates were nationalized—the latter to the annoyance of the peasantry, who had hoped to divide the land among themselves. A fierce anti-Semitic backlash followed Bela Kun's defeat and flight (eventually to Moscow), and in the 'White Terror' which ensued, 3,000 Jews were killed.

One of those who served under Bela Kun was a young filmmaker, Alexander Korda, who was imprisoned when the revolution failed. Korda moved first to Hollywood and then to England, where his films were among the most patriotic British productions of the inter-war and Second World War years: Churchill was a particular fan of the ultra-patriotic *Lady Hamilton* (set during the Napoleonic wars), and Korda was knighted in 1942—a Hungarian Jewish knight.

In 1920 a *numerus clausus* Act was passed by the Hungarian parliament, restricting the number of Jews in universities to five per cent. It was this Act, Auntie Fori, that led to you having to go to England to study, meeting Uncle Bijju . . . and the rest is (your) history.

In 1938, five years after Hitler came to power in Germany—and four years after you, Auntie Fori, had left Hungary for India—the 'First Jewish Law' was passed by the Hungarian Parliament. It restricted (and effectively more than halved) the number of Jews in the liberal professions, administration, and commerce. The term 'Jew' in the Law included those who had converted to Christianity after 1919. A 'Second Jewish Law' in 1939 extended the number of converts who were to be considered as Jews to 100,000, and further drastically reduced the number of Jews allowed to participate in economic activity, denying 250,000 of Hungary's 450,000 Jews their source of livelihood.

During the Second World War, of the 825,000 people considered Jews under Hungary's laws (this included most converts), an estimated 565,000 were murdered during the war, most of them deported to their deaths at Auschwitz in 1944. As many as 14,000 others had been killed in 1941 after being rounded up—mostly in Hungarian-annexed Ruthenia—and sent as slave labourers to the Ukraine, principally to Kamenets-Podolsk.

One miracle amid the horrors of the Second World War was that at least a hundred thousand Hungarian Jews survived, most of them in Budapest. Many did so as a result of the courageous intervention of several foreign diplomats in the city, among them the Swedish diplomat Raoul Wallenberg, who was later seized by the Russians, and disappeared, either shot in the Lubyanka prison in Moscow or dying in a Siberian labour camp. Ironically, Wallenberg was the great-great-grandson—on his mother's side—of the first Jew to settle in Sweden—in the eighteenth century. Named Benedicks, he had converted to the Lutheran faith and married a Christian woman.

The Hungarian Jewish community was reconstituted after the war; individual Jews were again—as in 1919—prominent in the Communist regime, among them Erno Gero, who had been active in the 1919 revolution, and was a leading member of the Communist ruling elite from 1950 to 1966. Other Jews were among the regime's opponents, and fled into exile, or were imprisoned, after the anti-Communist revolution of 1956.

Since the fall of Communism, Hungarian Jews have had renewed hope; as I write this letter, the Jews of Hungary number 100,000, of whom 80,000 live in Budapest. In Israel today and in the Diaspora there are many, many Jews of Hungarian descent.

Individual Jews made their mark on all aspects of Hungarian life. David Meir Gutman was among those who fought in the 1848–1849 Hungarian War of Independence. Disillusioned by Hungarian hostility to Jews, he emigrated to Palestine in 1876, settling in Jerusalem, and helping to buy land both for early Jewish agricultural settlements there and for the town of Petah Tikvah. Later he sold all his property in Jerusalem to pay the town's debts, and died impoverished.

Ignaz Goldziher, born Isaac Judah in 1850, was one of the founders of modern Islamic scholarship, teaching at the University of Budapest from 1872 and also at the Budapest Rabbinical Seminary. He was the first modern scholar of Islamic oral tradition, and also made a considerable contribution to the study of the various Muslim sects. A child prodigy, at the age of twelve he had published an essay on the Jewish prayers. After his death in 1921 his extensive library and scholarly correspondence was acquired by the National and University Library in Jerusalem, where it remains one of its treasures.

David Widder, who wrote under the name Janos Giszkalay, was a Hungarian poet who edited a Zionist newspaper in Budapest from 1918. He argued that anti-Semites had no moral right to demand patriotism of Hungarian Jews. As a result of his Zionist activities, many Hungarian Jews emigrated to Palestine, which he himself did in 1941, working as a shepherd on a kibbutz, and later translating his poetry into Hebrew.

Among the Jews active in the 1956 uprising against Communism, and forced to flee the country when the uprising was crushed, was the author and journalist Tamas Aczel, who edited an emigrant periodical while in exile. The Jewish poet Zoltan Zelk—his poems were specially loved by children—an orthodox Marxist, also joined the uprising, and was sentenced to two years in prison.

Many Hungarian Jewish sportsmen and -women competed in the Olympic Games, and won gold medals. In the first modern Olympic Games, held in Athens in 1896, Alfred Hajos-Guttmann won two golds—the first-ever for swimming. Later, as an architect specializing in designing sports facilities, he was awarded an Olympic silver medal for architecture, the highest award given in that competition. He was also a member of Hungary's national football team for three consecutive years, 1901, 1902 and 1903. He survived the Second World War, but his fellow Olympian, the fencer Oszkar Gerde, did not. Gerde had won gold medals in the team events in both 1908 (in London) and 1912 (in Stockholm). A medical doctor, he died as a prisoner of the Nazis in Mauthausen concentration camp in October 1944. He was sixty-one years old.

The Hungarian national heavyweight wrestling champion Richard Weisz won a gold medal in the 1908 Olympics in the Graeco-Roman heavyweight class. He had a twenty-inch neck and a fifty-inch chest! In fencing, Janos Garay won three Olympic medals for Hungary, a silver and a bronze at the 1924 Olympics, and a gold at the 1928 Olympics. He is believed to have perished in a Nazi concentration camp towards the end of the war, when he would have been fifty-five years old.

Among the gold medal winners in 1924 was another Jew, Budapest-born Ferenc Mezoe. He was not a sportsman but a writer—the first official historian of the Games. He won his medal for his book *The Olympic Games in Antiquity*—do you remember, Auntie Fori, when I wrote of how Herod was one of the patrons of the Games in that era? For many years, Mezoe was President of the Hungarian Olympic Committee, and in 1948 was elected to the International Committee. He died in Budapest in 1961.

Four members of the same Hungarian-Jewish family won Olympic gold medals. One of those family members, Eva Szekely, set ten world and five Olympic swimming records and held an astonishing sixty-eight Hungarian national swimming titles. In 1944 she and her family were sheltered from the Hungarian fascists in a Swiss-protected safehouse in Budapest. In order to keep up her exercises, she would get up at night, climb over the others asleep on the ground floor, and run up and down five flights of stairs, one hundred times. In the Helsinki Olympics in 1952 both she and her husband, Dezso Gyarmati (a Hungarian water polo champion whom she had just married), won gold medals. Her 200-metre breaststroke was an Olympic record.

Another Hungarian Jew, Agnes Keleti, had been removed from the

Hungarian athletic national team during the Second World War because she was Jewish. In 1944 her father was deported to Auschwitz and murdered there. Her mother and sister were given a secure haven in one of the Swedish 'safe houses' set up in Budapest by Raoul Wallenberg; she herself managed to buy 'Christian' identity papers which enabled her to leave Budapest and survive outside the city. After the war she won eleven Olympic medals for Hungary, including five golds: first in 1948 at the London Olympics (to which I went as an eleven-year-old schoolboy), then in 1952 in Helsinki, and finally in 1956 in Melbourne, where she won three gold medals.

While Agnes Keleti was in Melbourne the Soviets crushed the Hungarian revolution—she immediately sought asylum, which was granted. In 1957 she emigrated to Israel where, at the Maccabiah Games that year, before gymnastics had become a competitive sport, she gave two special public performances. Later she trained several Israeli national gymnastic teams.

Victor Barna, one of the world's greatest table tennis players, the holder of twenty-three world championship titles, was a Hungarian Jew. He played his first game in 1924, at a Bar Mitzvah party in Budapest, where his best friend, the Bar Mitzvah boy, had been given a table tennis table among his presents. In 1944 his younger brother, also a table tennis champion, was murdered by Hungarian Fascists. Learning that his own table tennis trophies had been saved by a Christian neighbour, Victor Barna said, of his brother: 'Imagine, he won the Hungarian title, he followed in my footsteps, he had a great future in table tennis, and they killed him. I wish the people could have saved him, and not my trophies.'

Born in Budapest five years after you, Auntie Fori, was Andrasz Friedmann—he had your surname. Taking the name Robert Capa, he became one of the twentieth century's foremost war photographers. As a young man, he left Hungary for Paris and became a darkroom assistant. One of the photographs he took during the Spanish Civil War, of a soldier at the moment of death, is one of the enduring photographic images of war. From Spain he went to China, to photograph the Sino-Japanese War. During the Second World War he was in North Africa,

Normandy and Northern Europe. In 1948 he was a photographer in Israel's War of Independence. Six years later, while photographing the French struggle in Indo-China, he stepped on a land mine and was killed. He was only forty-one years old.

Among Hollywood's Jews, Adolph Zukor was Hungarian-born. At the age of fifteen he emigrated to the United States and with the establishment of 'penny arcades' in 1903—five years before you, Auntie Fori, were born—created what were to be the movie houses of the twentieth century and beyond: eight years later, in 1911, he helped build and manage a chain of film theatres across the United States. He lived until one hundred and three: on his hundredth birthday, in 1973, he quipped: 'If I had known I was going to live this long, I would have taken better care of myself.'

Three Hungarian Jews who achieved international fame were Felix Salten, the creator of the cartoon character Bambi; Dennis Gabor, the inventor of holography; and Erno Rubik, the inventor of the Rubik Cube, one of the most popular game-challenges of the late twentieth century.

Two Hungarian Jews added enormously to the spice of life in Britain: the cartoonist Vicky and the humorist George Mikes. Vicky, born Victor Weisz, of Hungarian parents, studied in Germany, publishing his first anti-Hitler cartoon there in 1928. He left for Britain in 1935. During the Second World War his cartoons, published in the *News Chronicle,* were a perceptive, witty, often acidic, always eye-opening commentary on the war: the plight of refugees was one of his themes.

George Mikes, born in Hungary four years after you, Auntie Fori, emigrated to Britain in 1938, working for ten years for the Hungarian Service of the BBC. His first humorous book, *How to Be an Alien,* was published in 1946, followed over the next forty years by forty more books. Some were serious, such as his book about his friendship with his fellow–Hungarian Jewish writer Arthur Koestler, and his book about the Hungarian Revolution of 1956. But mostly he wrote amusing tales gently poking fun at all the ridiculous aspects of daily life in many lands. His *Milk and Honey* is a witty and also perceptive panorama of life in Israel.

Two more Hungarian-born Jews have always fascinated me. One—whose books of travel and adventure I read as a schoolboy—was Arminius Vambery. Born Hermann Vamberger, he came from an Orthodox family background. In 1862 he disguised himself as a Muslim and explored the remotest regions of Central Asia. Returning to Hungary after three years, he became a Protestant, and was appointed professor of Oriental languages at the University of Budapest. Without that conversion the professorship would have been all but impossibe. It was Vambery who, in 1901, introduced the Zionist leader Theodor Herzl—another Jew born in Budapest—to the Turkish sultan.

Also born in Hungary was Aurel Stein, who explored the almost inaccessible region north of the Himalayas, locating the ancient caravan routes between China and the West. Stein became a British subject in 1904 and was knighted eight years later. When you, Auntie Fori, were born, he had just completed his second expedition. Many of his discoveries are in the Antiquities Museum in Delhi.

It was Stein who identified the site of the near impregnable fortress guarding the River Indus which was captured by Alexander the Great on his march to India. Stein was still exploring at the age of eighty: he died in 1943, just before his eighty-first birthday, soon after reaching Kabul on yet another journey. He left his personal library to the Hungarian Research Academy in Budapest. Neil Malcolm and I knew nothing of his death in Kabul when we passed through Afghanistan in 1958.

Neil and I also travelled through the former Armenian regions of eastern Turkey, which before 1922 and the Armenian massacres were very much part of the Armenian heartland. It was Franz Werfel who, in 1933, gave the most vivid literary expression to the Armenian massacres in his prose epic *The Forty Days of Musa Dagh,* which became a beacon for Armenians of their tragic fate.

Werfel was much attracted to Roman Catholicism, but while in the United States during the Second World War as a refugee from Nazism, he decided not to convert, as a sign of solidarity with the Jews persecuted by Hitler.

No. 91

Dearest Auntie Fori,

My last three letters were written to you as a Hungarian. This letter is written to you as an Indian. One of the most popular authors when I was a schoolboy was Louis Fischer, an American Jew born in Philadelphia. The book of his that I remember most vividly was his biography of Gandhi, published in 1950. Fischer had befriended Gandhi in 1939 and helped to make the mahatma's vision and courage known to a very wide public. The other day I was reading another book about Gandhi, Margaret Chatterjee's *Gandhi and his Jewish Friends*. Writing about Gandhi's struggle in South Africa before 1914, for the rights of Indians there, Professor Chatterjee comments: 'Among Gandhi's early associates, I am persuaded, there were few who shared as many of his ideas so well as his Jewish friends did.'

Gandhi's closest Jewish friend was Hermann Kallenbach, a German-born architect living in South Africa. Gandhi wrote to him in 1909: 'Our mutual attachment is the strongest possible testimony of our having lived in other lives than in the present ones.'

It was Kallenbach who, in 1910, gave Gandhi the use of his 1,100-acre farm some twenty miles from Johannesburg for his Tolstoy Farm settlement, where he and his followers lived according to the rules of self-sufficiency. In order to be a useful member of the farm, Kallenbach learned sandal-making. During a Jewish fast day, Gandhi wrote wishing him 'well in every respect'. When things were going badly for both of them, Gandhi wrote to Kallenbach: 'A man's worth is tried not in prosperity but in adversity. So therefore cheer up.'

In his pre-1914 struggle for Indian rights in South Africa, Gandhi understood the parallel experiences of his Jewish friends, also living in a Diaspora, and also subject to racial and irrational discrimination. 'We know that Jews in South Africa are not labouring against any particular disabilities,' Gandhi wrote in 1911, 'but the silent and insidious opposition against them now and then comes to the surface. . . .' Inside the South African Parliament it was a Jewish member, the advocate

M. Alexander, who was Gandhi's most vocal supporter with regard to Indian rights.

Gandhi's secretary from 1907 was a high-spirited Jewish woman, Sonia Schlesin, who had a first-class diploma in shorthand. One of Gandhi's Indian friends described her as 'more or less a suffragette'. Her devotion to Gandhi was widely noted. She teased him about being 'unbusinesslike'. He countered by commenting that her smudgy writing was not as tidy as it should be! Later she became a schoolteacher in South Africa.

One of those who helped Gandhi when he was in London in 1906, heading a delegation to champion the rights of South Africa's Indians, was Lewis W. Ritch, a Jew who had been a clerk in Gandhi's Johannesburg law office. In London he helped Gandhi raise funds and organize meetings. Another Jew who helped Gandhi during that London visit was J. H. Polak, who took him to the House of Commons to meet various Liberal Members of Parliament. Polak's son Henry was, after Kallerbach, Gandhi's closest Jewish friend.

Like Gandhi, Henry Polak was a vegetarian. British-educated, he had moved to South Africa as a young journalist. They first met in 1904, and from that moment Polak was a forceful contributor to *Indian Opinion:* he later became its editor. One thing that impressed him was, he wrote, Gandhi's determination to bring Hindus and Muslims together 'and to make them realize that they are one brotherhood of the same Motherland'.

It was Henry Polak who gave Gandhi his strongest support in the decisive switch from deputations and delegations and petitions—the accepted routines of protest—to non-co-operation. Polak went on a mission to India for Gandhi, to explain non-co-operation, and its potential in bringing British rule to a halt. He returned to South Africa with support for the idea, and with funds which he had raised for Gandhi to continue his work.

Among Gandhi's friends in the Johannesburg Jewish community were William M. Vogel, a draper, and Gabriel Isaacs, a jeweller, with whom he attended a number of synagogue services, and took part in a Seder meal at Passover. Isaacs helped collect subscriptions and advertising for Gandhi's newspaper *Indian Opinion,* and went to prison with

Gandhi when they were arrested during a protest march—the Great March—in 1913.

When war broke out in 1914, Hermann Kallenbach was in Britain. As a German citizen, he was interned by the British on the Isle of Man for the duration of the war (in the Second World War many German Jewish refugees from Hitler were likewise interned on the Isle of Man). While Kallenbach was being held on the island, Gandhi wrote to him: 'At every turn I think of you.'

On the day after Gandhi, returning to India, established his Ashram at Ahmedabad, he wrote to Kallenbach to tell him about it. In a letter a year later Gandhi wrote: 'I am using your favourite wooden pillow.' And, as he cleaned the closets and the compound, he told his absent friend: 'Your suggestions and your nose I miss so much.'

Kallenbach did not meet Gandhi again for twenty-three years, when he went to India in 1937 to seek Gandhi's sympathy for Zionism. Gandhi wanted the Jews to seek Arab support, writing to Kallenbach after their talks together: 'If the Jews would rely wholly on the Arab goodwill they must once and for all renounce British protection,' and he added: 'I wonder if they will adopt the heroic remedy.'

The fate of the Jews of Germany, to which Kallenbach alerted him, affected Gandhi greatly. When Kallenbach returned to South Africa in 1938, Gandhi wrote to him: 'Has the anti-Jewish wave travelled in your direction?' He also had, in the 1930s, a Jewish assistant in his Ashram, Margarete Spiegel, who had been thrown out of her teaching post in Berlin when Hitler came to power. Her disillusionment with life in Berlin, as it so adversely affected Jews, made her think of changing her religion. Gandhi dissuaded her. 'You don't need to be a Hindu but a true Jewess,' he wrote to her. 'If Judaism does not satisfy you, no other faith will give you satisfaction for any length of time. I would advise you to remain a Jewess and appropriate the good of other faiths.' Later he wrote to her: 'Your semitic origin will be least resented in India.'

Gandhi advised the Jews of Germany to follow his prescription for the Indians confronted by British rule: non-violence. But he did publish an article, shortly after the Kristallnacht pogrom in Germany in November 1938, in which he wrote: 'If there ever could be a justifiable war in the name of and for humanity, a war against Germany to prevent the wanton persecution of a whole race would be completely justified. But I do not believe in any war.'

Reading of Gandhi's support for the Arabs of Palestine, the Jewish philosopher Martin Buber, himself an exile from Germany, and a strong advocate of Arab–Jewish reconciliation, wrote to Gandhi from Jerusalem in February 1939 to point out that the Arabs were far from practising non-violence. Why, Buber asked, did Gandhi, the supreme advocate and practitioner of non-violence, cast 'a lenient eye on those who carry murder into our ranks every day without even noticing who is hit'. But with regard to Zionism and the Jewish National Home in Palestine, Gandhi had adopted the view, expressed in an article in the London *Jewish Chronicle* in 1931, that 'Zion lives in one's heart. It is the abode of God. The real Jerusalem is the spiritual Jerusalem.' For this reason, the Jews 'can realize this Zionism in any part of the world'.

With regard to Germany, Gandhi was determined to adhere to his advocacy of non-violence. 'If Hitlerism is to be destroyed,' he wrote to Margarete Spiegel at the end of 1938—after Kristallnacht—'it will be destroyed only by non-violence, and in no other way.' Jawaharlal Nehru—your kinsman, Auntie Fori—understood the contrary view more clearly. At an International Congress Against Imperialism, held in Brussels in 1927, he had befriended the German-Jewish revolutionary, playwright, poet and First World War pacifist Ernest Toller. An exile after 1934, Toller, who supported the Republicans in the Spanish Civil War, committed suicide in May 1939 after learning of the fall of Madrid to the Nationalists. Nehru penned an obituary of him in the Indian *National Herald,* writing of Toller: 'Gradually, and with painful processes of thought, he came to the conclusion that violence against the aggressor was not only justified but necessary to prevent the collapse of what he valued.'

No. 92

Dearest Auntie Fori,

In December 1944, even as the Allied armies advanced across Nazi-occupied Europe, the future of the Jews in Palestine was being discussed at the Labour Party conference in Britain. The conference's conclusions, embodied in a formal public declaration, fully supported an eventual Jewish majority in Palestine. They also advocated a population transfer of Arabs out of Palestine and into the Arab lands beyond. 'Let the Arabs be encouraged to move out as the Jews move in,' the declaration stated, and it added: 'The Arabs have many wide territories of their own.'

The Labour Party declaration went on to propose that there should also be an examination of 'the possibility of extending the present Palestinian boundaries,' by agreement with Egypt, Syria and Transjordan, as the existing area of Palestine might be too small for the number of Jews seeking to enter.

Such was the official Labour Party view in December 1944, at a time when several senior Labour Party figures, including Clement Attlee, Herbert Morrison and Ernest Bevin, were members of Churchill's all-Party War Cabinet. But, for the civil servants who controlled the day-to-day development of policy, the overriding concern at the end of 1944 still seemed to be to prevent the Jewish survivors and refugees from reaching Palestine, and making a Jewish majority there possible. On 24 December 1944, the new High Commissioner for Palestine, Lord Gort, telegraphed from Jerusalem to the Foreign Office in London to ask that the Soviet Government, whose troops had reached both Bucharest and Sofia, be asked to close both the Roumanian and Bulgarian frontiers on the grounds, as he put it, that 'Jewish migration from South-East Europe is getting out of hand.'

On 8 May 1945 the war in Europe came to an end. For six years the Jews had been caught between the evil designs of those who sought to destroy them, and the indifference of those who had no special desire to help them. Six million had been murdered; not only Jewish lives, but Jewish life had been blotted out. Traditions, possessions, culture, the natural evolution of future generations of many more millions: all had been destroyed, more than one-third of the whole of world Jewry.

No longer could the Jews entrust their fate to others. The Holocaust was a bitter, final culmination of two thousand years of persecution. By the winter of 1946 the arguments in favour of Jewish statehood were, for the Jews, of overwhelming clarity.

In Palestine, more than half a million Jews formed the basis of a Jewish entity. Most of them were there because of Britain's promise of 1917—and policy up to 1939—to establish a Jewish 'National Home' in Palestine. But since the 1939 White Paper, no Jewish majority was to be possible under the new British plan. Throughout 1946 it was conflict, not co-operation, that dominated British–Jewish relations in the 'National Home'.

The British were vigilant in their search for hidden Jewish arms. Jews caught in possession of arms were arrested, imprisoned, and even flogged. Following one such flogging, on 29 December 1946, members of a Jewish underground organization, the Irgun, determined to see an end to British rule even by the use of the most violent methods, seized a British major and three sergeants, and flogged them in retaliation. With the opening weeks of 1947 the violence increased: on January 1 another Irgun group, in attacking a British police post, killed a policeman. British newspapers began to urge the partition of Palestine into two States— one Jewish, the other Arab—and a British withdrawal.

The British Government was coming close to the end of both its patience and its self-confidence. On 1 January 1947, at a meeting of the Cabinet's Defence Committee, it was agreed 'that to continue this policy in Palestine in present circumstances placed the Armed Forces in an impossible position'. Three days later the Secretary-General of the Arab League, General Azzam Pasha, announced that the Arabs would vote against any partition scheme that might be put forward, and they would continue to oppose any further Jewish immigration.

Such Arab hostility was well known. But on the morning of 7 January 1947—the year that was to see Indian independence—a new factor was introduced into the Middle East discussion, which made Arab goodwill even more essential. That day a 'Top Secret' memorandum, written four days earlier, was circulated to the Cabinet, entitled 'Middle East Oil'. Its authors were Ernest Bevin, the Foreign Secretary, and Emanuel Shinwell, the Minister of Fuel and Power, a Jewish Member of Parliament.

These two Ministers submitted facts and charts to illustrate what they called 'the vital importance for Great Britain and the British Empire of the oil resources in this area'. The Middle East, they stressed, was likely to provide 'a greater proportion of the total world increase of production than any other oil-bearing region'. By 1950, the 'centre of gravity' would shift from Persia 'to the Arab lands', with Saudi Arabia, Bahrain, Kuwait and Iraq being the main oil producers.

Bevin and Shinwell went on to warn of the grave risks involved in offending the Arabs 'by appearing to encourage Jewish settlement and to endorse the Jewish aspiration for a separate State'.

Bevin himself now favoured a plan put forward by the Arab States for a 'Unitary' State in Palestine, and in a further 'Top Secret' memorandum on January 14, he made one last attempt to warn his colleagues against partition. 'The certainty of Arab hostility to partition is so clear,' he wrote, 'and the consequences of permanently alienating the Arabs would be so serious, that partition must on this ground alone be regarded as a desperate remedy.'

Such a decision, he wrote, would 'contribute to the elimination of British influence from the vast Moslem area between Greece and India', and would have consequences even beyond strategy. 'It would also,' he wrote, 'jeopardize the security of our interests in the increasingly important oil production in the Middle East.'

Bevin told his colleagues that he favoured 'an independent unitary State' in Palestine, with special rights for the Jewish minority, but incorporating 'as much as possible of the Arab plan'. He went on to explain that he did not accept Arab demands to halt Jewish immigration altogether, although, he wrote, 'steps must be taken to prevent a real flooding of the country by Jewish immigrants'.

Bevin argued that 'a Jewish Government' would not accept the partition lines as final, but would eventually seek to expand its frontiers. 'If Jewish irredentism is likely to develop after an interval', he commented, 'Arab irredentism is certain from the outset. Thus the existence of a Jewish State might prove a constant factor of unrest in the Middle East'.

For the Jews in Palestine, statehood still seemed an impossible dream, given Bevin's implacable opposition. But all this was to change almost overnight, even as—in the first months of 1947—the people of India were preparing to see the end of British rule before the end of the year. The British Cabinet, which had been responsible for Palestine since 1917, decided—on 14 February 1947—to hand over all decision making about the future to a United Nations Special Committee on Palestine, known from its initials as UNSCOP. After long discussions, and taking evidence from leading Jews and Arabs, this committee decided on partition, proposing the creation of two separate and independent States, one Arab and one Jewish, with the city of Jerusalem under international trusteeship.

Under these new proposals the Jewish State would contain 498,000 Jews and 407,000 Arabs. The Arab State would contain 725,000 Arabs and 10,000 Jews. The city of Jerusalem and its environs, including the predominantly Christian Arab towns of Bethlehem and Beit Jalla, would contain 105,000 Arabs and 100,000 Jews, but would be under United Nations control, as a separate entity. The Negev Desert would be part of the Jewish State. The fertile hills of Western Galilee would be part of the Arab State. The Palestinian Arabs intimated that they would not accept even this small Jewish State alongside their own.

No. 93

Dearest Auntie Fori,

On 15 August 1947, after many years of struggle, 'your' India became independent. You, Auntie Fori, became the proud citizen of a new nation. Like the Jews, the Indians had been sovereign in their own land in previous centuries. Now they could fly their own flag, defend their own borders, administer their own laws and courts of justice.

The Jews wondered if they would ever be able to do the same, in even a small part of Palestine. In September, the Arab Higher Committee rejected even the United Nations proposal for a 'mini' Jewish State. Subject to further discussions on the actual boundary lines, the Jewish Agency accepted the United Nations proposals, although it meant leaving a quarter of the Jews of Palestine outside the area of Jewish statehood. Abba Hillel Silver—head of the American Zionist Emergency Council—declared on October 2 that acceptance would involve a sacrifice, but that this sacrifice 'will be the Jewish contribution to a painful problem and will bear witness to my people's international spirit and desire for peace.'

On 29 November 1947 the General Assembly of the United Nations accepted its Special Committee's proposals by thirty-three votes to thir-teen, with ten abstentions. Britain was among those States who ab-stained. All six independent Arab States voted against the plan, as did Afghanistan, Cuba, Greece, Iran, and Turkey, and the two most recently independent States, India and Pakistan. Among those in favour of parti-tion were the United States, the Soviet Union, Australia, Canada, France, the Netherlands, New Zealand, Poland and Sweden.

For the Jews of the Diaspora, the news that there was to be a Jewish State in Palestine represented, as the American Zionist Emergency Council declared, 'a milestone in the history of the world', which had 'ended 2,000 years of homelessness for the Jewish people'. For the Jews of Palestine, the news that they were to have a State, albeit a 'mini' one, excluding even Jerusalem, led to rejoicing in the streets.

No. 94

Dearest Auntie Fori,

Among those who rejoiced when news of the United Nations vote reached Palestine was a young Palestinian-born Jewish soldier, Moshe Dayan, later Chief of Staff of the Israeli army, and later still Israel's Minis-ter of Defence and Foreign Minister, and one of the architects of the peace agreement between Israel and Egypt in 1979. He recalled in his memoirs, of the moment in 1947 when he heard the result of the United Nations vote: 'I felt in my bones the victory of Judaism, which for two thousand years of exile from the Land of Israel had withstood persecu-tions, the Spanish Inquisition, pogroms, anti-Jewish decrees, restrictions, and the mass slaughter by the Nazis in our own generation, and had reached the fulfillment of its age-old yearning—the return to a free and independent Zion.'

Dayan added: 'We were happy that night, and we danced, and our hearts went out to every nation whose UN representative had voted in favour of the resolution. We had heard them utter the magic word 'yes' as we followed their voices over the airwaves from thousands of miles away. We danced—but we knew that ahead of us lay the battlefield'.

Among those who were to die on that battlefield in the months ahead was Dayan's own younger brother Zorik. But the Arabs, both inside Palestine and beyond it, turned violently against the United Nations decision. Even the 'mini' Arab State which they were offered was of no interest to their leaders and propagandists, whose hatred was focused towards Jewish statehood.

From the moment of the United Nations vote, Arab terrorists and armed bands attacked Jewish men, women and children all over the country, killing eighty Jews in the twelve days following the vote, looting Jewish shops, and attacking Jewish civilian buses on all the highways.

For the Arabs outside Palestine, a similar wave of anti-Jewish hatred led to violence against Jews in almost every Arab city. In British-ruled Aden, scene of a savage attack on Jewish life and property, eighty-two Jews were killed on December 9. In Beirut, Cairo, Alexandria and Aleppo, Jewish houses were looted, and synagogues attacked. In Tripolitania more than 130 Jews were murdered by Arab mobs.

There followed, in Palestine, five and a half months of terrorism and violence. 'Jews will take all measures to protect themselves', the Jewish National Council declared on December 3. But the Jewish instinct for moderation was a strong one: On December 13 the Jewish Agency, representing a majority of Palestinian Jewry, denounced the mounting tide of Irgun reprisals, calling them 'spectacular acts to gratify popular feeling'.

Nevertheless, as the Arab attacks rose in viciousness during the first four months of 1948, as Jewish Jerusalem was besieged and its water supply cut off, the battles and the reprisals gained a cruel momentum. The killing of more than a hundred Arabs in the village of Deir Yassin on April 9, and of seventy-seven Jewish doctors and nurses while on their way to the Hadassah hospital on Mount Scopus four days later, were but the most widely publicized episodes in a series of attacks and counter-attacks, random killings and military operations, which claimed several thousand lives on both sides.

While these killings were at their height, the British announced that they would withdraw from Palestine altogether on 15 May 1948. During the six weeks before they did so, the Arabs did everything in their power to break communication between the Jewish settlements, to prevent Jews from reaching Jerusalem, and to disrupt all Jewish life within the city itself. Many of the Arabs involved in these military acts, and in the sniping and killing of Jewish civilians, were regular soldiers from outside Palestine, from Syria, and even from Iraq. It was these Iraqi troops who had cut off Jerusalem's water supply.

During April and early May, every isolated Jewish village was subjected to a massive attack: on April 13 four hundred Arab troops attacked Kfar Etzion, just south of Bethlehem. Beaten off, they attacked again on May 12, when a hundred Jews were killed, and only four survived. Fifteen Jews captured at Kfar Etzion were machine-gunned to death after they had surrendered, while being photographed by their captors.

Despite the Arab attacks the Jews were determined not to be driven out of their promised 'mini' State. In the full-scale battles that developed during April between the Arab and Jewish armed forces, Tiberias, Haifa, Acre, Safed and Jaffa were occupied by Jewish forces between April 19 and May 14, while in Jerusalem Arab troops were driven from several suburbs. Between November 1947 and May 1948, more than 4,000 Jewish soldiers and 2,000 Jewish civilians had been killed, nearly one per cent of the total Jewish population.

As May 15, the day of the British withdrawal, drew near, the Jewish situation, despite the capture of the main towns, was still precarious; especially as four well-armed Arab armies, those of Egypt, Transjordan, Syria and Lebanon, were massing on the southern, western and northern borders preparing to invade at the very moment of British withdrawal.

At the last moment, the British advanced the withdrawal date by twenty-four hours to May 14. On May 12, Yigael Yadin, the Chief of Operations of the Hagana—the Jewish Agency's defence force—told Ben-Gurion and the other leaders: 'The regular forces of the neighbouring countries, with their equipment and their armaments, enjoy superiority at this time'. However, he said, the future of the Jews in Palestine 'cannot be merely a military consideration of arms against arms and units, since we do not have those arms and that armoured force. The problem is to what extent our men will be able to overcome enemy forces by virtue of their fighting spirit, of our planning and our tactics.'

For the first time since the defeat of Bar Kochba by the Roman forces more than 1,880 years before, the Jews were preparing to defend their sovereign rights. On the morning of May 14 the last British High

Commissioner left Jerusalem. Britain's thirty-year rule was at an end. That same afternoon, in the Jewish city of Tel Aviv, Ben-Gurion declared the independence of the Jewish State. In a moving address he announced that it would be called 'the State of Israel'. Among those who listened to it, on their army radios, were many soldiers huddled in dugouts and trenches, awaiting imminent Arab attack.

No. 95

Dearest Auntie Fori,

One of those present during the Israel independence ceremony in Tel Aviv was Golda Meir, a future Prime Minister of Israel, and a veritable matriarch of the new Jewish State during its first thirty years. She later recalled how, when Ben-Gurion spoke the words 'the State of Israel', she was overwhelmed with emotion. 'My eyes filled with tears and my hands shook,' she wrote. 'We had done it. We had brought the Jewish State into existence—and I, Golda Mabovitch Meyerson, had lived to see the day. Whatever price any of us would have to pay for it, we had re-created the Jewish national home. The long exile was over. From this day on, we would no longer live on sufferance in the land of our forefathers. Now we were a nation like other nations, masters—for the first time in twenty centuries—of our own destiny. The dream had come true, too late to save those who had perished in the Holocaust, but not too late for the generations to come.'

The coming into existence of the State of Israel was opposed by every Arab State, and in the war that followed the Jews—Israelis now—suffered considerable losses. But their State survived, forming a small but viable entity on the eastern shore of the Mediterranean. More than 550,000 Palestinian Arabs had fled from the area which became Israel. More than two-thirds of them fled to other areas of Palestine—the West Bank and the Gaza Strip—which had been allocated under the United Nations Partition Plan to Arab sovereignty, areas which were at once occupied by Transjordan and Egypt respectively.

For Jews, not only in Israel, but throughout the Diaspora, the establishment of their State was the culmination of centuries of longing, and of decades of struggle. Non-Zionists as well as Zionists often ask: If there had been a Jewish State in 1939, who knows how many Jews might not have been saved from the Holocaust? Since the establishment of the State of Israel in 1948, whenever anti-Semitism threatened Jews in the Diaspora, they had somewhere to which they could turn. Between 1948 and 1952, more than half a million Jews living in Arab lands as far apart as Morocco and Yemen flocked to Israel and rebuilt their lives without the stigma of second-class citizenship. It was not always easy, the new-comers were not welcomed by everyone or integrated all that easily, but the challenge of being one's own master brought forth great reserves of energy and courage. Similar problems were faced, and similar cour-age shown, by more than 120,000 Jews who, in the decade after 1967, reached Israel from the Soviet Union, a number that later grew to almost half a million.

Jews such as those from Arab lands or from the Soviet Union did not necessarily turn to Palestine because they were Zionists whose basic creed—based on the Bible, with secular nationalist overtones—was a Jewish homeland in the land of the Patriarchs. They did so because they were Jews who, in their corner of the world, had been rejected, perse-cuted, humiliated yet again, and whom Israel welcomed.

On 19 May 1948, five days after the establishment of the State of Israel, its first Prime Minister, David Ben-Gurion, spoke of how Jewish statehood had been achieved, and of how it should be maintained. 'We know,' he declared, 'that not by the grace of nations was our freedom won, not upon their bounty will its continuance depend.'

The Jewish community in Palestine had been built, said Ben-Gurion, 'with our own flesh and blood: so too we build, so too we shall guard the State', and he continued: 'Never have we lost faith in the conscience of mankind. Always we shall demand of the world what is justly ours. But morning and evening, day in and day out, we must remind ourselves that our existence, our freedom and our future are in our own hands. Our own exertions, our own capacity, our own will, they are the key.'

Israel also remembered its origins. Theodor Herzl had been buried in Vienna in 1904, a visionary with a dream of Jewish statehood: in 1949 his remains were re-interred on Mount Herzl, the hilltop to the west of Jerusalem that was to become the burial place of Israel's heroes, leaders and fallen soldiers. Herzl's study, likewise brought from Vienna, was re-created near his tomb.

More than once, Israel had to fight to ensure its survival. In 1956, in 1967 and in 1973 it was threatened by the Arab States around it. Each of the wars was, mercifully, short. But each involved heavy loss of life for the small, isolated State. My own first visit to Israel was in 1971. Many of my British contemporaries had gone earlier, to work on a kibbutz or study at the Hebrew University of Jerusalem, or Tel Aviv University—at both of which I later taught. My travels in my twenties, however, had taken me elsewhere, including India in 1958, and to your door, dearest Auntie Fori.

In 1973, two years after my first visit to Israel, I returned there, and by chance was in Jerusalem on the day the October War broke out—on Yom Kippur, the Day of Atonement. It was a frightening moment, during which Israel's fate seemed to hang in the balance. The two attacking armies were beaten off, but the three weeks of the 'Yom Kippur War' were a testing time for the people of Israel. The fact that the Syrian and Egyptian attack (Jordan under King Hussein refrained from joining in) came on the holiest day of the Jewish calendar, the Day of Atonement—a day of prayer and fasting—gave the war a momentous aspect.

In the immediate aftermath of that war, on my return to Oxford—where I was then teaching—I designed and drew an atlas on the subject of Jews and Arabs in Palestine and Israel since the earliest times, *The Arab-Israeli Conflict: Its History in Maps.*

For Israel, peace with its neighbours was slow in coming, but there were nevertheless amazing moments of hope and optimism. The visit of the Egyptian President, Anwar Sadat, to Israel, in 1978, was a high point, unexpected and dramatic. It began a process which has seen two peace treaties and a falling-away of tensions. First came peace with Egypt, negotiated with the support of an American President, Jimmy Carter, at Camp David. Then, twenty years later—a short period of time in the wide sweep of Jewish history—came peace with Jordan, signed on the White House lawn under the watchful eyes of another American President, Bill Clinton. As I write this letter, in the summer of the year 2000, peace with Syria has yet to come. But a new Israeli Prime Minister, Ehud Barak—a former Commander-in-Chief of the Israeli Defence

Forces—is determined to try to put such a peace in place, with President Clinton spending hundreds of hours to try to bring the conflicting parties together.

So Jewish life goes on in Israel and throughout the Diaspora. You have lived through nine decades of that history—almost a full century. It is a period that, despite the terrible Holocaust years, saw a flourishing of Jewish life and creativity throughout the Diaspora, the establishment of a Jewish State—for the first time in two thousand years—and many contributions by individual Jews to the life and well-being of mankind. That, I think, should be the subject of my next letters to you, bringing the history of the Jews up to the twenty-first century. It will be good to end the historical story on a note of celebration.

After that, I will write to you about the Jewish religion: the mortar which for five thousand years has held together the bricks of Jewish life, and the secured survival of the Jews as a people.

No. 96

Dearest Auntie Fori,

Here is the first of seven letters which will span the last fifty years of the twentieth century, or will at least try to do so.

This letter begins behind the Iron Curtain. After the Soviet Union had voted in the United Nations in 1947 in favour of a Jewish State, it soon found its interests best served—in the forty-year Cold War confrontation with the United States—by being the patron of as many Arab States as possible, which it helped to arm and incited against Israel. Internally, Stalin moved to suppress such manifestations of Jewish culture as had survived the long years of his autocracy. Many Soviet Jews felt that, with the defeat of Hitler, they might have a renewal of religious and communal life. But it was not to be, and what became known to Jews as the 'Black Years' of Stalin's rule began. Jewish religious worship was mocked and condemned, and most synagogues were closed down. Links between Jews in the Soviet Union and those outside—even close relatives—were stopped. People were taught to look with suspicion, both at the workplace and in their apartment blocks, on any Jew who showed the slightest interest in his religion, history, or traditions, and to report such behaviour to the authorities.

In 1948 the great Soviet-Jewish actor-manager, Solomon Mikhoels, was murdered on Stalin's orders. Within three years, dozens of leading Jews—many doctors among them—had been murdered. Others had been imprisoned, or sent to forced labour in Siberia. Only Stalin's death in 1952 stopped what might have been a widening and savage pogrom. Some Soviet Jews did well under the Communist regime. In 1962, General Jacob Kreiser, a Second World War Hero of the Soviet Union, and commander of the Soviet Far East region, became a Deputy in the Supreme Soviet. Veniamin Dymshyts, a Soviet Deputy Prime Minister, who had played a central part in developing the Soviet Union's economic links with India, was made head of the National Economics Council in 1962: he made his main task the modernising of distribution, which had been one of the black spots in the Soviet economy. In 1964 a Jewish ballet dancer, Maya Plisetskaya, then prima ballerina of the Bolshoi Ballet, won the Lenin Prize.

Stalin's successors still refused to let Jews emigrate. But in 1967 the Jews of the Soviet Union felt a sudden collective upsurge of affinity with Israel, as the Soviet newspapers and State-controlled radio announced with unconcealed glee the imminent destruction of the Jewish State by the armies of Egypt, Syria, and Jordan. Six days later, Israel emerged from that war victorious, and the awakened consciousness of Russian Jews was ignited. Tens of thousands asked for permission to leave and were refused. Thousands more, wanting to study Jewish history, learn Hebrew, or participate in some form of Jewish communal life, were confronted by a series of obstacles—and at times the threat of arrest and imprisonment.

In the 1970s and early 1980s a worldwide Jewish campaign to persuade the Soviets to 'let my people go' had the effect of uniting Jews throughout the Diaspora. In Moscow, Elena Dubianskaya led a women's group that helped the wives of more than twenty imprisoned Jewish activists, known as Prisoners of Zion. The group also challenged the Soviet authorities when they distorted Soviet Jewish history. When the 1941 Nazi massacre at Babi Yar, a ravine in the suburbs of Kiev, was commemorated in 1985 without any mention of Jews—who were in fact its sole victims—Elena Dubianskaya and members of her group journeyed from Moscow to Kiev to protest. The KGB prevented them from reaching the ravine.

Only with the disintegration of Communism itself were the gates finally opened. An era of often harsh and at times demoralising struggle came to an end, as half a million Jews went to Israel, a quarter a million to the United States, and thousands more to other countries with Jewish communities. But more than a million stayed, hoping that the new Russia and its successor States would be more fair. Only time will tell.

Behind another sort of Iron Curtain of isolation and discrimination, in Syria, lived 3,266 Syrian Jews. Their cause was taken up in the 1990s, amid strictest secrecy, by a Toronto Jewish woman, Judy Feld Carr, who managed to persuade the Syrian government to release 3,228 of them. The thirty-eight who remained had elected to do so. Among those who left was the Chief Rabbi of Syria, Avraham Hamra, who lives today in Israel.

No. 97

Dearest Auntie Fori,

The growing success of Zionism after the Balfour Declaration of 1917, and the immigration of Jews into Palestine in the 1920s and 1930s, had led to a mounting protest from all Muslim lands, and from each of the newly independent Arab States. These protests were not only directed against the Jews coming into Palestine—from Muslim lands as well as from Europe—but against the Jews who were living under Islam and who, for all their problems, wished only to remain in their homes of so many generations.

In Yemen anti-Zionist feeling led, as early as 1922, to a special law which demanded the conversion to Islam of all Jewish orphans under the age of thirteen. Between the two world wars laws forbidding Jews to travel to Palestine were passed in the Yemen and in Iraq. In Tunisia in 1932 local Jews were attacked by an Arab mob protesting against the immigration of European Jews to Palestine. In Egypt in 1938 riots broke out and Jews were attacked in Cairo, Alexandria, Ismailia and Port Said, as part of a Muslim protest against the immigration of German Jews to Palestine. Similar anti-Jewish violence took place in Damascus, after emissaries from Nazi Germany had 'explained' the anti-Jewish policy of the Third Reich to the local Arabs.

During the Second World War those Jews who lived in Muslim lands which came under Nazi control were subjected to slave labour, deportation and physical attack. In many cases local Muslims used the shield of Nazism to carry out their own pogroms. In Iraq in June 1941 following the collapse of a pro-Nazi regime, local Arabs destroyed nearly a thousand Jewish houses and murdered 175 Jews. Even with the defeat of the Nazis their propaganda continued to have its effect throughout the Muslim world, and anti-Semitic cartoons and accusations, once the particular speciality of European prejudice, now joined with existing Muslim attitudes to reinforce anti-Jewish feelings.

The immediate post-war years saw an upsurge of anti-Jewish activity throughout the Muslim world, as the growing number of independent Arab States sought to oppose a Jewish State in Palestine, and to do so by creating anti-Jewish riots within their own borders. Wild rumours were spread. In one town in Iraq a Jew was accused of trying to inject cholera germs into water drunk by Arab children, while in Baghdad a Jew was beaten to death by a mob which had accused him of giving poisoned sweets to an Arab child.

As a result of Israel achieving statehood, the Jews of Muslim lands faced increased hostility. Age-old prejudices now combined with political propaganda. In Aden the United Nations' vote in favour of Jewish Statehood was followed by three days of anti-Jewish rioting, in which 82 Jews were killed and four synagogues burnt to the ground. In Morocco in June 1948 mobs in two eastern towns killed 43 Jews. In Basra, in Iraq, a Jewish millionaire was hanged and his fortune seized. In Baghdad, Zionism was declared a crime. In Cairo, Jewish property was confiscated and more than fifty Jews killed in 'anti-Zionist' riots. In Damascus, the Jewish community council was dissolved. In Libya nearly three hundred Jews' houses were destroyed and twelve Jews murdered.

There then began one of the largest population movements of the twentieth century: the flight of the Jews of the Muslim world to the new Jewish State. This replaced second-class citizenship and the threat of ever-recurring violence by the security of their own sovereignty. In 1945 there were more than 870,000 Jews living in the Arab world. By 1952 more than 500,000 had reached Israel, refugees whose homes, property, inheritances and personal possessions had mostly to be left behind. As Albert Memi, who had been born in Tunis, wrote: 'We should have liked to be Arab Jews. If we abandoned the idea, it is because over the centuries, the Muslim Arabs systematically prevented its realization by contempt and cruelty.' Memi added: 'Not only were the homes of Jews in Germany and Poland torn down, and scattered to the four winds, and demolished—but our homes as well.'

After the return of half a million Jews from the Muslim world to Israel and the flight of a further quarter of a million to Europe, only a fragment of the once large two-thousand-year-old communities remains in the vast area of the Islamic world. The largest, in Iran, 25,000 Jews in all, seems continually threatened by the uncertainties of a religious fanaticism which has already executed one of its leading figures, and brought others to trial on trumped-up charges of spying for Israel. In Egypt, at the time of the Anglo-French-Israeli attack in 1956, following the nationalization of the Suez Canal, more than 10,000 Jews were expelled or fled: some went to Europe, Israel and the United States, others to Britain, among them the future cookery writer Claudia Roden and the future book publisher Martine Halban.

In Egypt, in the aftermath of the Israeli–Egyptian peace treaty of 1979, the small remnant—150 in Cairo and 50 in Alexandria—of a once large and flourishing Jewish community does seem to have a chance of being allowed to live in peace. But for the Jews who still live under Muslim rule, or in lands where Islam is the dominant religion, there can be no possibility of a return to the numbers, the prosperity, and the hope of a distant, past golden age of co-operation and tolerance. The cruel onward march of history has already mocked, and pushed aside, that golden age.

That is not to say that other ages, burnished bronze perhaps, or even silver, should not arise in the Muslim-Jewish firmament. When the Israeli leader Shimon Peres went to Casablanca in 1995, for a meeting between Israelis and Muslim Arab leaders, he saw a brighter future than most. It has not yet emerged. But like all visionaries, Peres understood that without a combination of dream and effort, humanity would not untangle its troublesome knots. Why should the Arab–Israeli conflict not be any less resolvable, in the long run, than the conflict between Germany and France (the conflict between 'Teuton and Gaul' as it was once described) which, after three destructive wars in seventy-five years, evaporated away, leaving only friendship, trade, and open borders?

No. 98

Dearest Auntie Fori,

I write now on a theme of importance in the modern Jewish story, Jews were active in the sphere of human rights in the twentieth century. Victor Basch, who was born in 'your' Budapest in 1863, and educated at the Sorbonne in Paris, founded the League of the Rights of Man in 1926—it was the forerunner of Amnesty International. At the age of eighty-one he was shot, together with his wife, by the pro-German Vichy French militia. His crime: to have been a Jew, to have been a supporter of resistance against the German occupation of France, and to have championed the rights of all mankind. His wife's crime: to have been at his side.

In 1951, six years after the end of the Second World War, the United Nations Convention on the Prevention and Punishment of the Crime of Genocide (known as the Genocide Convention) came into force. Its definition of genocide was inspired by Raphael Lemkin, a Jew who had earlier taken up the cause of the Armenian Christians massacred by the Turks both during and after the First World War.

While the Armenian massacres were at their height, Lemkin, who was then a twenty-one-year-old law student at Lvov University, discussed with his professors the recent assassination by an Armenian of a Turkish politician who had been involved in the massacres. Lemkin's professors defended the Turkish action against the Armenians, invoking the argument about 'Sovereignty of States'. But 'Sovereignty of States,' Lemkin answered, 'implies conducting an independent foreign and international policy, building of schools, construction of roads, in brief, all types of activity directed towards the welfare of people. Sovereignty cannot be conceived of as the right to kill millions of innocent people.'

In 1933, shortly after Hitler came to power in Germany, Lemkin—having coined the term 'genocide'—submitted a proposal to the International Conference for the Unification of Criminal Law, held in Madrid under the auspices of the League of Nations, 'to declare the destruction of racial, religious or social collectivities a crime under the law of nations'. Lemkin defined genocide as 'the criminal intent to destroy or to cripple permanently a human group'. Genocidal acts, he added, 'are directed against groups, as such, and individuals are selected for destruction only because they belong to these groups'. This definition, although rejected—with the whole concept—by the League of Nations, was to form the basis of the United Nations Convention on the Prevention and Punishment for the Crime of Genocide which was promulgated after the Second World War in 1948.

Another of those who made his contribution to the global protection of mankind was a Polish-born Jew, Joseph Rotblat—he is exactly your age, dearest Auntie Fori. During the Second World War he was part of the team that worked in the United States on the development of the atomic bomb. Deeply concerned about the implications of nuclear conflict, in 1957 he was among the founders of the Pugwash conference, dedicated to eliminating the threat of nuclear war. Pugwash named after a remote Canadian village where they first met—brought together scientists from both sides of the Iron Curtain. In Britain, Rotblat worked for more than twenty-five years (1950–1976) at St Bartholomew's Hospital Medical College on how radiation affects living tissue. In 1995 he was awarded the Nobel Peace Prize (and a few weeks ago he was knighted by the Queen).

An American Jew, Luis Kutner, taking up the torch of Victor Basch, was the inspiration behind Amnesty International, which was founded in 1961. The *Chicago Tribune* noted when he died: 'In some parts of the world, especially where there are dictators, people are thrown in jail and can't get out. You are locked up and no writ can reach you. His achievement was that he worked to change that throughout the world.'

In South Africa, Helen Suzman, the daughter of Jewish immigrants from Lithuania—like so many South African Jews—and a Member of Parliament for thirty-six years, campaigned indefatigably against apartheid. Aron 'Ali' Bacher, a leading player in the South African cricket team which beat Australia in 1966, led the campaign for multi-racial sport amid the inequalities of apartheid. Many Jews participated directly in the African National Congress struggle: Joe Slovo, who was charged with treason but later released, drafted the Freedom Charter in 1955 (his parents had brought him from Lithuania when he was nine years old). In 1982 his wife and fellow anti-apartheid activist, Ruth First, was killed when she opened a parcel bomb intended for him. In 1990 he was appointed General Secretary of the African National Congress, and in 1994 he became Minister of Housing in Mandela's government.

Earlier this year, Professor Kadar Asmal, Nelson Mandela's Minister of Education, told a Jewish audience after the ending of apartheid: 'Against the tide of white opinion, the Jewish community produced arguably more heroes and saints than any other so-called white group—including a good few battling rabbis. . . .'

Individual rabbis also played a leading part in the anti-segregation struggle in the United States in the Kennedy and Johnson era—the years Uncle Bijju was Indian Ambassador in Washington. One of them, Rabbi Seymour J. Cohen of Chicago, coordinated the 1963 National Conference on Religion and Race—while you, Auntie Fori, were in Washington—and introduced the keynote speaker, Martin Luther King. Rabbi Cohen was also one of the first activists to champion the emigration of Soviet Jews, making a pioneering visit, also in 1963, to Jewish communities inside the Soviet Union.

No. 99

Dearest Auntie Fori,

The search for excellence has been a driving factor in many Jewish homes. In times of discrimination, Jewish parents were determined that their children would be able to make their way in a hostile world. When that discrimination waned, and the hostility—in many countries—almost totally disappeared—the search for excellence remained. Since it was inaugurated in 1899, the Nobel Prize has been awarded to a higher proportion of Jews than any other group. Since 1945 these have included the first Nobel Prize for a writer in the Hebrew language, the novelist S. J. Agnon, born in Buczacz, in Eastern Galicia (then in Austria–Hungary), writing and living in Israel. The only Nobel Prize for Literature awarded to someone who wrote in Yiddish went to Isaac Bashevis Singer. It was awarded in 1978. Born in Poland in 1904, Singer—whose brother I. J. Singer was also a gifted writer—emigrated to the United States before the Second World War, but continued to write in Yiddish. His novels, with their powerful insight into pre-war Jewish life in Poland, were published as weekly part-works in the New York Yiddish newspaper, the *Jewish Daily Forward*. Translations of his work were a popular feature in both *Playboy* and *The New Yorker*.

Other Nobel Prizes since 1945 have gone to the German-born poet of the Holocaust, Nellie Sachs, and to the South African novelist Nadine Gordimer, who was a leading opponent of apartheid. In 1945 a refugee from Nazi Germany, Ernst Chain, won the prize for his wartime work in Britain in turning penicillin into an effective and life-saving remedy. In 1985 Joseph Goldstein and Michael Brown, American geneticists, won the prize for revealing the process of cholesterol metabolism in the human body. Another 'Jewish' Brown, Herbert Brown, also an American, had won the Nobel Prize for Chemistry six years earlier for his work on organic synthesis which, like his namesake's work on cholesterol, held considerable benefits to the well-being of mankind. Milton Friedman received the prize for his work in support of free trade and the free market, of which he was the economic guru. He believed, as he explained, that economic controls 'have not only restricted our freedom to use our economic resources, they have also affected our freedom of speech, of press, and of religion.'

The Soviet Jewish mathematician Lev Landau won the Order of Lenin, the Lenin Prize, and the Stalin Prize before being awarded the Nobel Prize in 1962. A French Jew, René Cassin, who drafted the Universal Declaration of Human Rights for the United Nations—and whom I mentioned in one of my First World War letters—won the Nobel Peace Prize, as did Elie Wiesel, who had been deported from the town of Sighet, then in Hungarian-occupied Transylvania, to Auschwitz, and whose writings gave the survivors of the Holocaust a powerful voice, reminding the world of how evil grows in the face of apathy.

In 1960 Victor Weisskopf, an Austrian-born physicist and Nobel Prize winner, was appointed Director-General of CERN, the European Council for Nuclear Research, near Geneva. In 1965, Zena Harman, a British-born Israeli, travelled from Jerusalem to receive the Nobel Peace Prize on behalf of United Nations International Children's Emergency Fund (UNICEF), of which she was then board chairman. The American Jewish comedian Danny Kaye, who had devoted much time and energy to helping the Fund, attended the ceremony with her.

On 10 December 1979 a former underground fighter against the British, the Polish-born Menachem Begin, travelled to Stockholm where he received the Nobel Prize for Peace, together with the President of Egypt, Anwar Sadat. They were not to be the last to win the Nobel Prize for trying to bring peace to the Middle East. Two Israelis, Yitzhak Rabin and Shimon Peres—both at different times Prime Minister—and the Chairman of the Palestinian Authority, Yasser Arafat, each received the prize for their efforts to bridge the many gaps of misunderstanding. One can only hope that a few more Nobel Prizes for peacemaking in the Middle East will reward the successful completion of the considerable task that still remains before peace throughout that region is a routine fact of life.

No. 100

Dearest Auntie Fori,

I cannot resist sending you, as my hundredth letter, a letter about Jews in sport, over and above the Hungarian Jewish sportsmen and women I have already written to you about. Jews—who competed in the first modern Olympics in Athens in 1896—continued to show sporting prowess, although non-Jews seldom think of them as being particularly sport-oriented. In the following random examples, decade-by-decade, I have restricted myself to sportsmen and women from America, South Africa and Israel. Since the 1920s, Jewish athletes have competed not only in the Olympics, but in their own sports championship, the

Maccabiah, known as the 'Jewish Olympics'. Held in Palestine on several occasions between the wars, it is now held every four years in Israel, just outside Tel Aviv.

While you, Auntie Fori, were beginning your life in India in the 1930s, Marshall Goldberg—nicknamed 'Biggie' and 'Mad Marshall'—was beginning his championship American football career in which he played from 1939 to 1943, and from 1946 to 1948, for the Chicago Cardinals. In American baseball, Sandy Koufax played for the Los Angeles Dodgers. When the opening game of the World Series fell in 1965 on Yom Kippur, he declined to play, but on the following day returned to the team and by the end of the season won the deciding game, and gave the Dodgers the World Series that year. This year, a Jew from the American South, Bill Goldberg, won the world championship wrestling title.

As I was finishing this letter, I read an obituary of a boxer, Sammy Luftspring, who had just died in Toronto at the age of eighty-five. He would have boxed for Canada in the 1936 Olympics, but his parents pleaded with him not to go. 'They figured I might get hurt, and being an obedient son, I consented.' In 1938 Luftspring was the Canadian welterweight champion, and number three in the world welterweight ranking. Two years later he lost an eye in a warm-up match in New York, and his boxing career came to an end: he was twenty-three years old.

In the 1948 Olympics, Henry Wittenberg, a New York policeman, one of the world's greatest wrestlers, won a gold medal. Between 1938 and 1952—the year in which he won a silver medal at the Helsinki Olympics—he won 400 consecutive matches. In 1949 he was named America's 'best Jewish athlete'. In retirement he became a professor of health education. In 1955, Sylvia Wene Martin became America's woman bowler of the year. The three perfect games (knocking down 300 pins) which she won in her career created a world record which stood for fifteen years.

In 1967 Ron Blomberg began his astonishingly successful baseball career: New York's Jewish fans nicknamed him 'the Messiah'. Once, when it looked as if his team—the White Sox—would have to play on the Jewish High Holy Days, he commented: 'In that case, I've talked to a couple of rabbis who say they'll pray for me at the ballpark'.

Among Soviet Jews who excelled in sport was Alexander Gomelsky, 'father' of basketball in the Soviet Union. He was the coach of the gold medal–winning Soviet basketball team in the Munich Olympics in 1972, the Olympics at which the American swimmer Mark Spitz won seven gold medals, setting a new world record in each event; he has been called the greatest Jewish athlete of all time. Tragically, that was the Olympics at which eleven members of the Israeli team were seized by Palestinian terrorists, held hostage, and killed.

In 1980 the South African Jody Scheckter completed twelve years of successful motorcar racing; among his wins was the American Formula 5000 championship. In 1992 Yael Arad, Israel's women's judo champion, won Israel's first Olympic medal—a silver. The 'most exciting part', she said, was standing on the podium as the band played the Israeli national anthem, 'Hatikvah'—Hope.

No. 101

Dearest Auntie Fori,

Since 1945, Jews have benefited as much as any minority from their unimpeded right to participate in the political life of the democracies. In France two post-war Prime Ministers, Pierre Mendès-France and René Mayer, were Jewish. A leading French civil servant, Olivier Wormser, who during the Second World War was with de Gaulle's Free French movement in London, became French Ambassador to the Soviet Union in 1966. Three years later he was appointed Governor of the Banque de France.

The first President of the European Parliament, inaugurated in 1979, was a survivor of the Holocaust, Simone Weil, a former French Minister of Health. In 1944, at the age of thirteen, she had been deported to Auschwitz with her sister and her mother. Deported elsewhere, her father and brother were never seen again. Her mother died of typhus at Auschwitz. On becoming President of the European Parliament—a post she held until 1982—Simone Weil told the Associated Press: 'As a Jew, as a concentration camp survivor, as a woman, you feel very much that you belong to a minority that has been bullied for a very long time. As for deportation, what remains with you most is the memory of humiliation,

and that is a feeling many women have, too, of trampled dignity.' Stressing the wider, universal aspect of her experiences, Simone Weil added: 'If
this Parliament has a Jew, a woman, as its President, it means everyone has
the same rights.'

In Britain, Jews held senior positions in the administrations of each
post-war Prime Minister. Harold Wilson took several initiatives to press
the Soviet Union to let Jews leave, and was especially proud of having
secured the emigration from Russia of the Panovs—husband and wife
ballet dancers. Wilson had several Jewish advisers: one of them, the Hungarian-born Thomas Balogh, was his adviser on economic affairs in
1964. Balogh had earlier advised the United Nations on the economic
development of India.

In 1960 a Labour Member of Parliament, and former First World
War conscientious objector, Sydney Silverman, piloted the Abolition of
Death Penalty Bill through the House of Commons.

Jews were among the leading members of Margaret Thatcher's Conservative government from 1979 to 1992. Michael Howard was Home
Secretary, and Malcolm Rifkind Secretary of State, first for Scotland and
then for Transport (and later, under John Major, Secretary of State for
Defence, and Foreign Secretary). Both were the grandchildren of Jewish
immigrants from Tsarist Russia, as was Jeremy Isaacs, General Director of
the Royal Opera House from 1988—whose brother, Michael, an immigrant to Israel, had been killed by a terrorist bomb in Jerusalem in the
1970s.

In the countries of the British Commonwealth, Jews were also active
in political and cultural life, and could rise to the top of their profession.
In Australia, Zelman Cowen, a Professor of Public Law, became Governor-General. In New Zealand, Sir Michael Myers, a former Chief Justice, represented his country on the United Nations Committee of Jurists
and was on several occasions Deputy Governor-General.

In Canada, Maxwell Cohen, a member of the Canadian delegation
to the United Nations, later served as chairman of a government commission on hate and propaganda. Borah Laskin was appointed in 1970 a
Judge of the Canadian Supreme Court, the youngest person to be so
appointed; three years later he became Chief Justice. Also in Canada,
David Lewis—who had been born in Poland in 1909, as David Los—led

the New Democratic Party from 1971. His son Stephen was one of Canada's ambassadors to the United Nations.

Elsewhere in the Americas, the Caribbean island of Jamaica benefited in the 1960s from the efforts of a Jew, Sir Neville Ashenheim, the first Jamaican ambassador to the United States, who obtained loans for the creation of an industrial base, and for the tourist industry of his newly independent country. In Brazil, Horacio Lafer served as Foreign Minister for three years, until 1961.

Beyond national politics, Jews have flourished since 1945 in the arts and sciences, in commerce and technology, as teachers and thinkers. In medical research they have brought to bear an unusual dimension: drawing upon the ethical codes in the Bible to try to resolve some of the troubling questions with which modern doctors have to deal: among them abortion, artificial insemination, autopsies and the prolongation of life by mechanical—and most recently, genetic—means. Jewish medical ethics seeks a moral path in these matters, based upon Jewish traditional values and precepts. One of its leading exponents was not a doctor but a rabbi, Immanuel Jakobovits, a refugee from pre-1939 Germany who became Chief Rabbi of Britain and the Commonwealth. As a rabbi in New York in the 1960s he was a pioneer in bringing rabbis and physicians together to discuss areas of ethical concern in medical practice, of which he was an authority throughout his life. Working in Britain, Robert Winston, pioneered techniques of in-vitro fertilisation which enabled women who had not hitherto been able to have children to do so.

Respect for doctors is an integral part of Jewish tradition: it is they who are trained to carry out the highest Jewish precept: to save a life. The Talmud even advises scholars not to live in towns which have no doctors!

No. 102

Dearest Auntie Fori,

It was in the United States that, for fifty years and more after the Second World War, the largest number of Jews lived: more than five million.

Before the war, the next largest other national group had been the 3,500,000 Jews of Poland, of whom more than three million were murdered during the Holocaust. Israel had only 500,000 Jewish citizens in 1945: fifty-five years later, it had still not (quite) caught up with the United States.

Emigrating to the United States after the war was the Italian neurobiologist Rita Levi-Montalcini. Her work had been interrupted when Mussolini's Fascist decrees forbade Jews from holding university posts or practising medicine. In 1951, within five years of reaching the United States, she made a breakthrough in work relating to nerve growth, bearing on both Alzheimer's and Parkinson's diseases. For this pioneering research she was awarded the Nobel Prize in medicine.

America's first Jewish Secretary of State in the twentieth century, Henry Kissinger, was a refugee from Nazi Germany—where he had celebrated his Bar Mitzvah shortly before emigrating. Madeleine Albright, Secretary of State during Bill Clinton's Presidency, was of Czech Jewish origin: her parents had left Czechoslovakia for Britain on the eve of the Second World War. On the memorial wall of the Pinkas Synagogue in Prague, among the names of the 77,297 Jews of Bohemia and Moravia who were murdered by the Nazis, is that of Arnost Korbel, Madeleine Albright's grandfather.

In 1967 the American actor and humorist Milton Beile (born Milton Berlinger) completed his sixth consecutive television series. Known affectionately as 'Mr Television', he had first appeared before the American public in silent films in 1913, at the age of five, and was still appearing in films seventy-five years later. Joan Rivers (born Joan Molinsky) became a star of night-clubs, stage and screen, especially the television screen, from the 1960s. Jackie Mason (born Yacov Moshe Maza), who began his adult life as a rabbi, is a Jewish humorist who makes Jews laugh at themselves.

Another American Jew, Abe Fortas, who in 1945 had been closely involved in the founding of the United Nations, achieved a landmark legal victory in 1963, when the Supreme Court upheld his assertion that poor defendants in criminal cases had the right to free legal counsel. Under President Reagan, Max Kampleman was at the forefront of negotiations between the United States and the Soviet Union for an end to

Soviet human rights abuses, a cause for which another American Jew, Morris Abram, worked in Geneva at the United Nations Human Rights Commission. In the two years (1984 and 1985) when I was a Non-Governmental Organisation participant at that Commission, a Washington law professor, Marshall Breger, rallied Western European countries to a more stalwart position in challenging Soviet human rights violations, particularly in the imprisonment and harassment of Soviet Jews.

American Jews who had fallen under the frown of Senator McCarthy during his anti-Communist witchhunt made careers elsewhere: Carl Foreman, who became President of the Writers' Guild of Great Britain, produced the film *Young Winston* in 1972, and Sam Wanamaker—who was to campaign for the restoration of Shakespeare's Globe Theatre in London—directed Prokofiev's *War and Peace* at the Sydney Opera House a year later.

No. 103

Dearest Auntie Fori,

For many Jews, the experiences of the Jewish people during the Holocaust made the killing of civilians anywhere on the globe something about which they felt particularly strongly. During a ceremony on 27 January 1995 to mark the fiftieth anniversary of the liberation of Auschwitz, Elie Wiesel—whom I mentioned briefly in my 'Nobel Prize' letter—himself a survivor of Auschwitz, told those gathered there: 'As we reflect upon the past, we must address ourselves to the present, and the future. In the name of all that is sacred in memory, let us stop the bloodshed where it is still being conducted. Let us reject, and oppose more effectively, religious fanaticism and racial hate.'

Remembering is seen by Jews not only as a pious gesture to a vanished past, but as a means of drawing the attention of contemporary societies to the dangers that lie along the path of prejudice and intolerance. Francesca Klug, one of the architects of Britain's recent Human Rights Act, a Jewish woman from London who had been born a decade after the Holocaust, reflected in the year 2000: 'My parents brought me up to make the connection between the Holocaust and the history of persecution against the Jews, and the suffering of other minorities.' In the 1980s she had worked for the anti-apartheid movement.

Since the Holocaust, concerns with non-Jewish tragedies have been high on the Jewish intellectual and practical agenda. In 1996 Adam Yauch, one of three Jewish boys who had founded the rock band The Beastie Boys fifteen years earlier, gave a concert in San Francisco to protest against China's cultural repression in Tibet: More than 50,000 people attended. Jewish communities have also raised money to help the victims of 'ethnic cleansing' in both Bosnia and Kosovo.

Since 1945, Jews have participated more actively than ever before in the life and culture of all the democracies in which they live. They have also been as active as at any time in Jewish history in helping Jews in countries where life is not so easy, where prejudice rules, and where persecution rears its hateful head. The World Ort Union, based in Geneva and London, has since 1880, when it was based in Tsarist Russia, given technological training to more than three and a half million Jews. Today it is training 260,000 Jews in sixty countries. World Jewish Relief—which between 1933 and 1939, as the Central British Fund, helped Jews escaping from Hitler—brings food and clothing to elderly, poor Jews throughout the former Soviet Union.

Jewish philanthropists, and uncounted numbers of ordinary Jewish families who respond repeatedly for appeals for funds, have been at the forefront of providing the financial resources needed by the State of Israel to absorb the influx of needy immigrants, most recently from Ethiopia, from Albania—with the collapse of Communism there in 1989—and from Bosnia. Wherever violence and civil war threaten, Jews seek to leave. In 1995, as a member of a British Joint Israel Appeal mission, I accompanied a group of Jews from Chechnya by bus across part of the North Caucasus and then by plane from Russia to Israel: they had no resources of their own to make the journey.

The World Union of Jewish Students, as well as combating anti-Semitism in universities worldwide, provides educational and leadership programmes for Jewish youth wherever they might live. A careful scrutiny of books and newspapers to see whenever the Holocaust is denied or minimized is carried out by, among others, the Anti-Defamation

League in New York, the Simon Wiesenthal Center in Los Angeles, and the Vidal Sassoon Centre for Anti-Semitism at the University of Tel Aviv. Deborah Lipstadt openly and powerfully exposed the Holocaust deniers in her book, *Denying the Holocaust*.

Based in New York, the Ronald S. Lauder Foundation is bringing Jewish education and communal facilities to the former Communist lands of Eastern Europe, including 'your' Hungary. I myself recently visited the school which Ronald Lauder established in Warsaw for more than two hundred children. The headmistress, Helise Lieberman, came from the United States eight years ago.

Worldwide, the Maimonides Foundation works to bring Jews and Muslims closer together. Here in Britain, the Inter-Faith Network for the United Kingdom, founded in 1987, works tirelessly to develop good relations between people of different faiths. Its members include members of the Baha'i, Buddhist, Christian, Hindu, Jain, Jewish, Muslim, Sikh and Zoroastrian faiths. One of its early stalwards was Hugo Gryn, my rabbi and friend who died in 1996. For him—a survivor of Auschwitz—goodwill between all faiths was an article of faith, for the future well-being of mankind.

A substantial volume could be written on these institutions and foundations—of which there are many hundreds—and their good works. But now I must settle down to write you my promised letters about Judaism—the faith, the festivals, the traditions and the pattern of life that have inspired, fortified and sustained the Jews century after century, through good times and bad.

Part Four

FAITH AND WORSHIP

No. 104

Dearest Auntie Fori,

As many of my hundred and three historical letters have shown, the history of the Jews is bound up with the Jewish religion. For several thousand years Jewish laws and traditions have held the Jews together as an identifiable group. As Jewish communities grew and were dispersed throughout the globe, their traditions and beliefs linked them, however far apart they were.

You and I are both part of that dispersal, known as the Diaspora, and of those traditions, however much we may have drifted from them, or even forgotten them altogether.

This letter will be about the Jewish New Year, Rosh Hashana—'The Head of the Year'—one of the holiest and most solemn days in the Jewish calendar. It is also known as Yom Ha-Din, 'Judgment Day', and as Yom Ha-Zikaron, Remembrance Day, as God remembers all his creatures on that day.

On the eve of the New Year, and throughout New Year's Day until sunset, Jews pray in synagogue to God, asking him directly: 'Inscribe us in the Book of Life.' Again and again during the liturgy, worshippers are reminded that three things can 'avert the evil decree'—penitence, prayer and charity. Rabbinical tradition asserts that each Jew's spiritual destiny is written down on New Year's Day. It is then sealed ten days later, on the Day of Atonement. It is written down on the New Year with penitence and a deep quest for forgiveness. It is sealed on the Day of Atonement with a solemn vow.

Because the New Year falls at the beginning of the month, and depends for its start on the sighting of the new moon, it was—and still is—celebrated for two days, the first and second days of the Hebrew month of Tishri. In this way, had the ancients not seen the thin sickle of the new moon on the first day, they would surely have seen it on the second. Reform Jews only celebrate one day, arguing that in modern times one does not have actually to see the new moon to know that it is there.

The Day of Atonement begins on the tenth of Tishri. The New Year and the Day of Atonement are known as the Days of Awe, days on which all religious Jews reflect on their failings and their sins of the previous year, and seek forgiveness, and a purer, more worthy path in the year that lies ahead. Even for non-religious Jews, the Day of Atonement and the New Year services give them an opportunity—every year—to reconnect with God.

The central prayer recited in all synagogues during the New Year service is believed to have been written by one of the great Babylonian teachers, Rabbi Abba Areka, known by the acronym of his name and rabbinical calling as Rabh. He was born in 160 AD and died in 247 AD at the age of eighty-seven. From Babylon he had gone as a young man to Palestine, where he studied in the rabbinical academies there. He then returned to Babylon where he founded the rabbinical academy at Sura—an academy that was to remain a centre of Jewish learning for eight hundred years. The prayer which he contributed to the New Year liturgy speaks of God as the one 'who rememberest the pious deeds of the patriarchs—Abraham, Isaac and Jacob—and in love will bring a redeemer to their children's children'.

Rabh also wrote the words that are recited as part of the daily Amidah prayer, describing God as the one who 'sustaineth the living with lovingkindness, revivest the dead with great mercy, supportest the falling, healest the sick, freest the bound, and keepest faith to them that sleep in the dust'.

Among Rabh's sayings was that 'the world is a beautiful world, and man will be called to account for every lawful occasion on which he has deprived himself of its goodness'. He also said that 'whoever is devoid of pity is no child of Abraham'. Central to the New Year liturgy is the recital in synagogue of the story of the *akedah*—the 'binding'—Abraham's willingness to bind his son Isaac on the sacrificial altar: that decisive moment when God called for total obedience, even if it meant the sacrifice of one's child. That day Jews ask in their prayers: 'Remember in our favour . . . how Abraham suppressed his fatherly love in order to do Your will.'

The principal synagogue ritual on the New Year is the blowing of the shofar, the ram's horn. The ram's horn was favoured because it was a ram that was caught in the thicket when Abraham was about to sacrifice his son Isaac, and which thus provided the alternative sacrifice that saved Isaac's life, thereby enabling the Jewish genealogy to begin. The horn of a sheep, goat or antelope may also be used. The only horn which is forbidden is that of a cow, lest there be heard some echo of the pagan worship of the Golden Calf by the Israelites in the wilderness, when Moses left them to speak with God on Mount Sinai—an episode which to this day pious Jews recall with shame. The ram's horn is not blown when the holiday falls on a Sabbath, as the laws of the Sabbath—forbidding all work—take precedence.

In the Book of Numbers the first day of the seventh month is described as a day when 'ye shall have an holy convocation; ye shall do no servile work: it is a day of blowing the trumpets unto you'. In ancient times there was considerable rabbinical discussion about why the horn should be blown at all. The prophet Amos had asked: 'Shall a trumpet be blown in the city, and the people not be afraid?' The prophet Zephaniah speaks of the Day of Judgment as 'a day of the trumpet and alarm against the fenced cities, and against the high towers'. The sound of the ram's horn would instantly bring back the mind of the sinner to contemplation of repentance.

Since earliest times a curved horn has been used, as a visual symbol of man bowing in submission to God's will. Maimonides, in the twelfth century, summing up the reasons for the trumpet call, wrote that it was as if to say to all Jews: 'Awake from your slumbers, ye who have fallen asleep in life, and reflect on your deeds. Remember your Creator. Be not of those who miss reality in pursuit of shadows, and waste their years in seeking after vain things which neither profit nor save. Look well to your souls and improve your character. Forsake each one of you his evil ways and thoughts.' What a wise man Maimonides was!

As the New Year begins the Book of Life is believed to be open: Jews greet each other with the words, 'May you be inscribed for a good year.' Sephardi Jews add to this greeting, 'May you be worthy of abundant years.' In some communities bread is baked on the New Year in the form of ladders, as a symbol of the fate and fortune that lies ahead: some men will rise up the ladder of life, others will go down it. In other communities the bread—the *challah*—is round; sometimes it has raisins in it.

The New Year celebrations at home include eating apple and honey, in anticipation of the sweet year that, we hope, and with God's blessing, lies ahead. The blessing is succinct: 'May it be thy will, O Lord our God and God of our fathers, to renew us unto a good and sweet year.' Nuts are not eaten, because they produce phlegm, which would make it more difficult to recite the day's prayers. Also, the numerical value—and every Hebrew letter is given a numerical value—of the Hebrew letters for the word nut (*egoz*) is the same as that for the word sin (*het*).

On the first day of the New Year, or the second day if the first falls on the Sabbath, a tradition has grown up based on the words of the prophet Micah: 'He will turn again, he will have compassion upon us; he will subdue our iniquities; and thou wilt cast all their sins into the depths of the sea.' In Hebrew, 'wilt cast' is *tashlikh:* and the Tashlikh ceremony involves finding some running water—the sea, or a stream, or even a pond—at which symbolically to throw one's sins into the water, while reciting this verse from Micah, and praying for God's forgiveness. According to one ancient tradition, running water is chosen for the Tashlikh ceremony because the fish in the river, whose eyes never close, remind us of the ever-watchful eyes of God, who is always looking down on his creatures on earth—in mercy.

In the last hundred and fifty years a custom has grown up among Jews—derived entirely from Christian practice—to send each other New Year cards. It is at this moment that the annual Jewish calendar begins. The next year that will begin after you receive this letter, the year 5761, starts on 30 September 2000. I will try to remember to send you a Jewish New Year card then, to your Himalayan foothills!

No. 105

Dearest Auntie Fori,

Ten days after the Jewish New Year comes the Day of Atonement, Yom Kippur—or, more correctly, in the plural, Yom ha-Kippurim, the Day of Atonements. It was on this day, the holiest day in the Hebrew calendar, that the armies of Egypt and Syria chose to invade Israel in 1973. It was, bizarrely, a blessing in disguise for Israel. Instead of the reserve soldiers who make up the bulk of the Israeli army being at the seaside or at picnic places throughout the countryside—as they might well have been on a public holiday or festival—they were mostly in synagogue. Thus it was far easier to call them to their army units than had the attack been made on a holiday, or indeed on an ordinary weekday, when they would have been at work in tens of thousands of different places: shops, offices, classrooms, factories, fields. From the synagogues many of them went straight to the front. Although caught unawares, Israel was able, after a few days of heavy fighting and heavy losses, to halt the attackers.

On that Day of Atonement in 1973 the strict religious injunction not to drive cars was swiftly broken, as soldiers were hurried to the threatened borders, and the rabbis permitted the violation of the rules, on behalf of the protection and preservation of the life of the nation.

The sense of history is never absent from the Day of Atonement. Among the hymns that are sung is one that was written by Rabbi Yomtob of York, who was almost certainly one of the Jews massacred in the British city of York in the year 1190. In the concentration camps during the Holocaust, even at Auschwitz where Jews died every day of starvation, there were those who managed, somehow, to fast that day, and to save their meagre scrap of bread until after sunset at the end of the fast.

Like the Sabbath day, the Day of Atonement is one of rest from worldly pursuits. Indeed, it is called in the Bible 'a Sabbath of Sabbaths'. Like New Year's Day it is a day of the most solemn reflection, prayer, and repentance. The Day of Atonement is also a day of fasting. Eating and drinking, as well as working, are forbidden. In the Book of Leviticus, the Day of Atonement is described as 'a Sabbath of rest unto you, and ye shall afflict your souls; it is a statute for ever. For on that day shall the priest make an atonement for you, to cleanse you, that ye may be clean from all your sins before the Lord.' Since the Temple and animal sacrifice no longer exist, each person makes his own atonement—through prayer.

The forgiveness of sins sought, and hopefully obtained, on the Day of Atonement is for sins committed by man against God. For sins committed by man against his fellows, full restitution, and a specific pardon by the person who has been wronged—as well as repentance—is needed and sought. The confessions recited throughout the day are of Biblical origin. In the Book of Leviticus the High Priest expresses them thus: 'I have sinned, I have committed iniquity, I have transgressed.' The Jewish sage Mar Samuel, who died in 257 AD, expressed the atonement in the words, 'Verily we have sinned'. The Rabh, about whom I have written to you earlier, addressed God with the words: 'Thou knowest the secrets of eternity.' These phrases and supplications remain an integral part of the confession to this day.

The prayers of the Day of Atonement begin in synagogue immediately after sunset on the first evening, with Kol Nidre, the prayer—with its haunting melody in the Ashkenazi tradition—with which the congregation ask God to release them from vows made during the previous year. To listen to, and to participate in the singing is a deeply moving experience, no less so year after year. In the words of Judah the Pious, in the thirteenth century: 'Chant your supplications to God in a melody that makes the heart weep, and your praises of Him in one that will make it sing. Thus you will be filled with love and joy for Him that seeth the heart.' The fast has already began.

In the Middle Ages, Christians mocked the Kol Nidre prayer, saying with contempt that in it the Jews reneged on the vows they had made to non-Jews, cancelling all debts, turning their back on all promises and pledges. But the vows for which, in Kol Nidre, the Jews seek annulment, are those made by man to God.

The origins of the prayer are obscure. Two versions predominate. One is that it had its origins in seventh-century Spain, where, at the time of the persecutions carried out by the ruling Visigoths, whole Jewish communities faced torture, and death by burning at the stake, unless they gave up their religion and denounced their God. They had also to promise not to take part in any further acts of Jewish worship, and to forgo their Jewish religious practices altogether. To save their lives—and in Jewish tradition the saving of human life is a commandment that overrides all others—these Jews swore to give up their religion. When Visigoth rule eventually disappeared, and better times came for the Jewish communities of Spain, they felt that they and their ancestors had perjured themselves before God by the vows made to the persecutors. The Kol Nidre prayer released them from those vows.

A second tradition asserts that the prayer for the annulment of all vows arose in the early Middle Ages, with regard to those within the Jewish community who had been excluded from it, who refused to join in communal work and had refused to be bound by the laws of the community. For such self-expulsion, they were expelled from the congregation, and put under a ban, or *herem* (excommunication). But when the Day of Atonement came—the most solemn day in the Jewish calendar—those who had been excluded because of their transgressions wanted to return to their people and to its public worship. The religious authorities agreed that they should do so. Hence the Kol Nidre prayer, and indeed the whole Day of Atonement service, is proceeded by the words: 'In the name of God, and in the name of the Congregation, with the sanction of the Court Above, and that of the Court below, we declare it is permitted to pray together with those who are transgressors.'

Throughout the first evening of prayer, and throughout the following day, the whole community, in synagogue, make their confession of sins. In all, during the Day of Atonement, that confession is repeated ten times. A white robe, known as a kittel, is worn by many of the male worshippers. The reasons for this have—as with almost every Jewish custom—a variety of possible origins and explanations. One is that the kittel is the actual shroud in which that person will be laid in the grave, and that wearing it during the atonement service will inspire repentance by reminding the wearer of death. This explanation can be traced back to the early Middle Ages in both Italy and Provence.

Other rabbinical commentators point out that the Day of Atonement is also a festival: and that men dress in white that day, in synagogue and in the street, not as reminders of the grave, but as a sign of the festive nature of the day. According to one rabbinical tradition: 'When men are summoned before an earthly ruler to defend themselves against some charge, they appear downcast and dressed in black, like mourners. The Israelite appears before God on Atonement Day dressed in white, as if going to a feast; because he is confident that, as soon as he returns penitently to his Maker, He will not condemn, but will abundantly pardon.'

Many customs have come down from the Day of Atonement in the Middle Ages to its celebration in modern times. In one such custom, two candles are lit in the home, one for the souls of the living and one for the souls of the dead. The giving of charity is encouraged on the Day of Atonement—although no money may pass hands until after sunset the following day.

On the afternoon of the Day of Atonement, during the Biblical readings, the Book of the Prophet Jonah is read in its entirety. God had told Jonah to go to the pagan city of Nineveh, to 'cry against it' because of its wickedness. Jonah was unwilling to obey, in case (in the view of some commentators) the Nineveh-ites repented, were saved, and then turned against the Israelites. Seeking to avoid God's command, he went on board a ship at Joppa—today's Jaffa, just south of Tel Aviv—which was sailing to Tarshish, a town as far from Nineveh as possible. God then created a tempest, the sailors cast lots as to who was responsible, the lot fell on Jonah. He begged the sailors to throw him in the sea in order to save themselves. At first the sailors would not do so, but when the tempest continued they 'took up Jonah, and cast him forth into the sea: and the sea ceased from her raging'.

By God's design, Jonah was then swallowed by 'a great fish'—much later commentators call it a whale—whereupon he cried out to God to save him. The fish then spewed out the prophet, who made his way to Nineveh and warned the king and citizens that in forty days the city would be overthrown. The king and his people repented and prayed to God, 'and God saw their works, that they turned from their evil way; and God repented of the evil, that he had said he would do unto them; and he did it not'.

God's mercy 'displeased' Jonah, 'and he was very angry'. Leaving Nineveh, he made a booth and sat under it in the shadow, waiting to see if God would destroy the city. But God, who had decided to spare it, made a gourd grow that cast a shadow over Jonah's head as he slept, and then prepared a worm which penetrated the gourd the next morning so that it withered and died. Then God prepared a hot east wind and when the sun beat down on him he fainted and wanted to die. 'It is better for me to die than to live', he said. God then asked Jonah if he was angered by the fate of the gourd. Jonah says he was, 'even unto death'. God then told Jonah—in the words with which the Book of Jonah ends: 'Thou hast had pity on the gourd, for that which thou hast not laboured, neither madest it grow; which came up in a night, and perished in a night: And should I not spare Nineveh, that great city, wherein are more than six score thousand persons that cannot discern between their right hand and their left hand; and also much cattle?'

Jonah's story is read in its entirety on Yom Kippur to give two messages. The first is that it is impossible for a man to escape from doing God's will. The second, which many rabbis suggest in their sermons that day is the more important, is that God is concerned with all his creatures, even if they are heathens: if their repentance is genuine, God will accept it. Rabbi Louis Jacobs comments: 'By a stroke of religious genius, the tradition has set aside the Book of Jonah, with its universalistic message, for reading . . . on the afternoon on Yom Kippur, the special Day of Atonement when the Jewish people becomes reconciled with its God.'

On Yom Kippur—and also on Shavuot and Shemini Atzeret and the last day of Passover—a memorial service, *yizkor* ('God shall remember') is held. It consists of special prayers for deceased parents and other close relatives, as well as the prayer *el male rahamin* (O God, full of compassion), for martyrs, for the six million Jews murdered in the Holocaust, and for the soldiers killed in Israel's wars. In some synagogues it is customary for those who have two living parents to leave while Yizkor is being recited. *El male rahamin* originated in Western and Eastern Europe, where it was recited for those who had been murdered during the Crusades, and later in the Chmielnicki massacres in the seventeenth century.

The Day of Atonement service ends in synagogue, as the sun sets, with the Neilah service—the closing of the Heavenly Gates. God has listened to the confessions of sins; the time has come for him to ponder and remit them. Both Ashkenazi and Sephardi Jews pray to God: 'Open unto us the gates of mercy, and forgive our iniquities, at the time of the closing of the Heavenly Gates.' Among the most powerful hymns of the

Day of Atonement is the one, originally from the Sephardi ritual, with which the Neilah service begins: *El Nora Alila* ('God whose work is awesome'). It was written by Moses ibn Ezra, who lived in Christian Spain (he died in 1135):

> *God whose work is awesome,*
> *God whose work is awesome,*
> *help us to forgiveness,*
> *as the Gates of Mercy close.*

> *We are not great but 'few in number',*
> *yet to You our vision rises.*
> *We tremble but we dare ask,*
> *because the Gates of Mercy close*

> *Their souls they pour out to You,*
> *wipe out their sin, their shame!*
> *Help them to forgiveness*
> *before the Gates of Mercy close*

At the end of the Neilah service, the ram's horn is sounded, and the whole congregation recite—call out in unison—'*Le'shanah haba'ah bi-Jerushalayim*': 'Next Year in Jerusalem'.

With that pious hope, the cry of Jews throughout the ages—including the many centuries when any chance of seeing Jerusalem was remote in the extreme—the gates of the old year are closed, and the hours of fasting and repentance come to an end.

Even amid the sombre thoughts of the Day of Atonement, Jewish tradition did not forget the call of the positive and the joyful. The meal before the fast begins is meant to be a festive one. From earliest times, there was much feasting on the eve of the fast, not just to stock up on food before the twenty-four-hour prohibition, but to fulfill the commandment to 'rejoice in and honour' the festive day. Again, when the Day of Atonement ends, an air of festivity is permitted, and indeed encouraged. The meal with which the fast is ended is one of festive gathering of family and friends, of singing and laughter. It is a religious duty that night to enjoy oneself, and to eat well. An ancient rabbinic commentary states that after the fast has ended a heavenly voice proclaims: 'Go thy way, eat thy bread with joy, and drink they wine with a merry heart, for God hath already accepted they works.'

As the bonds of the Jewish faith weaken, as assimilation grows in scale and pace, the Day of Atonement remains, for many Jews, the one occasion when they go to synagogue. That day, in almost every synagogue, can be found Jews who have no idea of the form of service, no knowledge of the prayers or even any means of following them, but who wish to be present at a Jewish moment—at the most solemn moment in the Jewish calendar. 'In recent generations,' writes Dr Moshe David Herr, of the Hebrew University of Jerusalem, 'the Day of Atonement has become the last concrete bond with Judaism for many Jews.'

No. 106

Dearest Auntie Fori,

This letter will be about one of the 'joyous' festivals, Shavuot, the Festival of Weeks, which celebrates the proclamation of the Ten Commandments on Mount Sinai, the Day of Revelation. The central part of the synagogue service that day is the reading of the Ten Commandments. In some traditions, the synagogue is decorated with flowers and plants, reflecting some pre-Mosaic agricultural celebration, and making the day a harvest festival as well as one of religious revelation.

Throughout the night leading up to the festival, many Orthodox and pious Jews spend the time in synagogue, reading passages from the Bible from dusk to dawn, as a preparation for the solemn moment of reading the Ten Commandments. According to tradition, a Jewish child is first introduced both to the study of religion and to the study of the Hebrew language on Shavuot, so that for him, as for his elders, the festival will be understood as the Day of Revelation, when God revealed the basic tenets of the religion to Moses. You may remember the letter in which I wrote of that dramatic moment in the history of the Children of Israel and their wanderings in the wilderness.

On the second day of Shavuot, the Book of Ruth is read in synagogue. It is also read by many Jews in their homes. It tells the story of a woman who, giving up the worship of idols, entered into the Covenant of Sinai of her own free will, and joined the Household of Israel. Indeed, the end of the Book of Ruth shows that King David was her great-grandson, and therefore, according to Christian belief, Jesus was also her descendant.

Ruth herself was a Moabite who became the first convert to Judaism. Her first husband, Mahlon, was the son of an Israelite couple, Naomi and Elimelech, who had left Judaea at a time of famine, crossed the River Jordan, and settled in Moab (today's Kingdom of Jordan). Ruth chose to follow the ways and the people of her mother-in-law Naomi. Ruth, Mahlon, Elimelech and Naomi lived in Moab for ten years, during which time Mahlon died. When Elimelech also died, Naomi urged Ruth to remain in Moab while she went back to Judaea. But Ruth refused to leave her mother-in-law, explaining, in words which move many who recite them in synagogue to tears: 'Entreat me not to leave thee, or to return from following after thee: for whither thou goest, I will go; and where thou lodgest, I will lodge: thy people shall be my people, and thy God my God.'

When, at the beginning of 1941, Winston Churchill was desperate to know how closely the United States would support Britain, he asked Roosevelt's close friend Harry Hopkins where the United States stood. Hopkins answered with Ruth's words 'whither thou goest, I will go . . .'. Churchill then knew that Britain would survive.

As her second husband, Ruth married Boaz, another Israelite. David (and Jesus) were their descendants. Because in Jewish belief the Messiah will be descended from David, Jews are taught to accept converts willingly—although they do not proselytize for conversions. Ruth, the first convert, became the 'patron saint' of converts.

No. 107

Dearest Auntie Fori,
Sukkot, the Festival of Tabernacles, and the last of the three Pilgrim Festivals of the Jewish religion, when, in Temple times, Jews went up

on foot (and still go today, though usually by bus) to Jerusalem to celebrate.

During the seven days of Sukkot, observant Jews eat and sleep in a
booth—known as a sukkah—erected in or near their home. Its pre-
requisite is that its roof is open to the sky. The original instruction comes
from the Book of Leviticus, at the time when the Children of Israel were
living in the wilderness, after the Exodus from Egypt: 'Ye shall dwell in
booths seven days; all that are Israelites born shall dwell in booths. That
your generations may know that I made the Children of Israel to dwell
in booths, when I brought them out of the land of Egypt: I am the Lord
your God.'

The roof of the booth has to be made of the branches of trees—
including willow—and from leaves. No man-made material is allowed,
lest it be tainted with some impurity. The fruits that hang from the roof,
as decoration, may be eaten during the festival. The roof has to be put up
in such a way that, while open to the sky, the shaded area which it casts
will exceed the unshaded area. During the seven days of the festival, the
sukkah is regarded as the main abode of the males of the family: they
must take all their meals in it, and sleep in it. Women and young children
continue to sleep in the house.

Today, most synagogues will build a communal sukkah, often beautifully decorated with fruits. Jews build their sukkahs on their roofs, on
balconies, and in their gardens, recalling the description, in the Book of
Nehemiah, of God's commandment to Moses:

> *Go forth unto the mount, and fetch olive branches, and pine branches, and*
> *myrtle branches, and palm branches, and branches of thick trees, to make*
> *booths, as it is written.*
>
> *So the people went forth, and brought them, and they made booths,*
> *every one upon the roof of his house, and in the courts of the house of*
> *God, and in the street. . . .*

On the first day of Sukkot, Jews take the four species—*arba'ah
minim*—of plant, according to the words in the Book of Leviticus: 'And
ye shall take you on the first day the fruit of goodly trees, branches of
palm trees, and the boughs of thick trees, and willows of the brook'. The

'fruit of goodly trees' is represented by the citron (*etrog*)—a type of lemon—and the 'boughs of thick trees' are represented by myrtle twigs (*hadasim*). The palm branch (*lulav*) and willow branches (*aravot*) make up the four. On the first day of Sukkot, every observant Jew holds these four species in the right hand, while reciting psalms and blessings.

In the sixteenth century the kabbalists (Jewish mystics) who were followers of Rabbi Isaac Luria—who died in 1572—introduced a new custom for Sukkot. On each of the seven days a 'guest' is welcomed into the sukkah: these special guests are the three patriarchs Abraham, Isaac and Jacob, followed by Joseph, Moses, Aaron and King David. Tradition relates that the Children of Israel were divinely protected while living in booths in the wilderness solely because Abraham had given shelter to three strangers under his tree in Hebron. When they arrived at his home, he said to them: 'Let a little water, I pray you, be fetched, and wash your feet, and rest yourselves under the tree: And I will fetch a morsel of bread, and comfort ye your hearts; after that ye shall pass on. . . .' This is the first recorded act of spontaneous hospitality.

The seven guests—known in Hebrew as *ushpizin*—are also said to represent the seven sefirot—the seven spheres or dimensions through which God manifests himself to man: lovingkindness, power, beauty, victory, splendour, foundation and sovereignty.

Two Jewish philosophers, Philo of Alexandria two thousand years ago, and Maimonides in the twelfth century, both suggest that the sukkah is built to remind us of misfortune at a time of good fortune, and specifically to remind the rich of the plight of the poor. There is so much homelessness today, in almost all the world's cities—and London, where I am writing this letter, is no exception—that these booths may have a modern application, to enable thought and reflection about those less fortunate.

No. 108

Dearest Auntie Fori,

The seventh day of Sukkot is known as Hoshana Rabba, the Great Hoshana, which since the Middle Ages has been regarded as the last possible day on which one can seek and obtain forgiveness for the sins of the previous year. The name comes from the word *hoshana*—'Save, I Pray', which appears frequently in the prayers during that day. These prayers are for a good harvest. They are recited during a procession that takes place inside the synagogue, around the *bimah*—the elevated platform at the centre of the synagogue, from which prayers are read (or, if the bimah is at the eastern end of the synagogue, as it sometimes is, the procession goes around the floor).

During the procession the four species, tied together, are waved and shaken in recollection of the time, two thousand years ago and more, when they used to be taken around the altar in the Temple in Jerusalem. One Jewish custom is to spend the whole night of Hoshana Rabba in prayer and study, especially of the Book of Deuteronomy, beginning with its opening explanation: 'These be the words which Moses spake unto all Israel on this side Jordan, in the wilderness, in the plain over against the Red Sea. . . .'.

According to one mediaeval superstition, if a man does not see his shadow on the night of Hoshana Rabba, he is fated to die during the following year.

The eighth and final day of Sukkot is a festival in its own right, Shemini Atzeret (the festival of Solemn Assembly). It derives from the verse in the Book of Numbers: 'On the eighth day ye shall have a solemn assembly: ye shall do no servile work therein.' A memorial service, and a prayer for rain, are recited in synagogue that day, and the Book of Ecclesiastes is read in its entirety, with its powerful opening verses:

> *Vanity of vanities, saith the Preacher, vanity of vanities; all is vanity.*
>
> *What profit hath a man of all his labour which he taketh under the sun?*
>
> *One generation passeth away, and another generation cometh: but the earth abideth for ever.*

The Book of Ecclesiastes ends with the words, recited as the last day of Sukkot comes to an end:

> *Let us hear the conclusion of the whole matter: Fear God, and keep his commandments: for this is the whole duty of man.*

For God shall bring every work into judgment, with every secret thing, whether it be good, or whether it be evil.

No. 109

Dearest Auntie Fori,

One more festival is associated with Sukkot, and takes place two days after the eighth and final day of Sukkot. It is called Simhat Torah (Rejoicing in the Torah). On this day, in synagogue, the annual weekly reading of the Torah is concluded, and then begun again.

Throughout the service, all the Torah scrolls are taken from the ark, and carried in joyous procession around the synagogue, seven times in all, as songs of praise are sung. In many communities, congregants dance with the scrolls in their arms. All the men present in the synagogue are called up to read from the scrolls. Children, too, join in the festive parade of the holy books. As the final verses of the fifth book of Moses, Deuteronomy 33 and 34, are read, all the children in the synagogue who have not yet had their Bar Mitzvah—all those under the age of thirteen—are called up to the bimah to hear the reading of the verses:

The eternal God is thy refuge, and underneath are the everlasting arms; and he shall thrust out the enemy from before thee; and shall say, Destroy them.

Israel shall then dwell in safety alone: the fountain of Jacob shall be upon a land of corn and wine; also his heavens shall drop down dew.

Happy art thou, O Israel: who is like unto thee, O people saved by the Lord, the shield of thy help, and who is the sword of thy excellency! and thine enemies shall be found liars unto thee; and thou shalt tread upon their high places.

The person who is called up—who is given an *aliyah*—to read the final passage of Deuteronomy is known as the *Hatan Torah*—the Bridegroom of the Torah. A second person is then called up, known as the *Hatan Bereshit*—the Bridegroom of Genesis—who begins the reading of the first of the Five Books of Moses, from its first words, 'In the beginning God created the heaven and the earth. . . .'

Thus the cycle of reading begins again without a break. According to one tradition, this was done in order to 'refute Satan', who might otherwise say that the Jews, having finished their readings from the Five Books of Moses, were unwilling to start them again, being happy to set them aside and ignore them.

When the service ends, both 'bridegrooms' invite the congregants to a festive party in honour of the day.

In the 1960s in the Soviet Union—thirty years before the collapse of Communism—the celebration of the Rejoicing of the Law became the focal point for Jews who wished to return to Judaism, and to obtain permission to leave Russia for Israel. A main meeting place in Moscow was the Archipova Street synagogue, and the street itself. KGB officials kept a careful watch, but the gatherings became an annual and exciting moment in Soviet Jewish life. Greetings were exchanged, pages of scripture and even whole books were passed from hand to hand. The few Jewish visitors from the West, especially those from Israel, were welcomed, embraced, and quizzed about every aspect of Jewish and Israeli life, by men and women eager to rejoin the Jewish community—*Am Yisrael*—the People of Israel—from whom, for three long decades, they had been almost totally cut off.

How well I remember those eager questions, bright eyes and keen anticipations of life in Israel: so much so that I called the book which I wrote about one of my visits to the refuseniks in Moscow, Leningrad and Minsk, *The Jews of Hope*. The struggle for the right of Soviet Jews to live in Israel galvanized the Diaspora throughout the 1970s and early 1980s. Thousands of Jews visited the Soviet Union to meet and give moral—and material—support to those who had been refused the right to leave. Those refused an exit visa were even given a name, 'refuseniks', coined by Michael Sherbourne, a British Jew who was at the forefront of the campaign for their release. Eventually, with the collapse of Communism, the refuseniks were allowed to leave. Some had been in the dark limbo world of refusal for a decade and even more, thrown out of their jobs, harassed by Soviet officials, and uncertain if they would ever be allowed to leave.

Today, they can participate in the Rejoicing of the Law with the memory of their seclusion and captivity still fresh in their minds.

No. 110

Dearest Auntie Fori,

Tisha B'Av ('Ninth of Av')—that is to say, the ninth day of the Hebrew month of Av—is a day of fasting. It came into being to remember the destruction of the First Temple by the Babylonians in 586 BC. After the building of the Second Temple by Herod, it remained as a fast day to recall the earlier destruction. Then, with the destruction of the Second Temple by the Romans in 70 AD, the fast, with an even greater intensity of feeling, came to commemorate both destructions. To this day—no Third Temple having been built, even during the time of the British Mandate or after Israel's conquest of the Temple Mount from the Jordanians in 1967—the fast day remains a poignant moment in the Jewish religious calendar. There is also some feeling that the Holocaust should be remembered on Tisha B'Av.

In synagogue the fast is marked by the recitation of the Book of Lamentations, with its plaintive opening refrain: 'How doth the city sit solitary, that was full of people! how is she become as a widow! she that was great among the nations, and princess among the provinces, how is she become tributary! She weepeth sore in the night, and her tears are on her cheeks: among all her lovers she hath none to comfort her. . . .'

Jewish historical tradition holds a tragic place for the fast day of Tisha B'Av. The fortress of Betar, the last of Bar Kochba's fortresses to hold out against the Romans, was said to have been captured by Hadrian's legions that day in 135 AD. It was also on Tisha B'Av, on 18 July 1290, that King Edward I signed the edict whereby all Jews were banished from England—in which they had lived for almost two hundred years. This was the first time in European history that a Jewish community had been expelled in its entirety. In the expulsion from Spain in 1492 the last Jew to have left is said to have done so four days before Tisha B'Av.

As the accumulated disasters grew, so the custom arose of observing a solemn period during the three weeks leading up to the fast day. On the eve of the fast itself, a light meal is eaten, with an egg symbolizing mourning. In some Sephardi communities the food is dipped in ash as a further sign of mourning. In synagogue, an atmosphere of gloom prevails. Ashkenazi communities remove the ark's colourful decorated cover—the *parokhet*. Sephardi communities, whose arks have no outside cover, drape the ark in black on Tisha B'Av. The worshippers, as in mourning, wear cloth or rubber footwear, sit on low stools or on the floor, and do not greet one another.

After the reading of the Book of Lamentations, special *kinot* (elegies) are read. These are religious poems, drawn from across the ages, which lament the destruction of the First and Second Temple, and look forward to their restoration. Like other fasts, the rabbis believe that Tisha B'Av will eventually become an occasion for rejoicing. The Book of Zechariah indicates this, when the prophet quotes God as saying that these fasts 'shall be to the house of Judah joy and gladness, and cheerful feasts'. In line with this note of optimism and hope, some mediaeval rabbinical commentators identified Tisha B'Av as the birthday of the Messiah.

Tisha B'Av is observed in Israel as a day of public mourning. Restaurants, theatres and cinemas are closed. Radio and television transmit programmes which match the solemn tenour of the day. Vast numbers go on foot to the Western Wall—to the large, beautifully hewn Herodian stones which have supported the Temple Mount since Roman times, and on which both the destroyed Temples once stood.

Against those ancient stones—now two thousand years old—which tower 58 feet—18 metres—above the worshippers, Jews mourn the destruction of both the First and Second Temple: destructions which at the time seemed to mark an end to their existence as a people.

No. 111

Dearest Auntie Fori,

Tu Bi'Shvat, the Hebrew for 'the 15th day of the month of Shvat', is the Jewish New Year for the Trees, a name by which it is also known in Hebrew: *Rosh Hashanah la-Ilanot*. It is one of the few festivals celebrated

each year which is not mentioned in the Bible. It first makes its appearance in Jewish writings in the Second Temple period, two thousand
years ago.

The concept of a New Year for the Trees arose from the need to reg-
ularize the rabbinical taxation system of that time. Trees planted before
the date of the festival would be taxed—at one-tenth their value—for
the current year. Trees planted after the New Year for the Trees would
only be taxed in the following year.

Following the destruction of the Second Temple and the imposition
of Roman rule, Jewish autonomy was destroyed, and with it the internal
taxation system, so that the reason for the New Year for the Trees disappeared. But the festival continued. In the Diaspora it served to remind
Jews—especially those living in the harsher climates and dense forests of
northern Europe—of the warmer climate and more luxuriant landscape
of the Land of Israel.

On the New Year for the Trees the ancient days are remembered with
joy, not sorrow, and fasting is forbidden. In the Middle Ages, the mystics
whose spiritual leader was Isaac Luria—whom I mentioned in a recent
letter—introduced a fuller ritual for the festival: fruits were eaten, and
hymns and prayers recited which gave praise to the Holy Land for its fertile agriculture. This more elaborate form of the festival was particularly
adopted by the Sephardi communities both in Europe and under Muslim rule. The first published selection of readings for the festival was
printed in 1753, entitled 'Goodly Fruit'. The principal fruits to be eaten
were those of the carob and almond trees.

The enhanced ceremony included the drinking of four cups of wine,
as at Passover—making Passover and the New Year for the Trees the only
two occasions in the whole year on which Jews were encouraged to
drink more than the single cup of kiddush wine on the Sabbath. As to
drinking on a third festival, Purim, I will write about that in a later letter.

In Israel today, on the day of the New Year for the Trees, schoolchildren plant trees throughout the land. In recent times many Diaspora
communities have followed this tradition, or, in a proxy adaptation of it,
have encouraged the purchase of trees for planting in Israel, through the
Jewish National Fund, which was established in the 1920s. I wonder if,

when you were a girl, trees were planted in Palestine in your name? When I was a boy in the late 1940s and early 1950s a certificate showing that one had given money for a tree to be planted in Israel was a prized possession (I think I may still have a few in one of my boxes of youthful ephemera).

Since Israel's independence in 1948, Jews throughout the Diaspora have given money to plant copses, groves, small woods, and even whole forests, often in the name of a loved one or of a public figure. One such forest, now thirty or forty years old, full of mature trees, is in honour of the Zionist leader Chaim Weizmann, Israel's first President. Another forest honours the memory of A. J. Balfour, the British Foreign Secretary whose 1917 declaration promised a 'Jewish National Home' in Palestine. Yet another honours Winston Churchill, whose 1922 British Government White Paper opened the doors for the immigration of half a million Jews to Palestine in the following fifteen years. It was the 'Churchill White Paper'—as it was known—that stated that the Jews were in Palestine 'of right, and not on sufferance'. From a Zionist perspective, that certainly deserved a forest.

In recent years, with the growing concern about the planet's resources, Jews have examined their traditions for guidance with regard to ecology. The New Year for the Trees has a place here, as does the sabbatical year—*shmita*—laid down in the Bible (in the Book of Leviticus) so that farmers' fields will lie fallow for a year to enable those fields to recuperate. The Bible tells us (in the Book of Deuteronomy): 'When thou shalt besiege a city a long time, in making war against it to take it, thou shalt not destroy the trees thereof by forcing an axe against them: for thou mayest eat of them, and thou shalt not cut them down to employ them in the siege—for the tree of the field is man's life.' This year, Arthur Waskow edited a book called *Torah of the Earth: Exploring 4,000 Years of Ecology in Jewish Thought*. Rabbi Gunther Plaut, of Toronto, in reviewing it, noted in the *Canadian Jewish News:* 'As the Jewish saying goes, when a tree is cut down its voice of pain resounds throughout the world.'

No. 112

Dearest Auntie Fori,

The greatest and the oldest of the Jewish festivals, Passover, celebrates the Exodus from Egypt. I have already written to you about some aspects of the festival, as when, during the family celebrations on the night of Passover, a place is set at table and a cup of wine poured out for the Prophet Elijah, and the door kept open in case he comes in to announce the imminent arrival of the Messianic age.

Passover is a spring festival. It lasts for seven days in Israel, eight days in the Diaspora. On the first and seventh days—and on the first and last two days in the Diaspora—work is not allowed. The Roman-Jewish historian Josephus records that no fewer than three million Jews went up to Jerusalem for the Passover of 65 AD. Throughout the festival, the only bread eaten is unleavened bread, the *matza* (plural *matzot*), in memory of how quickly the Jews had to act in order to leave Egypt: they did not have time to wait for their bread to rise.

In the words of the Book of Exodus:

And Moses said unto the people, Remember this day, in which ye came out from Egypt, out of the house of bondage; for by strength of hand the LORD brought you out from this place: there shall no leavened bread be eaten.

Seven days thou shalt eat unleavened bread, and in the seventh day shall be a feast to the LORD.

Unleavened bread shall be eaten seven days; and there shall no leavened bread be seen with thee, neither shall there be leaven seen with thee in all thy quarters.

The Saturday before Passover is *Shabbat ha-Gadol,* the Great Sabbath. In synagogue that day a portion of the Passover recitation is read, and the rabbi explains the whole Passover story. The night before Passover, in houses which by tradition have been cleaned and polished as never before, members of the family search for any traces of *chomets:* unleavened bread or food that is not 'kosher for Passover'. Cooking utensils, dishes and cutlery, for use only at Passover, are brought out of storage for the week of festivities, and all the regular ones put away.

Families gather at home, often with many guests, to recall the miracles of the Ten Plagues and the parting of the Red Sea. So central is the story of the Exodus to Jewish life and tradition—as it was to Jewish survival—that Passover comes first in the calendar of Jewish festivals.

On the seder night a lamb shank is set on the table in memory of God having 'passed over' (*passah*) the Hebrew first-born sons while slaying all male Egyptian first-born males.

As I wrote to you in my letter describing the Exodus, God had called the Israelis to put the blood of a lamb on the doorposts and lintels of their houses so that the Angel of Death would pass them by.

Bitter herbs are also put on the table, in memory of the bitterness of life under Egyptian rule. The fruit paste—called *charoses*—eaten at Passover is symbolic of the mortar which the Jews had to mix when making bricks as slaves of Pharoah.

In Roman times Jews spoke openly on Passover of the deliverance from Egypt, but hoped secretly for the deliverance from Rome. It was Rabbi Akiva—about whom I have written to you—who inserted at the end of the Passover meal the Day of Atonement prayer: 'Next Year in Jerusalem'—a rebuilt Jerusalem. In discussing the ten plagues, the sages are said to have sat all night, long after the meal and the prayers and the singing were over, scrutinizing the actual words used in the Bible to describe the departure from Egypt, and explaining that the number of plagues was not a 'mere' ten, but many hundreds.

These calculations are now part of the family readings during the evening. It has been said that the story of this all-night discussion masks the rabbis' true purpose, to plot rebellion against Rome.

Jews are instructed in the Book of Exodus: 'And thou shalt show thy son in that day, saying, "This is done because of that which the Lord did unto me when I came forth out of Egypt".' The Biblical injunction is understood as being personally received and personally connected with everyone present, individually: I was in Egypt, I crossed the Red Sea, I stood at Mount Sinai with the Children of Israel. The Haggadah does not even mention the name Moses: he is not to be deified. The Exodus is

God's miracle and His alone: the defining moment when He enabled His 'chosen people' to survive as an independent nation. From this Biblical injunction arose the ceremony held at home on the first night of Passover—and in the Diaspora on the second night as well—known as the *seder* ('order'—that is, the order of the proceedings).

The seder begins with the youngest child present asking the four questions, beginning with 'Why is this night different from all other nights?' The rest of the seder before the festive meal begins consists of the answer to the youngster's questions, sometimes given by the father, but more usually these days by each of those present, turn by turn around the table.

The questions and their answers, and the discussion about the historic Passover and its meaning, together with prayers, the grace before and after meals, stories, Psalms and songs, are set out in a book read every Passover by everyone at the table: called the *haggadah* (the word means 'telling'), it is often lavishly illustrated with the themes of the story of the Exodus. Mediaeval examples of this book are magnificent. Reproduced in facsimile, they too are among the varieties of the Haggadah read at the table. The British Library here in London has a superb fourteenth-century Barcelona Haggadah. Also originally from Barcelona is the particularly resplendent 'Sarajevo Haggadah', found in that city in the nineteenth century. The earliest known printed Hagaddah is from Guadalajara, in Spain, dated 1482, ten years before the expulsion of the Jews from Spain. (That same town saw fighting in the Spanish Civil War in 1936 in which Jewish volunteers, including those from America, Britain, France and Hungary took part.)

Editions of the Hagaddah are among the earliest Hebrew printed books from Prague (1526), Augsburg (1534), Mantua (1560), Venice (1599) and Amsterdam (1695). It was in this last edition that there appeared, as a folding page at the end, the first known printed map of the Land of Israel in a Jewish book.

Special *haggadot*—the plural in Hebrew of Hagaddah—have been issued for the use of soldiers in both world wars, for survivors of the Holocaust still in Displaced Persons camps in spring 1946, and for Israeli soldiers on front-line duty on the Syrian and Egyptian borders in the spring of 1967—only two months before the outbreak of the Six-Day War.

As I write this letter, I have in front of me the Haggadah used in Munich for the nights of 15–16 April 1946, for the two seder nights held in the restaurant of the Deutsches Theatre. Hundreds of American Jewish soldiers took part, as well as survivors of the Holocaust from the Displaced Persons camps in the area. For them, the Haggadah translation was in Yiddish. Instead of beginning with the traditional 'We were slaves to Pharaoh in Egypt,' that evening in Munich began with 'We were slaves to Hitler in Germany.' An introductory note reflected: 'And the khaki-clad sons of Israel . . . gathered together. . . . The driving spirit of the victory they felt was the same, but the leadership had changed. Great Allied armies replaced the ancient handful and in the sacred conviction of Moses now stood General Dwight D. Eisenhower.'

In all, more than 2,700 different printed editions of the Hagaddah have been recorded. Many years ago I began my own personal collections, but failed to persevere.

The reading of the Haggadah, both before and after the meal, is done with much chanting, and culminates in a dozen and more rousing songs. For a small boy, reaching the songs was a welcome sign that the evening was almost over; at the same time, the enthusiasm with which they were sung could rouse the sleepiest youngster.

Passover had one negative aspect. It often coincided with Easter, which was the Last Supper of Jesus, and when it did, Christians used the coincidence to attack Jews and often murder them, accusing them of using the blood of Christian children to bake the Passover unleavened bread. This blood libel gained frequency in the thirteenth century. It was at that time that an extra prayer was added to the Haggadah, beginning with the forceful words: 'Pour out thy wrath upon the heathen . . .'. Many Jews today, especially teenagers, dislike the bellicose 'anti-Christian' tone of this prayer and refuse to read it. Some families have dropped it altogether. I remember being embarrassed at it myself, as a teenager. Only when I was in my thirties was it explained to me!

Among Moroccan Jews, and Jews of Moroccan origin, most of whom live in Israel and France, the last evening of Passover is a time when people go from house to house to wish each other a happy year, and on the day after Passover it is customary for the whole community to go outside the town and recite a blessing over the trees.

No. 113

Dearest Auntie Fori,

The festival of Hanukah celebrates the victory of the Macabbees over the Seleucid Greeks. That story was the theme of one of my historical letters—many months ago. The word *hanukah* means 'dedication'. A candle is lit for each night of the eight-night miracle, when the Maccabees, coming into Jerusalem and determined to re-dedicate the Temple, found only one small jar of oil that was sealed with the High Priest seal, and thus pure. The oil in this jar was enough for only one night, but it lasted for eight nights—until uncontaminated oil could be produced in sufficient quantities for daily use.

On successive nights of the eight-day festival, a candle for each of the previous nights is lit again, so that on the last night, eight candles are burning, plus a ninth—the one which is used each night for lighting the others. It is known as the *shamash*—the servant.

The eight-branched candelabrum in which the Hanukah candles are lit is called the *hanukiyah* (as opposed to a regular six-branched candelabrum, the *menorah*). It has become an expression of Jewish creativity and art. Every type of style is used: antique, classical ornate, modern, austere, plain, elaborate. The candle holders can even be in the form of small silver or copper birds, and can burn with oil or a wax candle. Each member of the family may light his or her own.

In recent times, a large public Hanukiyah—with electric lights rather than candles—is set up in many civic locations, especially in Israel. Each year one such large Hanukiyah is set up quite near me here in London, in Golders Green, by the Lubavitch Hasids—about whom I have written to you. One is also set up each Hanukah outside the White House in Washington: this custom began when Jimmy Carter was President. A group of ultra-Orthodox Hasidim asked him to authorize the Jewish equivalent of the annual Christmas tree that already graced the White

House lawn. Carter's Domestic Affairs adviser, Stuart Eizenstat, an observant Jew, prevailed upon the relevant—and initially sceptical—authorities to let the *Hanukiyah* be set up. And there it is now, every year.

It is the culinary custom of Hanukah that all can agree on. Hanukah's two leading culinary delights are both fried in oil: potato pancakes—*latkes*—and doughnuts—*sufganiot*. Also at Hanukah there is the tradition of eating cheese delicacies, including cheese pancakes. According to one legend, the custom of eating cheese arose because a Hasmonean woman, Judith, fed cheese to the enemy Seleucid general, who became very thirsty and, to quench his thirst, drank too much wine and became drunk. As he lay prostrate, she cut off his head. This is clearly an echo of the Biblical story—about which I wrote to you in one of my early letters—of Jael and Sisera: 'she brought forth butter in a lordly dish'—before driving a tent peg through his head.

Another reason given for eating cheese is that milk is nourishing both to the young and old. Yet another view—there is no Jewish custom that does not have a wealth of legend and explanation attached to it—is that when in Biblical times the Jews were given the dietary laws they were not certain what to do with regard to meat, so they said 'we'll stick to cheese'. Then again, the rabbis of old compared the Torah to milk and honey, so eating cheese is a mark of respect.

Many games are played on Hanukah, including card games, and spinning a top known as a dreidel, each facet of which has a letter—N–G–H–S—representing **n**es **g**adol **h**ayah sham: 'a great miracle happened there.' When celebrating Hanukah in Israel, the letter P for **po**—'here'—replaces S and 'there'.

Hanukah, although a winter festival and a 'minor' one—not being a religious holiday—has become one of the most popular. A high point is the singing, after the candles are lit, of the thirteenth-century Jewish hymn *Maoz Tzur* ('fortress rock'), usually rendered 'Fortress, Rock of my Salvation'. The tune to which it is sung lustily, if not always in tune, is from the Jewish world of a fifteenth-century Germany.

Thanks to that most modern of inventions, the Internet, Jews and non-Jews alike who might wish to experience the full culinary delights of Hanukah can find different Web sites for every aspect of the festival's food. Mark Mietkiewicz, a Toronto-based television producer, has recently listed a number of Web sites which give recipes for many Hanukah dishes. For doughnuts—of all types, including cheese-filled and chocolate-filled. For latkes—the fried potato cakes usually served piping hot with apple sauce, or deliciously cool sour cream. For the appropriate music to play when busy with the fry-up. And for a variety of sauces for the latkes—among them Nectarine and Sweet Basil, and Hot Carrot and Salsa—this latter a Sephardi speciality. There is even a Web site—which I have just visited—to show you how to brew 'Adam's Channukah Ale'—with cardamom, cinnamon, oranges, ginger, nutmeg and cloves. Miracles will never cease, especially on Hanukah.

You may have noticed, in the last two sentences, two different spellings of Hanukah. Gloria Donen Sosin, an American correspondent of mine, has just sent me an article in which she notes no less than eighteen different spellings—in English transliteration alone—of the five Hebrew letters that make up the name of the festival: Kh-N-V-K-H. Among the variant spellings she has found—and most of which I myself have probably used over the years—are Khannukah, Channuka, Channukah, Chanuka, Chanuko, Hannukah, Hanukah, as well as my version here, Hanukah with one 'n'. As Gloria Sosin points out, the double 'n', which is popular in so many of the English versions of the name, has no rational basis, since Hebrew does not use double letters (unless there is a vowel between them). It seems there is no aspect of the Jewish story which does not have a world of exploration and explanation.

No. 114

Dearest Auntie Fori,

This letter is about the way in which the annual events in the Jewish calendar has been influenced by the establishment of the State of Israel in 1948, when three special days came into being.

The first of these days is Yom Ha-Zikaron, Memorial Day, which now commemorates the fallen soldiers and civilians in each of Israel's five wars: 1948–1949, 1956, 1967, 1973 and 1982, as well as the clashes of arms at other times—particularly the War of Attrition with Egypt in 1969–1970, in which more than 700 Israeli soldiers and civilians were killed.

In the War of Independence the death toll for the new nation of only half a million people was high: more than 10,000 dead. Because the body of every man and woman killed on the battlefield has been recovered, Israel has no Unknown Soldier memorial. But on Mount Herzl—where Theodor Herzl was re-interred—is the national military cemetery, which contains the graves of Israel's soldiers and of its leaders. The assassinated Yitzhak Rabin was buried there in 1995.

Each year on Memorial Day, a ceremony is held on Mount Herzl attended by the President and the Prime Minister and a host of dignitaries. In homes throughout Israel memorial candles are lit and memorial prayers recited. Throughout the country, the relatives of soldiers who have been killed visit the military cemeteries in which their loved ones are buried.

It is a sad day. Although Israel's wars resulted in victories there is no sense of triumphalism. It was Rabin who, in the immediate aftermath of Israel's dramatic and swift victory in 1967, when he was Chief of Staff, told a public meeting gathered to honour him at the Hebrew University—whose Mount Scopus campus, cut off from Israel by the Jordanians since 1948, had just been liberated by Israeli forces in a war in which more than 750 Israeli and 2,000 Arab soldiers had been killed: 'The warriors in the front lines saw with their own eyes not only the glory of victory but the price of victory: their comrades who fell beside them bleeding. And I know that even the terrible price which our enemies paid touched the hearts of many of our men.' Rabin added: 'It may be that the Jewish people has never learned or accustomed itself to feel the triumph of conquest and victory, and therefore we receive it with mixed feelings.'

The second special day celebrated each year in Israel is Yom Ha-Atzmaut, the Day of Independence. It takes place one day after Memorial Day, and commemorates the declaration of Jewish statehood on 15 May 1948. It is a religious as well as a secular holiday, for which the Chief Rabbinate devised a special morning and evening service for worshippers in synagogue. As it is a day of secular celebration, sporting events, marches and flagwaving, it never takes place on the Sabbath, but—whenever it falls on a Friday or the Sabbath—is celebrated on the previous Thursday.

Despite celebrating a day which was followed by ten months of war, and victorious survival, the Day of Independence is not a day of bellicose remembrance. The original practice of holding a military parade that day in Jerusalem has been disbanded, and the reading from the Book of Isaiah chosen for the day includes the verses:

> *The wolf also shall dwell with the lamb, and the leopard shall lie down with the kid; and the calf and the young lion and the fatling together; and a little child shall lead them.*
>
> *And the cow and the bear shall feed; their young ones shall lie down together: and the lion shall eat straw like the ox.*
>
> *And the suckling child shall play on the hole of the asp, and the weaned child shall put his hand on the cockatrice' den.*
>
> *They shall not hurt nor destroy in all my holy mountain. . . .*
>
> *And it shall come to pass in that day, that the Lord shall set his hand again the second time to recover the remnant of his people. . . .*

Throughout Independence Day, cars driving in the streets fly Israeli flags and pennants. It is a day of celebration for the survival of the State during the War of Independence and for its fifty and more years of creative endeavour, often amid hardship and setback, but never without zeal and hope.

The third annual day of remembrance which came into being only after the establishment of the State of Israel is Yom Ha-Shoah, the Day of the Catastrophe, also known as Holocaust Memorial Day, in memory of the six million Jews murdered during the Holocaust. The day chosen was the anniversary of the first day of the Warsaw Ghetto uprising in April 1943. Thus mass resistance as well as mass murder is recalled.

On that day in Israel radio and television devote most of their programmes to films and talks about the Holocaust, and to interviews with survivors. A service of remembrance is held at Yad Vashem, the Holocaust memorial built on a hilltop just to the west of the military cemetery on Mount Herzl. Individual survivors are invited to light the memorial candles. Some ten years ago a Holocaust memorial stone was set up in London, in Hyde Park, where, each year on Yom Ha-Shoah, Jews gather in solemn memorial.

As the Holocaust became more and more the subject of books, television programmes and even, in Britain, the school curriculum, a new date, January 27—the day on which Soviet troops entered Auschwitz in 1945—was chosen by most European governments as the day on which non-Jews as well as Jews would remember the victims of the Holocaust, its partisans and fighters, and remember also those non-Jews, as many as 20,000, who risked their lives to save Jewish life: men and women known to the Jews as 'Righteous Gentiles', about whom have written to you in one of my Second World War letters, and about whom I am even now researching, with a view to writing a book. As part of my researches, on a recent visit to 'your' Budapest, I went to a number of convents, Christian orphanages and private homes in different parts of the city, in which Jews were hidden, and saved, in 1944.

The fourth Israel-oriented day of celebration and memorial, which is now part of the Jewish calendar, came into being in 1967, as a result of the Six-Day War: Jerusalem Day, celebrated on the day in the Hebrew calendar, 28 Iyyar—a day which in 1967 fell on June 7—when Jerusalem was re-united.

That day was the first time that the whole of Jerusalem, including the Temple Mount and the Western or Wailing Wall, had come under Jewish sovereignty since the Second Temple period, and the rule of Herod.

In synagogues all over Israel, Jerusalem Day is celebrated by reciting the Hallel service: the recitation of Psalms in praise of God. The word *hallel* means praise—one form of it is 'hallelujah'. The Psalms that are recited are Nos. 113 to 118. The first begins with a veritable flurry of hallels: 'Praise ye the Lord. Praise, O ye servants of the Lord, praise the name of the Lord. . . . From the rising of the sun unto the going down of the same the Lord's name is to be praised.'

No. 115

Dearest Auntie Fori,

In this letter I want to write about the synagogue, the focal point of Jewish communal worship. The word comes from the Greek for an assembly. In Hebrew the word used is Beit Knesset—'House of Assembly' (the Israeli parliament is known simply as the Knesset, or Assembly).

The origin of the synagogue is obscure. No such place or concept exists in the Five Books of Moses. It may be that the first synagogues were created during the period of the Babylonian exile, small houses of prayer or meeting places for those who were so far away from the Temple. Thus the Book of Ezekiel relates God's words: 'although I have scattered them among the countries, yet will I be to them as a little sanctuary in the countries where they shall come.' Jewish rabbinic tradition identifies this 'little sanctuary' with the synagogue.

Another Biblical reference, which is regarded by some commentators as relating to the synagogue, is in the Book of Psalms. In Psalm 74 the enemies of the Jews are described as having 'burned up all the meeting places of God in the land'. The King James version of the Bible—the version I use in these letters—goes so far as to use the word 'synagogues' in this verse, though that is clearly an anachronism, and may even be a mis-translation.

Archaeologists have uncovered the remains of synagogues from Roman times, when they certainly existed in Rome itself, and in Alexandria, which had a large Jewish population. In the New Testament, Jesus preaches in synagogues in Galilee, Paul in Damascus, Asia Minor and Cyprus. The synagogues of those days, as of today, are always built on an axis facing towards Jerusalem. Thus the ancient synagogue in the Roman city of Jerash—now in Jordan—which I visited five years ago, faces more or less west. The synagogue in Herod's palace-fortress of Masada faces north. The London and Budapest synagogues face southeast. The New York synagogues face east.

On the synagogue wall that faces towards Jerusalem is the *aron hakodesh,* the holy ark. This is where the Torah scrolls are kept when they are not on the reader's table during the service. It is towards the ark that the individual directs his prayers.

Near the ark is a small light, the *ner tamid*—or eternal light—which is there to remind the congregation of the eternal light that was on view in the First Temple. The origin of this light is in one of God's commands to Moses, concerning the Temple: 'And thou shalt command the Children of Israel, that they bring thee pure olive oil beaten for the light, to cause the lamp to burn always.'

The ark in the synagogue is one of the most decorated places. The cabinet in which the Torah scrolls are placed, itself often highly decorated and lined in velvet, is covered with a *parokhet*—the richly decorated curtain about which I wrote to you earlier. The scrolls are themselves covered with fine cloth or velvet covers. On top of each of the two wooden handles around which the scroll is wound is a *keter*—a crown, or *rimonim*—ornamental pomegranates—both usually made of silver.

The central element of the synagogue service is the Amidah: the 'standing' prayer. The rabbis tell us that the three Amidah prayers recited each day are replacing the three daily animal sacrifices of Temple times. The first three blessings in the Amidah are those of praise to God; the last three are of thanks to God. In between are thirteen blessings: for wisdom, repentance, forgiveness, plentiful crops and abundant water, the ingathering of the exiles, the restoration of the ancient judicial system, God's compassion, the rebuilding of Jerusalem, Messianic deliverance, and the acceptance of prayer.

One of the prayers in the Amidah was written by Mar Bar Ravina, the fourth-century Babylonian sage. Famous for his wisdom and his austere character, Bar Ravina fasted every day until sunset—including the eve of the Day of Atonement. Wanting to stress the seriousness of life, during his son's wedding, seeing the couple in a jolly mood, he broke a cup: this is regarded by many scholars as the origin of breaking a cup at a Jewish wedding ceremony. His prayer in the Amidah reads: 'O my God, keep my tongue from evil and my lips from speaking guile. And to them that curse me may my soul be silent; yea let my soul be as the dust to all. Open my heart in thy law, and let my soul pursue thy commandments.'

The Amidah is recited facing the ark—that is, facing Jerusalem. It is recited silently by each worshipper, each word being articulated clearly. As the prayer is begun the worshipper takes three steps forward, as if approaching God. At the end of the prayer he takes three steps backward.

No private conversation between congregants—such conversations are a feature of many synagogue services, though there should not really be private conversations at any time—is permitted during the Amidah.

The synagogue falls silent. When all the congregants have ended their silent prayer the Reader repeats the Amidah aloud.

The centrepiece of the Sabbath service is the reading of the Torah, the Five Books of Moses. Individual congregants are called up for the Reading of the Law: this 'aliyah' is considered an honour. The first aliyah is always given to a Cohen—the priestly family—and the second to a Levite—those who in Temple times attended to the daily ritual. Each congregant called up may read, or sing, part of that week's portion, or he may elect to recite the blessings, and have the Reader do the actual reading. Among the most beautiful words in the service are those sung to a moving melody when the Torah Scroll is returned to the ark:

> *For the sake of David thy servant, turn not away the face of thine anointed. For I give you good doctrine; forsake ye not my Teaching. It is a tree of life to them that grasp it, and of them that uphold it every one is rendered happy. Its ways are ways of pleasantness, and all its paths are peace. Turn thou us unto thee, O Lord, and we shall return: renew our days as of old.*

No. 116

Dearest Auntie Fori,

The most solemn portion of synagogue worship, remembering the deceased, is done collectively through Yizkor, the memorial service on the New Year, the Day of Atonement, Shemini Atzeret, Passover and Shavuot; and also individually through Kaddish, the memorial prayer which is a part of every synagogue service.

Kaddish means 'sanctification'. This prayer, which is introduced at various stages of the daily liturgy, indicating a new section of the prayers, begins with an evocation to praise God: 'Magnified and sanctified be his great name in the world which he hath created according to his will.' One version of the Kaddish, Kaddish De-Rabbanan, the Kaddish of the Rabbis, includes an additional prayer for the well-being of students of the Torah—the only students in ancient days.

Since the Middle Ages in Germany—where several current customs began, or are first recorded—individuals who are bereaved stand in their place in synagogue and recite the Kaddish known as Kaddish Yatom, Mourner's Kaddish. They do this every day for eleven months following the death of their relative. Jews who are not regular synagogue-goers often ask a relative or friend to say the daily Kaddish for them. The prayer itself is written and spoken in Aramaic, the spoken language of the Jews in Palestine two thousand years ago, and indeed of Jesus.

The Kaddish ends with a request to God, in one of the most frequently recited passages of the liturgy. It is a direct appeal to God: 'He who maketh peace in his high places, may he make peace for us and for all Israel; and say ye, Amen.' This particular English-language version is the one in my father's prayer book, published in the year he was born, 1902.

On the anniversary of a parent's death, the son (or sons) recite the Kaddish prayer in synagogue and, on the preceding Sabbath, are called up to read from the Torah. It is also a custom for them to distribute charity on each anniversary.

As well as reciting the Kaddish, every year on the anniversary of the death of a parent Jewish children light a memorial candle based on a verse in the Book of Proverbs, 'The spirit of man is the candle of the Lord . . .'. The candle, known in Yiddish as the *yahrzeit* (the 'time of the year'), burns for twenty-four hours.

The yahrzeit custom, like the Kaddish, can be traced back among German Jews to the fifteenth century, when those in mourning also fasted on that day, though they do so no longer. Sephardi Jews use the term *nahalah,* or inheritance, for the annual memorial.

In the days between the New Year and the Day of Atonement—the Ten Days of Penitence—Jews visit the graves of their parents and recite the memorial prayer at the graveside. It is also a custom to place a pebble or small stone on the tomb of a loved one.

No. 117

Dearest Auntie Fori,

This letter will focus on some of the personalities of the synagogue, first and foremost the rabbi. In recent times, Reform, Conservative and

Liberal synagogues have introduced women rabbis, something virtually unknown until the twentieth century, although women did teach religion in the past: the eighteenth-century Jerusalem-based Rabbi Azulai lists several them among the 1,300 scholars in his biographical dictionary *Shem ha-Gedolim* ('The Name of the Great').

The word *rabbi* cames from the Hebrew *rav,* and means—with the suffix '*i*'—'my teacher'. As I have written to you, Auntie Fori, Moses is known as Moshe Rabbenu, Moses our Teacher. The Sephardi word for rabbi is *hakham,* 'sage'. In earlier times there was also a tradition of the wandering preacher, not attached to any particular town or synagogue: he was known as the Maggid. In very large towns, like Vilna—where my mother's parents came from—in addition to the town rabbi there was also a resident Maggid, who drew a salary from the community.

The rabbi's tasks include giving sermons in synagogue, conducting the service, blessing the community, teaching, visiting the sick, conducting bar mitzvahs, marriages, services for the dead, and visiting those who have been bereaved. In the Reform movement, women can be rabbis, and officiate at services.

Working closely with the rabbi is the hazzan: the cantor, whose melodious voice helps to lead the congregation through the services. The high point of the cantor's art—and spiritual fervour—is the singing of the Kol Nidre prayer which opens the evening service at the start of the twenty-four hours of the Day of Atonement.

The gabbai, or warden, presides over the synagogue's officials and its organizational needs. The shamash, the 'servant' or beadle, supervises the synagogue service, giving out the tasks allotted to various members of the community, helping whoever has been asked to read the Torah, and organizing the festival services and celebrations. In mediaeval times the gabbai was a collector of charity from the community.

The parnas is a leading synagogue official. who has both administrative and religious tasks. Today he is usually a lay leader, elected by the community.

As well as the rabbi, some congregations—such as that of Britain— have created the office of Chief Rabbi. This is relatively new to Jewish tradition. Great rabbis there always were, men to whom Jews—and indeed other rabbis—came for guidance. For more than a hundred years there has been a Chief Rabbi of Great Britain and the Commonwealth. For many years this post was held by Immanuel Jakobovits, who as a teenager came to Britain shortly before the Second World War, from the East Prussian city of Königsberg. Today it is held by Jonathan Sacks, who has been an influential interpreter of Jewish religious traditions to the non-Jewish world.

Today in Israel there are two Chief Rabbis, the Ashkenazi and the Sephardi, known mischievously as the 'heavenly twins'. The Ashkenazi Chief Rabbi today, Rabbi Lau, is a survivor of the Holocaust. Born in the Polish city of Piotrkow, he was protected during the deportations and in the camps by his older bother, Naphtali. They were liberated together—by the American troops who entered Buchenwald concentration camp.

The Sephardi Chief Rabbi of Israel, Eliyahu Bakshi Doron, was appointed in 1993. When he and Chief Rabbi Lau recently—on 23 March 2000—received Pope John Paul II at the Chief Rabbinate in Jerusalem, on the first visit by a Pope to the State of Israel, John Paul told them that the Jewish religious heritage was 'intrinsic' to the Roman Catholic faith.

The school for higher rabbinical learning is known as the Bet Midrash (House of Learning). It is often attached to a synagogue and serves its needs. Communal rabbis have an important role to play as members of the rabbinical courts (the Bet Din, or House of Law). The head of the three-member court is known as the Av Bet Din (Father of the Bet Din), originally the title of the vice-president of the supreme court in Jerusalem at the time of the Second Temple. The members of the rabbinical court are known as *dayyanim* (judges). In Orthodox rabbinical courts they are all men, but Reform Jews here in Britain and Conservative Jews in the United States have women on their courts, just as they have women rabbis.

The rabbinical courts rule mostly on divorce between Jews, conversions to Judaism, and certifying that the dietary laws are being kept, that a foodstuff is kosher (I will write to you about this soon). Jews regard judges with the highest respect. You will remember, Auntie Fori, in some of my earliest letters the era in Jewish history when the Children of Israel were ruled by Judges. The Hebrew prayer, *baruch dayan emet,*

Blessed be the True Judge, refers to God. It is said on learning of a death, or in the presence of a dead person.

Whatever hierarchies exist, and the rabbinate is essentially a system of equality of authority, it is God who remains for the Jews the concept—the Shekhinah, or Divine Presence—from whom all authority emanates: judgment, punishment and mercy. As each Jew is in direct connection to God, a rabbi, even a Chief Rabbi, is a teacher—a conduit—albeit often a charismatic personality to whom many people look for guidance and moral support.

No. 118

Dearest Auntie Fori,

The synagogue is the scene of many special acts of worship: fast days and festivals alike. One special service is held on every Rosh Hodesh—the 'head of the month'—the day of the New Moon, which marks the beginning of each Hebrew month, based on a lunar calendar. This was a time of solemn convocation and special animal sacrifices in Biblical times. It was also a day of rejoicing, and family festivity. The festive aspect ceased with the destruction of the Temple. Today the focus is on asking God to make the coming month one of happiness and blessing: the Sephardi congregants ask that 'it will be the end of all our sorrows, and the beginning of our soul's salvation'.

Different branches of Judaism have different orders of service in the synagogue, or varying ways of carrying out the forms of worship. These different approaches are known as the *minhag,* or custom. Thus one has an Ashkenazi minhag and a Sephardi minhag, an Orthodox minhag and a Reform minhag.

The celebration of the New Moon has a facet which illustrates this variety of custom. In the sixteenth century Rabbi Moses Cordovero—who died in 1570 at the age of forty-eight—the leader of the mystics in Safed, in Galilee, inaugurated a fast day on the eve of the New Moon celebration. It was called Yom Kippur Katan—Small Day of Atonement. His followers fasted that day until the afternoon service, when they declared in unison: 'Following the custom of the very pious, one must repent of his ways, and make restitution both by mouth and personal acts, in order that he may enter the new month as pure as a new-born infant.'

This minor fast was soon being observed far beyond Galilee, but always on a voluntary basis. Even in England there are some congregations that still fast on the eve of the New Moon.

In several books of the Bible, Rosh Hodesh is compared with the Sabbath, but it long ago lost its importance. It is what we now call a 'minor' festival, on which it is forbidden to fast, but during which work is allowed. One tradition asserts that in Moses' day, in the wilderness, the Israelite women refused to join in the making of the golden calf, and were given the first day of every month—Rosh Hodesh—as a reward for their piety, and do not have to do any work that day. In recent times, women have begun to use Rosh Hodesh as a special time to meet with other women and study and celebrate together.

I will end these thoughts about the synagogue and its services with the words spoken on entering the building, words from the Book of Numbers which reflect the atmosphere and warmth of the place of worship, and of the liturgy:

'How goodly are thy tents, O Jacob, thy dwelling places, O Israel!'

No. 119

Dearest Auntie Fori,

One special Jewish festival, which perhaps you remember as a child, is Purim. It celebrates the bravery of a Jewish woman, Esther, who married the King of Persia. The king was Xerxes, one of the great warrior kings of Persia. He is known in the Bible as Ahasuerus. His Grand Vizier, Haman, plotted to kill the Jews of Persia—a large and flourishing community, descendants of the Jews seized and deported from Judaea by Nebuchadnezzar. Esther was of the tribe of Benjamin.

Haman was willing to pay in silver, casting lots to determine how 'to destroy all the Jews that were throughout the whole kingdom'. It is from the Persian word for 'lot'—*pur*—that the festival of Purim takes its name. The Jews were to be killed without exception. On Haman's orders, letters were sent to all the king's provinces, a stern decree 'to destroy, to kill, and to cause to perish, all Jews, both young and old, little children and women, in one day. . . .' The decree added that the belongings of the Jews were to be taken 'as a prey'.

Esther's cousin Mordecai obtained a copy of the decree, and got it to her, begging her to ask the King to save her people—and herself—from destruction. Haman, meanwhile, had prepared a special gallows for Mordecai, who had refused to bow down to him and do him 'reverence'.

A banquet was held in the royal palace. Esther had asked the King to invite Haman, who was flattered to be asked. She then told the King of the planned killings: 'For we are sold, I and my people, to be destroyed, to be slain, and to perish'. Who had planned such a thing, the King asked: 'Who is he and where is he, that durst presume in his heart to do so?'

The 'adversary and enemy', Esther replied, 'is this wicked Haman'. The King then ordered Haman to be hanged on the very gallows which he had prepared for Mordecai.

Esther then asked the King to reverse Haman's decree, 'For how can I endure to see the evil that shall come unto my people? or how can I endure the destruction of my kindred?' The King at once reversed the murder decree, sending out new letters to the rulers of all his 127 provinces which, the Bible tells us, 'are from India unto Ethiopia'. The one to India must have come quite near to where you live, Auntie Fori, in the foothills of the Himalayas.

The letters were in all the local languages, including one 'to the Jews according to their writing, and according to their language'. The King also granted the Jews the right, in every city in his kingdom, 'to gather themselves together, and to stand for their life, to destroy, and to slay, and to cause to perish, all the power of the people and province that would assault them. . . .' So afraid were local people of what the Jews might do to them that many 'became Jews'. And in every town where the royal decree was read, reversing Haman's instruction for mass murder, 'the Jews had joy and gladness, a feast and a good day.'

A whole book of the Bible, the Book of Esther, is devoted to this episode, which gave rise to one of the most lively of Jewish celebrations, the festival of Purim. Once a year, in synagogue, the Book of Esther is read from a special scroll devoted to it, the Megillat Esther, or Scroll of Esther. During the reading, there is much cursing of Haman and cheering of Esther, while children—many of the girls dressed up as Esther—enjoy themselves amid a riot of noise.

During the synagogue service during Purim the Torah reading is from the Book of Exodus, the story of that earlier enemy of the Jews, Amalek, the tribe of which God said that its memory should be blotted out. Jewish tradition tells us that Haman was a descendant of Amalek. Hence, whenever his name is mentioned during the reading of the Scroll of Esther the congregation, in particular the children, make loud noises with rattles and banging so that his name will not be heard above the din.

If one cannot go to synagogue it is permitted, indeed encouraged, to read the Scroll of Esther at home. It is the only book in the Bible in which God is not mentioned by name. Mediaeval Jewish commentators explained this by saying it was proof that God works behind the scenes, coming to the rescue when all seems lost. In the story itself it is very much left to Mordecai and Esther to save the day.

The Hebrew name for Esther is Hadassah (myrtle): it became a popular name for Jewish girls. According to the rabbis, just as myrtle spreads fragrance, so Esther spreads good deeds.

The Book of Esther tells us that the Jews celebrated their deliverance from Haman by 'sending portions one to another, and gifts to the poor'. For this reason, as 'portions' and 'gifts' are both in the plural, on Purim people give two gifts to two poor people, and two items of food—most popularly a sweet-filled pastry known as 'Haman's ears'—to a friend. Often gifts are given out, from door to door, to dozens of friends and neighbours.

The pastries are known as *Hamantaschen*—Haman's ears. They are three-cornered, as a reminder of the hat which Haman wore—based (anachronistically) on Napoleon's triangular-shaped hat. Others say the three-cornered pastry represents the three Patriarchs, Abraham, Isaac and Jacob, in honour of the strength Queen Esther derived from her heritage. Because the Hebrew word for poppy seed, *mohn*, is similar to the Hebrew pronunciation of the second syllable of Haman's name, the pastry has a poppy seed filling.

One more custom, based on the words 'joy and gladness, a feast and a good day': the Talmudic rabbis said that there should be a special meal at home on Purim with so much wine that a man no longer knew whether he was blessing Mordecai or cursing Haman! Not all rabbis approve of such excess.

Across the years, Purim has not been restricted to the ancient Persian story. Local Purims have been celebrated in many towns where Jews escaped from danger. In 1524 the Jews of Cairo were threatened with mass execution if they could not pay an exorbitant sum of money to the ruler of Egypt, Ahmed Pasha. The sum was far beyond their capacity to pay. Ahmed was overthrown in a palace coup on the very day he had set for the Jews' execution. That day was henceforth celebrated as 'the Purim of Cairo'.

The date of the return of the Jews of Frankfurt-on-Main, by order of the emperor, immediately after their violent expulsion from the ghetto in 1614 by the rabble-rousing anti-Semite Vincent Fettmilch, was commemorated each year by the Frankfurt Jews as 'Purim Winz'—the Purim of Vincent.

In 1648 the Jews of Medzibozh escaped the ravages of the Chmielnicki massacres. To mark their seemingly miraculous survival, a special Purim was celebrated on the day the violent horde passed them by. A hundred years later the founder of Hasidism, the Baal Shem Tov, was living in Medzibozh. In 1790 a special Purim was declared in Florence, when the local Roman Catholic bishop intervened to prevent a mob attack on the Jewish community there.

In Muslim-ruled Tangier, when the Jewish community of more than two thousand was left unscathed after the French naval bombardment of 1844, the Jews celebrated what they called the 'Purim de las bombas'— as they had suffered no losses.

In all, more than a hundred such special Purims have been recorded. They span every month in the Jewish calendar. There are also family Purims: days celebrated in a family in thanksgiving for some act of mercy or rescue. In an article on local and family Purims published in the *Canadian Jewish News* a few weeks ago, Rabbi Shlomo Jakobovits refers to some of these, including that celebrated by the family and descendants of Rabbi Avraham Danzig, who lived in Vilna. In 1804 an accidental explosion demolished the housing complex in which he lived. Thirty-one people were killed. Rabbi Danzig and his family, although injured, survived. The anniversary of their escape became a special Purim for his family. In his influential compendium of Jewish religious law, *Chai Adam* ('The Life of Man'), he, understandably, devoted more space to Purim than to any other aspect of Jewish law.

One last word about the festival of Purim. It is a time of jollity and dressing up, a time of fun for children: there is even a Yiddish saying that cautions us against taking it too seriously: 'A high temperature is not an illness and Purim is not a festival'!

No. 120

Dearest Auntie Fori,

The Jews have been called the People of the Book. The Five Books of Moses, which constitute the basic text of their faith, are the main 'book', but many other books have also influenced their religious thinking and practice.

The Five Books of Moses are also known, from the Greek, as the Pentateuch. The Hebrew names—for Genesis, Exodus, Leviticus, Numbers and Deuteronomy—are, respectively, *Be-reshit* ('In the beginning'), *Shemot* ('The names of—the Children of Israel'), *Va-yikra* ('And He called'), *Be-midbar* ('In the wilderness') and *Devarim* ('Words'). Each of the Hebrew words is derived from the initial words or first significant word of each book. Collectively these five books are known as the *Chumash* ('Five'—books).

In the fifth of the five books, Deuteronomy, we read: 'This is the Torah which Moses set before the Children of Israel'. In the King James version of the Bible, the one which all British schoolchildren read when I was a boy, and which is the version I have used in these letters, the word 'Torah' is translated in the passage above as 'law'. But this is a misreading by the Christian scholars of the early seventeenth century.

Although the Five Books of Moses do contain many laws, they are not only law books, but a complete presentation of the story of the Children of Israel and their relationship to their God, including God's com-

mandments, but much else besides. The word 'Torah' itself comes from
the Hebrew verb *yaroh,* to teach: it is often translated as 'teaching' or
'instruction'. Some call it the Divine Law.

Most visually, the Torah is the parchment scroll containing the Five
Books of Moses; the scroll which is used for reading in synagogue. It
is this Torah which is decorated with embroidered cloths and silver
crowns, taken in procession around the synagogue, and read with devotion each Sabbath morning.

The Torah—sometimes called 'the Torah of Moses'—and its teach-
ings provided the Jews in all ages with the written bedrock of their faith.
It was the will of God, as provided for them, and to which they adhered.
It was, for mainstream Jewish Orthodoxy up to today, what the rabbis
called *Torah Min-Hashamayim:* Torah from the heavens—Heaven meaning 'God'—and therefore not capable of revision.

The immutability of the Torah was the ninth of the thirteen principles of faith put forward by Maimonides in the twelfth century:
'Nothing is to be added to it nor taken away from it.' Interpretation
is another matter, although Moses Sofer, Rabbi of Bratislava—not far
up the Danube from your Budapest, Auntie Fori—took the view that
'Anything new is forbidden by the Torah'. But an earlier sage, Yom Tov
Lippman Heller, who died in 1654, wrote: 'Although there existed a
complete interpretation of the Torah and its commands there is no generation in which something new is not added. . . .'

'Added', but not changed. For the Jews the 'Old Testament' is the
only one that exists, the sole path along which God's will can be found.
Reform Jews—about whom I shall write to you in a few weeks' time—
also adhere to this concept of the centrality of the Torah, and of Torah
study. In the words of a the Central Conference of American Rabbis, in
its book *Reform Judaism: A Contemporary Perspective,* published in 1976:
'Torah results from the relationship between God and the Jewish
people . . . lawgivers and prophets, historians and poets gave us a heritage whose study is a religious imperative and whose practice is our
chief means to holiness.'

After the Sabbath Torah reading in synagogue the scroll is held up
and, in the short prayer that the congregation then recites, are two beautiful verses from the Book of Proverbs about the Torah which have

always moved me: 'She is a tree of life (*etz haim hi*) to them that lay hold upon her: and happy is every one that retaineth her. Her ways are ways of pleasantness, and all her paths are peace.'

No. 121

Dearest Auntie Fori,

Having written about the Torah in my last letter, in this one I will write about some of the other books of the Jewish faith, all of which derive, in one way or another, from the Torah.

First and foremost after the Torah is the Mishnah. Translated, literally, as 'teaching' or 'instruction', it is the earliest codification of Jewish Oral Law, based on almost five hundred years of Jewish oral tradition. It was compiled by the Jewish prince about whom I wrote to you in one of my earlier letters, the sage Rabbi Judah ha-Nasi. Compiled between 200 and 220 AD, it was devised to be of use to judges and teachers.

The laws set out in the Mishnah cite, for their authority, by name, almost 150 different sages. No discussion of Jewish law can take place even today without reference to this extraordinary compilation. Minority as well as majority views are always noted: indeed, the minority view is recorded first, to make clear that it had been taken into account, even if it had eventually been rejected.

The Aggadah—literally 'narration'—is the name given to all the non-legal elements in rabbinical literature over a period of a thousand years, until the beginning of Middle Ages. Greek and Persian words appear in it, testifying to the influence on it of early Diaspora communities. It includes those sections of both the Torah and the Mishnah which contain explanations of the Bible, legends, folklore, history, philosophy and ethical maxims. It also includes the biographies of great rabbis and Jewish heroes.

The concept of *aggadah*—the non-legal aspects of Jewish teaching and tradition—is paralleled by that of *halakhah,* those portions of the Talmud concerned with legal matters, in which the Diaspora influence is also to be found. Halakhah is also the general word for the body of Jewish religious law. The Talmud, from the verb 'to study' or 'to teach', is the accumulated discussions—largely in Aramaic—on the Jewish Oral Law as set out in the Mishnah. These discussions, which in the Mishnah are written in 'mishnaic' Hebrew—to differentiate it from both Biblical and modern Hebrew—are often vigorous in their content, as well as rigorous in their intellectual approach. They were put together by generations of Jewish scholars over several hundred years. The Palestinian Talmud—also known as the Jerusalem Talmud—was put together by sages living in Palestine 1,600 years ago. The Babylonian Talmud was compiled by sages living in Babylonia about a hundred years later.

During the last hundred years, three massive translations of the Talmud have been made: in German, by Lazarus Goldschmidt, between 1897 and 1909; in English, by Isidor Epstein, between 1936 and 1952; and in modern Hebrew—not yet completed—by the Jerusalem scholar Adin Steinsalz. A treasured book in my own library, signed by its author, is Rabbi Louis Jacobs' *Structure and Form in the Babylonian Talmud,* who notes (of interest to all authors and editors like myself) that in all its thirty or more volumes the Babylonian Talmud 'appears as if it dropped down from Heaven intact with not the slightest indication of how and by whom this gigantic compilation was put together.'

No. 122

Dearest Auntie Fori,

Four more books that have influenced Jewish thought through the ages deserve mention. The first is the Midrash, the collection of rabbinical interpretations of the scriptures, to explain legal points, or to derive lessons from stories and homilies. The word midrash comes from the Hebrew verb *darash,* 'to inquire', 'to investigate'. It continued to be added to until the thirteenth century, and is a font of material for Jewish preachers, teachers, and students. It has also influenced Islam: the Koran contains many Biblical stories which derive from their exposition in the Midrash.

Of tremendous importance to students of Jewish law and practice are the Responsa, collections of written answers, given by rabbis to questions that have been put to them, over many centuries, on the interpretation of Jewish law in difficult and contentious cases. On my last visit to Israel, early this summer, I was shown, at Bar Ilan University—just outside Tel Aviv—a massive project that is putting on computer the whole Responsa literature.

At the click of a mouse and the tap of a keyboard—for such is the modern world—I was shown on the computer screen a series of questions relating to nineteenth-century trading disputes in the Balkan city of Skopje and the British port of Liverpool. Today, here at my desk in London—or in the foothills of the Himalayas if I were visiting you—I could easily be turning to the Responsa literature on my computer.

Another book, and a controversial one, is the Zohar (the 'Book of Splendour'). It was written in Spain—in Castile—towards the end of the thirteenth century, mostly by Rabbi Moses de Leon, but with later additions by other rabbis. It runs to five books in all. The complete version was first printed in northern Italy—in Mantua—between 1558 and 1560. It consists of the mystical commentary on the Five Books of Moses, and became the main textbook of Jewish mystical tradition, the Kabbalah. Among the fictional characters in it are Sava ('Old Man') and Yenuka ('Child'), who reveal heavenly secrets. According to Jewish mystical tradition, Jewish knowledge of the Zohar is part of the process whereby the Messiah will appear.

Finally, in the array of books that have influenced Jewish thought to this day, is the Shulhan Arukh ('a set table'). It is a code of Jewish legal practice written in the sixteenth century by Joseph Caro, in Safed, in northern Galilee. It examines four central aspects of Jewish life: prayers, the Sabbath, festivals and fasting; dietary laws; women and marriage; and civil and criminal court procedure. Within a few decades of its first publication it became the authoritative code of Jewish law for Orthodox Jews wherever they lived.

Important annotations to the Shulhan Arukh were made by Moses Isserles, of Cracow: he called his work *mappah*—a 'tablecloth', to set on Caro's existing 'table'. Essentially, Caro established the Sephardi practices, and Isserles—who died in 1572, at the age of forty-seven—the Ashkenazi ones. Over the following five centuries, all rabbis consulted the two works before giving their verdict on a specific problem of religious conduct—of particular influence were the discussions of dietary laws, marital relations during the period of menstruation, and the laws of mourning.

In my next letter, I thought I would tell you something about Joseph Caro: one of the many fascinating characters who crowd the Pantheon (excuse a pagan, Hellenistic concept) of Jewish biography.

No. 123

Dearest Auntie Fori,

Here is the letter I promised you about Joseph Caro. He was born in the Spanish city of Toledo, from which he and his family—and all the Jews of Spain who refused conversion to Christianity—were expelled in 1492. At the time of the expulsion he was four years old. Living his adult life in the Turkish empire, he taught in Constantinople (Istanbul), Adrianople (Edirne) and Salonika. At the age of forty-eight he moved to Palestine—then also within the Turkish dominions—to live in the Jewish holy city of Safed, in northern Galilee.

As many as two hundred pupils attended Caro's lectures in Safed. His correspondence with rabbis and learned men, on every aspect of Jewish religious practice, spanned the whole Diaspora. Believing, with his fellow exiles from Spain, that they were at the dawn of the messianic age, he decided to produce a work that would serve as a central and unifying authority for Jews throughout the world. He did so, it filled many volumes; so he then abridged it in order to make it more accessible. It is this abridged version that is the Shulhan Arukh.

When Caro died in 1575, at the 'ripe old age' (for those days) of eighty-seven—five years younger than you are now, Auntie Fori—he had established the source and development of every Jewish law on the basis of all the sources. Over the years, his 'Set Table' was to go into hundreds of editions, including a pocket 'compendium' edition printed in Venice in 1574. The editor of this compact compendium explained in his preface that it had been printed in such a small format 'so that it could be carried in one's bosom, so that it may be referred to at any time and any place, while resting or travelling'.

Every author should strive to produce a serious, substantial work (already an abridgment) that is also capable of being put into the bosom—or at least the pocket.

No. 124

Dearest Auntie Fori,

In this letter I want to touch on the dietary laws, the laws of *kashrut* (fitness)—the laws pertaining to kosher food. Food that is not kosher is known as *terefah* (in Yiddish pronunciation, *trayf*) and cannot be eaten by observant Jews.

Fruit and vegetables are outside the laws of kashrut: they can be eaten at all times, unless they contain worms. The forbidden foods are laid down with great clarity, the first to be mentioned in the Bible being the limb of a living animal—prohibited in Genesis—and the consumption of blood—prohibited in Leviticus and Deuteronomy.

An animal must chew the cud if it is to be kosher: thus the pig is a forbidden animal, in all its manifestations (pork, bacon, ham). An animal without a split hoof is also forbidden: thus, although the camel chews the cud, as it does not have a split hoof, it cannot be eaten.

Animals that can be eaten have to be slaughtered in a special way, that drains them of as much blood as possible. In the small towns and villages of eastern Europe, the *shohet*—the ritual slaughterer—was a familiar figure. Without him, the Sabbath meal would have lacked its chicken dish.

Of the creatures living in the sea, only those with at least one fin, and one easily removable scale, can be eaten. This bars out crab, lobster, oysters and clams.

Meat and milk cannot be eaten together: this has led to the development of a massive industry producing parve ('neutral', that is, non-dairy) cream: an ersatz cream that is made without milk or milk products. The origin of the prohibition on any milk and any meat being mixed is a specific one: 'You shall not cook a kid in its mother's milk.'

This prohibition appears three times in the Five Books of Moses: twice in Exodus and once in Deuteronomy. It is believed that it originally arose because there was a pagan custom to prepare charms by seething a kid in its mother's milk. In the spirit of 'erecting a fence around the Torah', the prohibition was widened to include any milk and any meat. Orthodox Jews, to avoid the risk of such contamination even inadvertently, keep separate sets of 'milk' and 'meat' plates, cutlery, pots and pans.

After eating meat, different communities insist on a different period before which milk must not be drunk—or milk products eaten. Six hours is the maximum, though some communities have reduced the gap—to their intellectual satisfaction—to as little as one hour.

In the nineteenth century, the dietary laws were an early source of disagreement between the Orthodox and Reform communities. The German Reform movement took the view that the laws of kashrut were connected with the ritual of the Temple, and were not 'integral' to the Jewish religion.

At its Pittsburgh Conference in 1885, the American Jewish Reform movement declared that the dietary laws 'fail to impress the modern Jew with a spirit of priestly holiness', and concluded that 'their observance in our days is apt rather to obstruct than to further modern spiritual elevation.'

Among Orthodox Jews, the dietary laws are still maintained. In Israel, too, they are kept in most restaurants, and in the army catering service. There is even a kosher McDonald's on the road to Jerusalem, and innumerable kosher Chinese and Vietnamese restaurants throughout Israel and in cities with large Jewish communities. Of course, millions of Jews no longer observe the dietary laws—which even a century ago were almost universal among Jews—yet consider themselves Jews, and are Jews.

No. 125

Dearest Auntie Fori,

This will be a letter on gematria: the interpretation of a Hebrew word according to the numerical value of its letters. The word gematria comes from the Greek word *geometria*—numerology. It is the aim of those who believe that Divine revelation can be found in the pages of the Five Books of Moses to seek the true meaning of a word or phrase by looking at the numerical value of its individual letters.

Gematria as Biblical interpretation was first expounded by Rabbi Judah Bar Ilai in the second century AD. Taking the phrase from the description in the Book of Jeremiah, 'none can pass through them . . . and the beasts are fled', he suggested that this showed that the Kingdom of Judah was deserted for fifty-two years, because the numerical value of the Hebrew word for beast (*behemah*) is fifty-two.

Another second-century authority, Rabbi Nathan, said that because, in the Book of Exodus, the phrase Moses uses to introduce the prohibition of work on the Sabbath is 'These are the words . . .', and that this phrase has a numerical value of thirty-nine, it is evidence that there were thirty-nine categories of work forbidden on the Sabbath.

The principle of gematria is a simple alphabetical device, based on the fact that the letters of the Hebrew alphabet have numerical values. The first ten letters of the alphabet also represent the numbers one to ten. The eleventh to eighteenth letters have the values (in tens) from ten to ninety. The last four letters have the values 100, 200, 300 and 400.

The Hebrew alphabet also has five letters which take a different form when they appear at the end of a word: these 'final' letters, as they are known, have the numerical values 500, 600, 700, 800 and 900.

Using this method, by counting up the numerical value of all, or some, or even just one of its words, no sentence in the Bible is free from possible overlapping interpretation. When, for example, Jacob told his sons 'to go down' to Egypt to buy grain there, the numerical value of the Hebrew letters of the verb 'to go down' (*redu*) is 210. Thus the hidden meaning of Jacob's words was—according to those for whom gematria is a spiritual and historical guide—that the Jews were to live in Egypt for 210 years, until they were taken out by Moses.

Another example much cited by students of gematria is the reference in Genesis to Abraham arming his 'three hundred and eighteen' servants. As three hundred and eighteen is also the numerical value of the letters of the name of his servant Eliezer, it was inferred by devotees of gematria that in fact it was Eliezer alone with whom Abraham went off to rescue his nephew Lot, who had been taken captive.

Among those who favoured the search for hidden meaning revealed by gematria was Rabbi Moses Ha-Darshan, who lived in Narbonne, in southern France, in the eleventh century. One example he gave was this: when Jacob says (in Genesis) 'I have sojourned' with Laban, the fact that the numerical value of the words 'I have sojourned' is 613 means that even while staying with Laban, the pious Jacob observed the 613 precepts of Judaism, the *mitzvot,* or Divine Commandments—about which I will write to you in my next letter.

Gematria has also been used in less weighty, non-Biblical matters. The word for wine (*yayin*) and the word for mystery (*sod*) having the same numerical value, seventy, this led to the saying: 'When the wine goes in, the secret will out.'

In ancient times it was not only Jews, but also Assyrians, Babylonians and Greeks who explored the world of gematria. But the Jewish people, surviving those ancient days, brought gematria with them into mediaeval and then into modern times. The dangers that misinterpretation could cause were stressed by several Jewish thinkers. Abraham Ibn Ezra went so far as to warn that 'whoever wants can devise a gematria interpretation for good or for evil'. This could be done so as to use the Torah—the Five Books of Moses—in such a way as to go counter to the spirit, and even the letter, of what had been set down. The thirteenth-century Spanish rabbi, Moses Nahmanides (known by the acronym of his name as the Ramban), stressed that it was not by the device and skills of gematria, but chiefly through authoritative tradition, that the Torah could be explained. 'No one may calculate a gematria in order to deduce from it something that occurs to him', was his terse and wise comment.

Mediaeval rabbis who were attracted to the mystical aspects of Judaism turned repeatedly to gematria, determined to reveal hidden spiritual meaning in the most prosaic of Biblical phrases. Both Ashkenazi and Sephardi rabbis were equally affected. An early exponent of the art of gematria was the eleventh-century Ashkenazi rabbi Eliezer of Worms (Eliezer the Great), in the Rhineland. He found support for the Jewish laws and customs of his time by applying gematria to the Biblical texts. He was also, through his writings, a strong influence on the Sephardi rabbi, Rabbi Abraham Abulafia, who at different times in the second half of the thirteenth century lived in Spain, Palestine, Italy, Sicily and

Greece, and who made extensive—and in the view of those who followed traditional Judaism, extreme—use of gematria. Abulafia's work
was accused by one leading scholar of his time of being 'full of false per-
mutations'.

The attraction of gematria continued into more modern times. One
substantial study by the seventeenth-century kabbalist Rabbi Nathan
Nata Ben Solomon Spira, which explained certain passages in the Book
of Deuteronomy in a total of 252 different ways, was published in Cracow in 1637, and his wider interpretations of the Five Books of Moses
were published in Lemberg in 1795. As late as 1865 a new book on
gematria was published in Lemberg.

A high, or—depending on your point of view—low point for gematria was in the mid-seventeenth century, when Shabbetai Zvi declared
himself the Messiah (I hope have written to you about him: even in
London, in 1666, citizens took wagers on whether or not he was the
true Messiah, or a charlatan). His enthusiastic followers found proof that
he was the true Messiah by taking the numerical value of his name—
814—and pointing out that this was also the numerical value of one of
the many names given to God (*shaddai*), as well as to the words in
Deuteronomy, 'you shall sanctify'. Those who denied his claims to be the
Messiah mocked at the fact that 814 could also stand for *ruah sheker*—
false spirit.

In criticizing gematria, the Italian rabbi, author and poet Leon de
Modena, who died in 1648, noted that it could be used to make everything possible. Rabbi Louis Jacobs comments: 'It can yield the thought,
for instance, that a woman can be addressed as "honey", since the
numerical value of *devash* ("honey") and *ishah* ("woman") is the same.'

No. 126

Dearest Auntie Fori,

I want today to write something about the *mitzvot* (the Hebrew
word for 'commandments'; the singular is *mitzvah*). These are the 613
religious duties—each of them a good deed in the eyes of God—that are
to be found in the Torah—the Five Books of Moses.

In one of my earlier letters I wrote of how Johanan ben Zakkai was given permission by the Romans to set up a school at Yavne 'to teach his pupils' and 'to observe the mitzvot and to study the Torah'.

In the ninth century Saadiah Gaon, about whom I have also written to you—he compiled one of the earliest Jewish prayer books—described the mizvot as a gift given by God to man 'enabling him to attain constant bliss; for the person who achieves the good life as a reward for compliance with His commandments, obtains double the benefit gained by one who is not called upon to comply, but receives the good life only as a result of God's kindness'.

In the twelfth century the poet and philosopher Judah Halevi declared that carrying out the mitzvot elevated a person to the 'sublime crest' of prophecy. The greatest of all the mediaeval Jewish thinkers, Maimonides, who was six years old when Judah Halevi died, saw the mitzvot as protecting the individual who carried them out against *yetzer ha-ra*—the inclination to do evil, an inclination which the rabbis recognized as being never-ending in the earthly realm.

Based on the Talmud, Rabbi Simlai, a third-century Palestinian rabbi, stated that the 613 commandments were given to Moses on Mount Sinai, and that they consisted of two types of commandment: 248 positive ones (things to be achieved), corresponding to the number of the parts in the human body, and 365 negative ones (things to be avoided), corresponding to the number of days in the year. The rationale of this was as follows: each part of his body urges man to do good; every day of the year he is warned against committing sin.

The sages stressed that the performance of a mitzvah is only meritorious if it is accompanied by an awareness (*kanavah*) that it is God who has ordered that mitzvot be carried out, and that it is in obedience to this command that man carries out mitzvot. One must therefore precede each good deed by praising God for having commanded that such a deed be performed. There are a few exceptions to this rule: no prior praise of God is needed in giving alms, or in reciting the Haggadah on Passover—the story of the Exodus from Egypt.

The greatest mitzvah is the study of the Five Books of Moses—from which I have quoted so copiously in the last few letters.

A father is obliged to train his children—boys and girls—in the performance of good deeds, so that when they reach the age of Bar Mitzvah (thirteen for a boy) or Bat Mitzvah (twelve for a girl), they will be able to be responsible for carrying out the mitzvot properly.

Mitzvot must be carried out with joy. Those that involve making a booth on the festival of Sukkot, or making a ram's horn, or writing a scroll of the Torah, must be done beautifully. The eleventh-century commentator, Rashi, stressed, however, that the mitzvot were not given for our enjoyment, but as 'a yoke, to make known that we are His servants and the keepers of His commandments'.

A person who is carrying out one mitzvah need not worry—at that particular moment in time—about carrying out another. If a mitzvah presents itself, there must be no delay in carrying it out. A mitzvah that is near takes precedence over one that is more distant. The mitzvot related to observing the Sabbath have precedence even over those for the New Year. The mitzvah of saving life has precedence over those of observing the Sabbath. The reward for carrying out mitzvot—for keeping the commandments—is peace and prosperity. The sages say: 'He who performs one mitzvah . . . his days are lengthened and he inherits the Land.'

Among the 613 mitzvot is one enjoining a man to marry and have children: 'Be fruitful and multiply, and fill the earth, and subdue it' (Genesis 1:28). Another is to show consideration towards strangers, as you, Auntie Fori, did to me in New Delhi in 1959: 'Though shalt neither vex a stranger, nor oppress him: for ye were strangers in the land of Egypt' (Exodus 22:21).

The definition of a mitzvah can be wide. When, during the Second Temple period, the great sage Hillel went to the bathhouse, he told his disciples that he was going there to perform a mitzvah. How so, they asked. Because, he replied, it is a good deed to clean the body that is created in the image of God.

Above all, *tzedakah*—charity—is seen as the one good deed that can, and must, be carried out repeatedly, and at all times. Once is definitely not enough! 'But thou shalt open thy hand wide unto him, and shalt surely lend him sufficient for his need, in that which he wanteth' (Deuteronomy 15:8).

Rabbi Abraham Chill, the first Jewish chaplain at the United States Military Academy at West Point, the rabbi in Providence, Rhode Island, for twenty-six years, and author in 1974 of a standard work on the mitzvot, wrote: 'The distinguishing psychological feature of the Jew is his sense of duty. This sign of his Jewishness is stamped into the very essence of his make-up. In Jewish thought it is inconceivable to be a Jew and yet not be charitable. It is for this reason, that the Torah insists very emphatically that charity is not merely a virtue but an inescapable duty.'

There is only one occasion, only one day, in a Jew's life when he or she is not obliged to carry out any of the mitzvot, and I recently went through that day: it is the day on which a Jews buries a parent. On that day—which only comes twice in any person's lifetime—the need to deal with the procedures of a funeral and a burial sadly obviate all the other requirements of Jewish law.

No. 127

Dearest Auntie Fori,

In addition to the things that a Jew must strive to do, are the things he must strive not to do. 'Perhaps the least observed of the Torah's 613 commandments', writes my friend Joseph Telushkin—rabbi, novelist and humanitarian—in his book *Jewish Wisdom,* is the law that states 'that it is forbidden to say something negative about another person, even if it is true.' Such negative speech is known in Hebrew as *lashon ha-ra* (the evil tongue).

The only exception is if the person you are speaking to vitally needs the 'negative' information—say because he or she is thinking of marrying, hiring or going into business with the person about whom you are speaking.

The Amidah prayer, which observant Jews recite every day, at each of the three daily services, concludes with a paragraph in which each worshipper asks God—in the word of Mar Bar Ravina: 'keep my tongue from evil, and my lips from speaking guile'. A thirteenth-century Jewish scholar from Rome, Yehiel ben Binyamin, asked: 'Why are the fingers tapered like pegs?' and gave the answer: 'So that if one hears anything improper, we can insert them into our ears.'

In his book *Operation Shylock,* the American Jewish novelist Philip

Roth lists among the 'evil tongues' that Jews are urged to avoid: 'Derogatory information. Insulting witticisms. Disparaging anecdotes. Idle mockery. Bitchy chatter. Malicious absurdities. Galling wisecracks. Fantastic lies.'

Twenty years ago, Yitzhak Rabin wrote in his memoirs of how the Israeli Prime Minister Levi Eshkol was subjected to 'evil tongues' on the eve of the Six-Day War in 1967. As Rabin recalled (and he was Chief of Staff at the time), Eshkol was subjected to some cruel verbal backbiting:

'They mocked him and chipped away at his image and publicized his weaknesses and made false accusations. . . . The burden of the times and that slander campaign worked together to call his position into question. . . . With his wings clipped and his authority curtailed, he lacked the power to impose his will on the government.'

The power of such gossip was understood 1,600 years ago. In the Jerusalem Talmud it states: 'The gossiper stands in Syria and kills in Rome.'

Rabbi Telushkin recounts an old Hasidic story of a man who went about the town slandering the rabbi. One day, realizing how harmful his comments had been, he went to the rabbi and asked for his forgiveness. The rabbi told him he would forgive him on one condition, that he went home, cut up a pillow, and scattered the feathers to the winds. The man did so, then returned to the rabbi.

'Am I now forgiven?' he asked.

'One more thing,' the rabbi said. 'Now go and gather all the feathers.'

'But that's impossible,' the man said.

'Precisely,' the rabbi answered. 'And although you sincerely regret the damage you have done me, it is as impossible to undo it as it is to recover all the feathers.'

No. 128

Dearest Auntie Fori,

This letter is about the *minyan*—the word means number—the ten males who are needed as a minimum to conduct a synagogue or communal service. Since Talmudic times it has been considered specially meritorious to be one of the first ten men to arrive at a service. One prayer which can be recited only in the presence of a minyan is the Gomel prayer. Its name derives from the Hebrew *ha-gomel* ('bestows favours') and it is said, within three days of the event, by anyone who has just survived danger: a perilous journey, a serious illness or a near escape from death. Women recite it after childbirth. The prayer reads: 'Blessed are You, O Lord our God, King of the Universe, who bestows favours on the undeserving, and who has also bestowed favours on me.'

In synagogues where it is difficult to get ten male congregants on a regular basis, synagogues hire poor men to come in and make up the numbers: they are known as 'minyan men'. When I was just thirteen, and used to walk past a small synagogue each evening on my way home from school, there always seemed to be someone on the lookout for the likes of me, to ask me to make up the numbers: I was almost seized off the street—*khupped,* as my grandmother used to say in Yiddish.

Six years ago, when I took my youngest son, Joshua, then aged twelve, on a train journey to Zagreb—as part of a school project he was doing on inter-war Yugoslavia—we went on the Friday night to the synagogue there. It was a room in the Jewish community building. Only eight men were present when we arrived. I made the ninth. A tenth was needed for the service to begin.

Because Joshua had still not celebrated his Bar Mitzvah—his thirteenth birthday—he was not yet able to be part of a minyan. A debate began among the other participants. One of them, a Croatian Jew who had studied Judaism in Israel, recalled a tradition that, if only one person is missing to form the ten men needed for prayer, then a boy who is less than one year from his thirteenth birthday can constitute the tenth man. Josh was glad to do so, and the service began. As I wrote to you earlier, one ancient tradition asserts that the stranger whose unexpected arrival makes up the minyan is none other than the Prophet Elijah.

Varieties of Jewish worship have instituted new rules: Reform Jews no longer insist on ten men being present before the service can begin, and Conservative Jews allow women to be counted as well as men.

No. 129

Dearest Auntie Fori,

I would like in this letter to touch on some of the rituals and practices of the Jewish life-cycle. At the start of life, for all Jewish males,
comes circumcision. In Hebrew it is called *brit milah,* 'covenant of circumcision'.

Health permitting, every Jewish boy is circumcised on the eighth day
of his life. This ritual marks the covenant between God and Abraham, the
defining rite of Jewishness. In the words which God spoke to Abraham,
recorded in the Book of Genesis: 'This is my covenant, which ye shall
keep, between me and you and thy seed after thee: Every man child
among you shall be circumcised. . . .'

God explained: 'My covenant shall be in your flesh for an everlasting
covenant.'

The circumcision ceremony is followed by a festive meal, sometimes
in synagogue, but more usually in the home. All male converts, whatever
their age, are circumcised as part of the conversion process, in order to be
considered Jewish, but anyone with a Jewish mother—like your three
boys, dearest Auntie Fori—do not have to be circumcised in order to be
Jewish: having a Jewish mother is enough.

Some two thousand years ago the Roman governor of Palestine
asked the great Rabbi Akiva why, if God disliked man having a foreskin,
he created him with one in the first place, to which Akiva answered that
God created an incomplete world, leaving human beings to bring it to
greater perfection. Noting the wider Jewish aspect of this reply, Rabbi
Louis Jacobs comments: 'Jewish teaching rejects the idea, put forward by
those hostile to aeroplanes, that if God wanted men to fly He would
have provided them with wings.'

When a Jewish boy reaches thirteen he becomes *bar mitzvah* ('son of
commandment')—the coming of age, at which moment he is regarded
as responsible for his actions, and must carry out the precepts of the
Torah. The day of a bar mitzvah is is one of the most festive in the Jewish
life-cycle, a day of pride for the boy's parents in synagogue as he recites,

and usually chants, the portion of the Torah for that week, and then chants the weekly portion of the Prophets. After that the rabbi will remind him of the new responsibilities that are his. The boy's father will already have recited—when his son was called up to read the Torah portion—the benediction: 'Blessed be he who has freed me from the responsibility of this child.'

After the synagogue service the boy, his family and friends return home, or to a festive hall, where there is eating, dancing, speechmaking, and a plethora of gifts. I remember all too well how, in 1949, my own Bar Mitzvah presents containing an excessive number of shaving kits and shaving brushes, at least half a dozen, to the detriment, I thought, of other gifts I might have welcomed more. By the time I came to shave I was in the army, and those de-luxe leather kits, had they survived the five years, would not have been at all suitable in the austerity of an infantry barracks.

I also remember going to my grandmother's bedside before the synagogue service—she was too ill to go—and singing my portion to her. She was my father's mother, and had come to Britain from Eastern Europe at the end of the nineteenth century.

In recent years, many boys from Western Europe, Canada and the United States, and also from Latin America, travel to Israel for their Bar Mitzvah, which they celebrate at the Western Wall in Jerusalem, reading their portion of the Torah there. Others hold individual, and even collective Bar Mitzvah ceremonies in the two-thousand-year-old synagogue that was found at the top of the mountain fortress of Masada, overlooking the Dead Sea, whose north-west axis is towards Jerusalem, across the Judaean desert.

From the day of his Bar Mitzvah, a boy can take part in the *minyan*, the quorum of ten males required for communal prayers, about which I wrote you in my last letter. In recent times, girls have also been given a coming-of-age ceremony, the Bat Mitzvah, held when they reach the age of twelve.

Marriage, the next defining stage in life, is known as *kiddushin*—sanctification. In Jewish tradition, it is the ideal state. At its outset, in Biblical times, a newly married man was excused both military service and work for a whole year, and instead 'shall cheer up his wife'.

Jewish weddings take place under a *huppah,* or wedding canopy. This can be an ornate covering, or a large prayer shawl held aloft by close relatives. Before the groom places the veil over his bride-to-be's face, those present recite the blessing which Rebecca's father and mother blessed her as she set off to marry Isaac: 'Thou art our sister, be thou the mother of thousands of mothers, and let thy seed possess the gate of those which hate them.'

The wedding ceremony ends with the breaking of a glass underfoot by the bridegroom. This ancient ceremony—in mediaeval times the glass was often thrown against a wall—is thought to symbolise the destruction of the Temple. That evening, after the wedding meal, the Seven Benedictions are recited, thanking God for the fruit of the vine, for having created 'all things to Your glory', for having created man, for having made man 'in Your image, after Your likeness', for making Zion 'joyful through her children', for making the bridegroom and bride to rejoice, and for having created 'joy and gladness, bridegroom and bride, mirth and exultation, pleasure and delight, love, brotherhood, peace and fellowship'.

The benedictions continue, in what is surely one of the most eloquent moments in the Jewish life-cycle:

Soon may there be heard in the cities of Judah and in the streets of Jerusalem, the voice of joy and gladness, the voice of the bridegroom and the voice of the bride, the happy sound of bridegrooms from their canopies, and of youths from their feasts of song.

Marriage is a sacred covenant in the Jewish religion. Divorce, alas so common today, is not traditionally a part of the life-cycle as envisaged by the sages. The Prophet Malachi records: 'For I hate divorce, says the Lord, the God of Israel.' Yet divorce existed, and was provided for from the earliest days. In the stark words of the Book of Deuteronomy: 'When a man hath taken a wife, and married her, and it come to pass that she find no favour in his eyes, because he hath found some uncleanness in her: then let him write her a bill of divorcement, and give it in her hand, and send her out of his house.'

This Jewish 'bill of divorcement', known in Hebrew as a *get,* requires only the will and consent of the husband that his wife should be divorced. Documents from the Jewish community of Elephantine in Egypt, dating back to the fifth century BC, suggest, however, that a wife had the right to divorce her husband also.

The position of a former wife can be difficult, even tragic. An *agunah* ('forsaken', 'shut off') is a Jewish woman who, according to Jewish law, is unable to remarry, either because her husband refuses to give her a divorce, or because of his desertion and disappearance, or by the inability of the rabbinical courts to satisfy themselves that he is dead—he may have disappeared, or died without his place of death being known. This problem of such 'chained' women, unable to re-marry, has persisted to this day. Recently a rabbi here in London tried to shame a man into giving his wife a *get* by putting a full-page advertisement in the local Jewish papers.

No. 130

Dearest Auntie Fori,

This letter is about the final stage of the life-cycle: death and burial. A Jew who is dying has, if possible, to recite the Shema prayer—'Hear, O Israel: The Lord is our God, the Lord is one . . .' and then make confession, if only with the three words 'I have sinned'. The thirteenth-century Spanish Jewish scholar Nahmanides—who himself died in Palestine—recorded a fuller confession, which is now part of the Jewish prayer book—the *siddur*—and which ends with the words: 'Make known to me the path of life; in Thy presence is fulness of joy; at Thy right hand, bliss for evermore.'

In the home, after a person has died and before the body is taken to the cemetery, the mourners hold a short service at which, among the prayers, is a reading of three verses from Psalm 103:

As for man, his days are as grass: as a flower in the field, he flourisheth.
For the wind passeth over it, and it is gone; and the place thereof shall know it no more.
But the mercy of the Lord is from everlasting to everlasting upon them that fear him, and his righteousness unto children's children.

When my father died, I remember how powerful were the words we spoke next, words written by Rabbi Tarfon—a man of priestly descent who used to officiate at the Second Temple—two thousand years ago:

The day is short, and the work is great, and the labourers are sluggish, and the reward is much, and the Master of the house is urgent.

It is not thy duty to complete the work, but neither art thou free to desist from it.

Faithful is thy Employer to pay thee the reward of thy labour; and know that the grant of reward unto the righteous will be in the time to come.

Before the funeral service at the cemetery, the mourners tear their outer garments—today a small cut on a shirt front is sufficient. The tear or cut—*keriya*—is as a sign of mourning. In some communities it is made on receiving news of the death, or just after the funeral. For parents, the left-hand side of the garment is torn, as it is nearest to the heart, and children are closest to the heart of their parents. For a son, daughter, brother, sister or spouse the tear is made on the right. Strictly observant Jews always make the tear by hand, not with a knife or scissors. The origin of the tear derives from three Biblical examples: Jacob tearing his garment when his sons told him that Joseph had been killed by a wild beast; David tearing his clothes when he heard of the death of King Saul; and Job tearing his mantle when he began to mourn the loss of his children.

In the house of prayer at the cemetery a rabbi recites the burial service, which is poignant in the extreme: 'If a man live a year, or a thousand years, what profiteth it him? He shall be as though he had not been.'

God is then praised as 'the true judge, who ordereth death and restoreth to life . . . the true judge, all of whose judgments are righteous and true.'

Walking from the prayer hall to the graveside, at the head of the mourners escorting the coffin to its final resting place, the rabbi may stop three times, to avoid the impression that one is in a hurry to commit a loved one to the grave. At the graveside the adult males present, led by the mourners, each throw three shovelfuls of earth into the grave, on top of the coffin, until it is completely covered. Some Jews use the back of the spade, so as also to avoid the impression—once again—that one is in a hurry to bury a loved one, that one wants to hasten to complete the final task.

One tradition—which took place at my mother's grave this autumn—was to put into the grave, on top of the coffin, a bag containing old prayer books, as it is forbidden to throw away or burn books which contain God's name in them. So the books are buried in an actual grave. One tradition asserts that the person in that grave will be doubly welcome in heaven—both for his or her own sake, and also for the books being laid to rest.

At the graveside, Kaddish is recited by the mourners, who then return to the prayer hall, where those who have come to the funeral to pay their condolences greet them with the words: 'May the Almighty comfort you among the other mourners of Zion and Jerusalem.' Here in Britain it is customary to wish the mourners 'long life.'

Sometimes, when the number of mourners is particularly large, those present in the prayer hall after the funeral form two lines, and the mourners pass between them. For me, one of the most solemn and terrible of such occasions was when a young man whom I knew and greatly liked, Mark Tager, was killed in the Lockerbie air disaster—a decade ago now. The devastation of his family, and of his many young friends, was palpable; the prayer hall was packed to capacity.

Before leaving the cemetery, it is customary to pick a few blades of grass, and to recite from the Psalms the following verse:

> There shall be an handful of corn in the earth upon the top of the mountain; the fruit thereof shall be like Lebanon: and they of the city shall flourish like grass of the earth.

Another verse from the Psalms that is spoken while holding the blades of grass, on leaving the cemetery, is: 'For he knoweth our frame; he remembereth that we are dust.'

After a death the family 'sit shiva': shiva is the Hebrew word for seven. It is a seven-day period when the mourners are at home, and receive relatives and friends throughout the day. The mourners sit on low stools. They are not allowed to cook or do any work: those visiting them do all that is required, bringing the food, pouring drinks and making tea. Those visiting may not speak to a mourner until they are beckoned over. Each evening, prayers are said.

After thirty days comes the *shloshim* (thirty), a day of solemn remembrance. In 1995 I went to Jerusalem for the shloshim of Yitzhak Rabin, for prayers at his graveside and a memorial gathering in the Jerusalem Convention Centre at which his friends spoke about him, and films were shown of his life, including family films of him playing with his children and grandchildren.

For eleven months the children of the dead person recite Kaddish in synagogue. On each anniversary of the death they light the memorial candle, known in Yiddish as the yahrzeit candle. I light the yahrzeit candle for my father every February; and will now light one for my mother each November (but according to the Hebrew calendar, which is lunar, and not always the same 'Christian' day each year).

No. 131

Dearest Auntie Fori,

This letter is about some of the religious artifacts that Jews use. When I went to the eastern Polish city of Wlodawa with my University College of London students in 1996, many of them were shown in the museum that had been set up in what, before the Second World War, had been the main hall of the great synagogue. The Jewish community of Wlodawa had been destroyed during the war, when almost all 5,000 Jews of the town—including several hundred young children—were murdered. Their religious artifacts live on, under glass, as museum pieces; artifacts that had once been part of a vibrant life of piety and hope. Here are some of them:

The prayer book, or *siddur* ('arrangement'), is the book from which Jews follow the daily synagogue service. In it are set out the order of the service, and the form and traditions of prayer. The equivalent volume for the festivals and Holy Days is the *Makhzor* ('cycle'). Among the prayer books that set the pattern of the liturgy was the first, compiled in ninth-century Mesopotamia more than a thousand years ago by Amram Gaon, and the second, compiled a century after him by Saadiah Gaon (Gaon was the name given to the head of the Babylonian academies of Sura and Pumbeditha, which flourished between the sixth and eleventh centuries; later it was used by other heads of religious academies elsewhere; and by religious authorities generally).

Saadiah Gaon's prayer book included explanatory notes in Arabic, for the use of the Jews of Egypt. The prayer book from which I have quoted in these letters has explanatory notes in English: it was first published in 1902; the 1963 edition which I use belonged to my father. The first Ashkenazi prayer book was printed in Prague in 1512.

Kippot (singular, kippa), are the skullcaps worn by Jews at prayer, and, in recent times, by Orthodox Jews throughout the day. In my youth, almost all the skullcaps one saw were black. Today they come in a variety of colours, many of them multi-coloured. Many North African, Turkish and Iranian Jews wear large, colourful kippot. In Israel, many Jews wear a small knitted kippa, clipped onto the hair with a pin, and serving as a badge not only of religious but of political affiliation—veering to the right of the political spectrum.

Tallit (in the Yiddish pronunciation *taliss*) is the large four-corned prayer shawl with fringes at each corner, worn in synagogue. It is usually made of wool, but can also be made of silk. Each of its four corners has a fringe, made up of four threads doubled over, giving eight threads. These threads are then knotted into five double knots. The shawls were originally white, with black stripes woven into them, but recent custom, particularly in Israel, has led to colour being used, and even colourful designs, bright patterns, or scenes such as the walls of Jerusalem. Though the shawls were restricted for centuries to men, in Reform, Conservative and Reconstructionist synagogues, many women now wear them.

Tsitsit: these are the fringes on the small prayer shawl (the 'small tallit'), often worn underneath the outer items of clothing, and hanging down below them, peeping out under a shirt or jacket. The Book of Numbers provides the origin of these fringes, as it did for the fringes on the tallit prayer shawl: 'And the Lord spake unto Moses, saying, Speak unto the children of Israel, and bid them that they make them fringes in the borders of their garments throughout their generations. . . .'

When pious Jews read the Shema—'Hear, O Israel!'—in synagogue it is the custom to take out the tsitsit at the paragraph which refers to them, and to kiss the fringes each time the word is mentioned.

Tefillin are small, square, black leather boxes, also known as phylacteries, which contain four short passages from the scriptures, and which are fixed by leather straps to the forehead and forearm by Jewish men during the recital of morning prayers, except on the Sabbath. In Biblical times they had been worn throughout the day. On the box is written the Hebrew letter *shin* ('S').

In fixing the tefillin box to the forehead with its narrow leather straps, the person putting them on ties a knot in the shape of the Hebrew letter *dalet* ('D'). The box that is set on the forearm is fixed by its strap to form a knot resembling the letter *yud* ('I'). The three letters combined make the Hebrew word *shaddai:* one of the names of God.

How I remember struggling to get the knots right when I put on my tefillin, as I used to many years ago.

You know how I am always curious about Jewish surnames. Last year the government of Iran arrested thirteen Iranian Jews—members of one of the oldest Jewish communities in the world—and charged them with espionage for Israel. Ten of them were sentenced to long terms of imprisonment, despite world-wide protests that they were innocent. One of them, who was sentenced to thirteen years in prison, was named Hamid 'Danny' Tefileen. He was twenty-nine years old.

In Shiraz, where the trial took place, local Jews prayed in their synagogue for mercy: other than prayer, there was no public action they could take without danger of immediate arrest. Israel's Sephardi Chief Rabbi, Eliyahu Bakshi Doron, urged Pope John Paul II—then on his visit to Jerusalem—to intercede. A prayer vigil by Orthodox, Conservative and Reform rabbis was held outside the Iranian Mission to the United Nations in New York. The Iranians went ahead with the sentences.

No. 132

Dearest Auntie Fori,

A popular Jewish artifact, and symbol, is the *menorah* (candelabrum), which I mentioned in my Hanukah letter. There are in fact two types of menorah: the seven-branched oil lamp used in ancient times in the Temple, and the eight-branched candelabrum used during the festival of Hanukah, when one light is lit on the first day of the festival, and an additional light each successive day. The menorah used on Hanukah is also known as a Hanukiyah. On it, a ninth lamp holds the *shamash,* the candle used for the lighting ceremony.

As for so many Jewish artifacts and customs, the Bible provides the starting point and explanation. In the case of the menorah it is in the Book of Exodus, where God tells Moses: 'And thou shalt make a candlestick of pure gold: of beaten work shall the candlestick be made. . . . And six branches shall come out of the sides of it; three branches of the candlestick out of the one side, and three branches of the candlestick out of the other side. . . . And thou shall make seven lamps . . . and they shall light the lamps. . . .'

In recent times, the menorah has become a potent Jewish symbol. Its discovery during archaeological digs—as a decoration on ancient lamps, mosaic floor, and synagogue decorations going back two thousand years—has made it a strong visual link with the Jewish past. It has been found as a decoration on ancient glass, and on metal and ceramic objects. In recent times artists and craftsmen have delighted in designing versions that are modern, unusual, vivid and imaginative: out of wood, silver, even glass.

At the Bezalel Academy, founded in Jerusalem by a Russian Jew, Boris Schatz, in 1906, young artists frequently used the menorah as a motif for their designs in paintings, fabrics, tapestries and jewelry. As a symbol of Jewish life and continuity, it came during the twentieth century to rival the nineteenth-century favourite, the *Magen David,* the Star or Shield of David—the symbol with which the Nazis sought to isolate and humiliate the Jews. On a Jewish tombstone, a menorah is used to designate a woman, and a Star of David for a man.

The word 'menorah' can pop up in unexpected places. The *Menorah Journal* was first published in the United States in 1915—when you, Auntie Fori, were a little girl. It was dedicated to the promotion of 'Jewish humanitarianism'. In it, Jewish writers and scholars conducted a lively debate about the humanistic values in Judaism, which they sought to link in positive embrace with Jewish traditions and religious beliefs. In 1923 an illustrated journal, *Menorah,* published monthly, was founded in Vienna—scarcely a three-hour train journey from Budapest, where you, Auntie Fori, were then living. During the nine years in which it appeared, its aim was to discuss science, art and literature in a way that would 'serve as a bridge between the different sections of the Jewish people'. Articles were published in German, Hebrew and English.

The menorah, appearing as it does in the time of the Jewish revolts against Ancient Rome, has been given an aura of Jewish martial and national achievement. In 1948 it became the official symbol and seal of the State of Israel. The design chosen for it was that of the candelabrum which appears on the Arch of Titus in Rome, about which I wrote to you a while back. The menorah on that arch depicts the great ornamental candelabrum which had been taken from Jerusalem by the Roman conquerors from the Second Temple and paraded in Rome together with their Jewish captives. That Temple menorah has never been found. Legend has it that a Christian Roman soldier took it back with him to Palestine in the third century AD and hid it under the floor of the Monastery of the Cross, just outside Jerusalem, at the site of the tree where Adam ate the fruit of the tree of knowledge—so legend says, though Jerusalem is hardly the Turkish–Iranian border—and also the tree, the same tree, it is said, which was used for the wood of the crucifix of Jesus. To this day, however, the monks, whom I have visited on a number of occasions, have not chosen to dig in search of the precious relic.

Another set of Judaica is the braided candles with at least two wicks, and the spice box, used for *havdalah* ('separation'), the blessings over wine, candles and spices, recited in the home at the end of Sabbath, about which I will write to you at the end of my Sabbath letter.

The *mezuzah* (the Hebrew word means 'doorpost') is a small parchment scroll on which have been written selected verses of the Torah. The scroll, placed in a container—of metal, wood or porcelain, often finely ornamented—is then affixed to the outer doorpost and inner doors of Jewish houses. I have one on my front door. In the Book of Deuteronomy Jews are told, with regard to God's commandments: 'And thou shalt write them upon the posts of thy house, and on thy gates.' The mezuzah scroll contains the Jewish confession of faith, the Shema prayer, to love God and to study the Torah. On the case in which the parchment is put is inscribed the word *Shaddai*: 'Almighty'.

Among observant Jews, it is the custom on entering or leaving any house to touch the mezuzah with the hand, and kiss it as a sign that they realize the need to carry out God's commandments, and to show reliance upon God's protection.

When I was travelling in Poland in 1980, doing research for my book *The Holocaust: The Jewish Tragedy,* a young Polish Catholic came up to me in the street, after seeing me emerge from a ruined synagogue in the town of Dzialoszyce, and showed me something—somewhat surreptitiously—in his hand. It was a fine parchment scroll, a mezuzah, though without its case. How he had found it, I did not know. He wanted me to buy it from him, and I did.

Another Jewish artifact is the *yad,* the Hebrew word for hand. This is the pointer used by readers of the Torah to keep their place and follow the words as they read the weekly portion of the Torah in synagogue on Saturday, and during the Holy Days.

In Jewish writing, the first mention of a yad does not come until 1570. From then on, its use became frequent, its decoration enhanced. Sometimes it was studded with semi-precious stones or coral. In the Sephardi tradition, however, the yad is not used: the reader points with a cloth, or with the fringes of his prayer shawl. One inscription that is often engraved on the yad is from the Book of Deuteronomy: 'And this is the law which Moses set before the Children of Israel.' Another is from Psalm 19: 'The commandment of the Lord is pure, enlightening the eyes.'

Often the yad is made of silver, with delicately ornamental fingers at the end which will touch the Torah scroll. When my father was seventy, in 1972, I asked him where he would like to go for a birthday treat, and he said Istanbul. There, in the covered bazaar, we were offered by one of the stallholders a beautiful silver yad. The price was $400. It seemed just too high. Hardly had we left the city than we both realized that we ought to have bought it (he as a present for me, me as a present for him). Although the price by the standards of those days was so high, it was such a beautiful piece of work, and it would have returned into Jewish hands. I have often thought since then of that lost opportunity. Every time I return to Istanbul, I have a particular vivid memory of my father, who died in 1976, and of that yad.

No. 133

Dearest Auntie Fori,

A building that is connected with the synagogue, often an integral part of it, is the ritual bath, the *mikveh*. The word means a 'gathering' of water. In it Jewish men and women bathe, separately, as part of the age-old stress on cleanliness as an integral part of purity. Part of the ritual is complete immersion under the water.

As always in Jewish religious practice, the Bible provides the source, in this case a passage in the Book of Leviticus: 'Only a spring, or cistern or collection of water shall be clean.' It was Maimonides who pointed out in the twelfth century that the 'uncleanliness' which the mikveh purifies 'is not mud or filth which water can remove, but is a matter of scriptural decree and dependent on the intention of the heart.'

The mikveh is used in connection with a woman's change of status during her menstrual cycle. A full week after she has finished bleeding she cleans herself thoroughly—including taking off all her makeup—then immerses herself in the mikveh, and says a prayer, after which she is able to resume sexual relations with her husband.

Also taken to the mikveh by some—but not all—Orthodox Jews are all new utensils to be used in the preparation or serving of food and drink which have been made by a non-Jew, or bought from a non-Jew.

The blessing recited on these utensils thanks God 'who has commanded us regarding the immersion of vessels'. Once they have been washed, these utensils can be used in a home.

The Prophet Ezra is said to have insisted that men go to the mikveh after having had marital relations, to cleanse themselves before studying the Torah. This is known as 'The Immersion of Ezra': Maimonides tells us that he always observed it. Pious Jews also immerse themselves on the eve of the Day of Atonement, to be clean in body and mind for that solemn day of fasting and prayer.

The actual mikveh, the structure itself, is often one of the few remaining traces of very early Jewish communities. The one found in Cologne dates from 1170 AD. In the archaeological digs in Israel, great joy is always expressed when the remains of a mikveh are found. This was particularly true of the two-thousand-year-old ruins of the fortress of Masada. As soon as Professor Yadin, who was excavating Masada, found what was thought to be a mikveh, a group of learned rabbis were escorted on foot up the precipitous mountain-side path—then, before the building of a cable car, the only way to the top—to measure the structure. Despite the intense heat, and giddy height, the rabbis were thrilled when their measurements of the two-thousand-year-old structure were precisely those laid down for the mikveh in ancient times. Yadin once told me that the rabbis' enthusiastic discovery was one of the most dramatic moments of his archaeological career.

A few years ago I was the presenter for a three-part television series on the history of Jerusalem. In one scene I spoke about the mikveh while standing in one: it had been discovered near the steps leading up to the Temple Mount from the City of David. Dating from the Second Temple period, it too was two thousand years old.

On a recent visit to Budapest, not far from the Dohany Street synagogue where your father, dearest Auntie Fori, had his seat seventy years ago, I saw the mikveh which, during the terrible months of the ghetto in 1944, had to be used as a morgue, because there was nowhere else in the ghetto with the necessary space that had a pious association.

No. 134

Dearest Auntie Fori,

Jews worship only one God, but they worship their one God in many ways. As I have mentioned in some of my letters about the Holy Days and Festivals, Ashkenazi and Sephardi rituals and customs differ. In the last 150 years many reformist aspects have also entered into the religious community. Reform, Conservative and Liberal Judaism all flourish. My own synagogue here in London is a Reform one, where part of the service is conducted in English, and where a choir sings from behind a screen, as opposed to the traditional cantor chanting in front of the congregation.

It was the Haskalah movement—the Jewish Enlightenment about which I wrote to you some while ago—that, following the intellectual upheavals of the French revolutionary era, set the tone for religious change. It took its name from the Hebrew word *sekhel,* intellect, or wisdom. Those who followed the enlightenment were known as *maskillim,* the wise, from the Biblical verse in the Book of the Prophet Daniel: 'And they that shall be wise shall shine as the brightness of the firmament. . . .'

Neo-Orthodoxy, led by the German rabbi and thinker Samson Raphael Hirsch (who died in 1888), argued for the adaptation of Jewish religious practice to the styles and decorum of the nineteenth century, and the teaching of secular as well as religious concepts. Having studied classical languages, history and philosophy, Hirsch was convinced that traditional Judaism was fully compatible with Western culture. But he opposed the Reform movement, led by his fellow student and friend Abraham Geiger, who argued that there had to be a bridge between the Jewish religion and the secular environment in which Jews lived. Geiger (who died in 1874) was a pioneer of *Die Wissenschaft der Judenthums*—Jewish Science—the movement that used modern historical methodology to examine the sources of Judaism and how the religion developed.

The leading figure in the Jewish Science movement was Leopold Zunz, the German-Jewish historian who served for two years as a preacher at the Reform New Synagogue in Berlin. In 1832 he published

a study of the evolution of Jewish preaching through the ages. A pro-
found student of Jewish history, he wrote in 1855: 'If there are ranks in
suffering, Israel takes precedence of all the nations. If duration of sorrows
and the patience with which they are borne ennoble, the Jews can challenge the aristocracy of every land.'

Reform synagogues were first established in Germany at the beginning of the nineteenth century. That in Hamburg was set up in 1818,
with its own revised prayer book. The German language, as well as
Hebrew, became a part of the service. Sermons were also spoken in German, as opposed to Hebrew. In 1832, Zunz published a book in which
he showed that sermons given in the local language were an old and
established Orthodox practice that had fallen into disuse. Rabbis were
trained with an emphasis on learning that would extend beyond the Talmud to secular and scientific studies. It was in 1838 that Geiger, who had
been trained in this way, became the rabbi of the Breslau Reform community, in German Silesia. He devised a system of worship that was
based on the concept of the evolution of ritual.

Orthodox Jews were convinced, and remain convinced to this day,
that the laws handed down to Moses on Mount Sinai are not only the
basis of the faith, but the unchanging, Divine basis. Members of the
Reform movement do not accept that *Torah Min-Hashamayim:* Torah
from the Heavens, that is, given by God and not capable of revision, is
the last word in religious belief and practice. For them, the One God
could be worshipped in ways which the Bible does not touch on, and
can be worshipped in German, or English, or in any other language spoken in their daily lives by the congregants.

In the United States from 1824, in Britain from 1842, in 'your' Hungary, Auntie Fori, in 1867, the slow but steady growth of Reform
communities led to divided religious loyalties, but—from the Reform
perspective—to an invigoration of Jewish worship.

It was in the United States that the reformist tendencies gained their
greatest strength. The Hebrew Union College for the training of Reform rabbis was established in 1875 in Cincinnati, Ohio. The serving of
non-kosher food at a banquet for its first rabbinical ordination in 1883
caused widespread anger, even dividing the reformists. Two years later,
in 1885, the Pittsburgh conference of the Reform movement formally

denied—in its Pittsburgh Platform—the binding character of 'the Mosaic legislation'. The Pittsburgh Platform stated:

> *We recognize in the modern era of universal culture of heart and intellect the approach of the realization of Israel's great Messianic hope for the establishment of the kingdom of truth, justice and peace among all men. . . .*
>
> *We recognize in Judaism a progressive religion, ever striving to be in accord with the postulates of reason.*

The pattern of worship of reformist Jews is itself always changing. The Pittsburgh Platform of 1885 was itself amended in 1937 by the Columbus Platform, following a meeting of American Reform rabbis in Columbus, Ohio. Among other intensifications of religious practice, they called for greater emphasis in 'moral discipline and religious worship in the Jewish home'.

Change is part of the nature of Reform, and at the centre of its disagreement with traditional Orthodoxy. That change, in recent times, has been towards a greater acknowledgment of traditional Judaism. There was a time, for example, when the Reform movement gave up the fast of Tisha B'Av, regarding it as an 'anachronism' to mourn the destruction of the First and Second Temples, since so much of Jewish life had been restored and built up since then, and since, after 1948, the State of Israel had been created, reversing the intended end of Jewish sovereignty which the destruction of the Temple had brought about. In recent times, however, Tisha B'Av has been seen by many in the Reform Movement to deserve a place in the liturgy—especially the reading of the Book of Lamentations—even if they remain reluctant to treat it as a day of fasting.

No. 135

Dearest Auntie Fori,

In my next three letters I want to look at one of the most fertile and vibrant aspects of Jewish life: the Sabbath.

The story of mankind, as recounted in the Bible, which I wrote to you about in my very first letter, begins with God creating the earth, light, water, plants, animals, man and woman, and then resting on the seventh day from his labours. The Sabbath commemorates that day of rest, and puts it at the very centre of the Jewish experience, of the Jewish week, and of Jewish family life.

For Jews, the Sabbath begins every Friday night at sunset and continues until sunset on Saturday night. It is a time of rest and of reflection.

The Sabbath is known in Hebrew as Shabbat, in Yiddish as Shabbos. The Hebrew word *shabbat* is related to the verb *shavat,* to cease, desist, or rest. In each of the Five Books of Moses there is some reference to keeping the Sabbath. In the Book of Leviticus it is linked to every man fearing his mother and his father. I suppose today we would say 'honouring' rather than 'fearing'—perhaps even 'loving', as your three boys love you.

The Sabbath is seen, not just as a special day, but as a noble one. Before darkness falls and the Sabbath begins, the mother of the house— covering her eyes with her hands—lights the two candles and recites the blessing over the candles, thanking God for his bounty.

The first candle represents the injunction in the Book of Exodus: 'Remember the Sabbath day.' The second candle recalls the injunction in the Book of Deuteronomy: 'Observe the Sabbath day.' In the synagogue service each Friday night, as the sun sinks low on the horizon, all congregations sing—and some in Jerusalem turn to face the sunset as they do so—the prayer to the Sabbath queen: 'Come my beloved to greet the bride, the Sabbath. . . .'

In the sixteenth century, in the Holy City of Safed, in northern Galilee, it was the custom to have a special pre-Sabbath ceremony, *Kabbalat Shabbat* ('the reception of the Sabbath'), by going out into the fields around the town and, facing west towards the setting sun, welcoming the Sabbath, singing Psalm 92, 'It is a good thing to give thanks unto the Lord. . . .'

Returning home from synagogue after darkness has fallen, the family, and their invited guests—often including strangers whom they have seen in synagogue, who have no family Sabbath meal to attend— gather around the Sabbath table, its candles already lit. The table is always covered with a white cloth, with the best cutlery—silver where possible—two candlesticks, a silver cup, and two plaited loaves of white bread—the challot or challas.

Before the family celebrations begin the participants leave the room briefly to wash their hands, and to say a short prayer on doing so. Returning to the table, the father blesses his children, after which he raises the silver cup, known as the *kiddush*—the blessing, or sanctification—cup, and recites the blessing, during which he first welcomes the Sabbath, and then recalls the Exodus from Egypt. This historical narrative, with its recitation of God's crucial intervention, is central to Jewish tradition. Then, after blessing the wine ('Blessed art thou, O Lord our God, King of the Universe, who createst the fruit of the vine'), the father—or perhaps one of the children present—recites the blessing over the two loaves of bread, and having sprinkled them with salt, a symbol of hospitality, gives each person a piece.

The above is the Ashkenazi tradition of your parents, Auntie Fori, and of mine. In the Sephardi tradition the bread is torn with the hands rather than cut with a knife, and then thrown across the table to those present, rather than handed to them. The two loaves represent the double portion of manna which the Children of Israel received in the wilderness on the Friday, so that they would not have to gather manna on Saturday. While the father of the house is blessing the wine, the two loaves of bread are covered by a decorated cloth, to avoid insulting the bread—the 'staff of life'—while the blessing is being made over the wine.

Immediately before the Sabbath meal, the head of the household, who normally sits at the head of the table facing his wife, sings his wife's praises by reciting the *Eshet Hayyil* (A Virtuous Woman) from the final chapter of the Book of Proverbs—one of the most beautiful lyrical passages in the Bible:

Who can find a virtuous woman? for her price is far above rubies.
    The heart of her husband doth safely trust in her, so that he shall have no need of spoil.
    She will do him good and not evil all the days of her life.

She seeketh wool, and flax, and worketh willingly with her hands.

She is like the merchants' ships; she bringeth her food from afar.

She riseth also while it is yet night, and giveth meat to her household, and a portion to her maidens . . .

She stretcheth out her hand to the poor; yea, she reacheth forth her hands to the needy. . . .

Strength and honour are her clothing; and she shall rejoice in the time to come.

She openeth her mouth with wisdom; and in her tongue is the law of kindness.

She looketh well to the ways of her household, and eateth not the bread of idleness.

Her children arise up, and call her blessed; her husband also, and he praiseth her:

Many daughters have done virtuously, but thou excellest them all.

Favour is deceitful, and beauty is vain: but a woman that feareth the Lord, she shall be praised.

Give her the fruit of her hands; and let her own works praise her in the gates.

The Sabbath meal itself, certainly in your Hungary and in my Britain during the last hundred years, has followed a traditional culinary pattern: chicken soup (with noodles or dumplings), fish, or a chicken in some form or another, vegetables (and sometimes noodles), and a pudding (often noodle pudding—lokshen pudding—with raisins). As a child, I used to enjoy the triple-noodle element.

Other dishes often include radishes dipped in salt, chopped liver, chopped herring, chopped egg and onions, pickled cucumbers, sweet cooked carrots (tzimmes) and, to end the meal, apple strudel or fruit compote.

The Sabbath meal is followed by one of the most melodious of all Jewish occasions, Grace After Meals: prayers thanking God for the meal and for his blessings. Most of these prayers are sung by all those present to tunes which have been passed down through the generations. Many date from mediaeval times. The first of these songs, with which the Grace After Meals starts, is Psalm 126:

When the Lord turned again the captivity of Zion, we were like them that dream.

Then was our mouth filled with laughter, and our tongue with singing: then said they among the heathen, The Lord hath done great things for them.

The Lord hath done great things for us; whereof we are glad.

Turn again our captivity, O Lord, as the streams in the south.

They that sow in tears shall reap in joy.

He that goeth forth and weepeth, bearing precious seed, shall doubtless come again with rejoicing, bringing his sheaves with him.

This Psalm was my father's favourite. He used to sing it at his parents' table before the First World War, here in London. His parents used to sing it, at their parents' table, in the Polish provinces of Tsarist Russia, more than a hundred years ago.

As the Sabbath ends at sunset on the Saturday, a short but moving service is held around the Sabbath table, marking the division between the day of rest and the days of toil. It is called *havdalah* ('distinction') and contains a blessing over spices, to restore the soul saddened by the departure of the Sabbath; a blessing over light, the flame of which comes from a braided candle which has more than one wick, and which could neither be lit nor blessed during the Sabbath; and a blessing over wine.

Originally, the Havdalah service took place in synagogue after the Sabbath, but according to the 1,600-year-old Jerusalem Talmud—the repository of so much Jewish tradition and explanation—'for the sake of the children' it became a part of the family ceremony at home. Its first prayer speaks of how 'with joy shall ye draw water out of the wells of salvation'. In my father's pre-Second World War copy of the Daily Prayer Book, the then Chief Rabbi Hertz comments on the phrase 'with joy' that: 'The duty of cheerfulness is a commonplace in Jewish ethics and life.'

The main prayer of Havdalah thanks God for making 'a distinction between holy and profane, between light and darkness, between Israel and the heathen nations, between the seventh day and the six working days'. Following that prayer, many families end with one or more songs, including a hymn written by Isaac ibn Chayyat, who died in 1089, and which includes the lines:

> *From the clutch of sickness set me free,*
> *And lead me forth to day from night.*

Orthodox Jewish women, especially those in the nineteenth-century Jewish heartland of Russian Poland, used to sing a Yiddish prayer which contained a similar refrain:

> *May the new week come to us*
> *For health, life, and all good.*
> *May it bring us sustenance, good tidings*
> *Deliverances and consolations.*

This ends the Sabbath observance.

No. 136

Dearest Auntie Fori,

The scriptural basis of the Sabbath lies in the opening pages of the Bible, in the second verse of the second chapter of the Book of Genesis: 'And on the seventh day God ended His work which He had made; and He rested on the seventh day from all His work which He had made.'

Man thus imitates God, in whose image we are created, and follows His example. Just as it was God who first rested after His act of creation, so man too must lay down the tools of his trade, and take a day of rest. According to Halakhah—Jewish religious law—no work must be done on the Sabbath that involves adding to what was there before, or making something new. That included baking bread, or—for the Children of Israel in the wilderness—baking the manna which they had found in the field, 'the bread which the Lord hath given you to eat', as Moses had explained to them.

On that first Friday when manna had appeared, Moses told the children of Israel to gather twice as much as usual, explaining: 'Tomorrow is the rest of the holy Sabbath unto the Lord: bake that which ye will bake today, and seethe that ye will seethe; and that which remaineth over lay up for you to be kept until the morning.' There would be no manna in the field, Moses explained, on the Sabbath day. 'Six days shall ye gather it; but on the seventh day, which is the Sabbath, in it there shall be none.'

Then, as now, the Jews rested on the Sabbath day, from sunset on Friday to sunset on Saturday. The Bible explains that one reason for this is that slaves and servants must have a day of rest, as must beasts of burden, and that even visitors must be the beneficiaries of such a day of rest. The Book of Exodus expresses it thus: 'Six days shalt thou do work, and on the seventh day thou shalt rest: that thine ox and thine ass may rest, and the son of thy handmaid, and the stranger, may be refreshed.'

In the Book of Deuteronomy there is a fuller version and explanation: 'Six days shalt thou labour, and do all thy work: But the seventh day is the Sabbath of the Lord thy God: in it thou shalt not do any work, thou, nor thy son, nor thy daughter, nor thy manservant, nor thy maidservant, nor thine cattle, nor thine ass, nor any of thy cattle, nor the stranger that is within thy gates; that thy manservant and thy maidservant may rest as well as thou.'

Ceasing from work was to be the case even during critical periods of plowing, and of harvesting. Even the building of the Temple had to cease on the Sabbath. The penalty for breaking the Sabbath could be a severe one in Moses' time. Indeed, the Book of Numbers recounts the story of a man brought before Moses after he had been found gathering sticks for firewood on the Sabbath. He was held in prison until God himself pronounced sentence, telling Moses: 'The man shall surely be put to death: all the congregation shall stone him with stones.' He was then taken outside the camp and stoned to death, at the hands of the whole community of Israel.

It was immediately after this incident, and to try to avert its repetition, that God commanded the Israelites to make fringes on their clothes 'throughout their generations'—and on the fringes to put a riband of blue—'that ye may look upon it, and remember all the commandments of the Lord, and do them; and that ye seek not after your own heart and your own eyes, after which ye use to go a whoring.'

Strong words, and a harsh example. Later, the prophet Jeremiah rebuked the rulers and people of Judah for allowing goods to be brought into Jerusalem on the Sabbath for commercial purposes. 'Take heed to yourself,' he warned, 'and bear no burden on the Sabbath day, nor bring it in by the gates of Jerusalem. Neither carry forth a burden out of your houses on the Sabbath day, neither do ye any work. . . .' Jeremiah went on to report on God's behalf that if the Sabbath were dishonoured in Jerusalem, 'then I will kindle a fire in the gates thereof, and it shall devour the palaces of Jerusalem, and it shall not be quenched.'

The prophet Isaiah had further warnings. Observing the Sabbath was a precondition for Jewish national restoration after the exile to Babylon. If the Sabbath were observed, Isaiah reported God's promise, 'I will cause thee to ride upon the high places of the earth, and feed thee with the heritage of Jacob thy father.' When the Jews returned from exile, Nehemiah specifically mentioned only 'thy holy Sabbath' among the 'precepts, statutes and laws' of Moses that must be kept.

As governor of Judaea, Nehemiah was rigorous in insisting that the rules of the Sabbath were kept. Had not their ancestors, he asked the Jews of Jerusalem, desecrated the Sabbath, with the result that God had brought 'all this evil upon us, and upon this city?'

The threat of assimilation, and the ever-present attraction of other gods and cults, heightened the stress on Sabbath observance as an essential feature of the perpetuation and unity of the monotheistic faith. The destruction of the Temple, and the ending of Temple sacrifices as the centre of the religious experience, made the keeping of the Sabbath the new focus of religious worship, capable of being observed each week both in the Land of Israel, even without a Temple, and in the ever-widening Diaspora.

At the time of the Maccabees, and their successful revolt against the Seleucid conquerors of Judaea—about which I have written to you some months ago—the keeping of the Sabbath was adhered to with particular strictness, as part of the revival of Jewish national identity—so strictly, according to tradition, that the Maccabean soldiers allowed themselves to be killed on the Sabbath, rather than violate the holiness of the day of rest by putting up a fight.

During the Maccabean period of Jewish independence, the desecration of the Sabbath was again punishable by death, as it had been in the time of Moses: walking any great distance, or travelling on a ship on Sabbath, were both punishable by death; and sexual relations with one's wife were forbidden. However, later rabbinical teaching made it meritorious to have marital sexual relations on Sabbath.

Rabbinical tradition dating back two thousand years describes the keeping of the Sabbath as equal to all the other precepts of the Five Books of Moses. Mediaeval Jewish tradition held that the Messiah would come on the first Sabbath day when every Jew in the world observed the Sabbath rules. The mediaeval Jewish philosopher Maimonides said that the Sabbath was of twofold significance: it taught the essential truth that God created the world, and it gave man physical rest and nourishment. Another mediaeval Jewish sage, Judah Halevi, saw the Sabbath as an opportunity provided by God himself to enable men to have complete rest of both body and soul for a sixth part of their lives—something denied even to kings and rulers (and certainly to your Prime Minister, Atal Vajpayee, and mine, Tony Blair) who know little or nothing, during their period of power and responsibility, of the 'precious boon' of complete cessation from work and worry.

For observant Jews today—who are known as *shomreh shabbat,* 'Guardians of the Sabbath'—no work at all is done during the twenty-five Sabbath hours. Indeed, it is considered a good deed to start the Sabbath a little early, in order to extend its sanctity. There are thirty-nine main classes of work that are forbidden, and several hundred sub-classes: thus watering of plants is a sub-class of sowing, weeding is a sub-class of planting, and adding oil to a burning lamp is a sub-class of lighting a fire. Turning on an electric switch is a sub-class of lighting a fire: hence lights and ovens cannot be turned on.

The main classes of forbidden work are known as the fathers (*avot*) of work, the sub-classes as the offspring (*toledot*). All shops are closed. Money is not carried. Heavy burdens and bundles are not taken out of doors. Cars are not driven. Telephones are not carried or used. Letters are not written.

Even food is not to be cooked during the Sabbath, just as no manna was to be gathered on Sabbath in the wilderness. For many Jews since early mediaeval times, the basic Sabbath fare is a stew that is put in the oven before Sabbath begins, and is cooked slowly through the night and the next morning, and eaten at midday: a delicious concoction, known as cholent, in which meat, beans, barley and potatoes blend into an aromatic feast. Garlic and onions—no strangers to the Indian palate—are an added ingredient.

Until the Holocaust, throughout Eastern Europe—and in the Hungary of your childhood, especially in its eastern provinces—each Sabbath morning after synagogue would see young boys setting out on foot to the communal ovens in bakeries where the cholents had been cooked and kept warm, and then carrying them back in their pots through the town to their homes. Being under the age of thirteen—the age of Jewish adulthood—these boys could carry a heavy weight in the street without violating the Sabbath rules.

No one really knows the origin of the word *cholent*. Some say it is from early mediaeval French, *chaud lent*—heated slowly. Certainly many of the mediaeval French Jewish communities made their way, mostly after expulsions but also in search of trade, eastward, towards Poland and Lithuania, where cholent became the main Sabbath dish, and very delicious it was, too.

Also made before the Sabbath is a pudding known as kugel. It too is cooked slowly through the night in an oven that has been lit before the Sabbath. Often flavoured with raisins, or with spices, it provides a sweet ending to the meal, before an afternoon of restful contemplation.

No. 137

Dearest Auntie Fori,

At the end of the Sabbath a short ceremony is held at home, called *havdalah* ('separation') This ceremony, which dates back 1,500 years, marks the divide between the Sabbath and working week. Four blessings are recited. The first three are over wine; over spices, during which a spice box is shaken and sniffed; and over a braided candle with two wicks, which is lit and then doused in wine.

After these three blessings, those present recite a fourth: 'Blessed art Thou, O Lord our God, King of the universe, who makest a distinction beteen holy and profane, between light and darknesss, between Israel and other nations, between the seventh day and the six working days.

Blessed art Thou, O Lord, who makest a distinction between holy and profane.'

The cup of wine used for the blessing over wine, and held up during the fourth blessing, is always filled to overflowing, as an expression of hope that the week to follow will bring with it an abundance of goodness. Tradition asserts that an unmarried girl holds the braided candle high, so that she will get a tall groom. The spices are to raise the spirits and offset the sadness that the Sabbath has come to an end.

Women do not drink the Havdalah wine: medieval superstition was that any woman who did so would grow a beard. Another tradition assets that Eve caused Adam's downfall when she made him eat the wine she had squeezed from grapes (in Jewish folklore the Tree of Knowledge was a vine) and that, because of this sin, women do not drink the Havdalah wine.

'The Sabbath comes to an end weekly,' writes Rabbi Irving Greenberg in his recent book *The Jewish Way, Living with the Holidays*, 'but it creates an appetite and a satisfaction that lasts through the week until it is renewed again.' And he went on to comment, with reference to the deepest of all; the historic longings of the Jewish people:

This is how the Zionist dream survived for two thousand years without becoming a bitter mockery of life. How can people cry out every year for nineteen hundred years, 'Next Year in Jerusalem', without becoming depressed by the fact that 365 days later they are still in exile, still calling out the slogan of hope?

The answer is that on every Shabbat, Jews pre-enact the coming of messianic restoration. For a day, the sounds of joy and gladness, the voice of the groom and the bride, reverberate in the streets of a restored Zion. For twenty-five hours the heavenly Jerusalem exists on earth—in France and Poland, in Yemen and Bombay.

Your Bombay (if I may call it that), Auntie Fori. And also, of course, your Budapest.

Rabbi Greenberg added: 'No wonder that when the road to earthly Jerusalem opened up, there were Jews who knew exactly what to do and where to go.'

The holiness of the Sabbath affected Jews of every status and calling, in every land of the Diaspora, and in the Land of Israel, throughout the millennia. It was Ahad Ha-am ('One of the People'), the turn-of-the-century Jewish thinker—who in his commercial life, as Asher Ginsberg, was a tea salesman here in London for the Russian Jewish tea magnate Wissotsky—who reflected: 'The Sabbath kept the Jews more than the Jews kept the Sabbath.'

As I was writing this letter, I was thinking that the word 'Sabbath' or 'Shabbat' (in Hebrew) is not a common Jewish surname. Almost no prominent Jews bear such a surname. One exception was Adolf Joachim Sabath—he spelt his name with only one 'b'. Like your parents, he was born in the Austro-Hungarian Empire. At the age of fifteen he emigrated to the United States, and in 1905, aged fifty, he was elected to Congress for Chicago's Fifth District, as a Democrat. He served for twenty-three consecutive terms until his death in 1952, the second longest continuous service of any congressman. A strong supporter of Roosevelt's New Deal, he also supported United States military preparedness in 1939, and the despatch of crucial Lend-Lease supplies to Britain in 1941.

No. 138

Dearest Auntie Fori,

My last letter ended with a note about an American congressman, and now I am writing my 138th letter—in fact a postcard—in the United States—in a street in Anchorage, Alaska, looking at a plaque to Isadore 'Ike' Bayles, born 1876, died 1956. The plaque reads:

'Ike Bayles' contributions to Anchorage were hallmarks in the development of the community. Born in Lithuania, he first came to Alaska in 1899. Soon after the creation of the Anchorage townsite in 1915–16, he opened his clothing store near this location. He was instrumental in the incorporation of the city, served on the school board, completed eight terms on the City Council, was active in the Jewish community, was president of the *Anchorage Daily Times* and fostered aviation in Alaska.

Altogether, he served Alaska, and Anchorage for over fifty years in pro-moting orderly growth and sound government.'

Quite a life and quite an achievement.

No. 139

Dearest Auntie Fori,

The Jewish community here in Anchorage gave me dinner last night in a restaurant overlooking the bay—part of the Cook Inlet of the Pacific Ocean—in which whales played. Across the bay, as the sun set, the silhouettes of mountains (and even of an extinct volcano) were out-lined in gold. I was welcomed so warmly, it quite belied their witty name these northernmost Jews have given themselves—the 'Frozen Chosen'.

Jews first reached Alaska more than 250 years ago, not with the Americans, to whom it was then an unknown land of no interest, but with the Russians; with the explorer Vitus Bering, in fact, whose expedi-tion of 1741 made Russia keen to acquire the land that lay beyond Siberia. The Russians found no gold however, their small settlements failed to flourish, and in 1868 they sold the whole territory to the United States for $7,200,000. The American soldier who raised the Stars and Stripes over the town of Sitka that year was a Jew, Benjamin Levi.

The discovery of gold followed within a few decades, and Jews—including Levi—were among the first prospectors, as well as among those who opened stores for food and supplies. In 1901, in the gold rush town of Nome, a Hebrew Benevolent Society was organized by the bet-ter-off Jews to help those who had fallen on hard times. The General Store in Nome was owned and operated by a Jewish couple, Yetta and Isaac Kracower—whose family almost certainly came originally from Cracow, part of Austria-Hungary after 1867. Their Jewish New Year's greeting card for 1910 was engraved on a walrus tusk. Their daughter Bella, who spent her childhood in Nome, was the first woman pharma-cist to graduate from the University of Washington in Seattle.

Among the successful Jews in Nome were two brothers, Max and Charles Hirschberg. Having travelled by bicycle from the Yukon to

Nome in the winter of 1900, a two-month journey of considerable hardship, along the Yukon river—they ended up a decade later as managers of the profitable Sunset Mines.

Jewish prospectors and tradesmen made their way in all the bustling towns of the Gold Rush era—towns like Sitka, Juneau, Haines and Skagway. In 1908 Robert Bloom, born in Lithuania, founded the first synagogue in Fairbanks. His journey to Alaska had taken him through Dublin and Seattle. Ike Bayles, the Lithuanian-born Jew about whom I wrote to you in my postcard from Anchorage on my second day there, had reached Alaska in 1899. His father, Afroim Hessel Bayless, who had been born in Russian Poland, was a rabbi in Jerusalem. He died there in 1912 at the age of seventy-six. Ike Bayles had last seen his father when he was fourteen years old. News of his death took three weeks to reach Alaska. That year, among the Jews living in Alaska who applied for naturalization were Ben Bromberg from Warsaw and Samuel Appelbaum from Suwalki—on the Polish–Lithuanian border.

In 1900 two Russian-born brothers, Sam and Boris Magids, from the Ukraine, began working as trappers on the Kenai Peninsula. Their activities prospered, and they owned a number of trading posts on the Peninsula. Sam died in 1930 and Boris a decade later.

One of Anchorage's most-remembered Jews was Zak Loussac, who had also reached Alaska in Gold Rush days before the First World War, and worked as a pharmacist. A strong believer in education and democracy, he was convinced (as his daughter-in-law told me when we spoke in her bookstore) 'that libraries were the way to go', and was the benefactor of the city's library—which is named after him. For three years after the Second World War, when Anchorage began seriously to expand, he was the city's mayor.

On the eve of the Second World War a New York–born Jew, Ernest Gruening—a former artillery officer in the First World War, and a distinguished journalist—was elected Governor of Alaska. An advocate of statehood for Alaska, after that was achieved he became one of the state's first two Senators—in 1959, when Alaska was admitted to the union as a state. In the Senate he was one of only two Senators, of the hundred, who voted against the Gulf of Tonkin resolution, which authorized President Johnson to attack North Vietnam. His opposition to the war in

Vietnam helped lead to his defeat in the Senatorial election in 1968, after which he wrote a book, *Vietnam Folly*.

The Second World War saw an influx of American servicemen to Alaska to defend it against Japanese attack (the Japanese did succeed in occupying two of the Aleutian Islands for a while). When the tide of war turned Alaska was a base for the bombing of Japan. One of the newcomers in those war years was Burton Goldberg, who decided to stay on once the war was over. It was in his living room in 1958 that the first Jewish communal worship was held in Anchorage. To the annoyance of his young sons, the television set in the living room was covered over to provide a surface from which to conduct of the service. One of those sons, Art Goldberg, who is now a Natural Resource Officer for the State of Alaska, was one of my hosts.

I was in Alaska to give a lecture in the recently rebuilt Congregation Beth Sholom—the House of Peace—located on Northern Lights Boulevard. Among the congregation when I spoke was George Mohr, who had been born in Vienna, and who emigrated to Britain just before the outbreak of war. Continuing to America, he made his way to Alaska in 1952, with the army.

They say that 'Jewish Geography' is the ability to find a link between any two Jews, through a third Jew. George Mohr told me that he had been in London, as 'a penniless refugee' with his fellow-Viennese, George Weidenfeld. In 1963, Weidenfeld (now a British Lord) was the publisher of my very first book, and indeed of many of my later books.

Also at my lecture was a Holocaust survivor from Cracow, who had been liberated by the British army in Bergen-Belsen, at the age of six.

Visiting Alaska for the first time in 1978, and later settling there, was Myron Rosenberg. His photographs of Alaska are inspiring. To spend time in his studio in Anchorage, as I did on the day of my synagogue lecture—though alas he was out—is to bring the glories of the Alaskan landscape and its people vividly to life. Rosenberg's photographic searches have taken him and his camera as far afield as the Russian Far East, China, Malaysia, Turkey and Roumania. Anchorage Jews hold him in high regard.

Among those who had spoken in the Anchorage synagogue—more than two decades ago—was Moshe Dayan. Also from Israel, among the most recent visitors were two Jewish musicians, Luba Agranovsky and Dmitri Kasyuk, who had emigrated from Russia to Israel in 1990, and a neuro-biologist from the Weizmann Institute, South African–born Henry Markrom, who is doing research into Alzheimer's disease.

Without a rabbi at the moment, but actively seeking one, the Jews of Anchorage celebrate the current High Holy days—the New Year and the Day of Atonement—with a visiting rabbi, seventy-four-year-old Jack Stern, from Massachusetts. Before his retirement a decade ago he chaired the Ethics and Appeals Committee of the Central Conference of American Rabbis. He would be travelling more than 3,500 miles to carry out his rabbinical assignment.

Notices on the walls of the synagogue gave a vivid picture of the vibrancy of the community: adult Hebrew-language classes, Jewish cooking classes, Sabbath evening meals ('bring your own favourite dairy dish') and a summer camp in the nearby mountain woodlands of Susitna, where the activities for the youngsters included Israeli dancing and making Sabbath candles.

In Anchorage, as well as in the Conservative synagogue in which I spoke, which has two hundred families on its register, there is a small ultra-Orthodox Lubavitch synagogue, with a rabbi and some twenty families. In Fairbanks, seventy Jewish families, although without a rabbi, have rented a small house in which to worship; they call it Or Hatzafon, Hebrew for Light of the North. The Jews of Juneau also gather for prayer, as do those on the Kenai Peninsula, an hour or so drive south of Anchorage, amid the most majestic Pacific Ocean inlets, mountains and glaciers.

Shortly before the outbreak of the Second World War, the Seward Chamber of Commerce—I lectured in the town of Seward after a boat excursion to the glaciers, seals and puffins of the region—offered to take in Jewish refugees from Hitler and to settle them on the Kenai Peninsula. There were more than a million empty acres of agricultural and grazing lands there (some of which I could see from my hotel bedroom at the Alyeska Mountain Resort, an hour's drive south of Anchorage, where I lectured on Churchill and Russia, before my synagogue talk in Anchorage itself, on Churchill and the Jews).

The Seward Chamber of Commerce informed the Secretary of the Interior in Washington that the virtually empty Kenai Peninsula was 'easily' capable of supporting a quarter of a million inhabitants. But the other Alaskan towns—Fairbanks, Juneau and Anchorage—did not want Jewish immigrants, and the idea died.

A few months later, the new governor of Alaska—Ernest Gruening, himself a Jew—suggested bringing in German Jews to develop some of Alaska's hot springs, on the lines of the central European health spas such as Karlsbad, Marienbad and Bad Nauheim—in the development of which Jews had played an important part. The bureaucrats in Washington said they would 'study the proposal', but did no more.

What an opportunity for saving human lives was lost. And what an opportunity for Alaska. That thought made me sadder than I might have been, looking at the stunning scenery of the Kenai peninsula.

Yet Alaska did become a place of refuge, and renewal, for individual Jews after the war. Among the many survivors of the Holocaust who write to me on a regular basis is Henry Wilde, a Czech Jew who, as a teenager, was liberated from the concentration camp at Theresienstadt in May 1945, and is now a consultant physician at Juneau.

Throughout the world, Jewish life goes on, after five thousand years, vibrantly. The Jews of Anchorage, who live about as far from the Land of Their Fathers as anyone could, show that it will be vibrant for a long time to come. When the twentieth century began there were about 15 million Jews in the world, five million of them in Russia. In 1939, on the eve of the Second World War, there were almost 17 million, five million of whom lived in the United States. Today, at the start of the twenty-first century—and after the massive loss of six million in the Holocaust— there are again, as in 1900, an estimated 15 million Jews in the world, five million of them in Israel and almost six million in the United States. Thus Jewish life goes on, despite the Holocaust, and despite the demo- graphic (and spiritual) 'perils' of assimilation.

So ends my last letter on the history, life and customs of the Jews— your co-religionists and mine. I will post it tomorrow, and will make sure that it, like those that have gone before it, has some fine stamps on it for your grandson.

No. 140

Dearest Auntie Fori,

This final letter is an attempt to summarize and also to put into perspective the story I have been telling you—in a hundred and forty letters. I am sending it during the most solemn, reflective days in the Jewish calendar, the Ten Days of Penitence, which fall between the New Year (six days ago) and the Day of Atonement (in three days' time). During these days, every Jew who still believes, however remotely, in the faith of his ancestors, looks deep into his or her soul, ponders the failings of the year that has gone, and seeks the strength to move ahead with greater wisdom.

The core of Jewish history is the story of a people who are defined by a book—the Torah—the Old Testament—and who subscribe to the set of laws set out in that book, and who are continually trying to understand how those laws of two thousand years ago and more can be 'modernised'—can be made to fit with all the moods and paraphernalia and demands and changing moralities of modern life, be it electricity, the motorcar, advances in medical science such as organ transplants, or (most recently) the 'marriages' of gay and lesbian couples. All these are real issues, daily issues which the Jew can seek to look at through his age-old beliefs.

Modern Jewish thinkers—like Adin Steinsalz in Israel, or Joseph Telushkin in the United States, or Jonathan Sacks here in Britain—grapple with these problems from the perspective of the Jewish religion—the root of Jewish survival. Because, writes Sacks in his recent book, *Radical Then, Radical Now,* the Jews 'never forgot their ideals, even though they were often powerless to implement them, they were ready for great things when the moment came'. Sacks goes on to write: 'I am a Jew because I cherish the Torah, knowing that God is to be found not in natural forces but in moral meanings, in words, texts, teachings and commands, and because Jews, though they lacked all else, never ceased to value education as a sacred task, endowing the individual with dignity and depth.'

Many non-religious, non-spiritual events have filled Jewish history, as in these pages, and continue to inspire and also bedevil Jewish life, but the 'main event', if I can call it that, is the religion: God's promises to Moses and to his 'chosen people'—chosen to carry out commands and moral imperatives, and to adhere to ethical codes that are ancient, yet modern and comprehensive.

In the words of a Jerusalem rabbi, Naftali Schiff: 'The Torah we must share is the instruction manual for living life to the fullest. It is the sign-post to a world hungry for upright values and direction. This is our legacy to mankind and, no less, to our children.'

With the wise words of another, I will sign off for the last time—before I fly out to see you in your Himalayan abode. My promise to write you a history of the Jews in the form of letters has come to an end. I hope it has been an enjoyable journey, despite some hard historical moments along the way. It has been such a joy to try to set all this out in less space than most of my books—proof that if a subject is close to one's heart, it can also be presented within a modest span—or at least within four hundred printed pages.

With much love from your adopted son—which you ask me to be, and which I accept with delight,

your devoted
MARTIN

EPILOGUE

In the summer of 2001, having posted the last of my letters to Auntie Fori in a London letterbox, I flew to Delhi and made my way northward by train and car to the former British hill station in the foothills of the Himalayas, 6,200 feet above sea-level, to which my letters had been sent. 'I am in my ninety-third year', Auntie Fori said proudly when I arrived—speaking with the same vigour and directness as when we had first met forty-three years earlier. We spent eight days together. While I was with her the last of my letters arrived.

On her terrace, in her drawing room, in her study and at her table, we spoke of Auntie Fori's family, her recollections of Hungary, and her Jewish origins. She was born Magdolna Friedmann in Budapest on 5 December 1908. Her mother, Regina, neé Hirshfeld, was a member of the well-known and prosperous Bettelheim family, toy manufacturers, who had acquired in Austro-Hungarian times, the right—much prized but seldom obtained by Jews—to use the aristocratic prefix 'von'. 'For a Jew,' Fori reflected, 'that was a great honour, so the family was very proud.' Her father Armin's seat in the Dohany Street Synagogue 'was in the third, fourth or fifth row', but, she added: 'The only time I went to the synagogue was to pick up my parents on the Day of Atonement.' Every Friday night her mother had lit the Sabbath candles in two silver candlesticks.

Fori recalled how, in 1998 in Delhi, 'I being Jewish, told you that I

knew nothing.' Her father had changed the family name from Friedmann to Forbath, seeking, as did many assimilated Hungarian Jews at
that time, a less Jewish-sounding name. At school, the young Miss Forbath was given the nickname 'Fori'—for Forbath. When, five years later,
the Hungarian government rescinded the right for Jews to change their
names, the family became Friedmann again, but the nickname Fori
stuck. 'That is how I am still known all over the globe!' she wrote to me
in one of her letters, and she added: 'Actually my parents called me
Dundi, meaning little fatty. It seems I was a lovely little fat girl.'

In 1919, while Fori was still at school, Red revolution broke out in
Hungary, led by a Jew, Bela Kun. It was followed by counter-revolution,
in which many Jews were among those killed. 'My father was on a committee,' Fori recalled. 'They used to patrol the streets to make sure
nothing happened. Once a week my father would travel to the villages
to get food. He had a house on Lake Balaton. One summer we went
there—by train—and I saw people hanging from trees. It was terrible for
us children to look at.'

As Jews, Fori's family members were, in the main, fortunate in their
fate. Between the wars, her uncle Armin, her mother's eldest brother,
who had fought in the Austro-Hungarian army in the First World War
and been taken prisoner by the Russians, emigrated to Palestine. His son
later became a music teacher in Mexico. Her mother's youngest brother,
Louis, a poet and a philatelist, emigrated to Tangier. Her younger sister
Carlotta went to Australia, where she married a distant cousin.

Fori and BK met in 1930 when they were both students at the London School of Economics. 'We noticed each other in the history library,'
she recalled. 'But in those days you didn't talk to a boy unless you were
formally introduced. Easter holidays started. We were alone up in the
library—he, me, and another Indian student. I heard him say something
to the other student, who then left. We looked at each other and
laughed. It was three months since we had first seen each other.'

Fori and BK fell in love. When she went back to Budapest, people
said: 'An Indian can marry hundreds of wives. What will you do?' In
1932, BK's parents travelled to Budapest to meet Fori's parents: 'Just to
make sure I wasn't riffraff', Fori said. 'They were sitting in the sitting
room. I was crying in my bedroom. My future mother-in-law had to go

to the loo. She came by my room—saw me crying. She said: "We must let them do what they want to do." I went to India for a year, to see if I fitted in. They had to promise, if I didn't fit in, they would let me come back. I came to India in January 1934—and didn't go back.'

From the moment of her arrival in India in 1934, Fori entered heart and soul into the needs and aspirations of its people. 'You changed from one civilization to another,' BK commented as she told me her story. One of their wedding gifts, which she showed me with pride, on a sideboard, is an ornamental brass saucer holder, a gift from Gandhi's Jewish friend Henry Polak, about whom I wrote to her in my letter about Gandhi and the Jews.

On the eve of the Second World War, Fori's mother travelled to India, where she remained. The war brought terror and massacre to the Jews of Budapest. At one moment of danger, Fori's father was saved by his German housekeeper, Mimi, who, when Hungarian Fascists came to take him away, shouted at them: 'What do you mean, to come in here. It is my place. I am a German. You are only Hungarian. Get out.' And they left. Fori's brother Joseph, an officer in the Hungarian army, was saved by the captain of his unit—with whom he used to play bridge in the evenings. 'He was a clever enough player,' Fori's son Ashok commented, 'to win when he needed to, and to lose—just—when that was expedient.' One day the captain said to Joseph: 'You know, I could send you off to the gas chambers—but then what would I do in the evenings. I need you.' As the Russian army approached central Hungary the captain told him: 'You'd better go.' Joseph ran away and hid. When the war ended, Fori, in India, received a telegram from her father, 'Jossi is at home.' After the war, during the early Communist years, he escaped from Hungary by swimming the Danube to the Czechoslovak side, and made his way to Vienna. From there he emigrated to Australia, where he married a Hungarian Jewish girl.

Fori's best friend in Hungary, from the time when they were youngsters of ten or twelve, was a Jewish girl, Katy. She married a Hungarian, but was later divorced. Throughout the war she lived in Budapest. German officers were billeted in her villa. She hid her son in a room behind the bathroom. When the Russians entered Budapest in January 1945 she still hid her son. Later she managed to leave Hungary by car, smuggling him out in the trunk. They went to Australia, where Katy married again. Katy's sister Anne—like Fori herself—married an Indian before the war and went to live in India. When I asked Fori if any close or distant family members had been killed in the Holocaust, she replied: 'I know of none because by that time most of them had left Hungary, as did my friends. They survived.'

In India, BK had risen steadily through the ranks of the British administration. From 1934 to 1939 he was an Assistant Commissioner, in charge of administering a sizable district. In 1939 he became Under-Secretary at the Department of Education, Health and Lands, and in 1940 Under-Secretary in the Finance Department. In 1945 he was one of India's three delegates to the Reparations Conference in Paris. A year later he became Joint Secretary of the Finance Department. During all that period his cousin Jawaharlal was leading the struggle against British rule. As a member of the Nehru family Fori saw that struggle at first hand. When independence came in August 1947 she took an active part in the protection of Muslims in Delhi who had been forced to flee their homes to the Purana Qila refugee camp. She was on the Emergency Committee which looked after the refugees and decided how many left Delhi each morning by train to Pakistan. 'Can you imagine the horror?' she asked me. 'We heard one day that all the Muslims on that day's train had been butchered. For several days we sent no train.'

With the mass influx of hundreds of thousands of Hindu refugees from Pakistan, Fori was involved in establishing a centre where they could sell their embroidery work and handicraft. Later she was one of the founders of the All-India Handicrafts Board. BK was a civil servant in the new India headed by his cousin Jawaharlal; his first appointment was as a member of the delegation sent to London to deal with India's sterling balances. When Gandhi was assassinated in January 1948, both BK and Auntie Fori were in Delhi. Nehru asked Fori to accompany the foreign diplomats, who arrived to pay their respects, into Gandhi's room.

In 1949 Fori returned to Hungary with her three sons—then aged twelve, ten and eight. She had not seen her father for fifteen years. For three months she stayed in Budapest. 'It was the first time we had seen her in Western dress,' Ashok recalled. 'Every evening when she came back she was crying. Many of the people whom she had known had been killed in the war. It was a very unhappy time for her.' Her mother's sister Elizabeth had killed herself during the war, on being told that her husband—an army doctor—had been killed at the front. But her husband had not been killed, and not long after she took her own life he returned to Budapest to discover the terrible tragedy. He and their young daughter survived the war.

Whatever positions BK held in Indian public life, Auntie Fori was at his side, active in social work. When he was governor of Assam and the eastern tribal areas, her responsibilities were onerous. 'I had one million refugees on the Bangladesh-Magalaya border,' she told me. When BK was governor of Kashmir, Fori was head of the province's family planning association, and of its Social Welfare Board, establishing several schools for Buddhist children from the remote villages.

As we talked, my letter about not speaking evil arrived. Fori's daughter-in-law Chand—like the Nehrus, from a leading Kashmiri Brahmin family—recited the Sanskrit couplet 'Speak the truth, but speak the sweet truth; Don't speak truth which is hurtful.' Fori commented approvingly: 'It is exactly the same thing in Sanskrit and Hebrew.'

Halfway through my visit two more of my letters arrived, the one about Hungarian Jews, and the one about the Jews of the Soviet Union, including the ballerina Plisetskaya. 'This about Hungarian Jews,' Fori commented, 'I never knew. Even Plisetskaya—I never knew she was Jewish. I saw her dance at the Bolshoi and she came to the Indian Embassy in Moscow where I was staying. It never occurs to me to think—who is a Jew, who is not a Jew. It just isn't there.' Later we talked about the British economist Nicholas Kaldor, like Fori a Hungarian-born Jew. 'He came to India, and Bijju and I spent some time with him,' she recalled. 'We took him for a picnic. I had no idea he was Jewish.' Fori had also met the Soviet writer Ilya Ehrenburg when he visited India as the guest of the Indo-Soviet Cultural Society, but she had no idea that he was Jewish, or had been the object of much Soviet Jewish bitterness at his apparently protected status as one of Stalin's 'favourites'.

BK, who listened attentively to all Fori told me, commented that on the previous year's Holocaust Memorial Day held by the Israeli Embassy in Delhi, 'Ashok and I went to the ceremony. The Israeli Ambassador said he would reverse the order laid down by protocol, and would sing the

Indian national anthem before the Israeli anthem. He explained that he would do so because Jews had been persecuted all over the world, but that India was the only country where Jews had been welcomed—in ancient times, by the king. It was very moving.'

Fori and BK recalled visiting the Jewish community in Cochin. 'It looked so lost, so godforsaken, just a few coloured lamps,' Fori said. 'We met a Jewish woman who said, "I can't marry." "Why not?" I asked. "Because all the unmarried Jewish men here are only boys." "Why not marry a Jew from Calcutta?" "I can't. They are different Jews. I cannot marry them." ' BK comments, 'The caste system had overcome them,' and he adds: 'In the synagogue in Cochin there was a colour distinction. One black man—he was also a Jew—was kept separate from the rest—he was kept behind the others.'

Dining alone with Auntie Fori and Uncle Bijju one Friday night, I lit two candles, blessed the bread and wine, and recited 'A woman of valour . . .' Fori said that the candle lighting brought back memories of her mother—of candle-lighting eighty years earlier. As we discussed the Sabbath and the blessings, Fori suddenly asked: 'Why is the Sabbath so special? Everyone rests. Why is it so rigid? It is not rigid with the Christians—but they still rest. I see there must be sanctity—otherwise why should I listen—but the Jewish Sabbath is so rigid—you mustn't do this, you mustn't do that. It is not a time of enjoyment. It is so rigid.' When I started to explain the beauty of the Sabbath, it emerged that my 'Shabbat' letter had never arrived. I promised to send her a copy when I got back.

Auntie Fori was particularly keen that I should meet her friend Lieutenant-General J.F.R. (Jack) Jacob, the Governor of the Punjab. Jacob was born in Calcutta in 1921, the son of a Jewish family, originally—like so many Calcutta Jews—from Baghdad. He had begun his military career in 1942 as a young artillery officer in the British army, and had seen active service in the Middle East and Burma. It was he who, in the India–Pakistan war thirty years ago, when he was Chief of Staff of India's Eastern Army, took the surrender of the Pakistani forces in Bangladesh. Before becoming Governor of the Punjab in 1999, he had been Governor of Goa. He told me proudly that for some years he has been a member of the Commonwealth Jewish Council, headed by a British Labour peer, Lord Janner.

As we spoke about Indian Jews, BK remarked that when he was Chief Secretary at the Finance Ministry, one of his most trusted senior civil servants, Ezra Kolet—about whom I had written to Fori in one of my letters—was Jewish. 'He used to go to synagogue in Delhi,' Fori recalled, and added: 'I didn't go.' But she has not set aside her Jewishness entirely. 'I am not much of a Jew,' she reflected, 'but even today I can't shake hands with a German. I couldn't do it in Washington'—where BK was Indian Ambassador—'I would say to the German Ambassador, politely, "Good evening, Mr Ambassador," but I would not shake his hand.' Later, looking through one of my books on her shelf, *The European Powers*—which I had sent her in 1966—she chanced on the photograph of the young Jewish boy in the Warsaw Ghetto being forced out of a building at gunpoint, with his hands up. 'That is why I can't shake hands with a German,' she said. 'That is why I could only say "Good evening, Mr Ambassador" but not shake his hand.' Pausing, she said quietly: 'I have a feeling of guilt, I wasn't there, I was safe. The guilt feeling is still with me. Why should I not have suffered?'

To friends who had come to lunch, Fori again recalled our talk in Delhi in the winter of 1998: 'I told him that I'm so ashamed, being a Jew, that I know nothing about Jewish history.' That evening Fori wanted me to wear a jacket. I said it is not really cold enough. She insisted, and then laughed: 'The Jewish mother: I cannot help it.'

APPENDIX

While writing my letters to Auntie Fori, I received a number of letters from her. One of them, in her inimitable, lively style, was written just after I had sent her my letter about the Jews of Alaska. I print it here in full, to give a flavour of her style and interests:

Dearest Martin,

Your letters arrive in bunches and every one is more welcome than the other. On Saturday the 16th came bunch 89–94 (not 90). Two days previously arrived your long-lost No. 63 franked in London the 1st August. Where was the letter between the 1st August and the 14th September? However late, most welcome as it gave the important story of England promising freedom to Israel, etc.

I am still missing letters 59, 68, 69 and 90. Where, where, where are they?

Along with your final letter 93 came your short note saying that you were leaving for Alaska next morning to meet the Jews of Anchorage. I had no idea, as I have no idea of a million things about life, that there should be a Jewish community in Alaska. I am awaiting with great interest your letter on them.

Nota Bene we were in Alaska in 1967; we flew direct from Switzerland to Vancouver and caught a boat from there up to Juneau, the capital of Alaska—from there at different stages to different places (forgot their names) to Point Barrow whereto a US air force plane took us; (they put a special Thunderbox, covered with red velvet, for my use) finally down to Anchorage, where we had some friends. This was not long after the bad earthquake there, which destroyed many houses.

An amazingly interesting State. We met genuine Eskimos and we felt extremely sorry and sad for them. However, that should be a letter from me to you about the native American Indians.

You speak about the Diaspora of the Jews. What about the Diaspora of our Indians? On this very trip (I forgot the name of the town), we landed high in North of Alaska and I saw a lady in a sari receiving us. The story about her is that she met a young American in India, married him, he was posted in this truly far flung northernmost tiny town of the State. While Bijju did his official visit, I lunched with her, eating whale blubber, it was terrible; I could not chew it and that is what this young lady from India had to eat.

I have not written to you for ages (17th August) reason being that I waited for your fascinating most interesting letters to come in. They arrive in driblets—79 before 70 before 80, etc.

The stamps are getting more and more beautiful. England is suddenly spurting forth with such glorious philatelic prints. It is a delight for the eyes. I am keeping them all, as you desire, but would like to give some of them to my grandson Akhil when several duplicates of the stamps arrive.

You have described yourself as my adopted nephew. I have always thought of you as my adopted son.

· With much love, and blessings,

Yours, as ever,

A. FORI

BIBLIOGRAPHY

Listed below are the works consulted during the writing of these letters.

REFERENCE BOOKS

Calvocoressi, Peter. *Who's Who in the Bible*. London: Penguin Books, 1988.

Carlson, Ralph (editorial director). *American Jewish Desk Reference*. New York: Random House, 1999.

Cohn-Sherbok, Dan. *A Concise Encyclopedia of Judaism*. Oxford: Oneworld, 1998.

Comay, Joan. *Who's Who in Jewish History after the Period of the Old Testament*. London: Weidenfeld and Nicolson, 1974

Gilbert, Martin. *Atlas of Jewish History*. 5th ed. London: Routledge; New York: William Morrow, 1993

Jacobs, Louis. *The Jewish Religion, A Companion*. Oxford: Oxford University Press, 1995.

Johnson, Paul. *A History of the Jews*. New York: Harper and Row, 1987.

Millgram, Abraham E. *Jewish Worship*. Philadelphia: Jewish Publication Society of America, 1971.

Rolef, Susan Hattis (editor). *Political Dictionary of the State of Israel*. 2nd ed. Jerusalem: Jerusalem Publishing House, 1993.

Roth, Cecil (editor in chief). *Encyclopaedia Judaica,* 16 vols. Jerusalem: Keter Publishing House, 1972.

Wigoder, Geoffrey (editor-in-chief). *The Encyclopaedia of Judaism*. Jerusalem: Jerusalem Publishing House, 1989.

————. *Dictionary of Jewish Biography*. New York: Simon and Schuster, 1991.

GENERAL WORKS

Baron, Salo W. *The Russian Jew Under Tsar and Soviets*. 2nd rev. ed. New York: Macmillan, 1976.

Beizer, Mikhail. *The Jews of St. Petersburg: Excursions Through a Noble Past*. Philadelphia: Jewish Publication Society, 1989.

Chatterjee, Margaret. *Gandhi and His Jewish Friends*. London: Macmillan Academic and Professional Ltd., 1992.

Chill, Abraham. *The Mitzvot, the Commandments, and Their Rationale*. Jerusalem: Keter Books, 1974.

Cohen, Mortimer J. *Pathways Through the Bible*. Philadelphia: Jewish Publication Society of America, 1946.

Comay, Joan. *The Hebrew Kings*. London: Weidenfeld and Nicolson, 1976.

————. *The Diaspora Story: The Epic of the Jewish People among the Nations*. London: Weidenfeld and Nicolson, 1981.

Falstein, Louis (editor). *The Martyrdom of Jewish Physicians in Poland*. New York: Exposition Press, 1963.

Gilbert, Martin. *The Holocaust: The Fate of the Jews of Europe under Nazi Rule*. New York: Holt, 1987 (published in Britain as *The Holocaust: The Jewish Tragedy*, London: HarperCollins, 1987).

————. *Israel, A History*. New York: William Morrow, 1998; London: Doubleday, 1998.

Goodman, Philip. *The Yom Kippur Anthology*. Philadelphia: The Jewish Publication Society of America, 1971. Philip Goodman has also published *The Rosh Hashanah Anthology* (1970) and the *The Shevuot Anthology* (1974).

Grant, Michael. *The History of Ancient Israel*. London: Weidenfeld and Nicolson, 1984.

Greenberg, Rabbi Irving. *The Jewish Way, Living with the Holidays*. New York: Summit Books, 1988.

Howe, Irving (with Kenneth Libo). *World of Our Fathers: The Journey of the East European Jews to America and the Life they Found and Made*. New York: Simon and Schuster, 1972

Israel, Benjamin J. *The Jews of India, and the Jewish Contribution to India*. New Delhi: Jewish Welfare Association, 1982.

Kolatch, Alfred J. *The Jewish Book of Why.* Middle Village, N.Y.: Jonathan David, 1981.

Levine, Israel. *Faithful Rebels: A Study in Jewish Speculative Thought.* London: Soncino Press, 1936.

Lipstadt, Deborah. *Denying the Holocaust: The Growing Assault on Truth and Memory.* New York: The Free Press, 1993.

Locks, Gutman G. *The Spice of Torah—Gematria.* New York: Judaica Press, 1985.

Millgram, Abraham E. *Sabbath: The Day of Delight.* Philadelphia: Jewish Publication Society of America, 1965.

Moneypenny, W. F. and G. E. Buckle. *The Life of Benjamin Disraeli, Earl of Beaconsfield.* 2 vols. London: John Murray, 1929.

Prager, Dennis, and Joseph Telushkin. *Why The Jews: The Reason for Antisemitism.* New York: Simon and Schuster, 1983.

Rose, Aubrey (editor). *Judaism and Ecology.* London: Cassell, 1992.

Sacks, Jonathan. *Radical Then, Radical Now: The Legacy of the World's Oldest Religion.* London: HarperCollins, 2000.

Sarner, Harvey. *The Jews of Gallipoli.* Cathedral City, California: Brunswick Press, 2000.

Sassoon, David Solomon. *A History of the Jews in Baghdad.* Published by his son Solomon D. Sassoon, Letchworth, Hertfordshire, 1949.

Schauss, Hayyim. *The Jewish Festivals: History and Observance.* New York: Schocken Books, 1958 (previously published as *Guide to Jewish Holy Days*).

Scholem, Gershom. *Kabbalah.* Jerusalem: Keter, 1974.

Slater, Robert. *Great Jews in Sport.* Rev. ed. Middle Village, N.Y.: Jonathan David, 1992.

Solomon, Samuel. *Memories, with Thoughts on Gandhi.* London: Counter-Point Publications, 1983

Symons, Alan. *The Jewish Contribution to the 20th Century.* London: Polo Publishing, 1997.

Telushkin, Rabbi Joseph. *Jewish Wisdom: Ethical, Spiritual, and Historical Lessons from the Great Works and Thinkers.* New York: William Morrow, 1994.

Wouk, Herman. *The Will to Live On: This Is Our Heritage.* New York, HarperCollins, 2000.

———. *This Is My God.* New York: Little, Brown and Company, 1959.

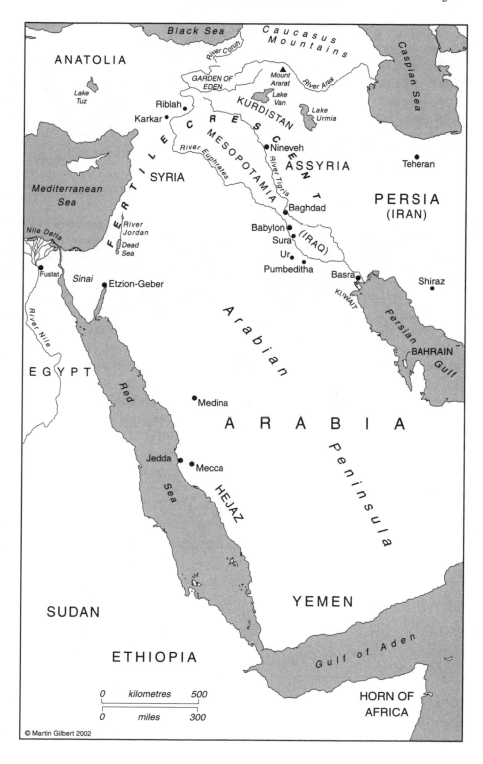

Black Sea

Caucasus
Mountains

ANATOLIA

River Çoruh

Caspian Sea

GARDEN OF
EDEN

▲ Mount
Ararat

River Aras

Lake
Tuz

Lake
Van

KURDISTAN

Lake
Urmia

Riblah

Karkar

FERTILE CRESCENT

MESOPOTAMIA

River Euphrates

River Tigris

Nineveh

ASSYRIA

Teheran

SYRIA

PERSIA
(IRAN)

Mediterranean
Sea

Baghdad

Nile Delta

River
Jordan

Dead
Sea

Babylon
Sura

(IRAQ)

Fustat

Sinai

Etzion-Geber

Ur

Pumbeditha

Basra

KUWAIT

Shiraz

River Nile

EGYPT

Arabian

Persian Gulf

BAHRAIN

Red

Medina

A R A B I A

Jedda

Mecca

Peninsula

Sea

HEJAZ

SUDAN

YEMEN

ETHIOPIA

Gulf of Aden

| 0 | kilometres | 500 |
| 0 | miles | 300 |

HORN OF
AFRICA

© Martin Gilbert 2002

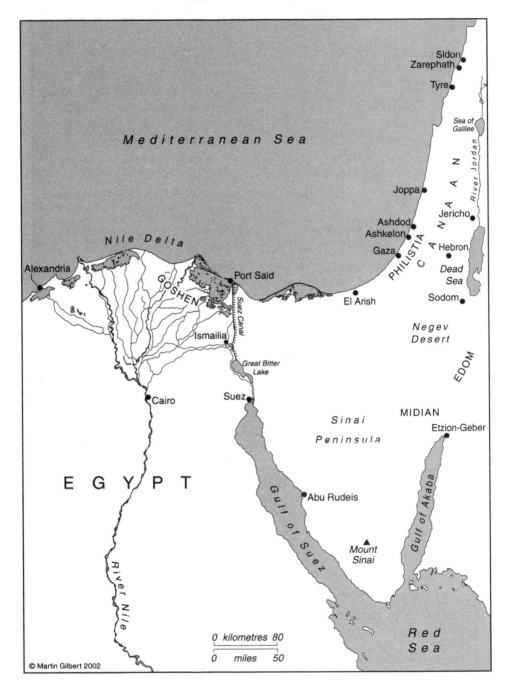

Sidon
Zarephath
Tyre

Sea of Galilee

Mediterranean Sea

C
A
N
A
A
N

River Jordan

Joppa

Jericho

Ashdod
Ashkelon

Gaza

PHILISTIA

Hebron

Dead Sea

Sodom

Nile Delta

Alexandria

GOSHEN

Port Said

El Arish

Negev Desert

EDOM

Ismailia

Suez Canal

Great Bitter Lake

Cairo

Suez

Sinai Peninsula

MIDIAN

Etzion-Geber

E G Y P T

Gulf of Suez

Abu Rudeis

Gulf of Akaba

▲ *Mount Sinai*

River Nile

0   kilometres   80

0   miles   50

Red Sea

© Martin Gilbert 2002

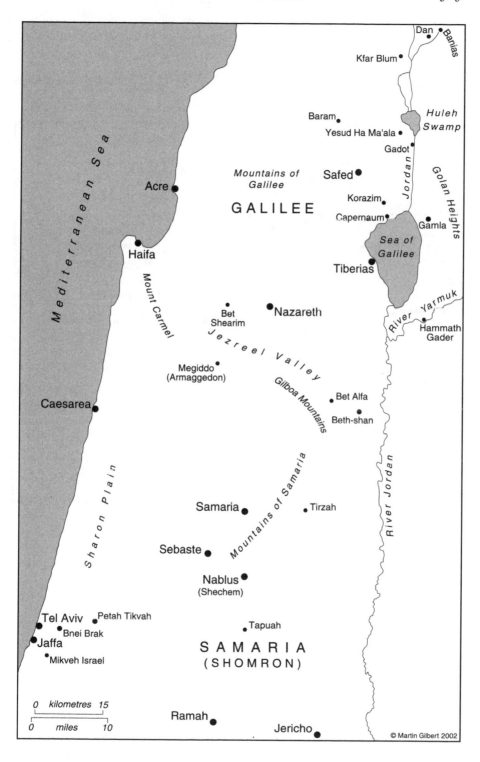

Galilee and Samaria

Dan
Banias
Kfar Blum
Huleh
Swamp
Baram
Yesud Ha Ma'ala
Gadot
Jordan
Mountains of
Galilee
Safed
Golan Heights
Korazim
Acre
GALILEE
Capernaum
Gamla
Sea of
Galilee
Mediterranean Sea
Haifa
Tiberias
Mount Carmel
Nazareth
River Yarmuk
Bet
Shearim
Jezreel Valley
Hammath
Gader
Megiddo
(Armaggedon)
Gilboa Mountains
Bet Alfa
Beth-shan
Caesarea
Sharon Plain
Mountains of Samaria
Samaria
Tirzah
River Jordan
Sebaste
Nablus
(Shechem)
Tel Aviv
Petah Tikvah
Bnei Brak
Tapuah
Jaffa
Mikveh Israel
SAMARIA
(SHOMRON)
0   kilometres   15
0   miles   10
Ramah
Jericho

© Martin Gilbert 2002

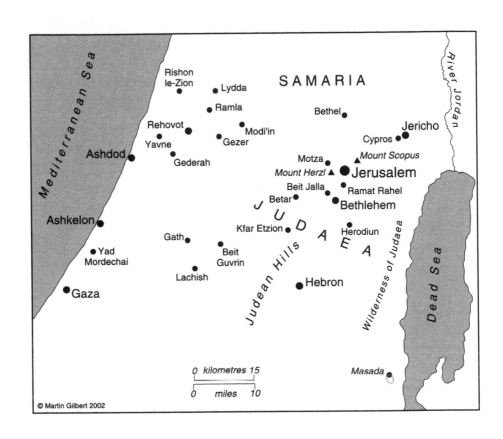

SAMARIA

Mediterranean Sea

Rishon le-Zion
Lydda
Ramla
Bethel
Rehovot
Modi'in
Jericho
Yavne
Gezer
Cypros
Ashdod
Gederah
Motza
Mount Scopus
Mount Herzl ▲ **Jerusalem**
Beit Jalla
Ramat Rahel
Betar
Bethlehem
Ashkelon
J   U   D   A   E   A
Kfar Etzion
Herodiun
Gath
Yad Mordechai
Beit Guvrin
Judean Hills
Wilderness of Judaea
Lachish
Gaza
Hebron

River Jordan

Dead Sea

0 kilometres 15
0   miles   10

Masada

© Martin Gilbert 2002

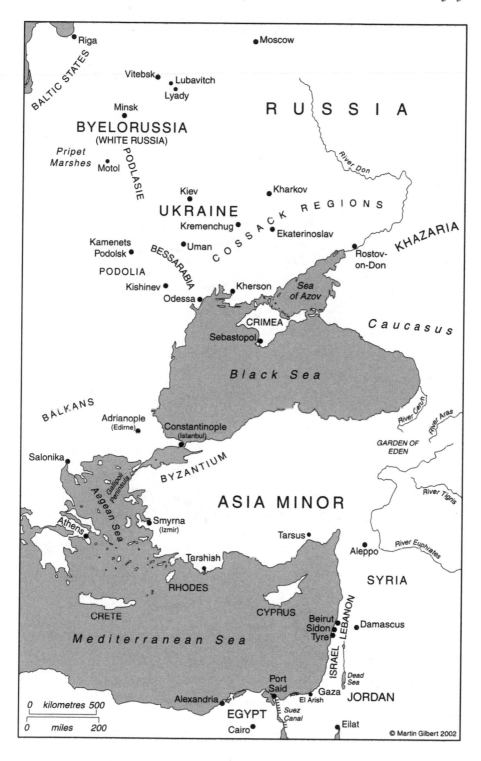

Riga

Moscow

BALTIC STATES

Vitebsk • • Lubavitch
• Lyady

Minsk
•

BYELORUSSIA
(WHITE RUSSIA)

R U S S I A

*Pripet
Marshes* • Motol

PODLASIE

River Don

Kiev • • Kharkov

UKRAINE

C O S S A C K   R E G I O N S

Kremenchug •
Uman • • Ekaterinoslav

Kamenets
Podolsk •

BESSARABIA

KHAZARIA

PODOLIA

Kishinev • • Kherson

Rostov-
on-Don •

Odessa •

*Sea
of Azov*

CRIMEA

C a u c a s u s

Sebastopol •

Black Sea

River Cur...

River Aras

B A L K A N S

Adrianople •
(Edirne)

Constantinople
(Istanbul)

*GARDEN OF
EDEN*

Salonika •

BYZANTIUM

River Tigris

Gallipoli
Peninsula

Aegean Sea

ASIA MINOR

Athens •

Smyrna •
(Izmir)

Tarsus •

Aleppo •

River Euphrates

Tarshish •

SYRIA

RHODES

CYPRUS

Beirut •
Sidon • • Damascus
Tyre •

LEBANON

CRETE

M e d i t e r r a n e a n   S e a

ISRAEL

*Dead
Sea*

Port
Said •

Alexandria •

Gaza
El Arish • **JORDAN**

0 kilometres 500

EGYPT

*Suez
Canal*

Eilat •

0 miles 200

Cairo •

© Martin Gilbert 2002

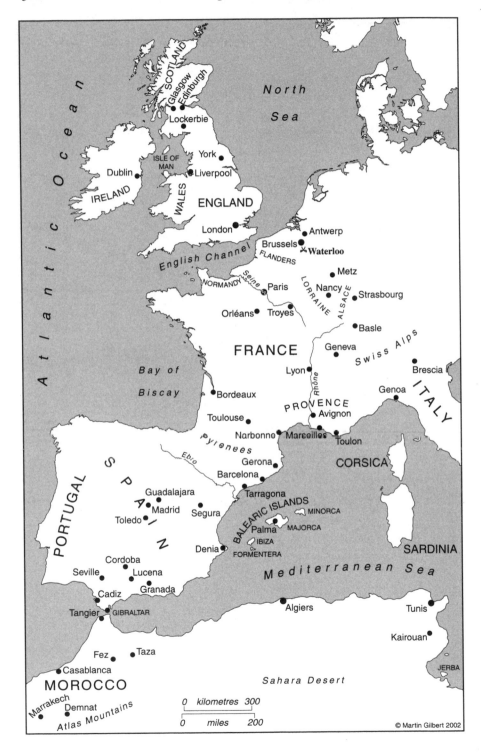

DENMARK

North
Sea

Baltic
Sea

Lübeck

Hamburg

MECKLENBURG

Bremen

Bergen-Belsen

HOLLAND

Amsterdam

Wannsee • Berlin

River Oder

GERMANY

River Elbe

Cologne

River Rhine

Pretzsch

RHINELAND

Bad Nauheim

Buchenwald

Frankfurt-on-Main

Karlsbad

Mainz

Trier

River Main

Worms

LORRAINE

Marienbad

Prague

Speyer

Nuremberg

Metz

Regensburg

ALSACE

River Danube

Augsburg

Mauthausen

Lake
Constance

Munich

BAVARIA

Basle

AUSTRIA

SWITZERLAND

0 kilometres 100

0   miles   75

© Martin Gilbert 2002

SWEDEN

Lake Peipus

ESTONIA

Lake Pskov

Baltic Sea

•Riga

LATVIA

LITHUANIA

Copenhagen

River Niemen •Kovno

•Königsberg   •Vilna

Danzig•

EAST PRUSSIA   Suwalki•

Stettin•

P O L A N D   Grodno•

Jedwabne• •Bialystok

Frankfurt-on-Oder•

River Oder

Vistula

Wsielub•   Treblinka

Plonsk• •Warsaw   •Kobryn

Chelmno•

Kalisz•

•Lodz

Piotrkow•

•Wlodawa

Sobibor•

Breslau•

Sosnowiec

Katowice

River Vistula

River Bug

•Theresienstadt

Dzialoszyce•

Majdanek•

•Prague

Cracow•   Belzec•

VOLHYNIA

BOHEMIA

•Wieliczka

Lvov•

Auschwitz

Wadowice•

Przemysl•   Przemyslyany•   Tarnopol•

•Medzibozh

SLOVAKIA

EASTERN GALICIA

Drohobycz•   Buczacz•

Carpathian Mountains

Vienna•

River Danube

Miskolc•   Bergszasz•

RUTHENIA

AUSTRIA

•Budapest

•Sighet

Lake Balaton

HUNGARY

ROUMANIA

0   kilometres 150

0   miles   100

© Martin Gilbert 2002

© Martin Gilbert 2002

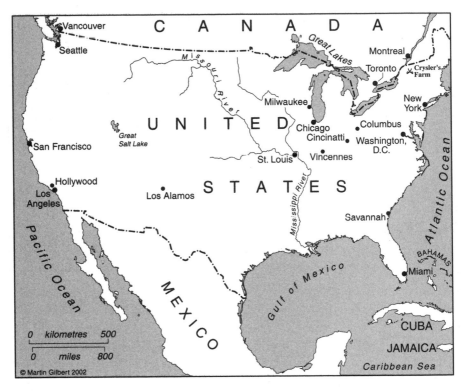

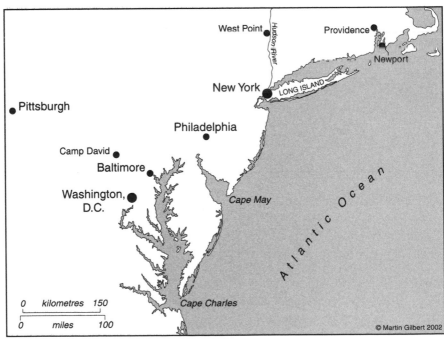

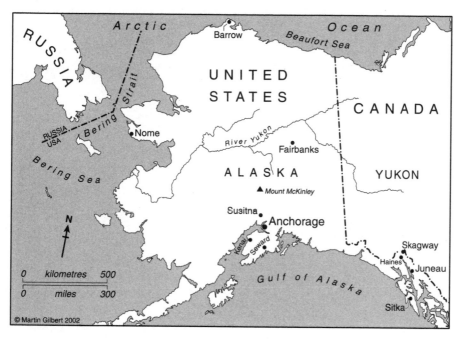

INDEX

COMPILED BY THE AUTHOR